BATTLE CHRONICLES
OF THE
CIVIL WAR
1863

JAMES M. McPHERSON, Editor
Princeton University

RICHARD GOTTLIEB, Managing Editor
Grey Castle Press

MACMILLAN PUBLISHING COMPANY
New York

COLLIER MACMILLAN PUBLISHERS
London

Text © 1989. *Civil War Times Illustrated*, a division of Cowles Magazines, Inc., Box 8200, Harrisburg, PA 17105.

Introduction, Transitions, Index and Format © 1989. Grey Castle Press, Inc., Lakeville, CT 06039.

Published by Macmillan Publishing Company
866 Third Avenue, New York, NY 10022

ILLUSTRATION CREDITS—Some sources are abbreviated as follows: BL, B&L (*Battles and Leaders of the Civil War*); CWTI Collection (*Civil War Times Illustrated* Collection); FL (*Frank Leslie's Illustrated Newspaper*); HW (*Harper's Weekly*); KA (Kean Archives); LC, Coll. of LC (Library of Congress); NA (National Archives); S (*The Soldier in Our Civil War*). Illustrations without credits are part of the *Civil War Times Illustrated* Collection.

Library of Congress Cataloging-in-Publication Data

Battle Chronicles of the Civil War.

    Includes bibliographies and indexes.
    Contents: 1. 1861—2.1862—3. 1863— [etc.]
    1. United States—History—Civil War, 1861–1865—
Campaigns.   I. McPherson, James M.
E470.B29   1989   973.7'3   89-8316
ISBN 0-02-920661-8 (set)

Printed in the USA

Contents

1863—AN OVERVIEW

In the East . . .

A new year began with cavalry action. In 1863 the principal figure was Colonel John S. Mosby, the legendary "Gray Ghost," who commanded a band of partisan rangers operating in northern Virginia. Mosby's most spectacular feat that year was a March 8 raid on Fairfax, in which he overwhelmed the Federal garrison and personally roused from bed General Edwin Stoughton. Meanwhile, Federal horsemen were trying vainly to match the daring of their Confederate counterparts. Late in April, General George Stoneman's 10,000 troopers made a dash on Lee's communication lines with Richmond. The ten-day foray accomplished little and it deprived the Army of the Potomac of much-needed reconnaissance at a critical time.

In January, General Joseph Hooker succeeded Burnside at the head of the Federal army. Hooker displayed great skill in reconstructing units and restoring morale among men demoralized by repeated setbacks. Soon the Union army was at a strength of 134,000 men. Hooker resolved to use strategy and weight of numbers to destroy Robert E. Lee. His plan called for a large portion of his army under General John Sedgwick to hold Lee in front of Fredericksburg, while Hooker and the main body marched westward and crossed the Rappahannock upriver. Then the two Federal wings would crush the Confederate flanks and ram their way to Richmond.

Lee responded with the greatest gamble of his career. He left General Jubal A. Early's division to confront Sedgwick while he and the rest of the army moved into the Wilderness to meet Hooker's main drive. Lee's shift knocked the confidence out of Hooker. The Federal general ordered his forces on the defensive. Lee now seized the initiative. He further divided his meager forces by sending Jackson's corps on a roundabout march to hit Hooker's unprotected right flank. Late in the afternoon of May 2, Jackson's men exploded from the woods and shattered an entire Union corps. Darkness prevented the Confederates from pressing their advantage. Near 9 p.m. that evening, while reconnoitering the Federal lines, Jackson was accidentally shot by his own men. General J. E. B. Stuart assumed temporary command of Jackson's corps.

The next day, Stuart's determined soldiers assailed Hooker from the west while Lee personally led the remainder of his forces against Hooker from the south. Hooker's wing crumbled and began filing back to the Rappahannock. Lee received word during this action that Early's line had broken in the face of Sedgwick's advance from Fredericksburg. Lee left Stuart to continue pressing Hooker while he took a portion of the Confederate army to stop Sedgwick. During May 4-5, Lee defeated Sedgwick at Salem Church and sent this Federal wing reeling northward. Lee countermarched his weary soldiers to deliver a death blow to Hooker—only to find that the other wing of a force Hooker had termed "the finest army on the planet" had retreated across the Rappahannock.

Chancellorsville was a brilliant success for Lee, but costly to both sides. Hooker lost 17,278 men. Numbered among the 12,821 Southern casualties was the incomparable "Stonewall" Jackson, who died May 10 of complications from his wounds. With Jackson's death, an era in Lee's tactics passed away. The startling flank attacks that brought smashing victory at Second Manassas and Chancellorsville never occurred again.

A Union charge at Gettysburg. The biggest and bloodiest battle ever fought on American soil was a victory for the North, a serious defeat for the South. (Harper's Weekly, August 8, 1863)

The decisiveness of the Chancellorsville victory, the need to gain supplies, the fading hope of European recognition, and the possibility of striking a final blow at the Union, persuaded Lee to initiate a second invasion of the North. On June 3 the Confederate army began maneuvering for a move across the Potomac. Six days later, 10,000 Federal cavalry under General Alfred Pleasonton struck a like number of Confederate troopers Stuart had assembled for a review on the previous day. For eight hours at Brandy Station the two forces exchanged saber-flourishing cavalry charges. The Confederates gained a hard-earned victory, but the Union cavalry gained a new-found respect.

Lee's army cleared Federals from Winchester on June 14-15 and then used the Shenandoah "avenue" to advance across Maryland and into Pennsylvania. Hooker's timidity in combating this invasion provoked Lincoln into appointing General George G. Meade to lead the Army of the Potomac. Meade, a dedicated soldier from Pennsylvania, had been in command but three days when the vanguards of the two veteran armies collided accidentally at the crossroads town of Gettysburg. "The greatest battle fought in the Western Hemisphere" erupted. For three days, more than 163,000 men waged a vicious, unyielding fight. Lee attacked repeatedly but could not dislodge the Federals from positions extending over a four-mile front.

The climax of the battle came on the afternoon of July 3, when Confederate General George E. Pickett led a heroic but fruitless charge against the center of the Union lines. Pickett lost 7,000 of 15,000 men. With fields drenched in blood, the battle of Gettysburg then ended. The two armies had suffered more than 51,000 casualties.

Again Lee was allowed to make an orderly retreat toward Virginia. Not until the night of July 13-14 were the Confederates able to ford the rain-swollen Potomac River. Thus Meade's decision to attack the strongly entrenched Confederates on the 14th came too late, and he lost the opportunity of possibly destroying Lee and ending the war in the East. This failure tarnished much of the luster gained from the victory at Gettysburg.

The armies of Lee and Meade spent the remainder of the year jockeying for position in northern Virginia. Lee in October made a feint toward Washington that caused Meade to retire to Centreville. Late in November, Meade assumed the offensive and pushed southward almost to Culpeper. For several days the two armies maneuvered at Mine Run. Lee held an almost impregnable position, and Meade prudently withdrew to the Rapidan River on December 1. This ended active operations in the East for the winter.

In the West . . .

Highlighting the 1863 actions in the West were Grant's extraordinary operations against the Confederate "Gibraltar of the West," Vicksburg. The campaign began in January, when General John A. McClernand led a Federal amphibious expedition fifty miles up the Arkansas River to capture Fort Hindman at Arkansas Post. An attempt by Sherman's men in January-February to cut a canal across the peninsula opposite Vicksburg failed and convinced Grant to concentrate his forces for an all-out offensive against the city.

To soften up the region, Grant that spring sent Colonel Benjamin H. Grierson and 1,700 cavalrymen on a raid Grant later termed "one of the most brilliant exploits of the war." Grierson's men fought their way from La Grange, Tennessee, to Baton Rouge, Louisiana; in the process they killed or wounded 100 Confederate soldiers, captured 500 others, destroyed 60 miles of railroad and 3,000 small arms, and set the torch to tons of Confederate government stores.

Meanwhile, Grant's army crossed the Mississippi at Milliken's Bend and marched southward through Louisiana to a point far below Vicksburg. Admiral David D. Porter's fleet blasted its way downriver past the Vicksburg defenses and joined Grant. With gunboats providing security on the river, Grant's 40,000 troops crossed into Mississippi. The Federal army was cut off from all supply bases; yet in less than three weeks a determined Grant led his forces to victories at Port Gibson, Raymond, Jackson, Champion's Hill, and Big Black River.

Having interposed between the Southern forces of Joseph E. Johnston and John C. Pemberton's Vicksburg defenders, Grant invested the town and initiated an ever-tightening siege. Union land and river forces slowly forced Vicksburg into submission. The defenders were reduced to living in caves and eating mules, dogs, and—according to some—rats. On July 4, Pemberton surrendered the city, its 30,000 defenders, 172 cannon, and 60,000 muskets. Five days later, the 6,000-man garrison downriver at Port Hudson struck its colors. "The Father of Waters," a joyful Lincoln exclaimed, "again goes unvexed to the sea!" In addition, the entire Trans-Mississippi had been sundered from the Confederacy.

Lost in the impact of the Vicksburg Campaign was John Hunt Morgan's dramatic but unrewarding "Ohio Raid" later that summer. With 2,500 mounted infantry, Morgan cut a swath through central Kentucky and crossed the Ohio River into southern Indiana, slashed through the suburbs of Cincinnati, and swept eastward

Federal troops move to take Fort Hindman, a huge fortification situated atop a cliff at Arkansas Post. The capture gave the Union a tremendous boost in morale. (Library of Congress)

Ulysses S. Grant and John C. Pemberton discuss the surrender of Vicksburg. (Mississippi Department of Archives & History)

until Federals dispersed the raiders. Morgan destroyed $500,000 worth of property before he and most of his band were captured and confined in a Columbus, Ohio, prison. Morgan escaped in November but died ten months later when Federal troops surprised him at Greenville, Tennessee.

By September 1863, Rosecrans had maneuvered Bragg from Chattanooga and occupied that strategic city. Bragg, a skillful organizer, now proved himself an inept field commander. On September 19, Bragg's 58,000 men engaged Rosecrans' 54,000 at Chickamauga Station, a few miles southeast of Chattanooga. The Confederate attacks reflected the general's lack of confidence and resourcefulness. General James Longstreet and 11,000 men from Lee's army arrived as reinforcements. In the second day's fighting, Longstreet's veterans drove through a gap in Rosecran's lines and sent the entire Federal right (along with Rosecrans himself) fleeing pell-mell back to Chattanooga. But the Federal left, under General George H. Thomas, refused to break in the face of repeated assaults by superior numbers. Thomas' stand earned him the sobriquet "Rock of Chickamauga," and possibly prevented the destruction of the whole Federal army. Rosecrans suffered 16,170 casualties; Bragg's losses were 18,454 men.

Bragg refused to exploit the victory, barren though it was. Instead, he posted his 40,000 men on the hills overlooking Chattanooga and laid siege to the city. Thomas replaced the stunned Rosecrans as head of the army. Grant, now supreme Federal commander in the West, began funneling reinforcements into Chattanooga via the

The Battles for Chattanooga: Patrick R. Cleburne's repulse of William T. Sherman at Missionary Ridge on November 25, 1863. Drawing by Alfred R. Waud. (Battlefields in Dixie Land)

Tennessee River line. Grant soon had supply lines open and 60,000 soldiers at hand. He then struck back. For three days (November 23-25), and from three directions, Federals hammered at the Southern lines. On November 25, Thomas' Army of the Cumberland scaled Missionary Ridge without orders and carried the heights. A demoralized Confederate army abandoned Chattanooga and retired into Georgia. Securing this remaining part of Tennessee cost Grant 5,824 troops. Bragg lost 6,667 irreplaceable soldiers.

Federal advances in the West during 1863 sounded the death knell of the Confederacy.

New Manpower for the North . . .

In addition to the era-ending campaigns of Vicksburg and Gettysburg, the year 1863 was epochal in another respect: For the first time, America made major use of Negroes as combat soldiers.

The opportunity for blacks to fight—and die—for their freedom did not come easily. Using former slaves as soldiers evolved over painful stepping-stones of hostility, discrimination, and ill will. Early in the war, Federal authorities were willing to employ ex-slaves as laborers in Northern armies. Yet because of the popular belief of whites in the Negro's biological inferiority, the North was extremely reluctant to uniform and arm blacks to fight alongside whites.

Attempts in 1862 to raise Negro regiments in Kansas and the occupied portions of South Carolina and Louisiana were ill-organized and too premature to be successful. In the autumn of that year, however, the Federal Government abandoned its lukewarm attitude toward the use of Negroes as soldiers. The war was then going badly for the Union; more manpower was needed; and Lincoln came to see that if the Emancipation Proclamation was ever to have real and lasting meaning blacks had to be given the chance to assist actively in the war for their liberation.

The War Department moved quickly in 1863 to implement the new policy. Recruitment was systematized, officer procurement regularized, training camps established, and a Bureau for Colored Troops created to administer the whole program. Yet the majority of Negro recruits were initially and justifiably unhappy. Underpaid, assigned mostly to menial tasks, and commanded always by white officers, black soldiers were stymied repeatedly in efforts to demonstrate their military worth. That the use of Negroes as soldiers ultimately succeeded so well is attributable to three factors: the indefatigable labors of Adjutant General Lorenzo Thomas (who personally stimulated 76,000 Negro recruitments and raised fifty regiments); a changing, more positive attitude among high-ranking Union officers toward the use of black soldiers; and—most importantly of all—the performance of Negroes in battle.

Negro soldiers and their families in Louisiana listen to an address on the duties of freedom. (Library of Congress)

The Union's siege of Petersburg: Negro infantry bring in captured guns amid the cheers of white Ohio troops. (Frank Leslie's Illustrated Newspaper)

While Negro soldiers of the Civil War participated in at least 39 major battles and 410 minor engagements, black troops are remembered principally for several 1863 and 1864 engagements. They demonstrated commendable valor in futile assaults at Port Hudson, Louisiana (May 27, 1863), and Fort Wagner, South Carolina (July 18, 1863), while other, equally untested black troops made a brief and disastrous stand at Milliken's Bend, Louisiana (June 7, 1863).

Southern reactions at the sight of Negroes in blue uniforms had overtones of barbarity in such 1864 engagements as Olustee, Florida; Fort Pillow, Tennessee; Poison Spring, Arkansas; at Petersburg, Virginia, in the "Battle of the Crater," and at Saltville, Virginia. Yet it was after two days of bitter fighting at Nashville that General George H. Thomas rendered the final verdict: "Gentlemen, the question is settled. Negroes will fight."

Indeed they did. A total of 178,895 Negroes flocked to the colors of 120 infantry regiments, twelve heavy artillery regiments, ten light artillery batteries, and seven cavalry regiments. Their numbers constituted 9 percent of the North's fighting forces. Their death rate was unusually high: 36,847 men, of whom 2,751 were killed in action. Most of the remainder were victims of disease. Fourteen black soldiers received the Medal of Honor. Color Sergeant Anselmas Planciancois of the 1st Louisiana Native Guards was not among that number. Yet on the morning before the assault on Port Hudson, Planciancois received the regimental flag with the vow: "Colonel, I will bring back the colors with honor or report to God the reason why." Mortally wounded in the action that followed, the sergeant's final act was to hug the flag to his breast.

—*James I. Robertson, Jr.*

The Northern Winter of Despair

The news of what happened at Fredericksburg on December 13, 1862, caused profound depression in the North. "If there is a worse place than Hell," said Lincoln as the first reports came in, "I am in it." *Harper's Weekly* commented angrily that for more than a year the northern people "have borne, silently and grimly, imbecility, treachery, failure, privation, loss of friends and means, almost every suffering which can afflict a brave people. But they cannot be expected to suffer that such massacres as this at Fredericksburg shall be repeated." Many other spokesmen expressed the defeatism that threatened to undermine the northern will to keep fighting. "The rebels could not be beaten," wrote a formerly staunch Chicago editor in a private letter. "An armistice is bound to come during the year '63."

Morale declined disastrously in the Army of the Potomac. Soldiers wrote home: "my loyalty is growing weak." "I am sick and tired of disaster and the fools that bring disaster upon us." "All think Virginia is not worth such a loss of life." "Why not confess we are worsted, and come to an agreement?" Intrigue and dissension became rife among high officers in the Army of the Potomac. Some of them went behind General Burnside's back to complain directly to Lincoln of the commander's incompetence. Even the weather conspired against Burnside. When he lurched the Army of the Potomac into motion for another attempt to cross the Rappahannock and engage the enemy in January 1863, the heavens opened to pour down several inches of rain and sleet that bogged the army hopelessly in the mud. In the aftermath of this notorious "Mud March" the already alarming number of desertions from the army multiplied threefold. Something had to be done to save the army from falling apart. Lincoln did it. On January 25 he removed Burnside from command and replaced him with Joseph Hooker.

Hooker's appointment was something of a surprise. Intensely ambitious, he had intrigued against Burnside. Something of a braggart, he had made numerous enemies. His reputation as a drinker and a womanizer did little to improve his standing in the eyes of many fellow officers. One of them observed that Hooker's headquarters was "a place which no self-respecting man liked to go, and no decent woman could go. It was a combination of barroom and brothel."

But Hooker had a reputation as a fighting general. That was what Lincoln wanted. And to the surprise of his detractors, he turned out to be a good administrator. He shook up the commissary and quartermaster services by dismissing inefficient and corrupt officers. He upgraded the food, cleaned up the filthy camps, improved the field hospitals, and instilled unit pride be creating insignia badges for each corps. By reorganizing the cavalry into a separate corps he accelerated the process whereby during 1863 this much-maligned branch rose to a fighting level equal to that of their Confederate counterparts. An amnesty for AWOL's brought many of them back to the army, and a liberal furlough program during these quiet winter months helped keep them there. By April Hooker had turned around the decline in morale. The Army of the Potomac was in fighting trim, ready for a new confrontation with the enemy.

But morale on the home front remained low in the spring of 1863. The legacy of Fredericksburg in the East and Grant's apparent failure to make any progress against Vicksburg in the West kept northern spirits depressed. Lincoln had issued the

Federal soldiers in dreary winter camps and their families back home strongly criticized President Lincoln, calling him "ignorant, self-willed . . . incompetent." (Library of Congress)

Emancipation Proclamation as promised on January 1. This did increase antislavery zeal for the war effort. But it also proved dangerously divisive, driving many Democrats into bitter opposition. The enactment of conscription in March 1863 (almost a year after the Confederacy had taken this step) increased the polarization between War Republicans and Peace Democrats. The latter, called Copperheads, stepped up their attacks against the war and their demands for an armistice. Since this would amount to a recognition of Confederate independence, Republicans branded Copperheads as traitors. They also organized Union Leagues throughout the North to promote public support for emancipation, the draft, and relentless war to victory. These Leagues became effective propaganda agencies. But no matter how effective, they could not win the war on their own. That could be accomplished only by the armies. And for a time news from the fighting front seemed only to get worse. Then, finally, it took a decisive turn for the better.

—James M. McPherson

THE BATTLE OF CHANCELLORSVILLE

by Joseph P. Cullen

14

ON A RAW, WINDY DAY in early April 1863, President Abraham Lincoln and Major General Joseph ("Fighting Joe") Hooker sat astride their horses as the Army of the Potomac, encamped on Stafford Heights overlooking the city of Fredericksburg and the Rappahannock River, passed in review. The ground was soft with melting snow, and the mud flew from the horses' hoofs. A reporter for the New York *Herald* described the scene: "Out upon a little swell of upland were crowded the President and his staff of generals, and over all the plain stretched the columns of the army. In the distance were the camps, the river, the spires of Fredericksburg, and the frowning batteries beyond; behind, miles of mud-walled villages, long, white-topped baggage wagons, and cannon on the hills. The sun danced on the bayonets and rifles and lingered in the folds of the flags; then the shadows drifted over the plains and melted away with the music."

Lincoln had come to visit the army for a few days, not only "to get away from Washington and the politicians," as he quaintly expressed it, but also to check on rumors about morale being low. Hooker's recent appointment as commander in chief of the army, replacing Burnside after the disaster at Fredericksburg in December, had not been particularly popular, as the President well knew. Consequently, when he appointed Hooker he told him, "I think that during General Burnside's command of the army you have taken counsel of your ambition, and thwarted him as much as you could, in which you did a great wrong to the country. . . . I much fear that the spirit which you have aided to infuse into the army, of criticizing their commander and withholding confidence from him, will now turn upon you. . . . Neither you nor Napoleon, if he were alive again, could get any good out of an army while such a spirit prevails in it."

After reviewing the troops, visiting with the sick, and talking with many of the officers, Lincoln was pleasantly surprised to find that morale was generally high. Hooker had realized his first job was to restore morale and discipline to the demoralized Union army, and in this he showed administrative ability that few suspected he possessed. Abandoning Burnside's unwieldy Grand Divisions, he reorganized the army on a corps level, forming the cavalry into a separate corps. The quality and quantity of the rations was increased, camp sanitation and living conditions improved, deserved furloughs granted. By the spring of 1863 the Army of the Potomac, numbering about 130,000 men, was certainly the largest and best equipped and supplied army the country had ever seen. "The finest army on the planet," Hooker called it.

Lincoln was reassured about the army, but he was still not convinced about its commander. It was not so much Hooker's constant boasting that bothered the President, as "Fighting Joe" had always been regarded as a braggart. "My plans are perfect," he had stated after his appointment to top command. "May God have mercy on General Lee for I will have none." But Hooker also had a reputation as a tough, aggressive corps commander, a good combat soldier, and

Repulse of Jackson's men at Hazel Grove by Federal artillery under (then) Brigadier General Alfred Pleasonton. (From B&L)

Lincoln was hoping that he would take this superb army and use it aggressively against the enemy. All he now heard from his general, however, was what he was going to do when "I get to Richmond." This brought forth Lincoln's mournful remark to his secretary, "It is about the worst thing I have seen since I have been down here." And he also stated in his characteristic way that "the hen is the wisest of all of the animal creation because she never cackles until the egg is laid."

Although a civilian with no formal military train-ing, Lincoln was acutely aware, unlike most of his generals, that the army's objective was not Richmond, it was the Confederate army. Now he feared that Hooker did not understand the problem, that his plan probably was to outmaneuver the enemy, à la McClellan and the Seven Days, with Richmond the major objective. Thus, as he departed for Washington, with a premonition of disaster, the President gave Hooker and Major General D. N. Couch, second in command, some sound advice. "In your next fight, gentlemen," he told them, "put in all of your men."

Review by President Lincoln of the cavalry of the Army of the Potomac in April 1863. Original drawing, A. R. Waud. (LC)

LEE'S PROBLEM

Across the river Lee's Army of Northern Virginia had its problems also, although of a different nature, to be sure. The winter had been long and unusually severe, with extreme cold and intermittent snow lasting into early April. Many of the men lacked blankets, while others wore coats and shoes that were in tatters. Horses were gaunt from lack of forage, and finally scurvy began to appear among the men when the ration was reduced "to 18 ounces of flour, 4 ounces of bacon of indifferent quality, with occasionally supplies of rice, sugar, or molasses." Each regiment sent out daily details to gather sassafras buds, wild onions, garlic, and poke sprouts, but the supply obtained in this manner was negligible. From his headquarters camp near Fredericksburg Lee wrote the Secretary of War that he feared the men "will be unable to endure the hardships of the approaching campaign."

This shortage of supplies, due primarily to the lack of efficient transportation and the general ineptitude of the commissary general, Colonel Lucius B. Northrop, also had a direct effect on the numerical strength of the Army of Northern Virginia. Lieutenant General James Longstreet, with Pickett's and Hood's divisions, had been sent south of the James River to contain the Federal forces at Newport News and in North Carolina, but his primary mission was to gather desperately needed supplies for Lee's army. When Longstreet completed the mission, Lee planned to recall him and mount an offensive against Hooker in order to relieve the pressure on the other Confederate forces in Tennessee and North Carolina and still keep Richmond covered. "I think it all-important," he wrote President Davis on April 16, "that we should assume the aggressive by the 1st of May. . . . If we could be placed in a condition to make a vigorous advance at that time, I think . . . the army opposite us could be thrown north of the Potomac."

In the meantime, however, Longstreet's absence reduced Lee's force to something over 60,000 effectives. If the Union army advanced before Longstreet could join him, Lee faced the prospect of having to fall back to the North Anna River, about halfway between Fredericksburg and Richmond, something he did not want to do because then the vital forage and provisions in the Rappahannock Valley would be lost. But to recall Longstreet now would mean that Lee, lacking provisions, would be unable to undertake an offensive. Therefore he decided to leave Longstreet's force south until its mission was accomplished. If necessary, he would face a Union advance with an inferior force.

In late April the weather turned warm and spring-like. Across the river constant activity could be observed in the Union camp. The Federals sent an observation balloon aloft every day, weather permitting; cavalry raids across the upper Rappahannock increased in number and intensity. Then on April 23 the Federals made a crossing and demonstration against Port Royal on the lower Rappahannock on the Confederate extreme right. This did not particularly disturb Lee, however, as he recognized it for what it was, a feint. He told Lieutenant General Thomas J. ("Stonewall") Jackson that he believed the "purpose is to draw our troops in that direction while he attempts a passage elsewhere," and "I think that if a real attempt is made to cross the river it will be above Fredericksburg." Until such time as some definite move on the part of the Federals could be ascertained, Lee had no intention of shifting any of his troops. Jackson's corps held the extreme right from Hamilton's Crossing to Port Royal. McLaws' division of Longstreet's corps, posted on Jackson's left, stretched from Hamilton's Crossing to Banks's Ford above Fredericksburg. Farther up the river Stuart's cavalry watched the various crossings, supported by Anderson's division of Longstreet's corps.

HOOKER'S PLAN

Finally, late in April, Hooker put the Army of the Potomac in motion, in furtherance of a bold plan. He would take at least three corps up the Rappahannock to Kelly's Ford, twenty-five miles northwest of Fredericksburg, then cross both the Rappahannock and the Rapidan Rivers to get on Lee's left flank and rear. Two corps would demonstrate actively in front of Fredericksburg to hold the Confederates in their defensive positions, while the remaining two corps would be held ready to go wherever the best opportunity might present itself. An essential part of the plan was for Stoneman's cavalry corps to precede the infantry by about two weeks, crossing the upper fords of the Rappahannock and, sweeping down upon Lee's lines of communication to Richmond, cut railroads and canals, block roads, and intercept all supplies. As it was known that the Confederates had great difficulty in keeping more than four days' rations on hand, Hooker believed that if Stoneman was successful Lee would run short of provisions, and with three Federal corps on his left and rear would be forced to retreat, thus giving the Federals a moral victory, at least.

→

Map 1. HOOKER'S PLAN. *Although generally excellent, this plan had two flaws. First, Sedgwick's secondary or "holding" attack was designated only as a "strong demonstration." Lee was never deceived by a feint. Sedgwick, however, did make a full-scale attack that might have achieved its purpose had Hooker himself done his part in the over-all scheme. Second, the timing of the grand cavalry raid was faulty. The Federal cavalry—especially under Stoneman—at this time was incapable of keeping the Confederate supply line interrupted for two weeks or more, even if it succeeded in penetrating the enemy rear areas deeply enough.*

Maps below and elsewhere in this chapter, prepared by Col. Wilbur S. Nye, originally appeared in Chancellorsville: Lee's Greatest Battle *by Lt. Gen. Edward J. Stackpole and are reproduced here by courtesy of Stackpole Books, Harrisburg, PA.*

It was an excellent plan with more daring and imagination than any Union commander in the East had ever shown before. Hooker, in effect, was splitting his army in the front of a brilliant and feared adversary, but if this were executed efficiently and aggressively it would almost guarantee the destruction of the Army of Northern Virginia. It was a risk well worth taking!

HOOKER'S OPENING MOVES

On the morning of April 13 Stoneman moved out at the head of 10,000 finely equipped and conditioned troopers to swing far out to the right, cross the Rappahannock, and fall on the unsuspecting Confederate rear. Before Stoneman left, Hooker reminded him that "celerity, audacity, and resolution are everything in war. Let your watchword be fight, fight, fight."

But after two days' march the skies opened up and halted the column. "During the night of the 14th a severe rain commenced and continued without cessation for thirty-six hours, which prevented the command from crossing the river," Stoneman reported. "The rain continued, with short intervals of fair

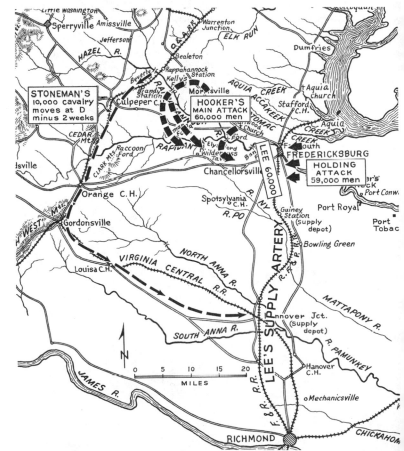

weather, and the river remained impassable for cavalry until the 28th of April, during which time the whole command remained in the vicinity of Warrenton Junction, on the Orange and Alexandria Railroad." Owing to this delay the battle would be over before Stoneman really got active, and his subsequent operations would have little or no effect on the outcome.

With this disruption of his timetable, Hooker became impatient and when the rains finally subsided he put his original plan into operation. Initially he displayed a boldness that augured well for the success of the campaign. On the morning of April 27 Meade's V, Howard's XI, and Slocum's XII Corps started up the Rappahannock, well screened from Confederate observers by the topography. Each man carried sixty rounds of ammunition and eight days' rations (twice the normal amount) of hardtack, salt pork, coffee, sugar, and salt. Each ration weighed three pounds. For the first time in the East, 2,000 pack mules were used instead of the usual supply wagons, to speed up the movement. "For miles nothing could be heard but the steady tramp of the men," wrote one campaigner, "the rattling and jingling of canteens and accouterments, and the occasional 'close-up-men-close-up' of the officers."

At dawn the next day Hancock's and French's divisions of Couch's II Corps marched to Banks's Ford, where a demonstration was made to keep the Confederates confused, while the road to United States Ford, farther up the river, was repaired. The third division of the II Corps, Gibbon's, was left behind because its encampment at Falmouth, directly across the river from Fredericksburg, was in full view of the Confederates and to withdraw it would have alerted them to the fact that some unusual movement was taking place. The other reserve corps, Sickles' III, was ordered to join Reynolds' I and Sedgwick's VI Corps below Fredericksburg where the Federals made

a strong demonstration in an attempt to hold the Confederates in their defensive positions until Hooker could complete his turning movement.

During the night of the 28th and early morning of the 29th, the three Federal corps crossed the Rappahannock at Kelly's Ford. Slocum and Howard then marched to Germanna Ford on the Rapidan, while Meade crossed lower down the river at Ely's Ford. Moving east, they uncovered United States Ford and were joined by Couch's two divisions. By early evening on the 30th, all were encamped around the rendezvous point, Chancellorsville (not a town, merely a farmhouse), a strategic crossroads at the edge of an area known as The Wilderness. Here Hooker joined them, establishing his headquarters at the Chancellor house. Receiving word from Sedgwick that although he had thrown two bridges across the Rappahannock below Fredericksburg the Confederates showed no disposition to attack, Hooker then ordered Sickles' III Corps to join him at Chancellorsville, which it did early next morning, via U.S. Ford.

THE whole plan had been executed perfectly. According to Couch, "It had been a brilliantly conceived and executed movement." The corps commanders realized that Hooker had successfully outflanked Lee and thus secured a great opportunity to destroy the Confederate army. Even the men in the ranks sensed they had stolen a march on the Confederates for the first time, and their confidence in Hooker increased. Major General Carl Schurz, commanding the 3d Division of Howard's XI Corps, reported that during the move "all orders were executed by officers and men with promptness and alacrity, and the men marched better, were in better spirits, and endured the fatigues and hardships of the march by night and day more cheerfully than ever before. I have never known my command to be in a more excellent condition."

In gaining this advantage, however, Hooker had split his army and it was now vital that he uncover

Pontoon bridges erected for Sedgwick's VI Corps to cross the Rappahannock in Hooker's planned diversionary move. (HW)

Banks's Ford, just a few miles above Fredericksburg, in order to place the two wings within easy support of each other, and to insure a safe route of retreat if necessary. Also, most of his men were still in the dark thickets of The Wilderness, a dense forest of second-growth pine and scrub oak, with numerous creeks, gullies, swamps, heavy tanglefoot underbrush, and few farms or open spaces. A few miles east toward Banks's Ford and Fredericksburg, however, would bring them to open areas where they could maneuver efficiently and bring their great preponderance of artillery to bear.

From Chancellorsville there were three roads that could be used. The Orange Turnpike, which passed through Chancellorsville from the west, and was the best and most direct road to Fredericksburg; the Orange Plank Road, which went southeast from Chancellorsville and then swung left to rejoin the Turnpike about five miles away; and the River Road, which ran almost north from Chancellorsville and then turned east, paralleling the Rappahannock to Banks's Ford and on to Fredericksburg. With Banks's Ford in Hooker's possession and his columns operating in favorable terrain, the Army of the Potomac would be in a good position to destroy Lee's army

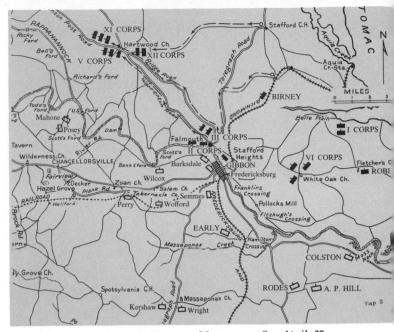

Map 2. START OF HOOKER'S TURNING MOVEMENT. *On April 27, 1863 Hooker's strong right wing started its march around Lee's left flank. Three corps reached Hartwood Church, undetected by Lee, and two others were ready to depart from the Falmouth area. The I and VI Corps are still in their camps.*

Lee's army is spread over a wide front, watching the river crossings. Jackson's corps, on the right, occupies the front from Moss Neck to Telegraph Road. Two of Longstreet's divisions are to the left; the other two, on a detached mission near Suffolk, are unavailable during the campaign.

Map 3. MOVEMENTS ON APRIL 28, 1863. *This shows Hooker's march from Hartwood Church to Kelly's Ford where, beginning at 10 p.m., the XI Corps starts crossing the Rappahannock. The remainder of this corps and the V and XII Corps are closing up and waiting for their turn to cross. Two divisions of the II Corps have marched from Falmouth to Banks's Ford, throwing out Carroll's brigade to U.S. Ford to cover their flank. The I and VI Corps have marched down to their assigned crossing sites, and the III Corps has been shifted over between them.*

Lee has made no material change in his dispositions. His first intimation of Hooker's threatening moves was a message from Stuart on the evening of the 28th that a Federal force of all arms (indicating a major unit) was moving up the Rappahannock in the direction of Kelly's Ford.

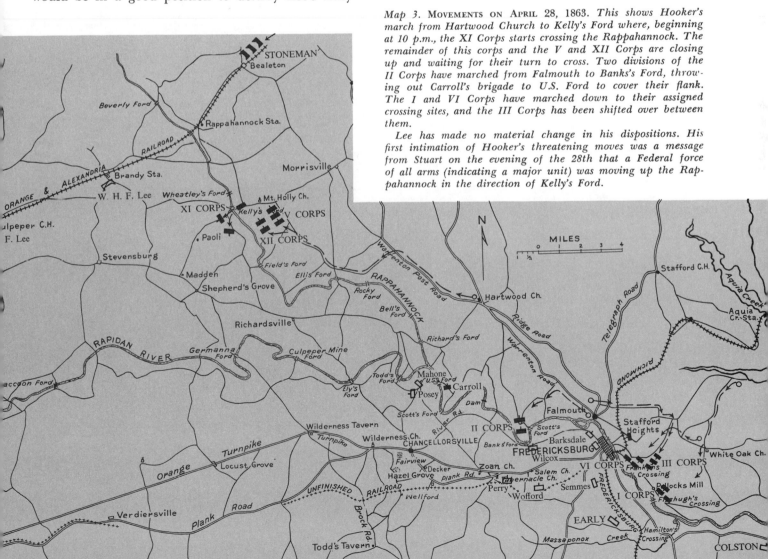

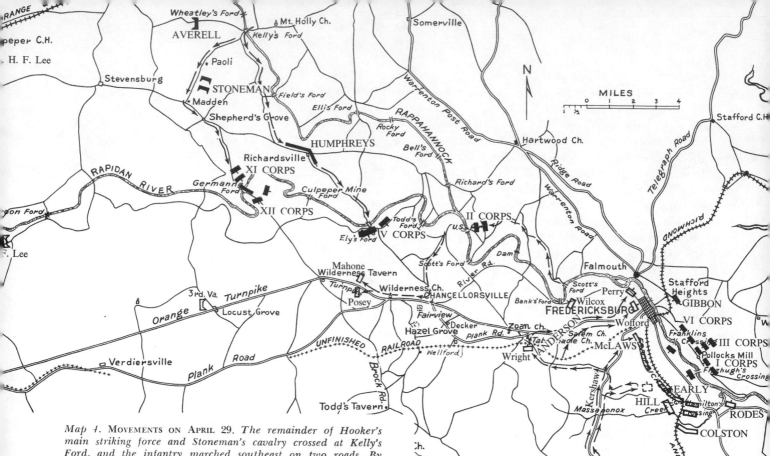

Map 4. Movements on April 29. *The remainder of Hooker's main striking force and Stoneman's cavalry crossed at Kelly's Ford, and the infantry marched southeast on two roads. By midnight the corps had reached the areas shown. The cavalry, now two weeks behind schedule, continued its raid during the following ten days to a point southwest of Hanover Junction, some forty miles below the Confederate army. They destroyed some rail and supply installations, but disturbed Lee not at all, and deprived Hooker of a large reconnaissance and screening force that he badly needed during the battle. Stoneman also succeeded in exhausting his troopers and killing off or crippling a great many of their mounts.*

Lee, on April 29, only partially informed by his cavalry of the Federal movements, was beginning to react. He was still inclined to believe that the Federal main effort might be made near Fredericksburg, although he previously reasoned that it would be near Chancellorsville. During the day he made a number of readjustments. Anderson was ordered to bring Posey and Mahone down from where they were covering U.S. Ford, and take positions west of Chancellorsville. Colston, Hill, and Rodes, of Jackson's corps, were moved over to the Hamilton's Crossing area. Early deployed in the old intrenchments along the railroad and McLaws occupied the high ground at

Lee's Hill and Marye's Heights. Wright was brought up from Massaponax Church to a reserve position in rear of Early, then later to near Tabernacle Church. Kershaw was also brought north and added to McLaws' line, and Wofford was moved from near Tabernacle Church to a position on the Plank Road overlooking Fredericksburg. Perry, of Anderson's division, was placed on the extreme left, at Dr. Taylor's. Stuart, with Fitz Lee's brigade, marched to Raccoon Ford. Three squadrons of the 3d Virginia Cavalry were pushed forward to Locust Grove.

Map 5. Federal Concentration Near Chancellorsville—Movements up to 2 p.m. April 30. *Meade's V Corps started from Ely's Ford at daylight, with Sykes's and Griffin's divisions; Humphreys' division was still en route between Kelly's Ford and Ely's. Meade, encountering a detachment of Rebels to his left front, detached Sykes toward Todd's and U.S. Fords to clear up the threat on that flank, meanwhile continuing the march with Griffin's division toward Chancellorsville. He arrived there at 11 a.m. and called in Sykes.*

Slocum's XII Corps marched from Germanna Ford, followed, at an hour's interval, by Howard's XI Corps. He brushed part of Stuart's cavalry aside at Wilderness Tavern and arrived at 2 p.m. at Chancellorsville. Here he was greeted by Meade, who was jubilant that Hooker had succeeded in getting a large force on Lee's flank and rear. Slocum sourly said that a new order from Fighting Joe directed them to stop and take up a defensive position.

Anderson has blocked the Turnpike at Tabernacle Church, with cavalry out to the front.

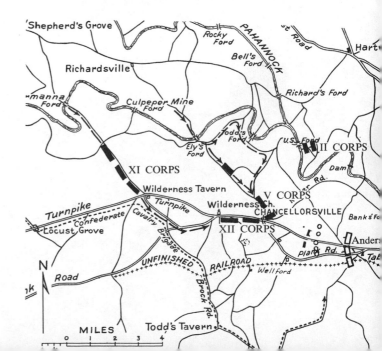

when it retreated from Fredericksburg, as the Federal commander believed it would have to do, with Sedgwick and Reynolds in hot pursuit. And Lee, in retreating would, in effect, be executing a flank movement across Hooker's front, a movement generally regarded as suicidal if performed in front of an aggressive enemy. As Hooker boasted: "I have Lee in one hand and Richmond in the other."

LEE'S COUNTERMOVES

But as darkness settled down that last day of April, Lee had finally decided on a plan of his own, and it did not conform at all to what the Federal commander hoped he would do. Before daybreak the previous day, Lee had been aroused by one of Jackson's staff officers sent to inform him that under cover of a heavy fog the Federals had thrown pontoon bridges across the Rappahannock just below Fredericksburg. Riding through the fog to Jackson's position, Lee found that the Federals had indeed crossed the river and driven back Jackson's pickets but were making no attempt to advance, although a large force could be observed on the other side of the river making preparations as if to cross. Everything seemed to indicate a general offensive, so Lee in a precautionary move withdrew all troops to the heights back of the river.

The Rappahannock at Fredericksburg takes a wide swing to the south to cut between two elevated ridges. If the Confederates tried to oppose the crossing, Federal artillery would have been looking down their throats. As Lee explained in his report: "As in the first battle of Fredericksburg, it was thought best to select positions with a view to resist the advances of the enemy, rather than incur the heavy loss that would attend any attempt to prevent his crossing."

As the morning wore on, however, and the Federals showed no inclination to attack, Lee became more convinced than ever that Hooker's main effort would be made in some other area. This view was confirmed when cavalry chief Major General J. E. B. ("Jeb") Stuart reported later that morning that a large Federal force had crossed at Kelly's Ford. A few hours later he informed Lee that he had captured prisoners from the V, XI, and XII Corps, and that heavy enemy columns were crossing the Rapidan at Germanna and Ely's Fords. Lee now believed that by the next day the entire Army of the Potomac would probably be south of the Rappahannock. In a dispatch to Jefferson Davis he stated: "Their intention, I presume, is to turn our left, and probably to get into our rear."

BUT not entirely sure of the strength of the turning column, Lee was reluctant to make any major shift of troops until he could be more confident of

where the major engagement probably would take place. In the meantime, however, he realized he had to do something to protect his left flank. A glance at the map showed him that the roads on which the Federals were advancing converged at Chancellorsville, from where several roads led directly to the rear of his position at Fredericksburg. Consequently, he ordered Anderson, whose brigades were guarding two fords immediately above the city, to advance his division towards Chancellorsville to cover the roads; and Stuart, in danger of being cut off by the Federal column, was ordered to rejoin the main force as soon as possible, delaying the enemy wherever he could. And he ordered McLaws to be ready to move his division at a moment's notice in case Anderson might need help. Now all Lee could do was wait to see what the next day might disclose.

Anderson moved out that night about 9 p.m. in a drenching rain and by early morning of the 30th had selected a strong position on a high rise a few miles east of Chancellorsville at the intersection of the Mine and Orange Plank Roads near Zoan [also called "Zoar" and "Zion"] Church. His left extended across an unfinished railroad and his right crossed the Orange Turnpike. Lee then ordered him to throw up strong fortifications and to extend his line in case additional troops were sent to him.

Accompanied by Jackson, Lee spent the morning carefully studying his intelligence reports and observing the lack of activity on the part of the Federals across the river at Fredericksburg. Finally convinced that the troops in front of the city were merely a diversion, he told his officers, "The main attack will come from above."

The question now was, what should he do about it? As Lee saw it, there were only two courses open to him: Either retreat southward or attack the Federal forces at Chancellorsville with the main part of his army. Retreat was definitely the easiest and safest course of action to take, but Lee undoubtedly reasoned that that was exactly what Hooker expected him to do, consequently he was reluctant to consider it. Also, by retreating now he would lose the desperately needed supplies and forage that the Rappahannock Valley could produce and, as he had stated in March when he argued against the evacuation of the Rappahannock line, "It throws open a broad margin of our frontier, and renders our railroad communications more hazardous and more difficult to secure." This consideration must have weighed on his mind now, but he was also seriously worried about his lack of strength. As he telegraphed Jefferson Davis on April 30, "If I had Longstreet's division [sic], would feel safe." [Lee was referring to the divisions of Pickett and Hood that Longstreet had taken on a detached mission to the Suffolk area.—Editor]

ABOVE: *Hooker's army on the march to the battlefield of Chancellorsville. From an original sketch by Edwin Forbes. (S)*

Even without these absent divisions, however, Lee decided to take the gamble. If it came to the worst, he believed he could always retreat and join Longstreet at the North Anna River. He hoped, however, that the unexpected nature and suddenness of his attack might surprise the enemy enough to disconcert him and force him to change his plans.

"It was, therefore, determined to leave sufficient troops to hold our lines," Lee wrote, "and with the main body of the army to give battle to the approaching column. Early's division of Jackson's corps, and Barksdale's brigade of McLaws' division, with part of the Reserve Artillery, under General Pendleton, were entrusted with the defense of our position at Fredericksburg, and, at midnight on the 30th, General McLaws marched with the rest of his command toward Chancellorsville. General Jackson followed at dawn next morning with the remaining divisions of his corps."

The renowned Jackson, always conscious of the value of time in battles, had his men moving long before daylight by the light of a brilliant moon that near dawn fortunately was obscured by a dense mist, concealing his movements from the ever-present Federal observation balloon.

BELOW: A Union battery posed for this photo made on the bank of the Rappahannock just prior to the Battle of Chancellorsville. From "Miller's Photographic History of the Civil War."

HOOKER VACILLATES

That morning, May 1, the Federal corps commanders at Chancellorsville were impatiently awaiting orders to advance. They realized that Hooker had outflanked Lee, but a delay now could lose all the advantages gained by the successful maneuver. With the aid of the bright moonlight, the troops should have been moving out before dawn, with no enemy in front of them but Anderson's division. But the sun came up, and the morning got hot, and still they did not move. Hooker, who until that morning had been all vigor, energy, and activity, suddenly became hesitant and cautious. Yet the only opposition he had encountered so far had been in a minor cavalry skirmish the night before between the 6th New York Cavalry and the 5th Virginia Cavalry on the road from Chancellorsville to Spotsylvania Court House.

Finally, about 11 a.m., Hooker gave the order to advance; but at 11 o'clock Anderson and McLaws were also moving out, supported by Jackson who had just arrived. Although Hooker by his vacillation had thrown away a great advantage, the day could still be won if the Federals with their superior numerical strength advanced vigorously and launched a determined and sustained offensive.

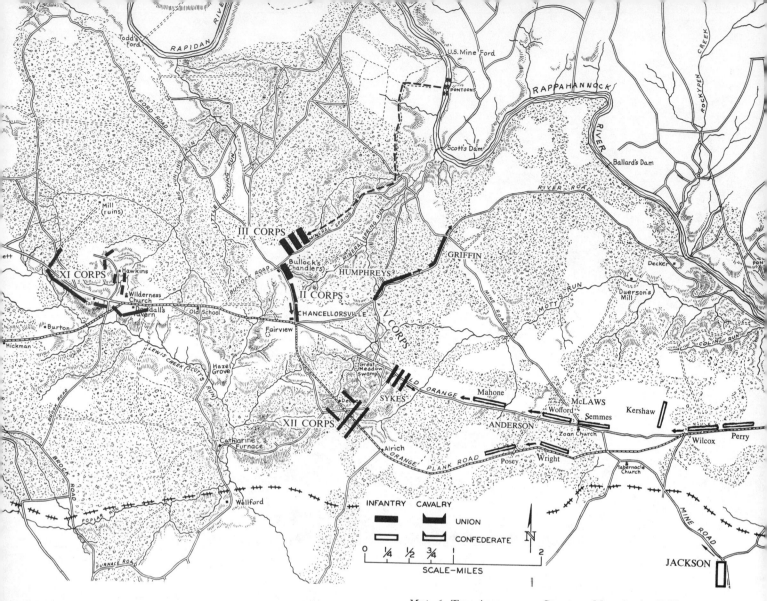

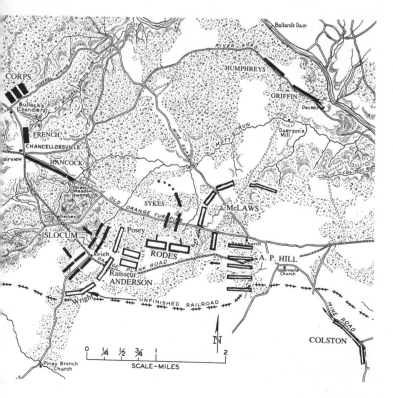

Map 6. The Advance to Contact, May 1. At 11:30 a.m. two divisions of the V Corps have marched east on the River Road and the other division, Sykes's, is advancing on the Turnpike. Couch, commanding the II Corps, has directed that French's division move from its bivouac north of Chancellorsville to Todd's Tavern, six miles south of Wilderness Church. But this unit's passage was blocked at Chancellorsville by the XII Corps moving on the Orange Plank Road. On the 30th Hooker had taken Sickles' III Corps away from Sedgwick's concentration below Fredericksburg and added it to his own force. It had crossed at U.S. Ford on the morning of the 1st and was now moving toward Chancellorsville. The XI Corps was in the defensive position it had taken up on the evening of the 30th.

On the Confederate side, Anderson's men had left their trenches along the line: Tabernacle Church-Zoan Church and were advancing west in two parallel columns as shown. Jackson's, shifting west from Hamilton's Crossing, is approaching on Mine Road.

The opening gun of the Battle of Chancellorsville has been fired, and in a few minutes Sykes will be fighting Mahone.

Map 7. The Situation at 1:30 p.m. May 1. The Confederate advance has isolated Sykes. Hooker, now at Chancellorsville, orders him to withdraw; Hancock is brought forward to cover the movement. Slocum, who had advanced a half mile, is also ordered to retire. Griffin and Humphreys, not informed until after 5 p.m. of these developments, reached Decker's. An order from Meade caused them to retrace their steps at a killing pace.

Rodes, at the head of Jackson's column, swung off the Plank Road and faced north against Sykes's flank. A. P. Hill came up in support, with Colston in reserve.

Meade sent two divisions (Griffin's and Humphreys') out on the River Road, leading to Banks's Ford, and another division, Sykes's, down the Orange Turnpike, followed by Hancock's division of Couch's corps. Slocum moved out on the Orange Plank Road, to be followed by Howard's corps. Sickles' corps was held back of the Chancellor house in reserve. Two miles out on the Turnpike Sykes ran head-on into McLaws, who had formed line of battle with his division astride the Pike; and Slocum's skirmishers tangled with Anderson on the Plank Road. Soon the area echoed to the roar of cannon, the crack of

musketry, and the angry, confused shouts of men trying desperately to kill each other. Then Anderson, on McLaws' left, sent Wright's brigade up an unfinished railroad south of the Plank Road, outflanking Slocum on his right, but not driving him back.

In the center, however, Sykes found himself partially outflanked on both his right and left when his advance carried him ahead of Slocum on his right and Meade's divisions on his left. He then fell back in an orderly manner behind Hancock, who took his place.

By 1 p.m. Slocum had advanced to the Alrich [often misspelled "Aldrich"] house, and was deployed astride the Plank Road with Geary's division on the right and Williams' on the left. Although outflanked on his right by Wright's brigade, the advance of Howard's corps behind him would in turn take Wright in flank. Meade's two divisions on the River Road had met no opposition and were within sight of Banks's Ford, the immediate objective.

Map 8. SITUATION UP TO MIDNIGHT, MAY 1. *From dark until midnight the opposing armies held the positions shown, except Wilcox's brigade, which owing to changing orders was kept marching back and forth between Duerson's Mill and the Turnpike. The divisions of Hill, Rodes, and Colston, except for Ramseur's brigade, have been kept "well in hand." Anderson's and McLaws' divisions, however, are somewhat intermingled.*

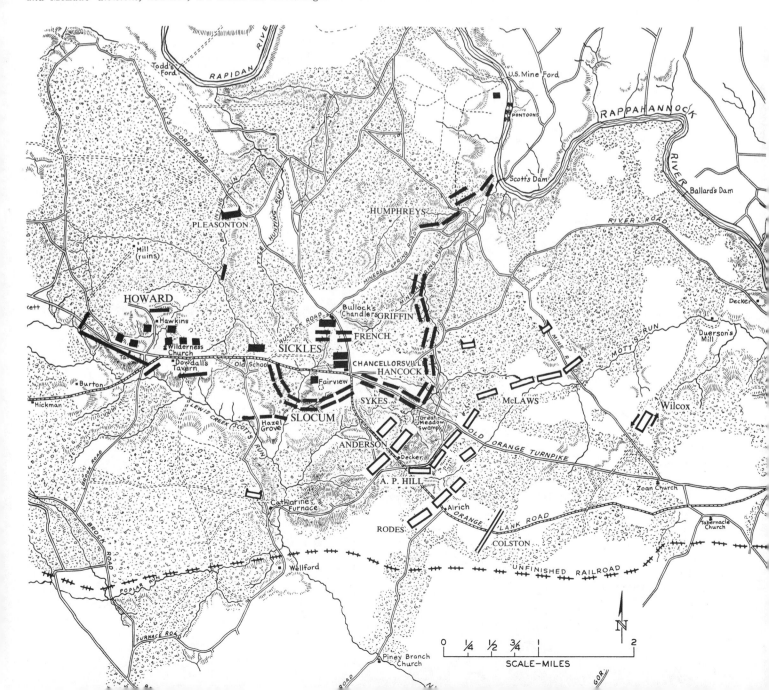

HOOKER ABANDONS THE OFFENSIVE

Then, to the consternation of the corps commanders, came Hooker's order for everyone to retreat to his original position! Fighting Joe was not willing to risk a fight, even with his superior numbers and artillery.

"The position thus abandoned was high ground," Couch reported, "more or less open in front, over which an army might move and artillery be used advantageously." Meade grumbled disgustedly, "If he can't hold the top of the hill, how does he expect to hold the bottom of it?" In a circular order to the corps commanders from army headquarters later came the excuse for the hasty retreat. "The major-general commanding trusts that a suspension in the attack today will embolden the enemy to attack him."

So by dark that evening most of the Army of the Potomac was entrenched in a defensive position around Chancellorsville. The terrain generally lent itself to defensive actions, rather than offensive, even though the superior Federal artillery could not be brought to bear effectively. It was rolling country covered with dense thickets and woods, with few open spaces, and commanded by two knolls south of the Turnpike at Hazel Grove and Fairview. The land between this position and the enemy was cut up by small streams, sharp ravines, and numerous marshes and swamps. Meade's V Corps held the left of the line, with its left resting on the Rappahannock, and facing east. Then came Couch's II, Slocum's XII, and Sickles' III Corps, curving around the Chancellorsville crossroads and stretching out along the Turnpike, facing east and south. The army's right flank was held by Howard's XI Corps, strung out about a mile west of Wilderness Church and generally facing south.

IT WAS now evident to every soldier in the ranks that the Army of the Potomac had suddenly gone on the defensive; and the men began to doubt the ability of their commanding general. "Troops were hurried into position," according to Couch, "but the observer required no wizard to tell him, as they marched past, that the high expectations which had animated them only a few hours ago had given place to disappointment."

When Couch went to headquarters Hooker tried to assure him that everything was just as he wanted it. "It is all right, Couch," he said. "I have got Lee just

where I want him; he must fight me on my own ground."

Couch, however, was not convinced. "The retrograde movement had prepared me for something of the kind," he stated, "but to hear from his own lips that the advantages gained by the successful marches of his lieutenants were to culminate in fighting a defensive battle in that nest of thickets was too much, and I retired from his presence with the belief that my commanding general was a whipped man."

Major General Abner Doubleday, commanding the 3d Division of Reynolds' I Corps, believed that

Hooker's headquarters at Chancellor house on May 1, 1863. (S)

BELOW: Action Friday afternoon, May 1, near the Chancellor house. This drawing (LC) by A. R. Waud is described in "Harper's Weekly" as follows: "The enemy made a vigorous effort to storm our position on the crossroads at Chancellor's. The house is on the right; about it the orderlies, servants, and pack mules of the headquarters—General Hooker and his staff, with Captain Starr's lancers. Slocum's battle line is formed in front, supporting the batteries near the burned chimney, which was surrounded by cherry trees in bloom. In the foreground are columns moving up to take part in the struggle."

28

"Hooker probably thought if Lee assailed a superior force in an entrenched position he would certainly be beaten; and if he did not attack he would soon be forced to fall back on his depots near Richmond for food and ammunition. In either case the prestige would remain with the Union general."

In any event, Hooker had no desire and no plans to attack, and thus by abandoning the offensive and assuming a defensive attitude he voluntarily surrendered the initiative to his opponent. This despite the fact that one clear lesson from all the campaigns of the great military commanders in history was that generally the defensive posture should not be assumed except as a temporary means, with the plan of passing to the offensive as soon as more favorable conditions obtained. The strength of the offensive lies in retaining the initiative, maneuvering at will so as to secure surprise, and to mass superior power at the opponent's weak point.

In retrospect, it is clear that Hooker lost the Battle of Chancellorsville on May 1. Initially he lost it by his hesitancy in moving out when he had Lee outflanked; then by his premature withdrawal before making any serious effort to carry out his plan; and finally by his unwillingness to assume the offensive at any time. Years later, on a visit to that open area

Lee and Jackson in the famous "cracker box" council on the night of Friday, May 1. Drawing by W. L. Sheppard. (B&L)

east of Chancellorsville, Hooker exclaimed grandly, waving one arm in the air, "Here, on this open ground, I intended to fight my battle. But the trouble was to get my army on it." He carefully neglected to mention that his army had been on it, but that at the first sign of a little opposition he hastily withdrew.

LEE DECIDES TO ATTACK

After the Federal forces' sudden and unexpected withdrawal, Lee rode out to his right to inspect the Federal left and see if an attack there might be feasible. He credited Slocum's withdrawal on the right to Wright's flanking movement up the unfinished railroad, but he was puzzled as to why Meade's divisions on the Federal left had retreated with no opposition in their front. Perhaps the enemy's left was weak and should be attacked. Instead, he found that "the enemy had assumed a position of great natural strength, surrounded on all sides by a dense forest filled with a tangled undergrowth, in the midst of which breastworks of logs had been constructed, with trees felled in front, so as to form an almost impenetrable abatis. . . . It was evident that a direct attack upon the enemy could be attended with great difficulty and loss, in view of the strength of his position and his superiority of numbers."

Darkness was approaching by the time Lee finished his reconnaissance and returned to his headquarters,

still undecided as to what action he should take. Here he conferred with Jackson, who expressed the belief that the Federal action had been either a feint or a failure, but in either event he insisted that "By tomorrow morning there will not be any of them this side of the river."

Lee, however, was not convinced. Then "Jeb" Stuart joined them with a report from Brigadier General Fitzhugh Lee that the Federal right extended west beyond Wilderness Church, was not resting on any natural obstacle, and seemed ill-prepared to resist a surprise attack. "It was, therefore, resolved," Lee reported, "to endeavor to turn his right flank and gain his rear, leaving a force in front to hold him in check and conceal the movement."

The risk was high, for the attacking force would have to make a flanking march of some twelve miles across the front of the Union army, traditionally one of the most dangerous military maneuvers. It was decided that Jackson would make this wide envelopment with his entire corps, some 28,000 men, thus leaving Lee with only Anderson's and McLaws' divisions to hold Hooker's whole force in check while the march was being made. Stuart's cavalry would screen Jackson's movement.

It was a bold and seemingly desperate gamble, but Lee apparently was willing to take the risk in order to seize and hold the initiative. That he was aware of the dangers involved and the possibility of failure is evident in what he wrote to Jefferson Davis: "It is plain that if the enemy is too strong for me here, I shall have to fall back, and Fredericksburg must be abandoned. If successful here, Fredericksburg will be saved and our communications retained. I may be forced back to the Orange and Alexandria or the Virginia Central road, but in either case I will be in position to contest the enemy's advance upon Richmond. . . . I am now swinging around to my left to come up in his rear."

JACKSON'S MARCH

It was almost dawn when Lee's conference broke up. The fading stars gave promise of a clear, hot day. Shortly after 7:30 a.m. the head of Jackson's column moved out past the crossroad near Decker's, to the southwest. A local guide had been found who knew a seldom-used woodcutter's road through the woods, which in turn led to a better road that ran northward beyond the Federal right flank and would put the column on the Orange Turnpike, well west of the enemy's position.

As the climbing sun burned down, the column, six miles long, wound its way across the Union front. Anderson and McLaws were ordered to press strongly against the Federal left to prevent reinforcements

being sent to their right, but Lee ordered them "not to attack in force unless a favorable opportunity should present itself."

Shortly after sunrise that morning Hooker rode out to inspect his lines. When he reached Howard's XI Corps on the west flank he found the three divisions spread along the Turnpike, generally facing south. Brigadier General Charles Devens' division held the extreme right, with only two regiments facing west at right angles to the Pike. Hooker seemed satisfied with the disposition of the troops and remarked about the unusually strong breastworks built by Devens. "How strong," he said to Howard, "how strong." And yet General Schurz, commanding the 3d Division of Howard's corps, later would report: "Our right wing stood completely in the air, with nothing to lean upon, not even a strong echelon, and with no reliable cavalry to make reconnaissances, and that, too, in a forest thick enough not to permit any view to the front, flank, or rear, but not thick enough to prevent the approach of the enemy's troops."

Map 9. START OF JACKSON'S FAMOUS FLANK MARCH. As was often the case with him, Jackson did not get an early start. The head of his column did not pass the crossroads at Decker's, on the Plank Road, until 7:30 a.m. (This late start, and its slowness, was to mean that he would not launch his attack against the XI Corps until too late to exploit his initial success before dark.)

Federals at Hazel Grove spied Jackson's column when, at 8 a.m., it was near Wellford, and Hooker later had Sickles attack the column near Catharine Furnace. During the entire march, however, Hooker failed to appreciate the significance of the movement—he thought the Rebels were trying to get away.

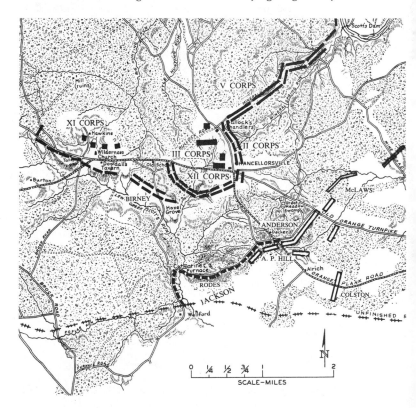

Hooker's headquarters at Chancellorsville on Saturday a.m., May 2. Picture faces south. From sketch by Edwin Forbes. (B&L)

ON returning to his headquarters at Chancellorsville Hooker was informed of strong demonstrations being made by the enemy in front of Meade's V Corps on the Federal east flank. Then, shortly after 9 o'clock, Federal observers posted in tall trees reported a heavy Confederate movement westward on the Catharine [usually misspelled "Catherine"] Furnace Road in front of Sickles' III Corps. Sickles immediately requested permission to attack, but Hooker was not yet willing to commit himself. He hoped, and tended to believe, that the movement signified that Lee was retreating to Gordonsville. Either that, or the Confederates might be preparing to attack his right flank. If he really believed the latter, he should have ordered Sickles and Slocum to attack immediately in front in order to break up the movement, and then ordered Meade to swing around and get on the Confederate rear. Instead, at 9:30 the following order was sent to Howard:

I am directed by the Major-General Commanding to say that . . . the disposition you have made of your corps has been with a view to a front attack by the enemy. If he should throw himself upon your flank, he wishes you to examine the ground and determine upon the positions you will take in that event, in order that you may be prepared for him in whatever direction he advances. He suggests that you have heavy reserves well in hand to meet this contingency. The right of your line does not appear to be strong enough. No artificial defences worth naming have been thrown up, and there appears to be a scarcity of troops at that point, and not, in the General's opinion, as favorably posted as might be.

We have good reason to suppose that the enemy is moving to our right. Please advance your pickets for purposes of observation as far as may be safe, in order to obtain timely information of their approach.

Howard later denied receiving this order, but admitted frankly that even if he had he would not have changed position without specific instructions to do so. The order was general in nature, he said, with no sense of urgency; Hooker had inspected the lines just a few hours previously; and Howard was firmly convinced that the heavy woods on his right would prevent any major attack from that direction. Yet he sent a message to Hooker's headquarters that stated, in part, "I am taking measures to resist an attack from the west."

But according to Schurz, "All the precaution that was taken against a flank attack . . . was the construction of a small rifle-pit across the Chancellorsville road in the rear of my division, near the house [Dowdall's Tavern] occupied by General Howard as headquarters."

AT 11 o'clock Devens reported a westward movement of the enemy in strength in his front. Still

Hooker hesitated. The previous night he had ordered Sedgwick to send Reynolds' I Corps to Chancellorsville, and when it arrived he would have approximately 90,000 troops at his immediate command. Even if Lee, instead of retreating, was preparing to attack his right, Hooker apparently felt secure in his defensive position and had no plans to attack. As the day wore on, with no word of a Confederate offensive anywhere along the line, Hooker convinced himself that Lee was fleeing to save his army. So, about 1 p.m., he ordered Sickles to "advance cautiously toward the road followed by the enemy, and harass the movement as much as possible." The word "attack" was not even mentioned, and only Sickles was ordered to move. Strange orders, indeed, for a commanding general who earlier had informed his cavalry commander that the secret of success in battle was to "fight, fight, fight."

At 2 o'clock Couch reported at headquarters, where Hooker greeted him with the exclamation: "Lee is in full retreat toward Gordonsville, and I have sent out Sickles to capture his artillery." Couch, who already believed that Hooker was a whipped man, thought to himself: "If your conception is correct, it is very strange that only the Third Corps should be sent in pursuit."

Map 10. MOVEMENTS BETWEEN 1:30 P.M. AND 2 P.M. MAY 2. This shows the march of Jackson's command around Hooker's army. Birney, of Sickles' III Corps, has moved his division south from Hazel Grove to attack the tail of Jackson's artillery column. Posey's brigade of Anderson's division and Thomas' and Archer's brigades of A. P. Hill's division are hastening to aid the 23d Georgia, which has been assailed by Birney. The remainder of the III Corps is coming to join Birney.

Jackson has just joined Fitzhugh Lee at Burton's farm, and is observing the disposition of Howard's unalarmed troops along the road near Dowdall's Tavern. Jackson sends word to Rodes, who had started to turn northeast at Hickman, to continue north and halt with the head of his column at the Turnpike three-quarters of a mile west of Luckett's. Colston and A. P. Hill are following Rodes. The cavalry is moving between the main infantry column and the enemy; the trains are on the outside route.

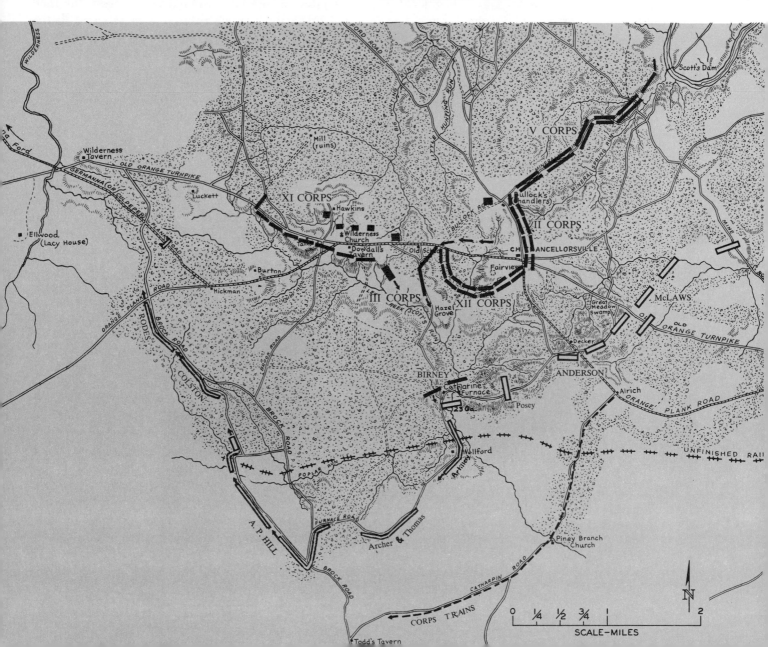

It is impossible, of course, to know what Hooker really did believe at this point, and there seems to be only one logical explanation for his actions, or lack of them. He was not willing, apparently, to disrupt what he considered a strong defensive position to risk an attack under any circumstances. He was hoping to win a great moral victory, which is the way Lee's retreat would be regarded in the North, without fighting a battle or risking his army or reputation. This, of course, was waging war in the classical European tradition of maneuvering rather than fighting.

Sickles moved out with two divisions. About 2:30 he hit Jackson's rearguard near Catharine Furnace and killed or captured most of the 23d Georgia Regiment. A veteran of the 8th Pennsylvania Cavalry reported: "Passing to the left of the Chancellorsville House, we crossed our line of battle at the edge of a wood and came up with a reconnoitering party that had captured the 23d Georgia. We had heard that Lee was retreating, and supposed that this unfortunate regiment had been sacrificed to give the main body a chance to escape; but while we were commiserating the poor fellows, one of them defiantly said, 'You may think you have done a big thing just now, but wait till Jackson gets round on your right.' We laughed at his harmless bravado." Not only the generals thought Lee was retreating; even the men in ranks believed it.

WHEN Lee learned of this attack on Jackson's column, he immediately dispatched Posey's brigade of Anderson's division to the support of Wright's brigade near Catharine Furnace. This successfully checked Sickles' advance, and as Sickles stated in his report: "Ascertaining from a careful examination of the position that it was practicable to gain the road and break the enemy's column, I so reported to the general-in-chief, adding that as I must expect to encounter a heavy force and a stubborn resistance, and bearing in mind his admonition to move cautiously, I should not advance farther until the supports from the Eleventh and Twelfth Corps closed up on Birney's right and left."

Hooker then ordered Barlow's brigade, 2,500 men, of the XI Corps over to support Sickles' right, although he knew this was the only force Howard had in reserve, and despite his earlier order to Howard that morning that he should "have heavy reserves well in hand." If Howard needed any convincing, this move certainly must have assured him that in Hooker's mind at least there was no thought of any attack on his right.

About the same time that Sickles was capturing the 23d Georgia, Jackson's leading regiment, the 5th Alabama, was already forming for the attack across the Turnpike west of Hooker's right flank. As the other Confederate regiments gradually came up and formed in the woods, the Union pickets were aware that something big was afoot. Junior officers of the line tried to alert corps headquarters, but Howard, by now imbued with Hooker's belief that Lee was fleeing, and convinced that the woods were too thick on his right for a major assault, refused to take any action.

Colonel Noble, commanding the 17th Connecticut Infantry, later reported: "Horseman after horseman rode into my post and was sent to headquarters with the information that the enemy were heavily marching along our front and proceeding to our right; and last of all an officer reported the rebels massing for

Howard's line at the moment of Jackson's attack on the evening of May 2. A. R. Waud's pencil drawing (LC) shows a part of the XI Corps line along the Old Orange Plank Road just before it caved in and was overrun. In the center of the picture is Dowdall's Tavern, Howard's headquarters. Across the pike (indicated by the line of troops) and to the right in the woods, is Wilderness Church, a landmark in the battle.

Map 11. JACKSON'S DEPLOYMENT. *Archer and Thomas reached Catharine Furnace at 3:30 p.m. to assist the 23d Georgia. An hour later they resumed the march. Meanwhile Anderson's and McLaws' divisions, under Lee's immediate charge, kept up a lively demonstration to divert the Federals' attention from Jackson's march.*

Sickles was having a private war of his own near the furnace. He saw a chance of cutting off part of the Confederate column, but needed help. Barlow's brigade of the XI Corps was sent to him. Slocum wheeled Williams' division around to assist. Sickles intended an advance against the flank and rear of Anderson, but Jackson launched his attack on the XI Corps before this could be executed.

Jackson had reached the Turnpike at 2:30 p.m., turned east at Luckett's, and deployed astride the Pike in the formation shown. The deployment was completed at 5 p.m. whereupon Jackson told Rodes to move out—although the last three brigades of Hill's division were not up.

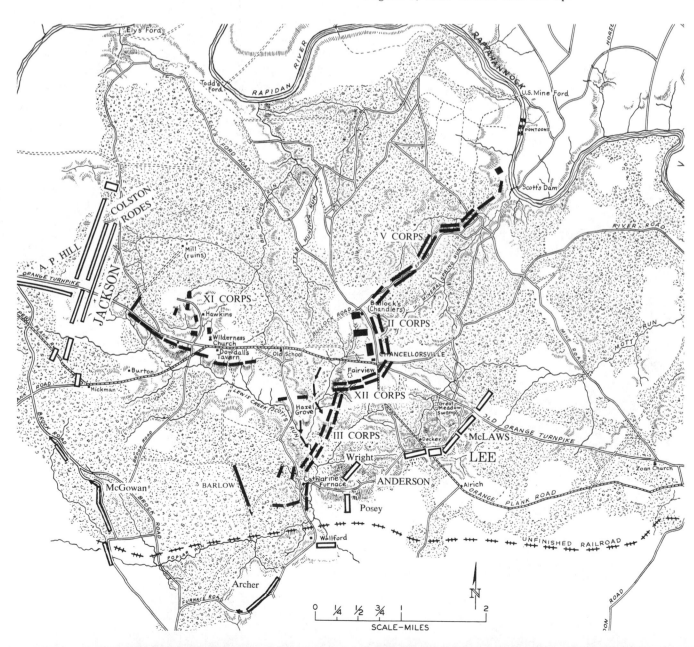

attack. Howard scouted the report and insulted the informants, charging them with telling a story that was the offspring of their imaginations or their fears."

In desperation, one officer in command of some pickets sent a final message to Howard that the enemy was forming in strength in the woods on his flank, and ended with, "For God's sake make disposition to receive him."

About this same time Hooker sent Sedgwick, back at Fredericksburg, a telegram: "We know that the enemy is fleeing, trying to save his trains."

By 5 p.m. all of Jackson's troops were up, and were eager to attack. But to be sure that they all moved forward in good order, Jackson spent almost an hour deploying them for a mile or more on either side of the Turnpike. In front was Rodes's division, with Colston's division 200 yards behind, and A. P. Hill's in the rear to support the other two. When Rodes reported he was ready, Jackson said calmly, "You can go forward, sir."

JACKSON STRIKES HOWARD

Most of the men in Howard's corps, their muskets stacked, were preparing supper, some were playing cards, others sleeping. Then the woods suddenly

Confederates carrying Howard's breastworks in Jackson's surprise attack on XI Corps. Drawing by W. L. Sheppard. (B&L)

echoed with bugle calls and the grayclad regiments, exploding into action to the sound of the fearful Rebel yell, proceeded to roll up Hooker's right flank.

"Its first lively effects," Howard described the assault, "appeared in the startled rabbits, squirrels, quail, and other game flying wildly hither and thither in evident terror, and escaping where possible into adjacent clearings." The first fierce rush struck the two regiments of Colonel Leopold Von Gilsa's brigade and his two guns on the pike, the only Federal force actually fronting in the direction of the attack. Devens' division, taken in flank, was driven back in disorder on Schurz's division, which in turn fell back in confusion and panic on Steinwehr's division.

"The noise and the smoke filled the air with excitement," according to Howard, "and, more quickly than it could be told, with all the fury of the wildest hailstorm, everything, every sort of organization that lay in the path of the mad current of panic-stricken men, had to give way and be broken into fragments."

Schurz in his report stated: "To change the front of the regiments deployed in line on the old Turnpike road was extremely difficult. In the first place, they were hemmed in between a variety of obstacles in front and dense pine brush in their rear. Then the officers had hardly had time to give a command when almost the whole of General McLean's brigade, mixed up with a number of Colonel Von Gilsa's men,

came rushing down the road from General Devens' headquarters in wild confusion, and, worse than that, the battery of the First Division broke in upon my right at a full run. This confused mass of guns, caissons, horses, and men broke lengthwise through the ranks of my regiments deployed in line on the road. . . . The whole line deployed on the old Turnpike, facing south, was rolled up and swept away in a moment."

And a soldier in the 13th Massachusetts Volunteers remembered that "along the road it was pandemonium; on the side of the road it was chaos."

IN THE deep, purple shadows of dusk the initial charge began to lose its momentum as scattered Federal units were brought into line to stem the tide. "Gathering up such troops as were nearest to the scene of action," Couch reported, "with Berry's division from the Third Corps, some from the Twelfth,

Hays' brigade of the Second, and a portion of the Eleventh, an effectual stand was made." Sickles was immediately ordered back from Catharine Furnace, several batteries were placed on Fairview, a knoll 750 yards west of Chancellorsville, and Brigadier General Alfred Pleasonton's brigade of cavalry, which had remained with the army, was ordered to Hazel Grove, a low but commanding hill just south of the Turnpike. Here his artillery, with other batteries from the III Corps and supported by Major General Amiel Whipple's division, enfiladed Jackson's right.

Their alignment broken by the charge through the woods, the darkness, and the growing resistance to the attack, the Confederates halted to reform. A confused clamor could be heard as officers and men sought to find their companies and regiments, now inextricably mixed, by the dim light of a rising moon. But Jackson, sensing his advantage, had no intention of stopping now. He ordered A. P. Hill to relieve Rodes and Colston and to prepare for a night attack. When Hill reported to him, Jackson directed: "Press them; cut them off from the United States Ford, Hill; press them." And then Jackson went forward on the Turnpike in the darkness to study the situation at first hand. Returning to his lines he and his aides rode into the 18th North Carolina Regiment, braced for an expected attack from the Federal cavalry,

Map 12. JACKSON FRACTURES THE XI CORPS. This shows the situation at 7:15 p.m. May 2, with the XI Corps fleeing the scene of its disaster. By 7:15 Sickles had broken off his movement to the south and had faced his three divisions back toward the Turnpike to stem the Confederate tidal wave. The first unit sent north to help Howard, the 8th Pennsylvania Cavalry, made a heroic but costly charge and was caught up in the general rout.

Federal artillery at Hazel Grove and Fairview is firing effectively. Sykes has moved northwest along the Ely's Ford Road. The I Corps, snatched early that day from Sedgwick, has reached U.S. Ford and is headed south into the battle.

Barlow's brigade of Howard's corps has not yet received orders to stop its advance southward to attack Jackson's supposed retreat.

Jackson's assault has lost its initial momentum. The front line units have become disoriented and intermingled in the darkening woods. Jackson, soon to be shot down by his own troops mistaking him for a Federal, has ordered Hill to pass through Rodes and renew the attack.

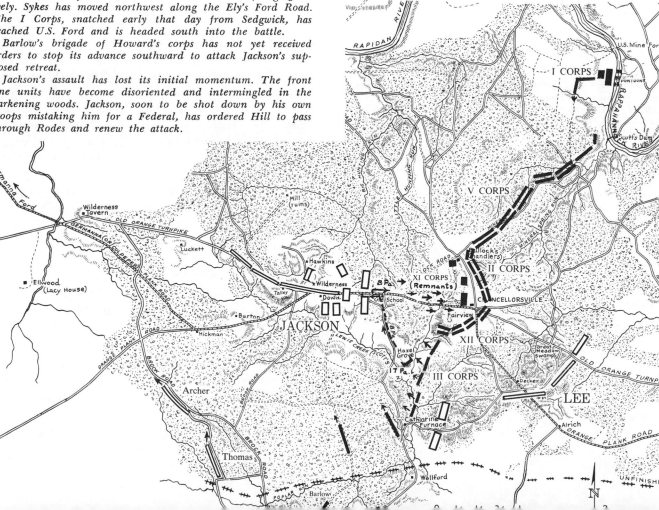

This drawing by A. C. Redwood shows the panic-stricken stampede of the XI Corps from position on the Plank Road. (B&L)

where he was shot and mortally wounded by his own men, thus ending any chance for another major assault before dawn. Command then fell to Hill, and when he was wounded by Federal artillery, Stuart took command of the corps.

Stuart, who arrived on the field at 10 o'clock that night, later reported:

> I found, upon reaching it, A. P. Hill's division in front, under Heth, with Lane's, McGowan's, Archer's, and Heth's brigades on the right of the road, within half a mile of Chancellorsville, near the apex of the ridge, and Pender's and Thomas' on the left. I found that the enemy had made an attack on our right flank, but were repulsed. The fact, however, that the attack was made, and at night, made me apprehensive of a repetition of it, and necessitated throwing back the right wing, so as to meet it. I was also informed that there was much confusion on the right, owing to the fact that some troops mistook friends for the enemy and fired upon them. Knowing that an advance under such circumstances would be extremely hazardous, much against my inclination, I felt bound to wait for daylight.

THE FEDERALS REORGANIZE

By 11 p.m. the Federal XI Corps had been re-formed north of Chancellorsville, Slocum and Sickles were in position across the Turnpike behind strong breastworks, Meade held the left flank securely based on the Rappahannock, and Reynolds' I Corps, after a 30-mile march, held the Federal right flank along the Ely's Ford Road, the right flank of the corps resting on the Rapidan and facing west generally. One veteran of that corps remembered: "Notwith-standing fatigue and weariness, we began at once to build earthworks, as every man felt that his own safety as well as that of the army might soon be at stake. Knives, bayonets, plates, and dippers were enlisted, and by continuous activity substantial breastworks were completed when daylight appeared."

Hooker, with the addition of the I Corps, was actually stronger after Jackson's attack than he had been before. Howard's corps, though temporarily routed in panic, suffered only 2,412 casualties during the whole campaign, whereas Sickles' corps, for example, lost 4,119 and Slocum's 2,824. During the night Howard reorganized his men, and by morning they were ready and willing to fight, if given the chance. As Couch expressed it: "It can be emphatically stated that no corps in the army, surprised as the Eleventh was at this time, could have held its ground under similar circumstances."

With the arrival of Reynolds' I Corps from Fredericksburg, Hooker had approximately 90,000 men around Chancellorsville to oppose Lee's divided 48,-000. Thus most of the advantages were still his; but the Union commander had lost his nerve the day before, and he was thinking only of defense. The only offensive action taken, if indeed it could be called that, was a panic-stricken message sent to Sedgwick at 9 p.m. ordering him to capture Fredericksburg immediately, drive the enemy off Marye's Heights back of the city, and proceed at once on the Turnpike to Hooker's relief, to "attack and destroy any force he may fall in with on the road . . . and march to be in our vicinity at daylight."

An easy order to give, but impossible to execute.

As Couch pointed out, "It was 11 p.m. May 2d when he [Sedgwick] got the order, and twelve or fourteen miles had to be marched over by daylight. The night was moonlit, but any officer who has had experience in making night marches with infantry will understand the vexatious delays occurring even when the road is clear; but when, in addition, there is an enemy in front, with a line of fortified heights to assault, the problem which Sedgwick had to solve will be pronounced impossible of solution."

LEE'S ATTACK ON MAY 3

There is no question that Lee's strategy and tactics had been successful. His whole movement had been a model of maneuvering, screening, and massing superior forces at the opponent's weak point. But the fact remains that as of 10 p.m. that night Lee had actually gained no material advantage. His situation

was just as critical as while the flanking march was being made. The Army of Northern Virginia was still split into three parts, with Sickles' corps and most of Slocum's between Lee and Stuart. And if Reynolds' comparatively fresh corps had moved out aggressively and attacked Stuart's left flank, while Meade simultaneously threw his V Corps at Lee's right flank, in all probability the Confederate army would have been destroyed. As the caustic Couch observed: "It only required that Hooker should brace himself up to take a reasonable, common-sense view of the state of things, when the success gained by Jackson would have been turned into an overwhelming defeat."

Lee was well aware of his potentially dangerous position. At 3 a.m. on May 3 he ordered Stuart, now commanding Jackson's corps, to resume the attack as soon as possible so as to unite the two wings of the army. Thirty minutes later he sent still another

Major General Oliver O. Howard trying to rally his men during the rout of the XI Corps at Chancellorsville. He lost his right arm at Fair Oaks. Drawing by R. Zogbaum. (B&L)

message to Stuart, stressing the urgency of the situation. "General: I repeat what I have said half an hour since. It is all-important that you still continue pressing to the right, turning, if possible, all the fortified points, in order that we can unite both wings of the army. Keep the troops well together, and press on, on the general plan, which is to work by the right wing, turning the positions of the enemy, so as to drive him from Chancellorsville, which will again unite us. Everything will be done on this side to accomplish the same object. Try and keep the troops provisioned and together, and proceed vigorously." And later in a note to the wounded Jackson he wrote: "Could I have directed events, I should

Map 13. THE MAY 3 FIGHT FOR CHANCELLORSVILLE. *This shows the situation at 7:30 a.m., as A. P. Hill's division (under Heth) advances against Fairview on the south of the Pike and Berry's division to the north of it. Archer's brigade has wheeled against Sickles' withdrawing column but is repulsed. Lane and Pender have crashed against the juncture of Berry's and Williams' divisions. Lee is wheeling Anderson's and McLaws' divisions to come abreast of Heth and make contact with the latter's right.*

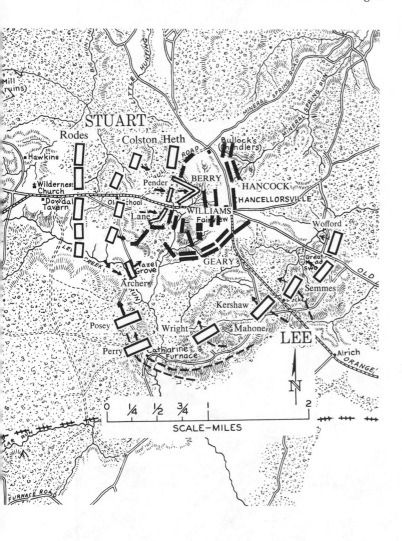

have chosen for the good of the country to be disabled in your stead."

At the first gray streaks of dawn Stuart sent Hill's division forward on the Turnpike, swinging his right flank, Archer's brigade, around to the south against Sickles' right, fighting desperately to hook up with Anderson's left. Colston was in the second line, Rodes in the third. Anderson, with his right resting on the Plank Road, pivoted his division on that point and swung his left flank, Posey's and Wright's brigades, forward from the vicinity of Catharine Furnace, against Sickles' left and Slocum's right. Meanwhile McLaws, between the Orange Plank Road and the Turnpike, moved straight ahead against Slocum's left and Couch's right.

THEN, suddenly, Hooker made it easy for the Confederates. The key to Sickles' position was the high ground at Hazel Grove which, since Pleasonton's cavalry had been withdrawn to Chancellorsville,

Whipple's division now held. But in order to strengthen his new, shorter defense line around Chancellorsville, Hooker ordered Whipple to be withdrawn from Hazel Grove and placed behind Berry's and Birney's divisions, straddling the Turnpike just west of Chancellorsville.

Stuart immediately saw that Hazel Grove was key terrain. Within a few minutes he had placed thirty pieces of artillery on it, and these guns soon began to play with devastating effect upon Sickles' troops and Geary's division of Slocum's corps. Sickles was forced to fall back, and with shouts of joy and excitement Stuart's right and Anderson's left linked up. Lee reported: "As the troops advancing upon the enemy's front and right converged upon his central position, Anderson effected a junction with Jackson's corps, and the whole line pressed irresistibly on."

For several more hours on May 3 the fighting raged furiously. Hill's men twice captured the knoll at Fairview and twice were thrown back; but with the Confederate artillery at Hazel Grove pouring in a deadly fire, the third time Fairview was captured and held. The Chancellor house was hit and set on fire and a cannon ball, striking a wooden pillar on which Hooker was leaning, hurled him to the ground and temporarily disabled him.

"The woods had caught fire in several places," wrote an observer, "the flames spreading over a span of several acres in extent where the ground was thickly covered with dry leaves; and here the conflagration progressed with the rapidity of a prairie-fire, and a large number of Confederate and Federal wounded thickly scattered in the vicinity, and too badly hurt to crawl out of the way, met a terrible death."

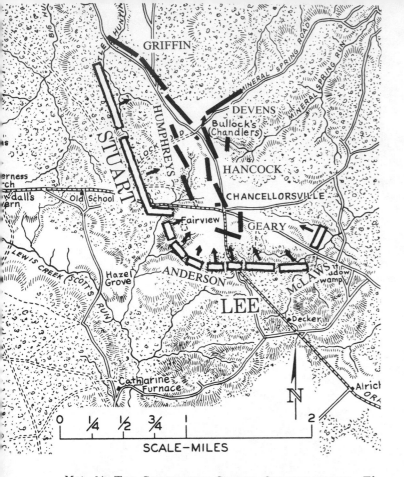

Map 14. THE CONFEDERATES CAPTURE CHANCELLORSVILLE. *The situation at 10 a.m. May 3, as Lee's two wings unite for the final drive to capture Chancellorsville. Hooker, in a semi-stupor, has ceased to function, and his divisions, though still full of fight, reluctantly pull out to the north.*

HOOKER IS DEFEATED

Almost out of ammunition and their requests for reinforcements refused, Sickles and Slocum were slowly driven back and the Federal front gradually melted away and passed to a new defensive line north of Chancellorsville, which Hooker's engineers had laid out the night before. In effect, the new position did nothing more than cover the bridgeheads across the Rappahannock. By 10 a.m. May 3 Lee was in full possession of the field, and by noon the Army of the Potomac was in its last defensive position before retreating across the river.

Hooker was reluctant to inform Washington of the results of the three days of fighting. In fact, for two days he had deliberately kept President Lincoln in the dark. Now, at 1:30 p.m., Major General Daniel Butterfield, his chief of staff, took it upon himself to let the President know something. "From all reports yet collected," he informed Lincoln, "the battle has been most fierce and terrible. Loss heavy on both sides. General Hooker slightly, but not severely wounded. He has preferred thus far that nothing should be reported, and does not know of this, but I cannot refrain from saying this much to

you." This, of course, told the President nothing, except that someone was fighting somewhere.

The anxious Lincoln frantically telegraphed Butterfield: "Where is General Hooker? Where is Sedgwick? Where is Stoneman?"

Finally at 3:30 p.m. Hooker reported: "We have had a desperate fight yesterday and today, which has resulted in no success to us, having lost a position of two lines, which had been selected for our defense. . . . I do not despair of success. . . . If Sedgwick could have gotten up, there could have been but one result. . . ."

It is interesting to note that while Hooker did not "despair of success," he offered no plans or information as to how this success was to be achieved in his present position, nor did he explain why, after ordering Sedgwick with 24,000 troops to come to the aid of the right wing of an army with 90,000 troops, he now withdrew the entire wing to a safe defensive position, leaving Sedgwick and his men to take care of themselves as best they could.

Lee was anxious to capitalize on the victory, but most of the men were scattered in confusion and many of them had been fighting since before dawn. He wisely halted to rest and to reorganize for a new attack. He stated in his report: "The enemy had withdrawn to a strong position nearer the Rappahannock, which he had previously fortified. His superiority of numbers, the unfavorable nature of the ground, which was densely wooded, and the condition of our troops after the arduous and sanguinary conflict in which they had been engaged, rendered great caution necessary. Our preparations were just completed when further operations were arrested by intelligence received from Fredericksburg." This intelligence was that Early had been driven off the heights at Fredericksburg, and a Federal force under Sedgwick was even now marching on Lee's rear.

Dilger's battery of Federal artillery on the Plank Road slowing Jackson's advance, Saturday evening, May 2. (B&L)

Rescuing the wounded from the burning woods. Many men were not so lucky. Based on wartime sketch by Edwin Forbes. (B&L)

SEDGWICK'S BATTLE AT FREDERICKSBURG

When Sedgwick at 11 p.m., May 2 received Hooker's order to cross the river at Fredericksburg and advance on Chancellorsville he immediately put his corps in motion even though he realized it undoubtedly would be impossible to reach Chancellorsville by daybreak, unless the Confederate force in his front had withdrawn. Of that he had no evidence. Also, it seemed apparent that Hooker either forgot or ignored the fact that on May 1 he had ordered Sedgwick to cross the river and make a demonstration down the Bowling Green Road, which Sedgwick had done with his whole command. "The [new] order to cross at Fredericksburg," Sedgwick reported, "found me with my entire command on the south side of the river, ready to pursue by the Bowling Green road," and he was already more than three miles beyond the city. "To recross for the purpose of crossing again at Fredericksburg, where no bridges had been laid, would have occupied until long after daylight. I commenced, therefore, to move by the flank in the direction of Fredericksburg, on the Bowling Green road."

But in the dark and unfamiliar country it took time to brush the Confederate pickets out of the way, and the column was slowed by the usual constant halts and false alarms of a night march in the presence of an enemy. It was close to daylight on May 3 when the advance reached the quiet streets of Fredericksburg. As the bright morning dawned, the dread Marye's Heights, the scene of Burnside's horrible disaster in December, came into view. "Several regiments were speedily moved along the open ground in the rear of the town toward the heights," a staff officer recorded, "and this movement discovered the enemy in force behind the famous stone wall at the base of the hill. They were protected by strong works

and supported by well-served artillery. It was at once felt that a desperate encounter was to follow, and the recollections of the previous disaster were by no means inspiriting."

On reaching the town, Sedgwick ordered Gibbon's division of Couch's II Corps, which had been left at Falmouth, to cross and take position on Sedgwick's right and try to outflank Early's left. He sent Howe's division to the south of Hazel Run to turn the Confederate right, and he held Newton's division in the center to await the results of the turning movements. Gibbon, however, was stopped by the canal and heavy artillery fire, and Howe found the terrain such that he could not move to his right. Consequently, Sedgwick concluded, "Nothing remained but to carry the works by direct assault."

Map 15. SITUATION ON SEDGWICK'S FRONT AT 7:30 A.M., MAY 3. During the early morning hours Sedgwick's VI Corps moved north from its pontoon bridges at Franklin's old crossing site, prepared to assault the Confederate works on the heights west of Fredericksburg. The bridges were then moved upstream, one to the position near the railroad bridge, the other to near the Lacy house. Gibbon's division, which was to cross at the latter bridge, was delayed in getting across, but at 7:30 a.m. was in the position shown. Newton's division led the VI Corps north into Fredericksburg, followed by Burnham's Light Division (a small provisional unit). Opposition was slight. Howe followed as far as Hazel Run, and Brooks as far as Deep Run, when skirmishing in his rear caused him to halt and face southwest.

The Confederates' fieldworks on the heights were occupied by Early's division. Wilcox came up to the vicinity of Taylor's Hill just in time to stall Gibbon's advance.

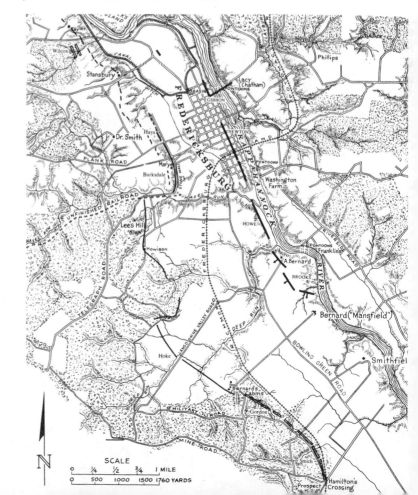

IT was now 10 a.m. and Major General Gouverneur K. Warren, who was at Sedgwick's headquarters as Hooker's representative, urged an immediate attack against Barksdale's brigade on the heights in the center of the Confederate line. Newton then formed three columns of assault in the center, based on the Plank Road, and at 11 o'clock Sedgwick, with much apprehension because the memory of the tragedy of the previous December was still fresh in his mind, gave the order to advance.

An observer noted: Both columns and line, in light marching order, advanced at double-quick without firing a shot. The enemy kept up an incessant artillery fire, and the noise was deafening. Their musketry fire was reserved until our men were within easy range. Then a murderous storm of shot from the stone wall, and grape and cannister from the hill, burst upon the columns and line. For a moment the head of the left column was checked and broken. The column on the right was also broken . . . Then, as if moved by a sudden impulse and nerved for a supreme effort, both columns and the line in the field simultaneously sprang forward. Along the wall a hand-to-hand fight took place, and the bayonet and the butt of the musket were freely used. The stone wall was gained and the men were quickly over it . . . and immediately after the wall was carried the enemy became panic-stricken. In the flight they threw away guns, knapsacks, pistols, swords, and everything that might retard their speed.

Map 16. SEDGWICK'S ATTACK AT FREDERICKSBURG. *This shows the VI Corps capturing Marye's Heights between 10:30 a.m. and 11 a.m. May 3.*

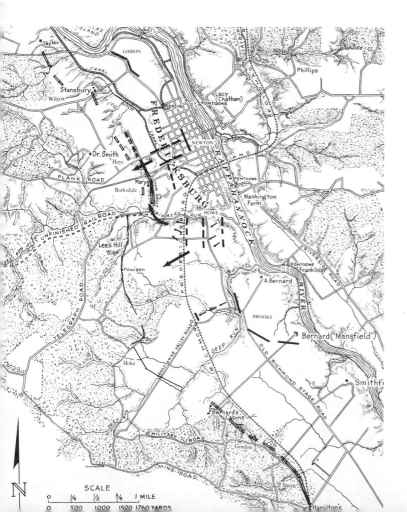

Attack on Sedgwick at Bank's Ford, Monday evening, May 4. From sandbag battery near Falmouth. Drawing, Edwin Forbes.

It was all over in fifteen minutes, as Early's troops retired along the Telegraph Road in confusion toward Richmond. It was a welcome but costly victory, as Sedgwick suffered almost 1,000 casualties.

Although he was still under orders to proceed as quickly as possible to Hooker's relief at Chancellorsville, Sedgwick now halted to reform and to rest Newton's division, exhausted by the night march, the weight of several days' rations and sixty rounds of ammunition, and by the heat, fatigue, and excitement of battle.

Brooks's division, which had been left to guard the bridges three miles lower down the Rappahannock, was now ordered up. Aware of the casualties Newton had suffered in the brilliant charge, Sedgwick was anxious to have Brooks, whose men had seen no action, take the lead in the move to Chancellorsville. Consequently it was 3 p.m. before Brooks moved out, followed by Newton and Howe.

Salem Church, from photograph made after the war. View is from the Plank Road. On the left is what remains of the Confederate trenches. The bricks on the four sides of the church are spotted with bullet marks, especially on the line of the upper windows toward the road, evidence that many Union soldiers aimed high. This church sheltered many Fredericksburg families during Burnside's battle. (B&L)

SCALE

0   ¼   ½   ¾   1 MILE

0   500   1000   1500   1760 YARDS

BATTLE OF SALEM CHURCH

The Plank Road running west from Fredericksburg passed through a gently rolling country with a series of low hills and sharp ravines at right angles to the road. Wilcox's brigade of Anderson's division, which had marched from Banks's Ford to Barksdale's assistance but arrived too late to help, now fell back slowly in front of Brooks, using the advantage of the terrain to impede the Federal advance. About four miles out, however, at Salem Church Wilcox halted and threw up breastworks across the road. The church, a small, unpretentious red-brick building, was situated on a long ridge covered with thick woods and tanglefoot underbrush. This position commanded the open approaches from the east. Here Wilcox was joined by McLaws with his three brigades and Mahone's brigade of Anderson's division, sent by Lee when he learned that Early had been repulsed and a Federal force was marching on his rear. The brigades of Kershaw and Wofford went into line on Wilcox's right, those of Semmes and Mahone on his left.

Coming up on this strong position, Sedgwick immediately deployed Brooks astride the road, and Newton on his right, and ordered an attack without waiting for Howe to come up. "After a sharp and prolonged contest," Sedgwick reported, "we gained the heights, but were met by fresh troops pouring in upon the flank of the advanced portion of the line. For a short time the crest was held by our troops with obstinate resistance, but at length the line was forced slowly back through the woods." Then darkness settled like a gently restraining hand over the field and the fighting stopped. When Howe came up, Sedgwick wisely had him form line of battle in the rear, facing east and south, and with his left flank resting on the Rappahannock protecting the Banks's Ford area. Sedgwick was now convinced that if Hooker did not attack to relieve the pressure on his front, he would have to retire across the river.

SHORTLY after dawn the next morning, May 4, Early, with his division reformed, advanced on the Telegraph Road to Fredericksburg and recaptured Marye's Heights and the adjacent hills without dif-

Map 17. BATTLE OF SALEM CHURCH. *This map also shows the position to which Hooker withdrew on May 3.*

The 29th Pennsylvania (of Kane's brigade, Geary's division, XII Corps) in the trenches under artillery fire, Sunday, May 3. From an original drawing by W. L. Sheppard. (B&L)

Map. 18. THE ATTACK ON SEDGWICK, MAY 4. *Anderson has marched from his position west of Salem Church to participate in Early's attack on Sedgwick's left flank. Gibbon has withdrawn to his bridge.*

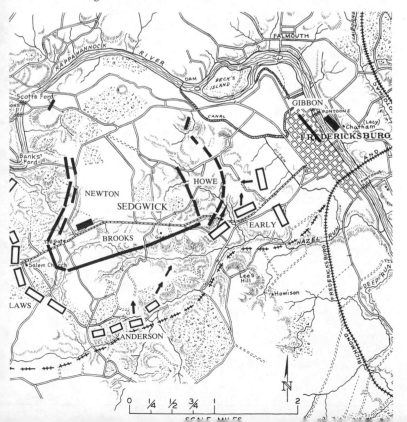

ficulty. Gibbon retired back across the river to Falmouth to protect the Federal camp and the supply line to Aquia Creek. Lee then ordered Early to march immediately to Salem Church so as to hit Sedgwick on the left and rear, while McLaws and Wilcox assailed him in front. McLaws, however, reported to Lee that he did not believe he was strong enough to make a frontal assault on the Federal position. Consequently, Lee decided to reinforce him. Showing his complete contempt for Hooker, he sent Anderson with his remaining brigade to Salem Church to swing around McLaws' right and effect a junction with Early marching out from Fredericksburg. This left Lee with only Jackson's three divisions and Stuart's cavalry to hold Hooker's force of approximately 90,000 men.

Anderson reached Salem Church about noon and continued on around McLaws' right flank to join Early. But, according to Lee, "Some delay occurred in getting the troops into position, owing to the broken and irregular nature of the ground and the difficulty of ascertaining the disposition of the enemy's force. The attack did not begin until 6 p.m., when Anderson and Early moved forward and drove General Sedgwick's troops before them across the Plank road in the direction of the Rappahannock."

McLaws failed to move in conjunction with Anderson and Early because, he claimed later, of the rapidly descending darkness and dense fog. Hence the attack fizzled out and Sedgwick's force crossed the river to safety that night under cover of darkness, after suffering approximately 4,500 casualties.

IT had been a trying day for Sedgwick. Believing that the Confederate force in his front had been reinforced by Lee, he was at a loss to explain why Hooker had not advanced to trap the enemy between them, and he was particularly disturbed because he had heard nothing from the commanding general. Early that morning he had sent a dispatch to army headquarters: "I am anxious to hear from General Hooker. There is a strong force in front of me, strongly posted. I cannot attack with any hope of dislodging them until I know something definite as to the position of their main body and ours."

Although Sedgwick was not aware of it, the main Confederate force was actually in his front. Finally he received a message from Hooker's headquarters telling him that he must look well to the safety of his corps and that if necessary he could fall back on Fredericksburg or retire across Banks's Ford. But, as Sedgwick reported, "to fall back on Fredericksburg was out of the question. To adopt the other alternative, except under cover of night, was especially so, for the enemy still maintained his position on Salem Heights, and was threatening my flank and rear from the direction of Fredericksburg."

Thus, facing in three directions, Sedgwick was forced to await attack, "determined to hold the position until dark and then fall back upon Banks's Ford." He frankly informed Hooker at 9 o'clock that morning (May 4) that "It depends upon the condition and position of your force whether I can sustain myself here." At 11 a.m. he sent another message: "The enemy threatens me strongly on two fronts. . . . Can you help me strongly if I am attacked?" The answer he received, signed by Hooker himself, stated: "I expect to advance tomorrow morning, which will be likely to relieve you. You must not count on much assistance without I hear heavy firing."

HOOKER WITHDRAWS ACROSS THE RIVER

Hooker had no intention of trying to advance the next morning or any other time. In effect, the VI Corps was being abandoned to its fate, while the main force of the Army of the Potomac, within three miles of it, did nothing. As Couch bitterly explained it: "Some of the most anomalous occurrences of the war took place in this campaign. On the night of May 2d the commanding general, with 80,000 men in his wing of the army, directed Sedgwick, with 22,000, to march to his relief. While that officer was doing this on the 3d, and when it would be expected that every

A. R. Waud describes this drawing as showing "an old mill near the front used as a hospital for Slocum's corps and as a rendezvous for skedaddlers." (HW) An examination of Map 17 indicates that the mill was on Mineral Spring Run.

effort would be made by the right wing to do its part, only one half of it was fought (or rather half-fought, for its ammunition was not replenished), and then the whole wing was withdrawn to a place where it could not be hurt, leaving Sedgwick to take care of himself."

And during the night of May 4-5, as Sedgwick was hastily crossing the river, Hooker, safe in a snug retreat north of Chancellorsville, called a meeting of his corps commanders. In a feeble explanation for his actions, Hooker told them that his main responsibility was to protect Washington, and that therefore he had no right to jeopardize the army. He then wanted to know if the corps commanders would vote to stay and fight, or retreat across the river. Although a majority voted to stay and fight, Hooker took upon himself the responsibility of withdrawing the army to the other side of the river. As the conference broke up Reynolds exclaimed angrily, "What was the use of calling us together at this time of night when he intended to retreat anyhow?"

Retreat of the Union army across the Rappahannock at United States Ford. From original drawing by Edwin Forbes. (B&L)

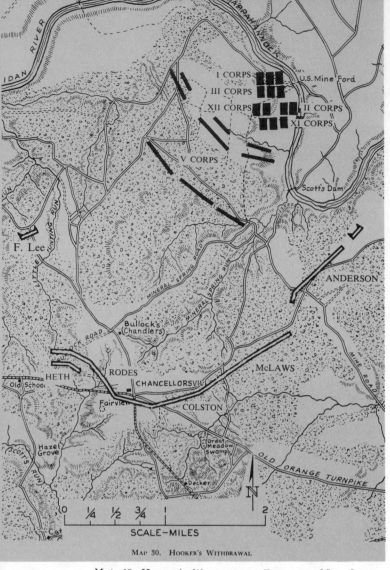

MAP 30. HOOKER'S WITHDRAWAL

Map 19. HOOKER'S WITHDRAWAL, EARLY ON MAY 6.

The withdrawal began the next day and continued into the night. By May 6 everything was safely transferred to the north bank of the Rappahannock, and the Battle of Chancellorsville was over. The Federal loss in killed, wounded, and missing was approximately 17,287; Confederate losses are estimated at 12,821.

COMMENTS

Unquestionably this was Lee's best fought battle of the entire war. Yet there was a striking similarity between his plan and Hooker's. They both divided their forces in the enemy's front to execute brilliant flanking movements. The main reason one succeeded and the other failed was not because of any difference in the two armies, but in the two commanders. One had the courage and conviction to execute his plan regardless of the circumstances; the other did not. One was willing and even anxious to fight; the other desired to avoid any decisive action. Hooker's basic plan really had as its major objective forcing the *withdrawal* of Lee's army, rather than the *destruction* of the Confederate force. There was nothing in it that

even anticipated a major attack or battle. Hooker simply did not have the nerve to commit the Army of the Potomac to a decisive test. As Couch succinctly phrased it: "In looking for the causes of the loss of Chancellorsville, the primary ones were that Hooker expected Lee to fall back without risking battle. Finding himself mistaken, he assumed the defensive, and was outgeneraled and became demoralized by the superior tactical boldness of the enemy."

While Richmond rejoiced at the brilliant victory, the deep despair in Washington was summed up by Lincoln's anguished cry, "My God! What will the country say?"

BUT the situation for the North was not as bad as it first seemed. In a sense, the Army of the Potomac had not been defeated, only its general. At no time during the battle had it been committed to action as an army. Over 40,000 troops had done no fighting at all, despite Lincoln's admonition to use all the men. The Federal losses were promptly made good by new recruits, and the Army of the Potomac was soon stronger than ever. Although few people recognized it at the time, while the North was losing battles it was at the same time inexorably winning the war by consistently whittling away at Southern resources.

And while Richmond celebrated, the truth was that the South had gained little if anything from the victory. Perhaps Lee alone realized this. His triumph was not an unmixed blessing. He had suffered a 22 percent loss whereas Hooker had lost only 13 percent of his strength. Since the recuperative power of Hooker's army was greater than his, and since Lee had not gained ground nor driven the invader from Virginia, his victory was a barren one. Lee was greatly depressed. In addition, he mourned the death of Stonewall Jackson, his "great right arm." In announcing it to the army he said: "The daring, skill, and energy of this great and good man are now lost to us."

To adjust the command structure of the Army of Northern Virginia and close the gap created by the loss of Jackson, Lee changed from a two-corps to a three-corps army, and placed A. P. Hill and R. S. Ewell in command of the troops formerly under Jackson. Both were to fail him repeatedly. He was never again able to take full advantage of his own aggressive fighting spirit and that of his troops.

Lee's great victory had two noteworthy effects: It removed any lingering objection on the part of the Richmond administration to his proposed invasion of Pennsylvania, and it confirmed him in his belief that his men were invincible. He said so, after Gettysburg, to explain his failure there. Thus the Battle of Chancellorsville led directly to Gettysburg, the turning point of the war.

THE BATTLE OF GETTYSBURG

by Jeffry Wert

After a string of victories that culminated at Chancellorsville, General Robert E. Lee convinced President Jefferson Davis and other Confederate officials that it was time to take the offensive and invade the North. The result: a three-day battle at Gettysburg, Pennsylvania—the largest and bloodiest battle ever fought on American soil. (CWTI Collection)

General Robert E. Lee stepped from a train at a depot on the corner of Broad and Eighth Streets in Richmond, Virginia, on Friday, May 15, 1863. The commander of the Army of Northern Virginia, Lee had been summoned to the capital of the Confederacy by President Jefferson Davis and Secretary of War James Seddon for an important conference. For the administration and the general a strategic crossroads had been reached; it was time to decide which road to take.

Lee came to the city with the reputation of a victor. He had commanded his army not quite a year, but in that span he had altered the course of the Civil War in the eastern theater and gained unrivaled influence and prestige with Confederate officials and the Southern people. His aggressiveness had resulted in a drum roll of victories—battles called The Seven Days, Second Bull Run (Second Manassas), Fredericksburg, and Chancellorsville. Lee's only failure, the September 1862 invasion of Maryland, which ended with the Battle of Antietam, had been decisive. But his masterful May 1863 victory at Chancellorsville, Virginia,

seemed to have erased that stain. The general arrived in Richmond at the apogee of success.

Events—some careening toward crises—were shaping the present and future this Friday in spring as Lee went to his meeting at Davis' executive mansion. To the north, along Virginia's Rappahannock River, supply and manpower shortages stalked the camps of Lee's army. In the Commonwealth's Shenandoah Valley, Lieutenant General Thomas J. "Stonewall" Jackson, the South's best strategist, was being buried. In the western theater, in Mississippi, Major General Ulysses S. Grant's Union forces had captured the state capital and were advancing southwest, shoving Lieutenant General John C. Pemberton's Confederates into a deathtrap at Vicksburg along the Mississippi River. If this city fell, Federals would control the river, and the South would be cut in two.

Davis' and Seddon's concern over Vicksburg's fate prompted their call for Lee. Seddon proposed detaching two divisions from Lee's army and sending them to Pemberton. But when the president and war secretary conferred with Lee on the 15th, the general countered Seddon's plan by outlining an invasion of Pennsylvania. It was an operation Lee had favored for at least two months. Impressed, Davis and Seddon asked Lee to return the next day and present the proposal to the entire cabinet.

Lee spent most of Saturday, May 16, sequestered with Davis and department heads. The general stated his objections to Seddon's scheme, arguing two detached Eastern divisions could not ensure success in Mississippi. Such a reduction in his strength would also surely require him to withdraw into the capital's fortifications. But an invasion of Northern soil, Lee argued, offered prospects of garnering desperately needed supplies, and would give Virginia a respite from the ravages of war and allow Shenandoah Valley farmers to harvest their crops.

The general had no real geographic target in mind, no specific city or railroad he believed he had to take and hold to make his plan successful. His movement would draw the Union's Army of the Potomac north, disrupting Federal operations in the Old Dominion and along the Virginia and North Carolina coasts that summer. This result alone would make the movement worthwhile. But if he could bring on a battle on Northern soil, if he could beat the Federals on their home ground, it might panic Union authorities and induce them to pull troops out of the Mississippi to defend the great cities of the East. In its way, victory in Pennsylvania might bring relief to Pemberton at Vicksburg. It was a serious hope, but one Lee did not stress as an objective of the movement.

Lee was an audacious general, a gambler flouting tactical arithmetic. He believed his invasion was the only course against a logistically and numerically superior foe. Subsequently, Lee understood there might be one more, final prospect—one he almost certainly did not expand upon at the conference, if he even mentioned it. It was this—that a crushing, decisive battlefield defeat of his opponent on Northern soil might finally end the war.

Not all the cabinet members concurred with Lee's proposal. Postmaster General John H. Reagan disagreed, arguing that Grant must be destroyed. Davis then called for a vote. A 5 to 1 tally favored Lee's plan. The meeting was adjourned. But Reagan remained unconvinced. The next morning, before dawn, he sent a message to Davis, urging another meeting. On Sunday, another long discussion ensued. Again the cabinet, by 5 to 1, endorsed an invasion of Pennsylvania.

The three-day Richmond conference set the course for the war in the East in summer 1863. When Lee's veterans marched northward, in one historian's words, they would carry "the undeveloped climax of the war with them." Unknown to them, they would march toward a Pennsylvania crossroads village named Gettysburg, into a deadly struggle that would be seared into the collective memory of Americans.

Before the Army of Northern Virginia could carry the war to enemy territory, it required refitting, refilling, and reorganization. From Lee's return to the army on May 18 until the start of the campaign on June 3, he concentrated his efforts on those urgent needs. Each branch of the army—infantry, artillery, and cavalry—underwent change. Units were added to replace recent casualties. Arms, cannon, wagons, and animals were accumulated.

The most significant alteration in the army resulted from Stonewall Jackson's mortal wounding at Chancellorsville. Lee wisely chose not to replace what was irreplaceable. For the better part of the previous year, the infantry had operated under a two-corps structure with steady, solid Lieutenant General James Longstreet leading the First and Jackson the Second. Lee thought corps of this size, with about 30,000 troops each, were too large, too unwieldy for one man to control, especially in heavily wooded terrain. But the army commander maintained the organization, believing he had no other officer with the skill, experience, and capability for corps command. Jackson's death forced him to reassess all that.

During the final weeks of May, Lee reorganized the First Corps, while two Virginians, Richard S. Ewell and Ambrose Powell Hill, became lieutenant generals and received command of the Second Corps and Third Corps, respectively. Ewell was 46 years old, a West Point graduate, a former division commander under Jackson with an excellent combat record. But "Old Bald Head" Ewell had been away from the army for nine months, convalescing from the loss of a leg during the Second Manassas Campaign.

"Powell" Hill, too, was a West Point graduate, nearly nine years younger than Ewell. Fiery, combative, Hill had led his so-called "Light Division" for nearly a year, making it one of the finest commands in the army. These two men were, in Lee's view, the best available for the new corps command positions, yet questions remained. Could each direct such large numbers of troops in battle? Had Ewell's wound sapped his martial spirit? Could Hill act with restraint and wisdom?

The three-corps reorganization necessitated changes at the divisional level. Lee assigned three divisions to each corps. This meant the creation of a new division for the army (bringing them to a total of nine) and the reshuffling of brigades. Of the nine commanders—all major generals—six were battle-tested at that position: Lafayette McLaws, John Bell

Hood, Jubal Early, Edward Johnson, Robert Rodes, and Richard Anderson. Lee promoted two of the remaining three—William Pender and Henry Heth—from brigadier and assigned them to Hill's corps, with Heth commanding the new division. The final officer, George Pickett, in division command for nine months, had never led his unit in combat.

After reorganizing the infantry, Lee next needed to obtain reinforcements. For several weeks, even as his troops were marching north, Lee negotiated furiously with Davis, Seddon, Major General D.H. Hill (commander of the Department of North Carolina), and others for the return of brigades detached from the army and for the loan of additional units from coastal defenses. Though Davis appreciated Lee's need for every available musket, he and his subordinates also viewed the stripping of troops from Hill's department and the Richmond defenses with nervousness. In the end, Lee added just three relatively untested brigades to his army.

Lee's long arm, the artillery, meanwhile underwent fine adjustments. On June 2, Lee placed five artillery battalions with each infantry corps—one for each division and two in reserve. Tactical control of the batteries went to the chief of artillery of each corps. Brigadier General William Pendleton, artillery commander of the army, was relegated to administrative direction of the battalions. He faced a couple of critical artillery problems: too little uniformity in the types of cannon within battalions and too much defective ammunition.

The army's third branch, the cavalry, under flamboyant, capable Major General J.E.B. "Jeb" Stuart, needed no structural changes. But an infusion of troopers and mounts was vital. For two years Stuart's horsemen dominated their opponents, but months of campaigning and combat had taken their toll in men and animals. Lee brought in two brigades to add to Stuart's three, and as the campaign progressed he attached two other mounted brigades to the army. The scarcity of good horseflesh persisted, but it was believed a source could possibly be found in the lush farmlands of Pennsylvania.

By the beginning of June 1863, the Army of Northern Virginia, even with its shortcomings and uncertainties, was a splendid instrument of war. Not since the spring 1862 Seven Days Campaign had Lee commanded such a host. The three infantry corps counted approximately 61,500 in the ranks, supported by 249 cannon served by 6,000 artillerists. Stuart's cavalry corps, with the addition of the four brigades, totaled nearly 12,400 officers and men, bolstered by thirty-one guns of horse artillery. In all, the army numbered between 79,000 and 80,000 men.

Numbers alone did not explain this army's prow-ess—that could be found only in its soul. From Lee to the lowliest private, these Southerners were infused with the belief that they, as Henry Heth said, "could accomplish anything." Even Lee spoke of this sense of invincibility, telling John Hood "there never were such men in an army before. They will go anywhere and do anything if properly led."

If the Army of Northern Virginia had been forged by victories, then its opponent, the Army of the Potomac, had been tempered by defeats. For two years these foes had bloodied each other and, except at Antietam, Southerner had prevailed over Northerner. Thousands of Yankees had died or bled because of political machinations and inept generalship.

The defeats had brought discouragement, even serious demoralization to the Union ranks after the 1862 Battles of Second Manassas and Fredericksburg. But the sacrifices made the men fighters, with a resilience and toughness some of their leaders seemingly did not understand or appreciate. One officer at this time likened them to an "English bulldog." "You can whip them time and again," he wrote, "but the next fight they go into, they are in good spirits, and as full of pluck as ever. They are used to being whipped, and no longer mind it. Some day or other we shall have our turn." Another officer argued that when properly commanded, they became the "best fighting men in the world."

The question remained, however: How many more lickings could this army withstand? The Chancellorsville battle, fought May 1–3, was an ignominious defeat, a thrashing the men blamed squarely on their commander, Major General Joseph "Fighting Joe" Hooker. Replacing former commander Major General Ambrose Burnside in January, he had come to his new position with a reputation for fighting and with important political connections. Forty-eight years old, West Point-trained, combat-tested, looking like a general, Hooker proved an excellent administrator and whipped the army into trim. But at Chancellorsville, when Lee turned and gave battle, he lost his nerve and the fight. The battle cost him his army's confidence.

On May 6, the day Hooker retreated from the battle area, President Abraham Lincoln and General-in-Chief Henry W. Halleck arrived at army headquarters. The pair visited only for a day, but Lincoln learned first-hand of the dissension among the officers. Major General Darius Couch, commander of the II Corps, told Lincoln he would no longer serve under Hooker and that Hooker should be replaced by Major General George G. Meade, V Corps commander. For the beleaguered president, Couch's words had a familiar ring. For two years, Lincoln had

Hot-tempered Major General George G. Meade, who commanded the V Corps at Chancellorsville, replaced Major General Joseph Hooker as commander for the Army of the Potomac. (PA-MOLLUS)

placed his trust in one general after another, and each had brought him only defeat. Now, another had failed.

Lincoln and others debated Hooker's future. And as they talked, the army commander and his troops remained quiet in their camps north of the Rappahannock. The Yankees needed time to heal. Chancellorsville cost 12 percent of the army in killed, wounded and missing. During May and June an additional 20 percent left the ranks as nine-month and two-year enlistment terms expired. Nevertheless, field returns for May 31 listed the army's strength as well in excess of 100,000.

On June 2, Lincoln offered command of the army to Major General John F. Reynolds, a first-rate combat officer and commander of the I Corps. Reynolds declined, arguing authorities in Washington would not promise him a "free hand." The next day, the Confederates started northward.

Lee had learned on the 2d that a Union force east of Richmond, the only one handy enough to monitor his movements, had withdrawn southeast toward the Federal's nearest large and secure encampment, Fort Monroe. At that point, with his force unobserved, he ordered the march. It started slowly, incrementally, with the divisions of Lafayette McLaws and John Hood leaving the Richmond area on the 3d. Robert Rodes' division left the next day, followed by those of Jubal Early and Edward Johnson on June 5. By the 7th the five divisions had concentrated near Culpeper Court House, where five of Stuart's cavalry brigades were located.

A.P. Hill's Third Corps remained behind in Vir-

ginia, at Fredericksburg. Lee, who had moved his headquarters to Culpeper on the evening of the 6th, directed Hill to dispose his troops "as will be best calculated to deceive the enemy, and keep him in ignorance of any change in the disposition of the army." If the Federals advanced against the Third Corps, Hill should resist, Lee added. But if compelled to retreat, Hill should retire along the railroad toward Richmond, delaying the Yankees until Lee returned.

Hooker, who had received warnings of an unspecified movement, learned of the Confederate activity on June 4. Within twenty-four hours, he concluded Lee was trying to cut him off from Washington. He alerted three infantry corps and ordered Brigadier General John Buford to push the Rebels at Culpeper with his cavalry division. "I am of the opinion," Hooker wired Lincoln, "that it is my duty to pitch into his rear, although in so doing the head of his column may reach Warrenton before I can return." He ended the message by asking for the president's views.

Lincoln wasted little time in responding: "I would not take any risk of being entangled upon the river, like an ox jumped half over a fence and liable to be torn by dogs front and rear, without a fair chance to gore one way or kick the other." Halleck followed Lincoln's telegraph with one of his own, advising that Lee's "moveable column" be the target, instead of Hill's entrenched troops.

Lincoln's and Halleck's messages dissuaded the army commander from carrying out his plan. Hooker spent June 6 and 7 sifting intelligence and preparing countermoves. He sent Major General John Sedgwick's VI Corps across the Rappahannock on the 6th on a reconnaissance-in-force. That same day Buford reported the Confederate concentration at Culpeper, but he mistakenly identified the force as consisting only of Stuart's cavalry. Consequently, Hooker directed his cavalry commander, Brigadier General Alfred Pleasonton, to take the entire mounted corps, supported by some infantry brigades, and "to disperse and destroy the rebel force assembled in the vicinity of Culpeper, and to destroy his trains and supplies."

Pleasonton, in command less than three weeks, completed preparations for the movement by dark on June 8. With a force of about 11,000, he proposed to cross the Rappahannock at two points, reunite his units at Brandy Station, a stop on the Orange & Alexandria Railroad, then advance the remaining six miles to Culpeper. His right wing—Buford's division and an infantry brigade—would move via Beverly Ford while the left wing—Brigadier Generals Davis McMurtrie Gregg's and Alfred N. Duffié's cavalry

Brandy Station early in 1863. The battle fought here on June 9 was the first of numerous engagements and skirmishes prior to Gettysburg. (U.S. Army Military History Institute)

divisions and an infantry brigade—would cross Kelly's Ford, downstream from Beverly. Duffié, instead of advancing directly toward Brandy Station, was ordered to seize Stevensburg, a town five miles to the south.

Buford started first, splashing across the river at dawn. Pickets from the 6th Virginia Cavalry responded with a ragged fire and fled. Other Virginians came up. The Yankees swatted them aside, pressing westward. Buford's men nearly captured a four-gun horse battery; it escaped only after two cannon deployed and shelled the Federals. The 7th Virginia Cavalry, with many men undressed and riding bareback, lashed the head of the Yankee force. Soon the remainder of Brigadier General William E. "Grumble" Jones' Confederate brigade entered the action, followed by Brigadier General Wade Hampton's four regiments and several squadrons of dismounted troopers from Brigadier General W.H.F. Lee's brigade. This resistance stalled Buford.

About 10:00 A.M., as the Confederates formed for an attack, they received word of a second Yankee column approaching from the southeast. These Federals belonged to Gregg, who had been delayed when Duffié lost his way *en route* to the ford. Once over the river, the two divisions rode directly on the Stevensburg road until Gregg turned off toward Brandy Station. Brigadier General Beverly Robert-

son's brigade of two large regiments protected this sector of the Confederate lines, and it was Robertson who sent the urgent message of Gregg's approach. He did not oppose the Northerners, giving them an unhindered route into the Confederate right rear. Gregg's men, unaware of Robertson's presence, closed on the station about noon. The only enemy in their front was Major Henry B. McClellan, Stuart's assistant adjutant general, and a gun crew manning a 6-pounder howitzer.

McClellan reacted immediately, ordering gunners to shell the Union column. The bluff worked; Gregg hesitated. Minutes later two of Jones' regiments thundered along Fleetwood Hill, the key position on the battlefield, and into the blueclad ranks.

It was a wild, swirling struggle. Mounted men engaged in hand-to-hand combat with sabers and pistols. The Yankees gained the crest only to be swept back as more Rebels galloped into the fury. But this day was not like days past when Union cavalry had been easily swept aside. The Federals stormed to the high ground again. But on came Hampton's brigade, ripping into the stubborn Union ranks and clawing them off the crest once more.

Additional Southern regiments finished the job, and Gregg's troopers pulled back to Brandy Station. Concentrating his brigades, Stuart consolidated his hold on Fleetwood Hill. Buford, who pressed forward when Gregg advanced, could go no farther. And at Stevensburg Duffié had his hands full with two Confederate regiments. He reached Gregg's position too late. Late in the afternoon, Pleasonton ordered a withdrawal when he learned enemy infantry were approaching. Stuart did not pursue him.

Brandy Station was the biggest cavalry engagement of the Civil War. Federal losses totaled 866, estimated Confederate casualties ranged from 375 to 485. Though Stuart claimed victory he had been surprised, even humiliated by the aggressive enemy horsemen. For the first time in the war in Virginia, the individual Yankees showed themselves to be equals in a fight with the men of Stuart's legions. The Southerners acquired new respect for their opponents. In Henry McClellan's words, Brandy Station *"made* the Federal cavalry."

The battle's importance in the unfolding campaign was minimal, however. Pleasonton neither destroyed Stuart's cavalry nor gained valuable intelligence. For Hooker, the mounted thrust was his only attempt to regain the initiative and disrupt Lee's operations for the summer. Once he failed to stall the Confederate movement, Hooker relinquished control of events to his opponent.

The Union commander's initial response was to reiterate to Lincoln on June 10 his earlier proposal of a movement on Richmond if Lee's infantry could be placed at Culpeper. But Lincoln again objected, stating, "I think Lee's army, and not Richmond, is your sure objective point." Follow Lee along the inside track, he added, and "if he stays where he is, fret him and fret him."

The next day and for three days thereafter, as evidence of Confederate marches mounted, the Union army moved away from Fredericksburg. On the 11th, Hooker shifted two infantry corps upriver and ordered all baggage and camp followers to the rear. The VI Corps returned to the north side of the Rappahannock on the 12th. When headquarters learned the next day that the Rebels were heading for the Shenandoah Valley, Hooker withdrew his entire command from the river and, on the 14th, moved his base of operations from Aquia Creek to a point on the Orange & Alexandria Railroad. Once again the luckless Army of the Potomac followed its opponent toward an unknown destination.

Ten Roads Lead To Gettysburg

Lee started his legions northward in earnest the day after the Brandy Station clash. The Second Corps, Stonewall Jackson's old troops, led the march, setting a blistering pace. By the 12th, these veterans

Army of the Potomac cavalrymen scouting in front of the Confederate advance. (Battles and Leaders of the Civil War)

covered forty-five miles, reaching Cedarville in the Shenandoah Valley, where Brigadier General Albert Jenkins' cavalry brigade joined the infantry. Corps commander Ewell's target was a Union garrison at Winchester, ten miles northwest of Cedarville.

These Federals, numbering 6,900 effectives, were commanded by Major General Robert H. Milroy, an officer with an undistinguished record. He possessed more bombast than sense. General-in-Chief Henry Halleck warned him of approaching Confederates and ordered him to abandon his post and retire to Harpers Ferry. Milroy ignored the signals and disobeyed orders.

Ewell, whose bald pate reminded people of either an eagle or buzzard, came after the myopic Milroy by three routes on June 13. Jenkins and Rodes advanced on Berryville, due east of Winchester; Johnson angled in from the southeast, while Early, on the Valley Pike, approached from the south. The infantrymen of Johnson and Early skirmished throughout most of the day as they closed the vise on the Federals. Milroy still could have escaped, but he did not want to be regarded as a coward, and somehow convinced himself that his troops had repulsed the graycoats.

Skirmishing resumed the next morning and continued into the afternoon. Ewell planned deliberately. While Johnson pressed the Yankees on Winchester's eastern fringe, Early swung his division to the west on a concealed route. About 6:00 P.M., twenty Confederate cannon opened on a fort on Bowers Hill at the southwest corner of town. The bombardment silenced six Union pieces in thirty minutes. A short time later, Brigadier General Henry Hays' brigade of Louisianans burst from concealment and overran the earthwork. At 9:00, Milroy convened a council of war and issued orders for immediate retreat.

Shielded by darkness, the Federals stole northward. Ewell, however, anticipating a retreat, had sent Johnson's division to a point north of Winchester. Johnson intercepted the column near Stephenson's Depot, less than five miles beyond Winchester. Milroy launched an attack, but the flashing Rebel lines repulsed it. Panic ensued among the Yankees; their organized resistance evaporated. The Southerners bagged nearly 4,000 prisoners while killing or wounding another 443 men. Ewell's men also seized 23 cannon, 300 loaded wagons, more than 300 horses and a large cache of quartermaster stores, suffering 269 casualties in the process. Milroy and some remnants of his command fled to Harpers Ferry while another column marched all the way to Pennsylvania. This fight at Winchester, "a humiliating fiasco" for the Federals, cleared the lower Shenandoah Valley for the Confederates, opening the doorway to Maryland and Pennsylvania.

While Ewell was chasing Yankees from the valley, the rest of the army was *en route* to the region. At one time Lee's force was stretched out over 100 miles. Both Longstreet, from Culpeper, and Hill, from Fredericksburg, started on the 14th. Their seasoned marchers usually did well in unmercifully hot weather, but the broiling sun and choking dust wilted columns, causing considerable straggling. (On June 15, for instance, 500 of John Hood's troops left the ranks because of exhaustion, and a number died from sunstroke.) By the 17th, Longstreet's command occupied two gaps in the Blue Ridge Mountains, with three cavalry brigades covering his front. Hill's corps was clearing Culpeper, heading into the mountains, and Ewell had Rodes' division in Maryland and his other two poised for a crossing.

East of the Confederates, paralleling their route, marched the Army of the Potomac. The Yankees suffered as intensely as their opponents from the heat wave. One Federal veteran described the trek along the Orange & Alexandria Railroad as "the hardest march in my experience." Hooker had ordered a concentration in the vicinity of Centreville, and by the 17th many units were near the destination or strung out along the railroad tracks. Pleasonton's cavalrymen probed westward toward the Bull Run Mountains, which screened Hooker's flank just as the Blue Ridge did Lee's.

Hooker's withdrawal to the Centreville area secured Washington, but in the process he had lost contact with the enemy. He knew of Milroy's disaster, but little else. He assigned Pleasonton the task of securing definitive intelligence. For most of the next week, the region between the two mountain chains, the Loudoun Valley, served as an amphitheater for war between opposing cavalry.

From June 17 until the 21st, the mounted antagonists clashed in engagements at Aldie, Middleburg, and Upperville. The combat escalated in numbers and fierceness each successive day. Much of the time

the troopers fought dismounted, but mounted counterattacks met mounted charges. Stuart, fighting in the shadow of Ashby's Gap in the Blue Ridge Mountains, stopped Pleasonton's probes, but only after using more of his units and meeting stiff resistance.

Not only did the Yankee horsemen give another good account of themselves in these actions, they supplied army headquarters with accurate intelligence on Confederate whereabouts. The reports confirmed information Hooker received from other sources. The signs clearly indicated a full-scale invasion, yet "Fighting Joe" was slow to realize he had to move into Maryland. As the crisis grew, Hooker began losing control of the situation and of himself, just as he had at Chancellorsville.

According to a historian of the campaign, the Union commander possessed a "disturbed state of mind," with an "abnormal tendency" to fault others for his failures. To Hooker, no one was more duplicitous, more villainous than Halleck. The general-in-chief had no confidence in Hooker's generalship, had been vague in defining Hooker's authority over other departments (thus slowing the accretion of reinforcements), and had opposed the army commander's proposal for abandoning Harpers Ferry—this was Hooker's view. Unfortunately for "Fighting Joe," Lincoln supported his principal adviser. The President would neither strip the capital's defenses of troops nor order away the Harpers Ferry garrison, which had retired to the dominating Maryland Heights above the town. Lincoln and Halleck eventually gave Hooker two infantry divisions, a cavalry division, and two batteries—15,000 men altogether. But the status of the force on Maryland Heights remained unresolved.

While these disputes flared between Hooker and the administration, the Union army consolidated its position in northern Virginia, east of the Bull Run Mountains. Gripped by indecision, Hooker undertook no major movements for a week, from June 17 to 24. Finally, on June 25, with certain knowledge that Confederates were on Northern soil, Hooker acted, ordering the entire army into Maryland.

The roads of northern Virginia and western Maryland brimmed with marching Yankees that day and the next two. Hooker's irresolution resulted in physically punishing forced marches by the men in the ranks. The I, III and XI Corps, under the overall command of John Reynolds, pushed northward to Middletown, Maryland, on the 25th, with the XI Corps covering nearly thirty miles. The army's remaining four infantry corps started over the Potomac on the 26th, and by nightfall of June 27 all components of the army were in Maryland, between Middletown and Frederick. The commanding general had acted with dispatch, and the soldiers, though grumbling, had responded.

The three days of hard marching still left the Union army short of its opponents. To the north, beyond the grasp of the Yankees, a flood tide of Rebels was engulfing southern Pennsylvania, with two currents coursing toward the Susquehanna River in the directions of the cities of Harrisburg and York. On June 22, with Hill at hand and the Union cavalry quiet east of the Blue Ridge, Lee ordered Ewell from Maryland into Pennsylvania and called Hill and Longstreet across the Potomac.

For the next five days, Confederate units poured into and across the Keystone State. By June 27, Ewell's divisions were knifing toward the Susquehanna and Hill's and Longstreet's were concentrated near Chambersburg, where Lee established headquarters.

A major objective of the invasion was the collection of foodstuffs, forage and livestock, and as soon as the Rebels crossed the Pennsylvania line the plundering began. Lee issued two general orders regarding the troops' conduct, which surely contributed to the men's restraint. But, like a swarm of ravenous locusts, the invaders cleaned out south-central Pennsylvania's brimming larders. The troops, Rebel division commander William Pender wrote his wife, "have done nothing like the Yankees do in our country. They take poultry and hogs but in most cases pay our money for it. We take everything we want for government use." A staff officer put it succinctly, saying that "the land is full of everything and we have an abundance."

The iron fist of war visited seven counties, an area 100 miles from west to east and 40 miles from south to north. Plundering was concentrated in Franklin and Adams counties, with Chambersburg the hardest hit community. Jenkins' cavalry—better raiders than fighters—ranged far, rustling horses and cattle. Ewell's corps, in the van, probably garnered most of the spoils. Jubal Early requisitioned clothing, supplies or cash from the citizens of Gettysburg and York, but neither community could meet all his demands. Robert Rodes collected $50,000 worth of medicine in the town of Carlisle. Overall, the army seized property valued at hundreds of thousands of dollars.

Civilians in the area either fled or submitted passively to the invaders. "I never saw a people so badly scared," averred William Pender. Some farmers made peculiar signs with their hands as Confederates approached. Apparently some slick operator had revealed to them, for a price, some magic to ward off any evil carried by the Rebels. It did not work.

Southerners viewed the Pennsylvanians with contempt. "This is the most magnificent country to look at," Pender confided to his wife, "but the most miserable people. They are coarse and dirty, and the number of dirty looking children is perfectly astonishing." An uncharitable Union officer even admitted that "altogether, they are a people of barns, not brains."

By June 27, the Rebels were positioned as well as could be expected. Lee's major concern was a lack of information about the Union army's location. He thought his foe was still south of the Potomac River; no contrary information came from Jeb Stuart. Lee had not exchanged messages with his cavalry chief since the 23d, when he granted Stuart permission to make his own way north. His route, "Stuart's Ride," then became a controversial aspect of the campaign.

Lee had issued Stuart two orders, on the 22d and 23d. In his initial instructions, the commanding general directed his cavalry chief to take three brigades, move ahead of the army, align himself on Ewell's right flank, and collect supplies and information. In the second message, Lee gave Stuart the option of crossing the Potomac either west or east of the Blue Ridge, depending upon whether the Federals remained inactive or marched northward. "You will, however," added Lee, "be able to judge whether you can pass around their army without hinderance, doing all the damage you can, and cross the river east of the mountains. In either case, after crossing the river, you must move on and feel the right of Ewell's troops, collecting information, provisions, etc."

The instructions were vague, discretionary, more suggestion than directive. Lee unquestionably expected Stuart to ride Ewell's flank as soon as possible. He did not, however, clarify the conditions for the movement. Subsequently, Stuart, an officer who avidly sought independent operations, chose to ride around the enemy. (Major John S. Mosby, an excellent partisan officer, may have precipitated this when he informed Stuart he could strike Hooker a "damaging blow.") Lee trusted Stuart's judgment and gave him wide latitude, but in the end the cavalry commander acted injudiciously, misusing, even wasting, three brigades at a time when his services were critically required.

Stuart started from Salem, Virginia, about a mile south of Upperville and Middleburg, at 1:00 A.M. on June 25. He took the brigades of Wade Hampton, Brigadier General Fitzhugh Lee, and Colonel John Chambliss, Jr., and left behind those of Beverly Robertson and William Jones as rear guards for the army. The mounted column soon encountered the Union's II Corps marching northward.

With the roads filled with Yankees, Stuart stopped.

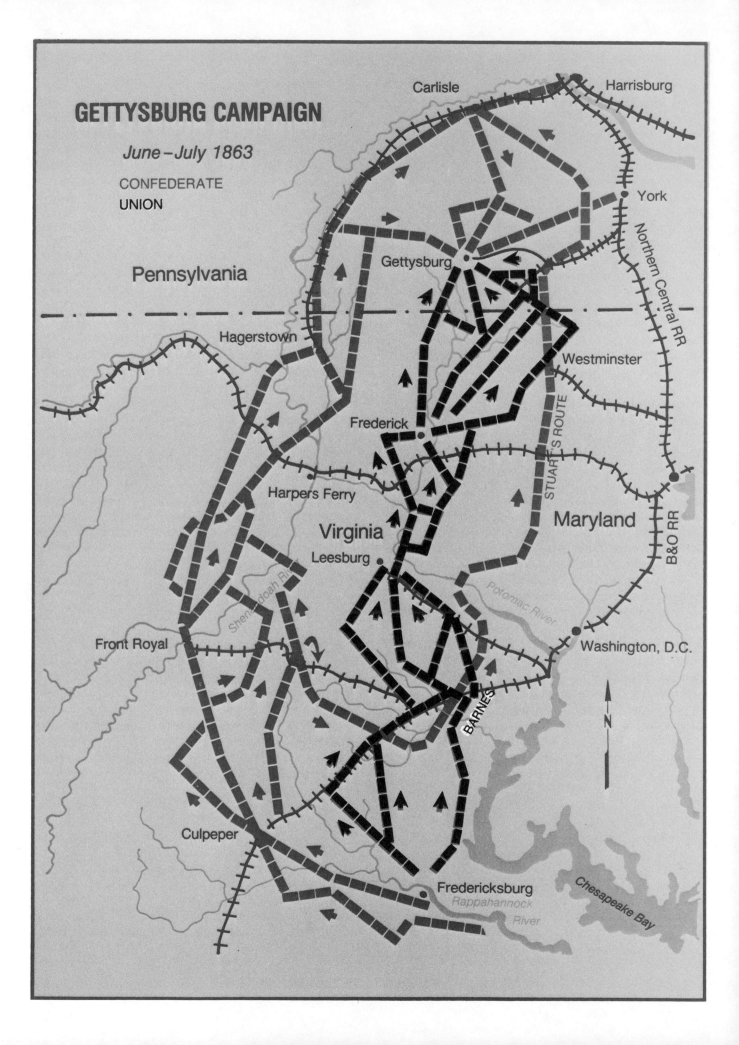

GETTYSBURG CAMPAIGN

June–July 1863

CONFEDERATE
UNION

Pennsylvania

Carlisle

Harrisburg

York

Gettysburg

Hagerstown

Northern Central RR

Westminster

Frederick

Harpers Ferry

STUART'S ROUTE

Virginia

Maryland

Leesburg

Potomac River

B&O RR

Shenandoah River

Front Royal

Washington, D.C.

BARNES

N

Culpeper

Fredericksburg

Rappahannock River

Chesapeake Bay

The next day the horsemen covered twenty-five miles, camping along the Occoquan River. It was another thirty miles on the 27th, through Fairfax Station to Dranesville, across the Potomac and into Maryland. They skirmished briefly with enemy cavalry and saw many signs of Union concentration north of the river.

Sunday, June 28, was a fateful day for both armies. Stuart's men were in the saddle again, clattering through Maryland, near Washington. At Rockville, Chambliss' men seized an eight-mile-long wagon train. In the ensuing pursuit, the Rebel units were scattered, the men exhausted, and precious time wasted. It took several hours to burn twenty-five wrecked wagons and untangle the jumble. Stuart unwisely decided to take 125 wagons with him, which slowed his march. The gray-jacketed troopers bivouacked that night at Brookville, ten miles north of Rockville. Stuart was about fifty-five miles, as the crow flies, from Lee's headquarters at Chambersburg, with the Union army barring the way.

In Pennsylvania that Sabbath, the Confederate invasion was reaching the extent of its northern penetration. Jubal Early, at York, sent Brigadier General John Gordon and his brigade to Wrightsville, where a key railroad bridge spanned the Susquehanna. Before Gordon could seize the structure, militiamen burned the bridge. North of Gordon, at Mechanicsburg, Jenkins' command dueled with a Union battery. The cavalrymen were only a few miles southwest of Harrisburg, the state capital, and some of them viewed it the next morning before retiring. This was the farthest north the Southerners would march. Jenkins received orders to withdraw south on the 29th; this signalled a major change in Confederate plans.

During the night of June 28, James Longstreet sent a civilian to Lee's tent outside Chambersburg. A staff officer introduced the man to Lee as Henry T. Harrison, a spy in Longstreet's service. Harrison reported the Union army was not south of the Potomac but in Maryland, concentrated around Frederick. Harrison, according to Longstreet's chief of staff, "gave us the first complete account of the operations of the enemy since Hooker left our front."

Lee was surprised. Evidently, he had inferred from Stuart's absence that the Yankees were still in Virginia.* But he still had time to modify his operations.

---

*Why did Lee allow himself to be without Stuart's troops, "the eyes" of his army, on this march? This is a perennial question in the study of Civil War history. And there is another. Scholars concede that Lee should have expected Hooker to pursue him, and that Stuart should have hewed to his instructions. But, to date, no one is certain why Lee, with Stuart absent, did not use those brigades still traveling with his columns—Jones' and Robertson's—to scout the Union army's movements.

The Confederate commander issued orders that night for a reconcentration of his scattered units. At first, he recalled Ewell's three divisions to Chambersburg. Then, the next morning, he changed this, redirecting them toward a point east of South Mountain at either Cashtown or Gettysburg. The second message, however, arrived too late to be received by Edward Johnson, whose division was already under way toward Chambersburg with the corps wagon train. (Johnson's march brought him to the Chambersburg Pike on July 1, where he added to the congestion on that vital roadway on a day that would prove critical.) Lee ordered Hill to Cashtown on the 29th, with Longstreet to follow. By June 30, Lee had fashioned a concentration. If his redeployment had a serious weakness, it was the need for seven of his nine divisions to use the Chambersburg Pike.

It was probably on the evening of June 30 when Longstreet gave Lee another piece of information— Joseph Hooker no longer commanded the Army of the Potomac. Lee's new opponent was Major General George G. Meade. Three days earlier, when General-in-Chief Halleck refused to comply with Hooker's recurrent demand to abandon Harper's Ferry, Fighting Joe submitted his resignation, arguing, "I am unable to comply with conditions with the means at my disposal." In a clear attempt to force acceptance of his strategy, Hooker requested that the matter be referred to Stanton and Lincoln. The President accepted the resignation without referring it to the Cabinet. At 3:00 A.M., June 28, Colonel James A. Hardie of Halleck's staff awoke Meade, informing him of the command change. A short time later, Hardie, Meade, and the general's son and aide, Captain George Meade, went to army headquarters. Hardie handed the order to Hooker, who responded graciously. At 7:00 A.M., Meade formally accepted the post in a message to Halleck. Hooker departed that evening after issuing a farewell sentiment to the troops. Fighting Joe was not finished; he was destined for service in the West.

George Gordon Meade was 47 years old and a Pennsylvania resident. An 1835 graduate of West Point, a Mexican War veteran, he had a solid antebellum record as a military engineer and had commanded at the brigade, division and corps levels. A businesslike officer, he shunned the intrigues so rampant in the army, performing his duties without concern for personal popularity. No political faction in Washington favored or opposed him, a fact Lincoln found appealing. One army staff officer characterized him as a "thorough soldier," a "mighty clear-headed man" with a "straightforward truthfulness" the like of which he had not seen before.

Within the army, Meade had a reputation for courage, skill, and prickliness. He had a temper feared by anyone who might be subjected to its explosion. Staff officer Theodore Lyman likened him to "a firework, always going bang to someone." "Woe to those," Lyman added, "no matter who they are, who do not do right!" The aide called him "the Great Peppering;" the men in the ranks described him more bluntly as a "damned goggle-eyed snapping turtle."

Although the new commander lacked dash, a soldierly handsomeness and popularity, he was a general soldiers trusted in combat. Meade, said Lyman, had "extraordinary moral courage," which, if circumstances required, made him a fighter. Lee, after learning of the Union general's promotion, allegedly said, "General Meade will commit no blunder in my front, and if I make one he will make haste to take advantage of it."

"Considering the circumstances," Halleck told Meade in the order promoting him, "no one ever received a more important command." The general-in-chief gave him authority to replace any officer he wished. And Halleck reminded Meade that the city of Washington had to be covered and headquarters in the capital should be kept fully informed. In response, Meade put his task succinctly: "My main point being to find and fight the enemy."

The commanding general went to work immediately. On the 28th, he reorganized the cavalry, giving Brigadier General Judson Kilpatrick command of the division sent from Washington and jumping three captains—Elon Farnsworth, George Custer, and Wesley Merritt—to brigadier, assigning them to brigades. For the infantry he issued marching orders. Unlike Hooker, Meade kept his corps commanders fully informed, treating them as colleagues.

On June 29 and 30, the Union army marched toward Pennsylvania. The weather was hot, but showers reduced the dust. Orders arrived late and snarls occurred, yet the Yankees covered the miles without too many delays. Meade acted boldly but prudently in a masterful performance. By nightfall the second day, he believed the Confederates were closing on Gettysburg, a small community where John Buford's two mounted brigades were positioned. He also had his infantry well at hand: the left wing— the I, III, and XI Corps under John Reynolds—was five to twelve miles south and southwest of Buford, and the other four corps were nine to twenty-five miles from Gettysburg. Kilpatrick's horsemen rimmed the eastern flank, Gregg's troopers covered the rear. The Federals, moreover, could advance on Gettysburg by five roadways.

Though Meade anticipated a collision of unknown extent in the vicinity of Gettysburg, he could not be certain. Consequently, on the morning of July 1, he

issued a contingency plan, the so-called Pipe Creek Circular. If the Confederates attacked, the Union army would fight a holding action before withdrawing to a strong defensive position on the high ground south of Pipe Creek in Maryland, roughly fifteen to twenty miles from Gettysburg. He had sound reasons for issuing the tentative orders, but the operation had serious flaws, most importantly the psychological effect that retiring before the enemy might have on the army. Critics of the general later cited the order as an example of his confusion and timidity. But when the armies engaged at Gettysburg Meade discarded the plan, demonstrating willingness not to avoid Lee but to fight him from an advantageous position.

The Confederates, meanwhile, continued their reconcentration on June 30. Rodes' and Early's divisions in Ewell's corps reached the area around Heidlersburg, nine miles north-northeast of Gettysburg. To their southwest, Hill's divisions under Heth and Pender were east of South Mountain, less than eight miles from Gettysburg. During the day, Brigadier General James J. Pettigrew's brigade of Heth's command, searching for a reported cache of shoes, entered Gettysburg but retired without the footwear when Buford's Union horsemen rode into town. Richard Anderson's division of Hill's corps, Edward Johnson's of Ewell's corps, and Longstreet's corps remained west of the mountain, from Fayetteville to Chambersburg and the town of Scotland. Lee, on the eve of his greatest battle, bedded down at a deserted sawmill near the community of Greenwood. He had brought his splendid army to this point; tomorrow's early work fell to others, friends and foes.

Two of the coming morning's leading Confederate characters had conferred before nightfall. Powell Hill and Henry Heth discussed Pettigrew's report of Union cavalry in Gettysburg. Both dismissed it. Then Heth said, "If there is no objection, General, I will take my division tomorrow and go to Gettysburg and get those shoes."

"None in the world," Hill replied.

A Carbine Fires
and A Battle Begins

In Gettysburg, after dark on June 30, Colonel William Gamble talked with his superior, John Buford. He said his brigade could handle any force coming their way the next day. Buford, an experienced, no-nonsense officer of highest caliber, responded: "No, you won't. They will attack you in the morning; and they will come 'booming'—skirmishers three deep. You will have to fight like the devil to hold your own until supporters arrive. The enemy must know the importance of this position, and will strain every nerve to secure it, and if we are able to hold it we will do well."

Nightfall in the bivouacs brought shared meals, conversation, and sleep. Some on both sides never forgot that night or their feelings. The members of a South Carolina brigade savored an uncommon ration of liquor. One of them, echoing the view of probably all in that army, affirmed that they believed "scarcely anything impossible to Lee's army." Around other fires, where bluecoated men sat, the attitude, with a different perspective, was similar. "We felt some doubt about whether it was ever going to be our fortune to win a victory in Virginia," a Yankee wrote later, "but no one admitted the possibility of a defeat north of the Potomac."

Light glowed elsewhere nearby: candles and oil lamps inside homes. For the 2,400 inhabitants of Gettysburg, it was the last night before American history claimed their village. Founded in 1780 by James Getty, the town was the seat of Adams County, noted for leather and carriage manufacturing, the Lutheran Theological Seminary, and the Pennsylvania (now Gettysburg) College. Ten roads met there, former avenues of commerce now pathways of war. These highways suddenly made the place important, and on them the future was coming with the morning light. The crack of a carbine ended Gettysburg's past.

Henry Heth started for the shoes early on July 1. His four brigades, numbering slightly less than 8,000, filed onto the Chambersburg Pike by 5:00 A.M. Light, misty rain carried by a gentle wind from the south, cooled the marchers. Brigadier General James Archer's Alabamans and Tennesseeans led the division. Behind the infantry brigades rumbled the artillery battalions of Majors William Pegram and David McIntosh.

The pace of the march was not forced. Few expected much of a fight that morning—the possibility of battle, said an officer, was earlier met with a "spirit of unbelief."

Thirty minutes into the march, the van approached Marsh Creek, about three miles west of Gettysburg. Archer halted his brigade there, shaking out a skirmish line from the 13th Alabama Regiment and 5th Alabama Battalion. Advancing south of the pike, the graycoats neared a bridge spanning the creek when a carbine fired up ahead. Lieutenant Marcellus E. Jones, 8th Illinois Cavalry was the man at the trigger. It was the first shot of the battle. Other Federals, concealed in tall grass and behind bushes and trees, opened fire. The Alabamans replied. So it went for the next two hours as the Yankees, armed with breechloading carbines, maintained an inces-

sant fire against the Rebels, armed with single-shot muzzleloading rifles. The Illinoisans fought doggedly but eventually retired to their brigade's main line.

The ground west of Gettysburg was chiefly meadows and cultivated fields lying between a series of ridges. The four ridges—Seminary-Oak, McPherson, Herr, and Belmont Schoolhouse—ran north to south and were the dominant terrain on this sector of the battlefield. Buford had deployed Gamble's 1,700 cavalrymen on the westernmost crest of McPherson Ridge, south of the pike, while Colonel Thomas Devin's 1,200 men extended the line northward, with videttes guarding the roads entering town from the north. The cavalry was dismounted, with every fourth man holding the horses. Battery A, 2d U.S. Horse Artillery, Lieutenant John H. Calef commanding, supported the troopers with six 3-inch rifles.

Heth viewed Buford's ranks from Herr Ridge before 8:00 A.M. The Confederate division commander was 37 years old, an authority on the rifle and the only officer Lee addressed by first name. This was his first real test at the division command level. He ordered Archer's brigade of 1,300 into line south of the pike. Across the roadbed he deployed the 1,800 men of Brigadier General Joseph Davis, nephew of the Confederate President. Heth also closed his last two brigades—those of Brigadier General James J. Pettigrew and Colonel John M. Brockenbrough. Lee's army was being drawn into a battle led by its weakest infantry division, a patchwork organization with inexperienced officers in key commands.

The Confederates stepped out about 8:00. Union skirmishers, rimming Willoughby Run, a shallow stream midway between the ridges, sniped at the Southern battle lines. The Rebels pressed on, back went the enemy skirmishers, and the Federal line flamed. Henry Raison of the 7th Tennessee in Archer's brigade fell, the first Southerner killed at Gettysburg. The graycoats waded the run and went not much farther. The breechloading carbines gave the Yankees an edge in firepower, and they laced the sloping ground with strings of bullets.

About 9:00, youthful, bespectacled Major William Pegram, looking more like a schoolmaster than a master of cannon, unlimbered three batteries on Belmont Schoolhouse Ridge and opened long-range fire on McPherson Ridge. Calef's Union gunners replied, fighting "on this occasion as is seldom witnessed," reported Buford. For another hour the cannon thundered, the rifles and carbines crackled. Throughout, the graycoats increased the pressure, edging up the rising ground. Buford had been correct—his men had to "fight like the devil," but their time was running out before the Rebel infantry and Pegram's booming guns. To the north, some of Devin's Union men had been engaging advance elements of another enemy

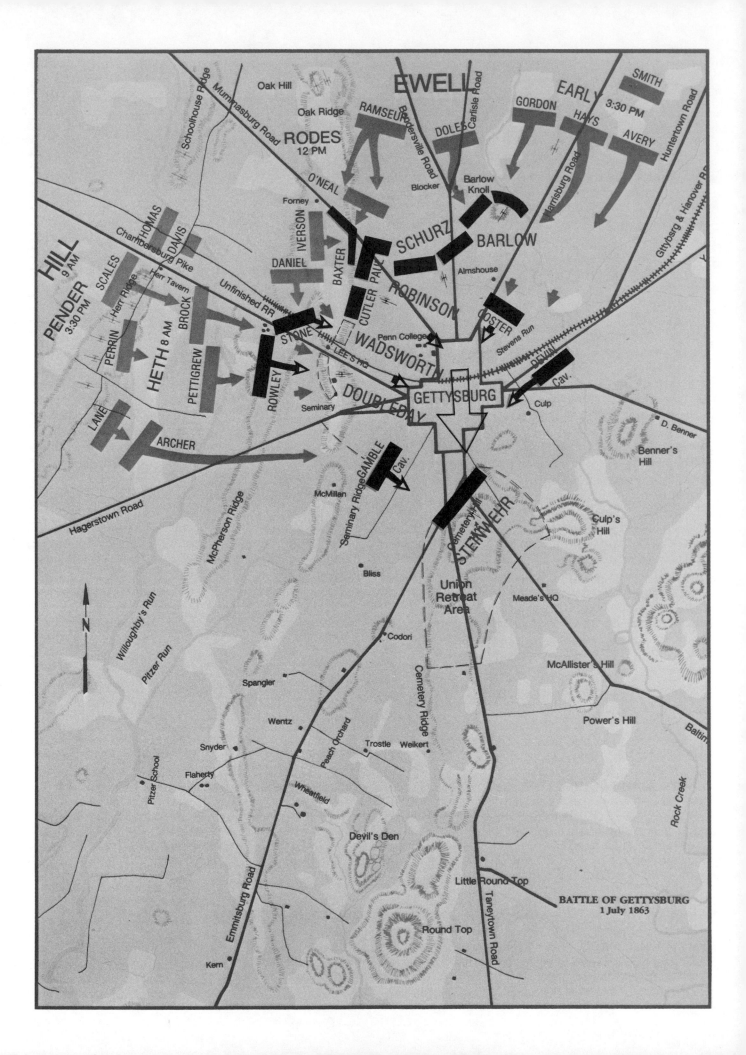

BATTLE OF GETTYSBURG
1 July 1863

·*On the first day: Confederate soldiers of Henry Heth's division fight past the stone barn of the McPherson farm. A.C. Redwood, who drew this scene, was a Confederate veteran of combat there. (Battles and Leaders of the Civil War)*

infantry force since 8:00. The 9th New York Cavalry, fighting on foot, repulsed the Rebels but one of its members, Cyrus W. James, was killed; his was the first Union battle death.

Buford was watching the combat from the cupola of the Lutheran Seminary when he saw help coming. About the same time Pegram's batteries entered the action, Major General John Reynolds, acting commander of the Union army's left wing, rode up to the seminary. Buford yelled down: "There's the devil to pay."

Reynolds dismounted and the two conferred. The infantry general was the most popular corps commander in the army and a combat officer second to none. He decided to make a stand west of town, told Buford to hang on, and sent a message to Meade, telling him the enemy was advancing but "I will fight him inch by inch, and if driven into the town I will barricade the streets and hold him back as long as possible." Remounting, Reynolds spurred his horse back to town to hurry his infantry forward.

Reynolds barely cleared Gettysburg's southern outskirts when he met the head of his own I Corps, Brigadier General James Wadsworth's 1st Division, marching up the Emmitsburg Road. Reynolds at once detoured the command into the fields on a direct path to Buford's position. Pioneers leveled fences before the column. Wadsworth's command was an excellent combat unit, numbering 4,000 effectives in two brigades. With them, rumbling past foot soldiers, was Captain James A. Hall's 2d Maine Battery. An orderly told Wadsworth "the rebs were thicker than blackberries ahead."

Hall's gun crews arrived first on McPherson Ridge where Reynolds, who had galloped ahead, ordered them into position. The artillerists unlimbered, rammed in charges and pulled the lanyards. The 3-inch rifles thundered in response to Pegram's cannon. Suddenly, to their right, about 50 yards away, the 42d Mississippi of Davis' brigade rose and blasted the Yankee gunners with a volley. Hall wheeled four cannon toward the gray-clad infantrymen, and raked them with canister—containers full of iron slugs, usually one inch in diameter, which converted cannon into giant shotguns. The Mississippians scrambled for cover behind a deep embankment where an unfinished railroad line cut through the ridge.

It was between 10:00 and 10:30 A.M. Wadsworth's leading brigade, Brigadier General Lysander Cutler's, hurried across the low ground between Seminary and McPherson Ridges. Wadsworth directed the 76th New York and 56th Pennsylvania north of the pike to support Hall's guns. Reynolds, who seemed to be everywhere, detached Cutler's two rear regiments, the 14th Brooklyn (84th New York) and 95th New York, sending them onto the western crest of the ridge, between Edward McPherson's house, his stone barn, and a triangular-shaped grove of trees south of the buildings known as McPherson Woods, relieving Buford's men. In the confusion, the 147th New York received no orders, so its commander massed it behind the barn.

A few minutes later, Reynolds saw Archer's troops charging up the slope toward the grove. The Union general rode toward the leading regiment of Brigadier General Solomon Meredith's "Iron Brigade," the 2d Wisconsin, now streaming across the depression between the ridges. "Forward men, forward for God's sake and drive those fellows out of those woods," Reynolds shouted. Loading rifles as they ran, the Wisconsin veterans entered the woods. Opposing lines exploded in an exchange of volleys. When the ranks fired, Reynolds, behind the 2d Wisconsin, turned in the saddle, looking for more troops. Suddenly he swayed and toppled to the ground. A stray bullet had struck him behind the right ear, killing him instantly. Reynolds' death, a Federal later wrote, "affected us much" for he was "one of the *soldier* Generals of the army." Major General Abner Doubleday took command of the corps.

Even as Reynolds lay dead, other regiments of the Iron Brigade—minus the 6th Wisconsin—raced past the fallen general and into the woods. The Midwesterners believed they were the best fighters in the army and wore black felt slouch hats as a distinctive badge. When told to hold the grove "at all hazards," they shouted back: "If we cannot hold it, where will you find men who can?"

They entered the trees none too soon. Archer's Rebels, after being momentarily checked by the 2d Wisconsin, were swarming across Willoughby Run, yelling as they charged into the grove. The Confederates fired, at a range of 40 to 50 yards. Solomon Meredith went down with a wound. But to the Southerners' shock, the Federals returned the volley and kept coming. "There are those damned black-hatted fellows again," exclaimed a Confederate. "T'aint no militia. It's the Army of the Potomac!"

The 19th Indiana and the 24th Michigan, swinging in from the south, raked the Rebels' flank. Combat escalated, but the "black-hatted fellows" had the best of it. Archer's ranks began receding, flowing down the slope and across the run. The Yankees pressed ahead; the flag of the 24th Michigan went down fourteen times, with nine members of the color guard killed or wounded. Scores of Confederates were captured, including Archer, who was seized by Private Patrick Mahoney, 2d Wisconsin. Archer was the first general captured since Lee took command of the army.

As Archer was led to the rear, Doubleday, who knew him before the war, extended a hand, saying "Archer! I'm glad to see you!" The prisoner refused the hand and shot back: "Well, I'm not glad to see you by a damn sight."

Cutler's Federals, meanwhile, were in serious trouble along the pike. When Wadsworth sent the 56th Pennsylvania and 76th New York to support Hall's battery, they met the 55th North Carolina of Davis' brigade. The opposing lines blasted each other. Davis advanced the 2d Mississippi on the 55th's right, and both commands charged. The North Carolinians overlapped the New Yorkers' flank, raking the Union line. Major Andrew Grover of the 76th died almost instantly and Colonel Hugh Connally, commanding the 55th North Carolina, fell grievously wounded as he grabbed his regiment's flag. In thirty minutes the New Yorkers lost 234 of their compliment of 370 men.

The 147th New York crossed the pike and came in on the 56th Pennsylvania's left. It collided head-on with the 42d Mississippi. "A continuous roar of musketry drowned all orders," asserted a New York officer. In the midst of the fury, Captain Thon Wright of the 147th was on his knees, pounding the ground, screaming, "Give them hell." But it was the Yankees who were caught in an infernal cauldron.

Wadsworth ordered all three regiments to retire. As Lieutenant Colonel Francis Miller of the 147th tried to shout the order, he was silenced with a bullet in the throat. Because of rifle smoke and an intervening fence, the New Yorkers did not see the other two regiments withdraw.

Davis' men concentrated on the solitary Union regiment and Hall's battery. Cannon spewed canister.

The Rebels pressed ahead, scorching the 147th New York at a distance of 6 to 8 yards. Hall ordered retreat. His gun crews pulled out section by section, lashing their horses into a gallop through a crossfire of musketry. "It was hellish," said Hall. Within minutes an aide of Wadsworth reached the New Yorkers, telling them to get out. This time the order was heard and they streamed eastward without organization. Their valiant stand cost them 75 percent of their members.

Wadsworth had already reacted to the disintegration of his line along the pike by sending an aide for the 6th Wisconsin, the division's only reserve. The aide ordered the regiment's commander, Lieutenant Colonel Rufus Dawes, to the right, admonishing him to "go like hell." Earlier that day, during the march, Dawes had his band play "The Campbells are Coming." Now his Iron Brigade veterans crossed the fields at the double-quick. They saw Davis' men swarm toward the roadbed. Reaching the fence along the pike's southern edge, the Federals rested their rifles on the top rails and fired. The Southerners recoiled at the blast and scampered back into the deep railroad cut. Dawes' men scaled the fence, crossed the road, cleared the second fence, and charged. At that point, the 95th New York and 14th Brooklyn attacked on their left.

The three Federal regiments hit in echelon, like successive hammers pounding an anvil. Davis ordered an immediate withdrawal from the cut, but numbers of his men never heard him. Those who stayed fought fiercely. Hand-to-hand combat ensued along the southern edge of the defile. Sergeant W.A. Murphy of the 2d Mississippi, trying to rip his flag from the staff, lost it in a duel with Corporal Francis Walker of the 6th Wisconsin. With the Federals sealing the cut, Dawes yelled to the trapped Confederates to surrender. Between 200 and 300 Southerners dropped their rifles; Major John Blair, 2d Mississippi, handed his sword to Dawes. The remainder of Davis' shattered command retreated to Herr Ridge while the three Union regiments fashioned a new line near the cut. It was a few minutes past 11:00.

A Full Day of Fighting

A lull in the fighting began at this time, lasting a full two hours. Both sides regrouped units that had been engaged and fresh ones arrived. What began as a foray for shoes had escalated into a major battle. Blame for this rested primarily with Heth and his superior, Hill. For reasons never fully explained, the pair committed Lee and his army to the campaign's decisive engagement without orders or prior notice. Buford and Reynolds answered Heth's advance with aggressiveness, selecting the area of combat and upsetting the Confederate timetable. The Federals, though suffering serious losses in an infantry division, wrecked half of Heth's division and held the ground. So far, the day belonged to the Northerners.

As fighting flickered out at the railroad cut, Doubleday brought his two other divisions into position. He placed Brigadier General John Robinson's two brigades in reserve on Seminary Ridge. Doubleday's own division, under Brigadier General Thomas Rowley, advanced to McPherson Ridge. Colonel Roy Stone's Pennsylvania brigade lengthened the Iron Brigade's right from the grove to the pike. As Stone's "Bucktails"—so called because of their marksmanship and the distinctive deer's tail they wore on their hats—filed onto the western crest, they chanted, "We have come to stay!" Colonel Chapman Biddle's four regiments formed on the Iron Brigade's left rear on the eastern crest. Biddle's left or southern flank was exposed because Gamble's cavalry brigade, repositioned by Buford, was too far south. Colonel Charles Wainwright, corps artillery chief, unlimbered two batteries with Robinson and two with Rowley. These deployments were completed under artillery fire from Pegram's and McIntosh's batteries.

In town, Major General Oliver O. Howard, commander of the XI Corps, surveyed the field from the roof of Samuel Fahnestock's three-story mercantile building at Middle and Baltimore Streets. On orders from Reynolds, Howard had hurried to Gettysburg ahead of his troops. He arrived in time to see Cutler's three regiments flee before Davis' men, but mistook the retreat as a collapse of the entire I Corps and reported this erroneous observation to Meade.* Next, Howard informed Doubleday that as ranking officer he, Howard, was assuming command of the field: the I Corps was to hold the left and the XI Corps, upon arrival, would protect the right in the fields north of town.

Howard, only 32 years old, was an experienced professional soldier who had lost his right arm in battle a year earlier. On July 1, 1863, his training and knowledge served the Union cause well. He entered the town and saw the tactical value of the high ground on Gettysburg's southeast corner, Cemetery Hill, and its southerly extension, Cemetery Ridge. He decided to hold the dominating terrain with part of his troops and established his headquarters on East Cemetery Hill, a spur of the higher eminence. Then he waited for his corps.

The three divisions of Howard's XI Corps—10,700 strong, with five batteries of twenty-six cannon—reached the Cemetery Hill area about 12:30 P.M.,

coming in on the Emmitsburg and Taneytown Roads. At the same time Howard received a report from the vigilant Buford, noting the arrival of Confederate infantry in strength at Oak Hill, a commanding height at the northern end of Oak Ridge beyond the I Corps' right flank. Howard had planned to extend Doubleday's flank by positioning two of his divisions on heavily wooded Oak Ridge, but because Southerners manned Oak Hill, he altered the corps' deployment. He held Brigadier General Adolph von Steinwehr's division and two batteries in reserve on Cemetery Hill while ordering the remaining infantry and artillery to the plain north of town.

It took more than an hour for three batteries and the divisions of Brigadier Generals Francis Barlow and Alexander Schimmelfennig to file through Gettysburg and form into line in the fields of clover and ripened grain. Major General Carl Schurz, temporarily commanding the corps, oversaw the movement. Contrary to Schurz' wishes, Barlow moved a mile and a half north of the town square, curling his two brigades around three slopes of a low knoll (known today as Barlow's Knoll) west of Rock Creek and the Harrisburg Road. Schimmelfennig's two brigades extended the line southwestward across the fields to within a quarter-mile of the crest of Oak Ridge. Schurz' entire front, held by 6,100 infantry and sixteen cannon, stretched for three quarters of a mile at an obtuse angle from Oak Ridge, where part of the I Corps was going into position.

The terrain offered no natural defensive advantages or anchors for either of Schurz' flanks. Barlow's aggressive movement to the knoll exposed the command's right flank. Howard personally inspected the completed line about 2:00, before examining Doubleday's front, which now embraced Oak Ridge just west of Schimmelfennig's left flank.

As the XI Corps filled the plain, Doubleday shifted Brigadier General Henry Baxter's brigade of Robinson's division from a position near the Lutheran Seminary to the northern end of Oak Ridge. Baxter aligned his six regiments along the Mummasburg Road, which skirted the southern base of Oak Hill. The Federals held a stone wall, facing north. Less than a quarter-mile northeast lay Schimmelfennig's command.

The deployment of Baxter's brigade and Schurz' two divisions was completed under artillery fire from Lieutenant Colonel Thomas Carter's Confederate battalion of sixteen cannon on Oak Hill, and rifle fire from Rebel skirmishers. The guns and infantrymen were the leading edge of Robert Rodes' division of five brigades, numbering 8,500 veterans.

Rodes reached the vicinity of Oak Hill about mid-

*Howard's error contributed to Meade's removal of Doubleday from corps command on July 2d.

day, after Ewell redirected him to Gettysburg on Lee's orders. Marching and the morning's heat exhausted Rodes' men; it took them nearly two hours to form for an attack. Carter's gunners, meanwhile, shelled the Federals on the plain and on McPherson Ridge from Oak Hill, a natural artillery platform and the key terrain feature of the afternoon's combat. Rodes' skirmishers also engaged the Yankees. In turn, they captured 600 Rebels. About 2:00 P.M. Rodes pressed a full-scale assault.

These troops had been Stonewall Jackson's cohesive strike force at Chancellorsville, but on this day their attack unraveled almost from the outset. Colonel Edward O'Neal's Alabama brigade in the center charged on too narrow a front, at the wrong place, and in some confusion. O'Neal, an undistinguished officer, used only three of his five regiments and did not personally direct the movement. Baxter's Federals, shielded by the stone wall, hammered back the Alabamans.

With O'Neal's quick repulse, Brigadier General Alfred Iverson's four North Carolina regiments, on the Alabamans' right, took up the assault. Iverson, like O'Neal, was not very capable, and neither he nor Rodes conducted an efficient reconnaissance. Telling his men to "give them hell," Iverson sent them forward without skirmishers. They advanced through a field of timothy west of Oak Ridge and into an ambush. "Unarmed, unled as a brigade, we went to our doom," wrote a captain.

Baxter, seeing Iverson's advance, hurried his men to the crest of Oak Ridge, faced them west, and hid them behind a stone wall. The unsuspecting North Carolinians flattened the timothy as they marched straight across the front of the concealed Union brigade. Ahead, some of Lysander Cutler's Yankees opened fire on the Rebels, who edged closer to the stone wall. When the Carolinians were only seventy-five paces away, Baxter's men stood up and the crest flamed with hellfire. Hundreds of Confederates toppled to the ground, the dead and wounded lying in a distinct, straight line as if they were in a dress parade of the macabre.

Numbers of Southerners regrouped in a gully about 100 yards to the rear, returning the fire. But the 20th North Carolina, closest to the ridge, was pinned down and helpless. "I believe every man who stood up was either killed or wounded," remarked one of its officers. Baxter, performing with skill, counterattacked with part of his brigade. The Federals surged down the slope into the timothy, shooting down Carolinians and capturing approximately 400. Every officer, except one in the 23d North Carolina, was shot. The shattered Confederate brigade streamed northward. The remnant of the 12th North Carolina

escaped by waving a white flag which briefly stopped the Yankees.

O'Neal's Alabamans resumed their attack, wrenching the north end of the stone wall from Baxter's troops. This success was temporary, however. Baxter's men were out of ammunition. Robinson sent Brigadier General Gabriel Paul's Union brigade to their relief and they engaged the Alabamans.

Paul formed his five regiments in an inverted "L," with the angle located where Oak Ridge intersected the Mummasburg Road. The Union brigadier positioned his command of more than 1,600 men behind the stone walls. Carter's gunners and some of O'Neal's and Iverson's troops opened a severe fire on the Yankees. Paul suffered a ghastly wound early in the action; a bullet carried away both his eyes. His successor fell minutes later. Colonel Adrian Root, 94th New York, took command.

The combat sharpened. The Southerners overran the angle, only to be swept back by the 104th New York, which lost seven colorbearers. A short time later, Brigadier General Stephen Dodson Ramseur's brigade of North Carolinians reinforced Iverson's battered ranks. Ramseur advanced against both sides of the Federal position. Paul's three regiments on the ridge repulsed this new thrust by counterattacking down the hillside into the fields. Ramseur's veterans stopped, a number were taken prisoner, and the action temporarily subsided. Rodes, like Heth earlier, had committed his brigades in piecemeal assaults, encountering stiff resistance and suffering severe casualties in two units. His direction of the division was substandard.

The entry of Paul's brigade into combat on Oak Ridge around 2:30 P.M. coincided with the renewal of battle on McPherson Ridge. After the debacle of Archer and Davis, Heth remained inactive for three hours. During that time the batteries of Pegram and McIntosh, assisted by some of Carter's crews, achieved artillery supremacy on this sector. Between 2:00 and 2:30 P.M. the Confederate gunners opened a sustained bombardment. Behind this blanket of metallic thunder and lightning came the infantry, Heth's two remaining brigades under Pettigrew and Brockenbrough.

Pettigrew's four regiments of North Carolinians, 2,740 strong, constituted "the largest, best equipped, finest looking brigade of the whole army," said an admiring artillerist. Both of Heth's fresh brigades were south of the Chambersburg Pike, with the Carolinians on the right, headed straight for McPherson Woods, which the Iron Brigade held. One Federal said they "came on with rapid strides, yelling like demons." As the Carolinians entered the stand of oaks and chestnuts, the opposing lines unleashed murderous volleys. On Pettigrew's left, the 26th North Carolina, under 21-one-year-old Colonel Henry King Burgwyn, fired at point-blank range into the 24th Michigan, which responded in kind. It was some of the fiercest, deadliest fighting of the day, even of the war. Burgwyn, nicknamed the "boy colonel," took a bullet through both lungs, a mortal wound. His successor soon had his jaw shattered.

The screaming Confederates pressed deeper into the woods. The "damned black hats" fought with a determination worthy of their reputation but the Rebels, overlapping a flank, bent back the Union line. The 24th Michigan formed three separate lines in the grove. The 26th North Carolina, still in the forefront, collided at twenty paces with the 151st Pennsylvania of Biddle's brigade. The exchanges were merciless.* The demonic combat raged for nearly an hour.

North of the grove, around the McPherson farm buildings, Brockenbrough's Virginians were pounding Stone's Pennsylvania Bucktails. Stone's three regiments were already engaged with Brigadier General Junius Daniel's brigade of Rodes' division when Brockenbrough attacked. Daniel had crossed the fields beyond Iverson's right and had driven toward the railroad cut. Stone changed front to the north, along the pike, repulsing Daniel's initial thrust. The Rebels renewed the assault only to crash into a counterattack. Stone, who suffered a severe wound, claimed the Bucktails "fought as if each man felt that upon his arm hung the fate of the day and the nation."

But when Brockenbrough attacked, the pressure crushed the Union brigade. The 150th Pennsylvania hurried back to the ridge to meet the oncoming Virginians. In the ranks of the Union regiment stood John Burns, a 70-year-old Gettysburg resident. Burns, a veteran of the War of 1812, grabbed an old musket when the battle began, walked to the Union line, and was permitted to fight with the Pennsylvanians. The old warrior was wounded three times and had to be carried into town.

The combined Confederate offensive against McPherson Ridge finally succeeded. On the right, part of Pettigrew's command turned the flank of Biddle's poorly placed brigade. Division commander Thomas Rowley was responsible for the shoddy disposition and was subsequently court-martialed for drunkenness. The collapse of Biddle's line exposed the Iron

---

*The Pennsylvanians lost 337 of 467 members. For the Carolinians it was even worse—11 colorbearers; among three sets of twins in the regiment, five men died; in one company of 89, all but one hit; in all, 588 of 800, or 82 percent, were casualties. The 26th had the heaviest losses sustained by any regiment in the army during the campaign.

Brigade's left, prompting the Midwesterners' retreat from the grove. Daniel and Brockenbrough also cracked Stone's front at the farm and along the pike. Most of the Yankees retired fighting to Seminary Ridge, where Doubleday and his subordinates fashioned a new line.

The Union front contained remnants of six brigades, supported by four batteries. The Northerners had barely finished their dispositions when Heth's second division, three of four brigades belonging to William Dorsey Pender, 5,300 veterans, passed over McPherson Ridge in serried ranks. "For a mile up and down the open fields in front," recalled Rufus Dawes, "the splendid lines of the veterans of the Army of Northern Virginia swept down upon us. Their bearing was magnificent. They maintained their alignment with great precision."

These Confederates, clad in butternut-colored uniforms, had been part of Hill's "Light Division" and Pender, their commander, was one of the finest combat officers on the field. When the left brigade, Brigadier General Alfred Scales' North Carolinians, reached a point 75 to 100 yards from the Federal ranks, a battery opened with canister. An artillery officer shouted: "Feed it to 'em, God damn 'em! Feed it to 'em!" The gray line melted before the furnace. Scales fell wounded, along with every field officer, except one. The bloodied command pulled back, re-formed, and charged again.

On Scales' right, the South Carolinians of Colonel Abner Perrin were breaching the Union defense in the sector held by Biddle. Perrin's men leaned into the murderous storm of bullets, ascended the slope, and seized breastworks beyond Biddle's left, enfilading the Federal ranks. With Perrin on the crest and Scales closing once more, Doubleday ordered a final withdrawal. The cannon went first, followed by the infantry, pockets of whom stood and fought, saving the guns.

The fleeing Yankees of the I Corps raced through the streets of Gettysburg, where they encountered men of the XI Corps; the entire Union front had collapsed almost at once. Schurz' men had been caught in a vise fashioned by Rodes' and Jubal Early's troops. The latter officer and his 5,700-man division arrived on the field just before 3:00, coming in on the Harrisburg Road, where Barlow's division held the knoll. Early was one of the Confederate army's characters, a crotchety, fault-finding man, liked by few, and the only officer known to swear in the presence of Lee, who affectionately called him "my bad old man." But Early was a fighter, and he went after Barlow's exposed line.

Early's assault began with a fearful bombardment by twelve cannon of Lieutenant Colonel H.P. Jones'

The retreat of the Union XI Corps through the streets of Gettysburg on the afternoon of July 1. What had begun as a minor engagement between a shoe-hunting party and "home guards" was about to become the greatest battle of the war. (Library of Congress)

battalion. Lieutenant Bayard Wilkeson's six-gun Battery G, 4th United States Artillery, replied from the knoll. One Federal shell opened the skull of a Confederate gunner, creating a gruesome sight as his brain lay on the ground "in two, bloody, palpitating lobes." But Jones' crews fired from an enfilading position with terrible effect. Wilkeson's leg was shattered by a round, so the 19-year-old officer calmly amputated it with a penknife. When the Federals retreated, Wilkeson crawled to an almshouse nearly half a mile to the south, off the Harrisburg Road. He died there that night.

About 3:30 P.M.—at approximately the same time Pender started—Early unleashed three brigades against Barlow's vulnerable flank. Brigadier General John Gordon's right brigade spearheaded the charge, and Brigadier General Harry Hays and Colonel Isaac Avery swung their units southwest to take the Union line in reverse. As Gordon closed, Brigadier General George Doles' Georgians of Rodes' division —men who had engaged Schimmelfennig's troops— shifted left to strike Barlow's front.

Schimmelfennig responded, advancing one of his brigades to gnaw at Doles' flank, stalling his attack. At this point, Gordon's veterans, also Georgians, screamed the "Rebel yell" and charged across a wheatfield. Barlow's line flamed; cannon scorched the grain field with grape and canister. Opposing ranks exchanged knee-buckling volleys at fifty paces.

Doles came on, as did Hays and Avery. Battered on three sides, Barlow's division abandoned the bloody knoll, retreating 500 yards south to the almshouse, where some units briefly re-formed and fought some more. Barlow, grievously wounded, was captured.

To the west, Schimmelfennig's ranks, hit on the right by Doles and on the left by Ramseur, were also cracking. Ramseur had launched another attack on Paul's I Corps' brigade on Oak Ridge. The Yankees once more resisted fiercely until their division commander, Robinson, ordered them back. Only the 16th Maine was left in place; Robinson had directed the unit to hold the angle "at any cost." The Maine troops, assailed by four regiments, made an heroic, deadly stand. Of the regiment's 298 members, 232 were casualties. Nearly surrounded, the survivors tore their flag into pieces to save it and then fled.

With Paul's withdrawal, Ramseur's "Tarheels" carved into Schimmelfennig's flank. The 75th Pennsylvania held this point in the line. The unit shifted its front to the left to resist the onslaught. In fifteen minutes, 111 Pennsylvanians fell. The plain north of town was filled with fleeing Northerners and pursuing Southerners. Howard rushed Colonel Charles R. Coster's Union brigade from Cemetery Hill as reinforcement. Coster's New Yorkers and Pennsylvanians reached Gettysburg's northern outskirts when the brigades of Hays and Avery descended on their front and right flank. The Union brigade held long enough for Barlow's troops to retire from the almshouse. Captain Lewis Heckman's Battery K, 1st Ohio Light Artillery, unlimbered on the Carlisle Road near the college and discharged 113 rounds of canister in thirty minutes, only to lose two cannon before escaping. When Coster retreated, Union resistance ended.

The Yankees' retreat was executed with reasonable order until they reached town. Caught in unfamiliar streets, pursued by a victorious enemy, the men suddenly became desperate, panic-stricken. Pandemonium ensued. Hundreds of trapped Federals surrendered. Division commander Schimmelfennig hid in a woodpile to avoid capture and stayed there until July 4, when the battle ended and the Confederates left. Most of the pursuers belonged to the brigades of Hays, Ramseur, and Perrin. At approximately 4:30 P.M., Perrin's 1st South Carolina planted its colors in the town square. Gettysburg was in the hands of a jubilant enemy.

On Cemetery Hill, Oliver Howard and Major General Winfield Scott Hancock rallied the shattered Federal units. Meade, acting through army Chief of Staff Daniel Butterfield, had sent Hancock to assume overall command of the field. In a 1:10 P.M. order,

Butterfield added, "if you think the ground and position there a better one to fight a battle under existing circumstances, you will so advise the general, and he will order all the troops up." After turning over command of his II Corps, Hancock hurried to the battlefield, arriving around 4:30 P.M. He met Howard, the senior officer, on Cemetery Hill and delivered Meade's order, which resulted in an exchange of words between the pair. But discussion over who should command ended abruptly when blue-coated fugitives began spilling out of town.

In chosing Hancock, Meade selected the best officer to meet this crisis. Tall, handsome, 30 years old, the native Pennsylvanian possessed a galvanizing presence. To one officer he was "a glorious soldier"; to another, he was "upon horseback I think the most magnificent looking General in the whole Army." He always looked like a leader, well-dressed, wearing "a clean *white* shirt (where he gets them nobody knows)." His appearance, his bearing, his actions were of inestimable value.

When Hancock saw the oncoming fugitives, he reacted instantly. Using Colonel Orland Smith's brigade and a battery as a rallying point, he and Howard

About 4:30 P.M., Major General Winfield Scott Hancock, now in overall command of the field, arrives on Cemetery Hill to save the day for the Federal army, transforming the disorganized mass of fleeing Union soldiers into a tenable line. (Library of Congress)

The gatehouse of Gettysburg's Evergreen Cemetery was a prominent landmark on Cemetery Hill. The fighting here is seen from Union lines around the gatehouse. (Library of Congress)

stopped the flight and re-formed the units. The troops, though defeated, even routed, were not demoralized, and by 5:00 P.M. most had rallied. Hancock directed tactical rearrangements, supplementing Howard's earlier decision to hold Cemetery Hill. Two of Doubleday's I Corps divisions fashioned a line on the hill, while Hancock, over Doubleday's objections, sent Wadsworth's division to Culp's Hill, a higher, wooded elevation a half-mile southeast of Cemetery Hill. Schurz' XI Corps held East Cemetery Hill, and Buford's cavalry formed near the Emmitsburg Road to protect that flank. Batteries unlimbered among the infantry, set to sweep approaches to the hilltops. At 5:15 P.M. Hancock sent a message to Meade stating he could hold the position until dark.

Hancock's confidence was bolstered by the arrival of reinforcements. Major General Henry Slocum's XII Corps, marching on the Baltimore Pike, reached the field about 5:00. In the next hour, the vanguard of Major General Daniel Sickles' III Corps marched in on the Emmitsburg Road. With the arrival of these two commands and some smaller units, the Union position was temporarily secured. By nightfall, Hancock's own II Corps was bivouacking near the Round Tops, hills roughly two miles from Cemetery Hill. About 6:30 P.M., Slocum, the senior officer, assumed command of all the troops. Nearby, a sign in the

Citizen's Evergreen Cemetery read: "All persons found using firearms in these grounds will be prosecuted with the utmost rigor of the law."

In the Confederate lines, officers reorganized their own victorious commands. More importantly, though, Robert E. Lee was now on the field. The army commander had learned of an engagement when he crossed the summit of South Mountain and heard the distant rumble of artillery fire. He became visibly annoyed, for he had neither expected nor wanted a general engagement without his army fully concentrated and equipped with accurate intelligence on the enemy's whereabouts. Spurring his horse, Traveller, forward, he rode swiftly to Cashtown, where he found Powell Hill, who was ill. Hill evidently never informed his superior of the ongoing battle or his and Heth's decision to escalate the struggle. Contrary to his expressed wishes, Lee found himself entangled in a general engagement against an opponent of unknown strength and composition. He could not hide his displeasure and spoke again of Stuart's absence.

Riding on, Lee met Heth at Marsh Creek about 2:30 P.M. "Rodes is heavily engaged," stated the subordinate. "Had I not better attack?"

"No," Lee replied. "I am not prepared to bring on a general engagement today. Longstreet is not up."

Heth returned to his troops on Herr Ridge, saw Doubleday's Federals engage Rodes, and relayed the information to Lee, requesting permission to attack. Confronted with these circumstances, Lee approved, and Pettigrew and Brockenbrough charged.

Some Curious Names and Some Places To Die

Lee witnessed a Confederate victory on Seminary Ridge. And as the attacking troops of Pettigrew and Brockenbrough pursued the enemy, the army's commanding general rode up behind them. He cut a magnificent figure.

"General Lee is, almost without exception, the handsomest man of his age I ever saw," wrote a British officer accompanying the army. He wore a long gray jacket with three stars on the collar, blue trousers tucked into Wellington boots, and a felt hat. He had the carriage and manners of "a perfect gentleman," but he possessed a temper. A difficult taskmaster to those closest to him, Lee was dubbed "The Tycoon" by his staff. And the burdens of his position had aged him beyond his 56 years.

Lee's looks and demeanor hid the flames burning within him whenever battle was joined. "General Lee, not excepting Jackson," argued Heth, "was the most aggressive man in the army." A pair of historians described this characteristic of Lee at Gettysburg as "blinding exhilaration." His temperament, his belief his troops were invincible, army tradition, and military concepts shaped the general's conduct and decisions from the time he reached Gettysburg.

A revealing exchange occurred between Lee and James Longstreet shortly after Lee's halt on Seminary Ridge. Longstreet found his general there and joined him in examining the high ground south of town. After viewing it for several minutes, "Old Peter," as Longstreet was nicknamed, proposed a vague flanking movement around the heights. "If the enemy is there tomorrow," Lee said firmly, "I will attack him."

"If the enemy is there tomorrow," rebutted Longstreet, "it will be because he wants you to attack."

Lee may have been disturbed at his subordinate's words, but he kept his composure. For the moment, Lee had more important matters to resolve. He saw clearly that Cemetery Hill and Culp's Hill gave the beaten enemy excellent defensive positions. If the hills could be taken immediately, the Federals fleeing through town would have no other ground on which to rally and construct a new line. Consequently, Lee sent Lieutenant Colonel Walter Taylor, a staff officer, to Ewell with a message. As Taylor recalled it, Lee believed "it was only necessary to press 'those people' in order to secure possession of the heights, and that, if possible, he wished him [Ewell] to do this." Ewell listened to Taylor repeat the general's wishes and "did not express any objection or indicate the existence of any impediment." The staff officer left, believing the order would be executed.

Ewell never advanced. This caused one of the battle's bitterest controversies. Ex-Confederates writing of Southern defeat years later made Ewell a major scapegoat. He unquestionably lacked the insight and relentlessness of a Stonewall Jackson, and clearly acted with excessive prudence during the late afternoon and evening of July 1, but most criticism of his generalship is undeserved. From the time the South Carolinians waved their flag in the square, around 4:30 P.M., Ewell had only about forty-five minutes, perhaps less, to undertake a vigorous assault. By 5:15 P.M., Hancock and Howard had stabilized their line, and within another fifteen minutes about 12,000 Yankees manned the heights. By 6:00 that figure reached 20,000, supported by scores of cannon. Ewell could not have attacked in that brief time because of disorganization in his ranks caused by fatigue, casualties, and pursuit. He probably could have mustered 6,000 to 7,000 troops for an assault, but not much before 5:30. The ultimate responsibility for the failure rested with Lee, who would have had to risk not only Ewell's divisions but Hill's, too, in an offensive at 5:00 or minutes later. Circumstances, more than failed leadership, prevented the Confederates from seizing Cemetery Hill.

After sunset, Lee rode to Ewell's headquarters at the Blocher farm, northwest of Barlow's Knoll. He conferred with Ewell, Early, and Rodes in an arbor. Lee proposed a daylight assault on Cemetery Hill with Ewell's corps, now that Edward Johnson's division was at hand. Early surprisingly acted as spokesman, opposing the plan. Ewell and Rodes concurred. Lee then asked if the corps should not be withdrawn through the town, thus shortening the army's lengthy line. Again Early voiced objections, listing the abandonment of the wounded and potential damage to the troops morale as defects of the plan. Lee was not pleased with this timidity. With the next day's operations unresolved, Lee departed, returning to his headquarters in a field across the Chambersburg Pike from Maria Thompson's stone dwelling. He had had his tent placed there, and a door from the widow's house was laid on braces or chairs for use as a map table. During the battle, Lee ate some meals in Mrs. Thompson's home but slept in his tent.

The Virginian, though aggressive and inclined to take the offensive, was a careful, studious planner. He weighed all aspects of a battle or campaign thoroughly. But when Lee bedded down for a few hours sleep that night, no one was sure of how to proceed on July 2. Later, in his report, all Lee could say was that he had not intended to fight unless attacked, but the army had stumbled into a major, bloody fight, making a battle at this crossroads "in a measure, unavoidable." "Encouraged by the successful issue of the engagement of the first day," he added, "and in view of the valuable results that would ensue from the defeat of the army of General Meade, it was thought advisable to renew the attack."

A full moon bathed the countryside that night, lighting the roadways for marching men. Most troops on the move were Federals, responding to Meade's concentration orders issued that afternoon and evening. Sometime before dawn on July 2, the Union commander arrived on Cemetery Hill. Meade, like Lee, had been drawn into a major engagement by subordinate officers. But unlike his counterpart, Meade had had his troops soundly defeated. Total Federal losses amounted to 8,900, of which nearly 3,500 were captured or missing. Given the number of troops involved, the Union forces had suffered 28 percent casualties; but the Yankees, in turn, had inflicted enemy losses of about 6,000, nearly 22 percent.

By the time Meade arrived on the 2d the Federals already enjoyed two major advantages: a formidable defensive position and the presence of most units of the army. By 7:00 A.M., all infantry corps except the VI were on the field, plus all their artillery battalions, four of the five artillery brigades, and Buford's two mounted brigades. A host of Federals, 93,500 of them, fought at Gettysburg. And Meade, allowing for his first day's losses, still had approximately 60,000 troops—a force surpassing his opponent's.

The terrain augmented Meade's numerical strength. In few major engagements of the Civil War did the battlefield's natural features provide such a significant advantage to one opponent as it did to the Federals at Gettysburg. Howard and Hancock were correct—this was a fine place to fight a defensive battle.

Union riflemen and gunners, in a line about three and a half miles long, found they had been positioned along a front that curved backward sharply at one end. It was later dubbed the "fishhook" line because of its literal resemblence to that sporting item. The barb of the "fishhook" was Culp's Hill, a wooded eminence towering 140 feet over its base; it anchored the army's right flank. From Culp's Hill, the line curved northwest one half-mile to Cemetery Hill, which had an elevation 60 to 80 feet. The shank of the "fishhook" was Cemetery Ridge, a plateau extending nearly two miles from Cemetery Hill to the base of Little Round Top. This latter height, its crest 170 feet above its base, lay a quarter-mile northeast of Big Round Top, looming 305 feet above the valley below. Little Round Top's western face was cleared of marketable timber in 1861 or 1862. Now it was the key to this sector of the field; it was accessible to artillery and stood as the natural sentry guarding the left flank and rear of the Union line on Cemetery Ridge. Complementing these natural strengths was a geometric feature of the line; its outward arc permitted Meade to shift units rapidly from one area to another behind the lines.

Seminary Ridge, stretched more than 1,000 yards, lying west of Cemetery Ridge. The bulk of the Confederate army deployed on its wooded crest, paralleling the sparsely forested Cemetery Ridge. The elongated valley between the ridges became the main amphitheater of combat. It was a battlefield where the fury of combat could be seen by thousands of the participants. But it was also a place of great beauty. Fields of wheat, corn, timothy, and clover, scarred by outcroppings of rocks, splotched by orchards of fruit trees, colored by farmhouses and farms, testified to the region's lushness. The Emmitsburg Road bisected the valley, its bed marked by post-and-rail fences. At the southern end of the field, opposite the Round Tops, the valley floor rose slightly, and there grew J. Sherfy's Peach Orchard.

Just before dawn Meade, with Howard and Brigadier General Henry Hunt, chief of artillery, began a careful survey of the field and Union dispositions. The XI Corps covered Cemetery Hill, with the I Corps extending the XI's right to Culp's Hill, where the XII Corps was positioned. The II and III Corps manned Cemetery Ridge from the hill to the low ground north of Little Round Top. Meade placed the V Corps in reserve behind Power's Hill, a mile south of Culp's Hill, near the Baltimore Pike, to await the VI Corps arrival. Until Lee revealed his hand, Meade and his army would hold the heights and wait.

Early in the morning, Meade established headquarters in "a shabby little farm house" at the eastern foot of Cemetery Ridge, beside the Taneytown Road. The white house belonged to Mrs. Lydia Leister, a widow who left her home during the battle. Though closer to the line's northern end, headquarters was within an easy ride of all Union positions. After examining the Federal terrain, Meade returned to headquarters and worked on preparations for an expected renewal of combat.

Like Meade, Lee spent the early daylight hours studying the enemy position. The Confederate commander was suffering from an intestinal disorder. He had gone to bed the night before with no certain plan other than his decision to resume the offensive. Before Lee slept, Ewell visited him and proposed an early morning attack on Culp's Hill. Ewell said two of his aides reported the rise unoccupied. Lee consented to Ewell's plan, though he probably knew the enemy would not leave such a dominating height long vacant. Shortly after dawn he cancelled the movement with a new set of orders for Ewell.

Between 5:00 and 6:00 A.M., Longstreet, Hill, Heth, and Hood joined Lee on Seminary Ridge. The meeting was relaxed, informal—Lee sitting on a log, periodically studying a map, Longstreet and Hood whittling. The commanding general outlined an assault on the Union left by Longstreet's two divisions. Longstreet once more disapproved of an attack on the Federals. But Lee was adamant.

About 8:00 Lafayette McLaws, riding ahead of his division, joined the group. Lee pointed to his map and showed McLaws that he wanted his division placed perpendicular to the Emmitsburg Road, between the road and the Round Tops. Again Longstreet dissented. "No, General," rebutted Lee, "I wish it placed as I have told General McLaws."

Historian Douglas Southall Freeman characterized the Confederate plan as "vague and misfounded," the result of Lee's mistaken belief about the location of Meade's left flank, and of Lee's resultant improvisation. Lee ordered an oblique attack that would envelop and roll back the Union flank toward Cemetery Hill. Once McLaws and Hood advanced, Hill's divisions would charge, moving forward en echelon from south to north. The plan required concerted action between units, subject to the interpretations of officers directing those units. So complicated an offensive also needed careful scrutiny and guidance, but Lee had too small a staff, and he did not believe such direction was his function as commander. Whenever he brought his army into battle and formulated a tactical plan, he left execution to subordinates. With Stonewall Jackson leading half the army, Lee's method achieved brilliant successes; but without Jackson at Gettysburg, the Confederate command system collapsed.

Lee ordered another reconnaissance of the Union flank by Captain S.R. Johnston, an engineer, then rode to Ewell's headquarters. After conferring again with Ewell, Lee ordered him to pressure the Union right flank once he heard Longstreet's guns; he was to exploit any advantage.

Lee then rode back to Seminary Ridge, arriving after 11:00. He found Captain Johnston had not returned from his mission and Longstreet had not moved. Lee told the corps commander to advance but Longstreet asked permission to wait until one of Hood's brigades, Brigadier General Evander Law's, arrived. Lee consented, though he showed his impatience with the slowness of developments.

After midday, McLaws' and Hood's divisions started, with engineer Johnston as guide. According to one historian, the march became "a comedy of errors." No one, not even Johnston, had sought a route that would keep the units concealed from Federal signalmen on Little Round Top. Consequently, soon after crossing the Fairfield Road at Black Horse Tavern, the head of the column reached the crest of a hill that was exposed to Union watchmen. The divisions backtracked, with Hood now in the lead, almost to their starting point before turning south again, following Willoughby Run until they reached Pitzer's School House. There they turned east. The countermarch had nearly doubled the four-mile distance.

It was near 3:00 when Longstreet's infantry began filing into attack formation. Hood placed his four brigades in two lines on Bushman Ridge, overlapping the Emmitsburg Road, facing northwest. McLaws' four brigades were similarly aligned on Warfield Ridge, extending Hood's ranks. Colonel E. Porter Alexander, acting corps artillery commander, had had three battalions of artillery parked in the area for nearly three hours. Alexander, an excellent officer, had discovered a concealed short cut the infantry had missed. When the foot soldiers deployed, Alexander massed two battalions, fifty to fifty-four cannon, along a half-mile front on Warfield Ridge. Major

M.W. Henry's nineteen-gun battalion was posted on the right flank to support Hood.

Confederate officers examined the ground and were amazed to see Union infantry and artillery in line from the Peach Orchard to the Round Tops. These blue-bloused troops belonged to Major General Daniel Sickles' III Corps. For much of the day, from his position on the low, southern end of Cemetery Ridge, Sickles fretted over the seemingly higher ground in his front along the Emmitsburg Road. He talked to Meade about the corps' placement, but Meade repeated an earlier order: Sickles was to connect his line with the II Corps' left. The III Corps chief requested authority to use his judgment in the disposition. Meade approved, provided Sickles would act within limits his commander had defined.

Sickles rode with Henry Hunt to the Emmitsburg Road for a closer inspection. Sickles told Hunt he wanted to occupy this ground. Hunt, unaware of Meade's instructions, told the corps commander to await directions from army headquarters.

Dan Sickles was probably the most colorful general in the army. A 43-year-old New Yorker, former lawyer, and U.S. congressman, he had killed Philip Barton Key, son of "Star Spangled Banner" composer Francis Scott Key, upon discovering his illicit affair with his wife. During his trial, Sickles achieved a legal first when he pleaded the "unwritten law," a man's right to protect the sanctity of his marriage, and was acquitted. A Democrat who supported Republican President Lincoln's war aims, Sickles was commissioned a brigadier in 1861 and given a brigade. He proved a capable, aggressive officer, with a pronounced streak of independence. He neither listened to opposing opinion nor took advice.

About 2:00, a 100-man detachment from Colonel Hiram Berdan's 1st and 2d U.S. Sharpshooters reported three columns of Confederate infantry moving toward the Union left flank. The sharpshooters, wearing green coats, had been skirmishing with Rebels nearly three hours. Sickles also learned Buford's cavalrymen had been withdrawn from the southern flank. This was enough for Sickles; he ordered his divisions, nearly 11,000 men strong, to advance.

Major General David Birney's troops led the movement. Not only did Sickles advance without authorization, his units marched as if on dress parade—bugles blaring, flags uncased, skirmishers rimming the front. Soldiers from other corps watched in admiration. Brigadier General John Gibbon, with Winfield Hancock on the ridge, asked his commander if their corps had not received an order for a general advance. "Wait a moment," Hancock said, "you'll see them tumbling back."

Birney's three brigades deployed on a broken ridge extending from the Emmitsburg Road to above Devil's Den, an aptly named pile of huge boulders about 500 yards southwest of Little Round Top. Brigadier General Charles Graham's brigade of Pennsylvanians occupied the Peach Orchard on the right. In the center, massed in column of regiments, was Colonel P. Regis DeTrobriand's command. Brigadier General J.H. Hobart Ward's brigade anchored the division's left on Houck's Ridge, which rose above Devil's Den. Skirmishers concealed behind stone walls covered the front. Birney was deployed by 3:30 P.M.

Sickles' second division, under Brigadier General Andrew Humphreys, moved into position during the next half hour. Humphreys placed Brigadier General Joseph Carr's brigade along the Emmitsburg Road, with Carr's left creating a salient at the Peach Orchard with Graham's right. The division's other two brigades, under Colonels William Brewster and George Burling, were kept in reserve. Humphreys finished his dispositions by 4:00. Some of the five Union batteries were already engaged with Alexander's artillery crews.

Minutes earlier, Meade had ridden to of Cemetery Ridge's southern end. He was astounded when he saw the III Corps down in the valley. Sending an aide for Sickles, he unequivocally told the subordinate the advance was contrary to what he wanted. Sickles offered to withdraw but at that moment the Southern cannon exploded, raking the III Corps with a deadly crossfire. "I wish to God you could," Meade shot back, "but the enemy won't let you." The two parted, Meade to summon help, Sickles to direct his troops, now under assault.

Lee's long-delayed, problem-plagued offensive finally began about 4:00. Behind shelling from Alexander's guns, the brigades of Evander Law and Brigadier General Jerome Robertson descended Bushman Ridge into plowed fields. Union skirmishers and Captain James Smith's 4th New York Light Artillery, on Houck's Ridge, opened fire. Law, on the right, angled eastward, contrary to Hood's orders. Robertson, in turn, drifted in that direction, pulling his left away from the Emmitsburg Road. From the outset, Lee's plan came unhinged as his men plunged into the rugged terrain east and south of the Round Tops. Twenty minutes into the attack, Hood was severely wounded in the arm and relinquished command to Law.

Law's Alabamans drove toward the lower slope of Big Round Top, called the "Devil's Kitchen," while Robertson's Texans and Arkansans moved against Houck's Ridge. Smith's gunners switched to canister, and Ward's ranks delivered volleys of musketry. For the next hour and a half, the struggle for Houck's Ridge and Devil's Den raged. Robertson's veterans hurled themselves against the Union cannon and

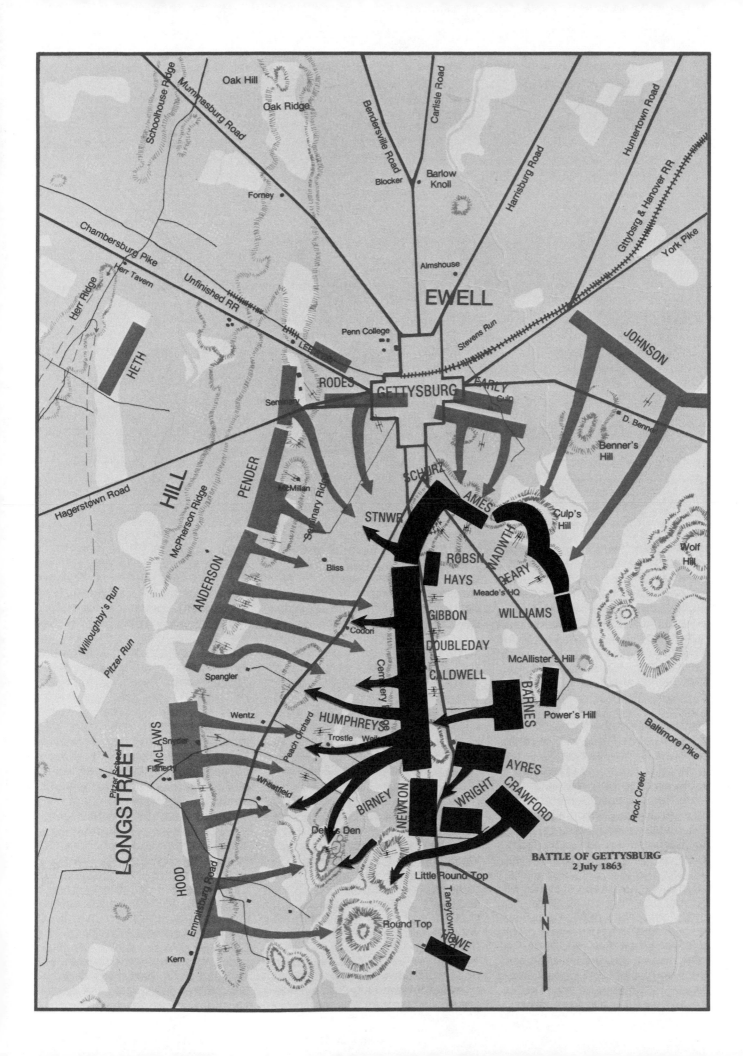

BATTLE OF GETTYSBURG
2 July 1863

infantry time and again. In one charge, the 1st Texas closed to within 50 yards of the crest before the 124th New York stood and blasted the Texans. The volley "seemed to paralyze their whole line," wrote a New Yorker. But the Rebels fired and came on, into a counterattack by the New Yorkers. The combat "defied description," claimed a Yankee. A Texan stated the action "was more like Indian fighting than anything I experienced during the war." One of his comrades asserted "every fellow was his own general. Private soldiers gave commands as loud as the officers; nobody paying any attention to either." Finally, the New Yorkers beat back the Texans.

South of Houck's Ridge, between Big Round Top and Devil's Den, in the area that became known as the "Slaughter Pen," the 44th Alabama charged. The 4th Maine met them with a volley but the Alabamans scorched the flank and front of the Union regiment. These opponents hammered each other for twenty minutes, and the Alabamans lost a quarter of their comrades. The Federals retired into the rock-strewn Devil's Den as the 48th Alabama entered the action on the 44th's right. Simultaneously, the 4th Alabama and 4th and 5th Texas advanced toward the western slope of Little Round Top, where the crisis shifted temporarily. To one Federal it seemed "the whole line was alive with burning powder."

Sickles' occupation of the Peach Orchard salient left Little Round Top uncovered. When the Confederates attacked, Brigadier General Gouverneur Warren, Meade's chief of engineers, was standing on the crest with a small coterie of aides and couriers, watching the gray lines advance. Warren at once recognized the peak's tactical value and the danger presented by the Southern movement. He hurried couriers to Meade and Sickles, asking for immediate help. Major General George Sykes and the V Corps, meanwhile, were marching to support Sickles under Meade's orders. Warren, bristling with impatience, descended the hillside, rode across country, and found Sykes at the head of Brigadier General James Barnes' division. The engineer explained the situation, requesting that a brigade be sent to Little Round Top immediately.

Sykes responded rapidly, sending aides to find Barnes, who had ridden to another part of the line. One aide asked brigade commander Colonel Strong Vincent for Barnes' whereabouts, adding that Sykes wanted a brigade sent to the nearby hill. Vincent, a Pennsylvania native and Harvard graduate, took responsibility himself, told his bugler to sound the advance and, waving his sword, galloped toward Little Round Top. Behind him came his four regiments, 1,330 officers and men, double-quicking on a road up the hill's northern slope. Vincent's men filed into line just below the crest as long-range Confederate artillery fire crashed into the trees behind them. The 20th Maine curled a line around the hill's southern face. On the 20th's right, along the western slope, were the 83d Pennsylvania, 44th New York, and 16th Michigan. These veterans hastily built crude breastworks from the numerous rocks.

The brigade had barely settled in when Colonel Joshua Chamberlain of the 20th Maine looked down into the swale between the Round Tops and saw two Confederate regiments advancing. These were the 15th and 47th Alabama of Law's brigade. During their advance, the two regiments separated and scaled Big Round Top, swatting aside a detachment of the 2d U.S. Sharpshooters. The 15th Alabama under Colonel William Oates was resting on the peak, awaiting the return of a detachment sent to fill the regiment's canteens, when an aide of Law found Oates and ordered him to press on toward the lower crest. Oates' men, with the 47th Alabama on their left, spilled down Big Round Top and into the small valley, where Chamberlain glimpsed their ranks.

Joshua Chamberlain, educated for the ministry, taught rhetoric, oratory and modern languages at Bowdoin College in Maine before the war. A man of letters and of peace, he became an outstanding warrior. When he saw Oates' Alabamans stalking through the trees, he shifted four companies to the left, facing them at a right angle to his main line. As the Rebels approached, these companies unleashed a withering volley into their flank. The Alabamans recoiled, then regrouped and stormed up Little Round Top. The foes clubbed, bayoneted and shot each other in hand-to-hand combat. "The edge of conflict swayed to and fro, with wild whirlpools and eddies," Chamberlain recalled.

The men sought shelter behind any available boulder or tree. Like automatons, they loaded, fired, and repeated the procedure. "The steel rammers clashed and clanged in barrels heated with burning powder," a Yankee private recounted. Also etched in his memory was the blood he saw "running in little rivulets and forming crimson pools."

In time, the outnumbered Maine volunteers repulsed the Alabamans, and a lull set in. But Chamberlain, seeing his men's ammunition was nearly expended, ordered a bayonet charge. Stepping to the front, he shouted: "Bayonet!" Some of the troops charged but many hesitated. The left wing went first, wheeling to the right, and the regiment moved "like a great gate upon a post." The attack surprised the Alabamans, who broke and scrambled across the swale and onto Big Round Top.*

Despite the 20th Maine's success the western face

---

*For this Chamberlain eventually received the Congressional Medal of Honor.

During wild fighting on July 2, Union soldiers successfully defend Little Round Top, one of the key eminences on the battlefield. Painting by F. B. Briscoe. (Library of Congress)

of Little Round Top was ablaze with musketry. Men of the 47th Alabama and 83d Pennsylvania killed and maimed each other. On their flanks, the 4th and 5th Texas and 4th Alabama ascended the hillside into the flames of Colonel Vincent's other regiments. The Union brigade commander was slain in one of the first volleys, ordering as he died: "Don't yield an inch." Lieutenant Charles E. Hazlett's Battery D, 5th U.S. Artillery was now on the crest, supporting the infantry with its rifled cannon. The Southerners kept coming. One of them, Private Joe Smith of the 4th Texas, soaked a white handkerchief in the waters of Plum Run and wrapped it around his head. When Smith was buried later, the detail counted eleven holes in the distinctive target.

Vincent's ranks on the western slope were starting to crumble under the pressure when Colonel Patrick O'Rorke came over the crest with his 140th New York. Sent by Warren, the regiment was the van of Brigadier General Stephen Weed's brigade of Brigadier General Romeyn Ayres' V Corps division. The New Yorkers rushed down the hillside, stopping the 47th and 4th Alabama. O'Rorke died at the head of his line. Weed soon arrived with his other three regiments. Weed was killed, and as Hazlett stooped beside the fallen brigadier, the artillery lieutenant died, too. In the Texas regiments, all field officers but

one were killed or wounded. At one point, a courier from Law rode up to Major J.C. Rogers, commanding the 5th Texas, extended Law's compliments and ordered the major to hold his position "at all hazards." "Compliments, hell!" groused Rogers. "Who wants compliments in such a damned place as this?"

Through The Wheatfield and Up Cemetery Hill

The Confederate thrust's momentum ebbed because of excess casualties, intermingling of units, and the rugged terrain. Ayres' other Union brigades arrived, and Little Round Top was secured. The gray-coated line receded down the slope. A Texan summarized the fight years later: "At the first roll of the war drum, Texas sent forth her noblest and best. She gave the Army of Northern Virginia Hood's matchless brigade—a band of heroes who bore their country's flag to victory on every field, until God stopped them at Little Round Top." The proud soldier conveniently forgot to mention the band of Yankee heroes.

West of Little Round Top, from Houck's Ridge to the Peach Orchard, the struggle continued. The duel for Houck's Ridge had drawn other units from both sides into the cauldron. Brigadier General Henry Benning's brigade of Hood's division added its might to Robertson's and Law's assault on the Union cannon and infantry. Ward's beleaguered Federals received two regiments from DeTrobriand's brigade and three from Burling's brigade of Humphrey's division. In the confusion and smoke, units became entangled with one another. From the fields and woods west of Houck's Ridge and from the "Slaughter Pen," Texans, Georgians, and Alabamans closed on the collapsing Union position. Benning, walking back and forth behind his men, shouted, "Give them hell, boys— give them hell." Opposing lines lashed each other in Plum Run gorge, known afterwards as the "Valley of Death." Finally three Georgia regiments and the survivors of the 1st Texas overran the crest, seizing three abandoned cannon. The 99th Pennsylvania, standing with the guns, was engulfed. Birney's left flank had been crushed, with appalling losses on both sides.

There was also fighting in a place that would be remembered as the "Wheatfield." Hood's 4th Brigade, comprising Brigadier General George Anderson's five Georgia regiments, was attacking Birney's center, held by DeTrobriand's remaining regiments and Ward's right flank units. The Georgians wrenched a triangular-shaped field of wheat from the defenders, only to encounter the brigades of Colonels Jacob Sweitzer and William Tilton of Barnes' V Corps division. Assisted by some of Burling's troops, these Federals stopped Anderson, who retired into the woods south of the wheat.

Help was coming for Anderson; the brigades of Brigadier Generals Joseph Kershaw and Paul Semmes of McLaws' division were on their way. For reasons never satisfactorily explained, Hood's troops had to battle for ninety minutes before this second Confederate division charged. Ultimate responsibility rested with Longstreet, who at 5:30 P.M. finally ordered Kershaw and Semmes forward. Kershaw's South Carolinians went first, with Semmes' Georgians directly behind. Union batteries, seeing the two gray-clad lines advance across the fields of the John P. Rose farm, opened with shell fire, cutting "great gaps or swaths" in Kershaw's ranks, according to a Southern officer.

The South Carolinians marched north and came in on Anderson's left, gaining the ridge overlooking the Wheatfield, southeast of a grove of fruit trees called the Peach Orchard. Tilton's Federals were overlapped on their right flank and gave ground, withdrawing into a stand of trees. This retirement exposed Sweitzer's flank, so Barnes ordered the brigade back into the wood. A Union battery, unlimbered east of the Peach Orchard, raked the Rebels' left flank with

the Battle of Gettysburg
the summit of Little Round Top on the evening of Thursday July 2nd, 18
view of the attack of Longstreet Corps. by the 5th Corps.
Sketched on the Spot. Sundown — E. Forbes.

Longstreet's assault troops, viewed from the crest of Little Round Top. This sketch was drawn on the spot by Northern news artist Edwin Forbes on the evening of July 2. Had the Confederates taken the hill and set up guns, the entire Union position could have been enfiladed. (Library of Congress)

canister. But Kershaw's greatest danger lay on the right, where he saw two Federal battle lines rushing toward the Wheatfield. These were part of Brigadier General John Caldwell's II Corps division, 3,300 fresh soldiers ordered into the battle by Meade through Hancock.

The brigade of Colonel Edward Cross spearheaded Caldwell's counterattack. As the four regiments stepped out, Hancock shouted to the colonel, "Cross, this is the last time you'll fight without a star."

"Too late, general. This is my last battle," replied the colonel, who had had a premonition of his death.

Cross' 850 veterans advanced diagonally across the Wheatfield toward the southwest corner. One of them remembered seeing the enemy's muskets resting on a fence; "the barrels of them glittered like a looking glass," he wrote. Anderson's and Kershaw's men, aligned along the wood's edge, fired, and Cross toppled with a mortal wound. "I noticed," recalled a member of the 148th Pennsylvania, "how the ears of wheat flew in the air all over the field as they were cut off by the enemy's bullets."

On Cross' left, the brigade of Colonel Patrick Kelly entered the maelstrom, hammering the Southern position. Before Kelly advanced Father William Corby gave the brigade's Irishmen absolution. Remitted of sin, Kelly's veterans went in like avenging angels. The Wheatfield reddened with blood.

The third of Caldwell's four brigades, Brigadier General Samuel Zook's, now joined the other two. Hit by these successive blows, Anderson's and Kershaw's commands pulled back toward a spot called the Rose Woods. Kershaw rode to the rear and ordered Semmes' Georgians to the right. Semmes had been mortally wounded in the early stages of the advance and Colonel Goode Bryan led the brigade. The Georgians ran head-on into Caldwell's last brigade, under Brigadier General John Brooke, and the Yankees shoved them out of the Rose Woods. The lines fought for fifteen minutes. Finally, the Georgians counterattacked, and with support from the 15th South Carolina drove Brooke's troops into the Wheatfield. Caldwell, meanwhile, secured Sweitzer's brigade from Barnes, and the unit locked onto

"The Whirlpool in the Wheatfield," painted by F.D. Briscoe. Battle lines wade through a sea of grain in this farm field south of Gettysburg, which changed hands several times in furious fighting on the second day. (Library of Congress)

Brooke's right and stopped the Rebel thrust. The combat in the Wheatfield subsided briefly.

The contest for the Rose Woods began about 6:00, when McLaws' final two brigades launched the afternoon's decisive attack in this sector. Brigadier General William Barksdale's Mississippians went first, emerging from the timber on Warfield Ridge screaming a savage yell and marching at the double-quick. Barksdale, 41 years old with a distinctive shock of premature white hair, had been chafing to enter the action. "He had a thirst for battle glory," said one of his men. When Longstreet finally gave the order, he hurled his brigade at the Yankees in the Peach Orchard in what a Confederate onlooker later called "the most magnificent charge I witnessed. . . ."

The 57th and 114th Pennsylvania of Charles Graham's brigade ran across the roadbed right into the Rebels' path. The lines collided near farm buildings belonging to the Sherfy family, and the Mississippians decimated the Pennsylvanians. On the Confederates came. The 141st Pennsylvania, positioned at the nearby John Wentz farm, lost 156 of 209 men within minutes. The 21st Mississippi overran the apex of the Peach Orchard salient, wounding and capturing Graham and routing the 68th Pennsylvania. "It was a terrible afternoon in that orchard," a member of that Union regiment asserted. North of the angle in the road, the 105th Pennsylvania "Wildcats" "fought like demons," shouting "Pennsylvania." But the Wildcats, too, were ripped apart, losing half their number.

As the Mississippians swarmed over the Emmitsburg Road and salient, Brigadier General William Wofford's Alabamans crushed the salient's southern front on Barksdale's right. The Pennsylvanians fled north toward the Abraham Trostle farm, some 300 yards away. Minutes before, Sickles, whose headquarters were at the farm, had his right leg crushed by a cannonball. The corps leader was out of the battle and out of the war. He would, however, outlive all the Union generals present at Gettysburg.

The destruction of the salient exposed the flank of the Union line running eastward on the ridge to the Wheatfield. Wofford's Alabamans and the 21st Mississippi wheeled to the right, following the Fairfield crossroad. Kershaw's, Anderson's and Semmes' troops joined the sweep and Barnes' and Caldwell's Yankees scrambled for their lives. The brigades of Zook, Kelly, and Sweitzer were nearly trapped between the converging Rebel lines. Zook was killed. The Federals suffered fearful losses, some men fighting hand-to-hand with attackers before escaping. Streams of blue-clad fugitives ran across Plum Run

gorge to the safety of Little Round Top. The Confederates pursued, across the Wheatfield toward the Valley of Death.

Many fleeing Yankees passed through the ranks of Brigadier General Samuel Crawford's V Corps division of Pennsylvania Reserves. Sykes had earlier moved them to Little Round Top, where the proud, tough veterans watched the collapse of the Union front in the valley. Once the fugitives cleared his two massed lines, Crawford grabbed a flag and led his command down the hillside. The Reserves triggered two volleys before storming into the disorganized enemy. The Confederates resisted fiercely for a few minutes, but the counterattack was too much and most of them retired to a stone wall along the Wheatfield's eastern edge. Crawford's assault ended the major fighting in this bloody area.

The embattled Northerners' focus shifted to the fields before Cemetery Ridge, where Barksdale's Confederates and three Rebel brigades from Richard Anderson's division were sweeping toward high ground. When Barksdale and Wofford charged, Anderson followed Lee's plan and sent three brigades forward in succession. Brigadier General Cadmus Wilcox's Alabamans went first, followed closely on their left by Colonel David Lang's Floridians, nearly 2,500 troops altogether. These men drove straight for the Emmitsburg Road and Joseph Carr's Union brigade of Humphrey's division. The Confederates advanced at the double-quick into a rain of canister from two batteries.

The assault was unrelenting, coupled with Barksdale's thrust through the Peach Orchard. Carr's six regiments, 1,700 Yankees, found themselves in a wild melee. Each command seemed to fight separately, forced to change fronts under searing musketry. When Battery K, 4th U.S. Artillery withdrew, the 11th New Jersey filled the gap, manning a small orchard south of a farmhouse owned by D.H. Klingel. Wilcox's Alabamans shredded the regiment's ranks. North of the Klingel house, the 12th New Hampshire wheeled to the south, opening their flank to the Alabamans, who ripped it apart. Next to the New Jersey men were the 16th Massachusetts and Battery F and K, 3d U.S. Artillery. Wilcox's veterans struck them squarely, capturing several cannon and dispersing the infantry. North of the overrun battery the 11th Massachusetts was wheeling south when it was lashed by part of Lang's brigade. Hit on three sides, the Bay Staters got out.

Behind Carr's collapsing front, Colonel William Brewster shifted six regiments of the famous New York Excelsior Brigade to meet Barksdale and

Another sketch by Forbes of Longstreet's assault across the "Valley of Death" to Little Round Top on the evening of July 2. Little Round Top is the hill on the left (#1); on it was Hazlett's battery (#2). The hill on the right (#3) is Big Round Top. (Library of Congress)

Wilcox. The 73d New York, fighting west of the Sherfy farm near the Peach Orchard, was nearly surrounded by the 13th and 17th Mississippi and suffered grievous losses. The New Yorkers could not stay the flood. Birney, who had replaced Sickles, ordered both brigades to retire. As they withdrew the Federals turned and fired at their pursuers twenty times.

On the left of the three Confederate brigades came Brigadier General Ambrose Wright's Georgians. Wright's 1,400 troops assailed the Union line at a farm owned by one N. Codori. Carr's final regiment and two II Corps regiments sent forward by John Gibbon were pounded back. The Georgians seized two cannon as they swirled toward the crest of Cemetery Ridge, coming on "like the fury of a whirlwind." Gibbon hurled two more regiments at them. This resulted in the near annihilation of the blue-coated units.

The scene between Cemetery Ridge and the Em-

mitsburg Road almost defied description. Acrid smoke blanketed the fields, making observation difficult. Shattered Union commands fled before the Confederate onslaught. One of the final islands of resistance was at the Trostle farm, where Captain John Bigelow's 9th Massachusetts Battery poured canister into the Southern ranks. Finally, with nearly all his horses lost, Bigelow withdrew two pieces, leaving four behind. The Bay Staters' stand gave their comrades in Colonel Freeman McGilvery's 1st Volunteer Brigade of the Artillery Reserve time to re-deploy on the ridge and blast the oncoming Southerners. The Union artillery fire was answered effectively by six Confederate batteries Alexander had rolled into position at the Sherfy and Wentz farms along the Emmitsburg Road.

The charge of the four Confederate brigades was moving toward final resolution. On the ridge Winfield Hancock, wearing a clean white shirt, was gathering any units at hand for a counterattack. He found Colonel William Colville's 1st Minnesota rushing south on the crest. He ordered them to charge Wilcox's Alabamans. The 262 Minnesotans stormed down the slope, hit the center of the Rebel line, and were shot to pieces. Only thirty-eight survivors, led by a captain, escaped. The regiment's 82 percent loss was the greatest sustained by a Union regiment at Gettysburg. Their brave act bought ten precious minutes for Hancock, who launched Colonel George Willard's brigade and re-grouped commands at the Confederates. These thrusts broke Southern ranks. Barksdale was mortally wounded by a bullet in his left breast. The Confederate warrior died in enemy hands the next day.

The Mississippians, Alabamans, Floridians, and Georgians now became the pursued. Wright's brigade was finally stopped by Union Brigadier General Alexander Webb's brigade. Once the Yankees regained the initiative, they won back several lost cannon, captured clusters of Southerners, and pressed on to the Emmitsburg Road. The Confederates retreated to Seminary Ridge and the Federals returned to the opposite crest. Combat was over by 7:30 P.M.

"History," said Longstreet, "records no parallel to the fight made by these two divisions [Hood and McLaws] on the 2d of July at Gettysburg." Their assaults, he added, commenced the "best three hours' fighting ever done by any troops on any battlefield." Longstreet's words were not far from the truth. The foes ravaged each other in some of the war's most fearful combat. Losses were about 15,000 on this part of the field—16,500 for the entire day. Federal casualties were 30 to 40 percent, a figure surely equalled by the Confederates. The Rebels temporarily knocked thirteen Union brigades out of battle; the Southerners were outgeneraled not outfought.

E. Porter Alexander, a perceptive student of Gettysburg, later argued, "it must be said that the management of the battle on the Confederate side during this afternoon was conspicuously bad. The fighting was superb. But there appears to have been little supervision." Scarcely at any stage in the combat did either Hood, McLaws, or Anderson charge simultaneously with all their brigades. Two of Anderson's brigades, because of misunderstood orders and Anderson's lack of assertiveness and management, never advanced. Longstreet performed below his standards and reputation, and Hill was conspicuously absent in supervising his corps in the offensive. Misfortune also plagued Southern operations, for when William Pender, an excellent general, prepared to support an assault by Ewell, he suffered a crippling wound that cost him his life seventeen days later. His successor, Brigadier General James Lane, did nothing.

This lack of control reflected the command system of the army and its creator, Robert E. Lee. The Confederate commander spent most of the afternoon near the Lutheran Seminary, sitting on a stump. He dispatched only one message and received only one. He had committed his army to battle, leaving the outcome to subordinates and providence. He surely should have exercised firmer control over Hill and Ewell. As a consequence, "the whole affair was disjointed," staff officer Walter Taylor judged. "There was an utter absence of accord in the movements of the several commands, and no decisive result attended the operations of the second day."

Lee's passive role contrasted sharply with Meade's active direction of Union commands. The major general was seemingly everywhere on the endangered center and left, confronting emergencies, drawing units from parts of the line, and directing them in well-timed counterattacks. Hancock rendered invaluable service, while unit commanders used the terrain to advantage and the men in the ranks proved their mettle. The outcome of July 2's fighting had remained unpredictable all day, but ultimately, Union advantages in position, tactics, numbers, and leadership prevailed.

The bloodletting and drama were not confined to the southern end of the field that day. Other soldiers had died on the slopes of Culp's Hill and Cemetery Hill. Ewell, as his role in the Confederate offensive prescribed, had opened an artillery bombardment on Union positions on the Culp's Hill-Cemetery Hill area as soon as he heard the sounds of Longstreet's attack at 4:00. From Benner's Hill, roughly three fourths of a mile northeast of the Federal lines, thirty-two cannon directed by Major J.W. Latimer pounded the heights for over two hours. Union batteries replied, and the duel lasted until about 6:30 P.M. Latimer, only 20 years old, was mortally wounded in the exchange.

When the cannon fire ceased, Ewell ordered an assault on Culp's Hill by Edward Johnson's division. Problems hounded the movement from its outset. Johnson detached a brigade to fend off Federal cavalry skirmishers on his left. Then he underestimated the time required to cover the ground and cross Rock Creek. By the time he reached the base of Culp's Hill it was almost dark. The men started to pick their way up the slopes, "a wild position," said a Union officer, "full of great detached masses of rock and hugh [sic] boulders." As the Rebels struggled, the wooded rise flamed with musketry.

The defenders belonged to Brigadier General George Greene's XII Corps brigade and the bloodied ranks of James Wadsworth's I Corps division. Meade had sent most of the XII Corps with John Robinson's I Corps division to the embattled left and center, and Johnson held a numerical advantage. But the Federals were solid veterans, protected by trenches. Greene's 1,424 men bore the brunt of the combat, occupying the northeast slope from the crest to the southern shoulder. Sixty-two-year-old Greene, a tough professional the troops affectionately called "Pop," maintained an incessant fire by shuttling reserves into the trenches to relieve the front-line men as they exhausted their ammunition. Wadsworth and Oliver Howard dispatched six regiments as reinforcements. The graycoats attacked fiercely but fighting darkness, terrain, and Greene's tactics, they gained little ground. Only Johnson's left brigade, Brigadier General George "Maryland" Steuart's, achieved some success when it stumbled upon abandoned trenches on the right end of the Union line. The action eventually subsided and flickered out, with each side sleeping on the ground they occupied.

While fighting raged on Culp's Hill, Jubal Early sent two brigades against the Union stronghold on Cemetery Hill. Forming in the fields of the William Culp farm, the 2,500 Louisianans and North Carolinians of Brigadier General Harry Hays and Colonel Isaac Avery, respectively, started forward shortly after 7:30 P.M. It took nearly an hour to cross the 700 yards from Culp's farm to the base of the hill, where the brigade of Colonel Leopold Von Gilsa and that of Brigadier General Adelbert Ames, led by Colonel Andrew Harris, were deployed behind a stone wall. When the Confederates came into view, four Union batteries opened from the heights. Avery, the only officer mounted, was hit early, suffering a fatal wound.

When the Southerners closed on the stone wall, Avery's Carolinians on the left executed a parade-ground right oblique. The movement, however, exposed their left and rear to Captain Greenleaf Stevens' Battery E, 5th Maine Light, positioned on a spur of Culp's Hill known thereafter as Stevens' Knoll. The Maine gunners poured canister into the gray-clad ranks, while the 33d Massachusetts, to the west and rear of the battery, let go volleys. But, in the words of one of their officers, the Rebels charged "with heroic determination." Von Gilsa's and Harris' men offered feeble resistance, before fleeing up the hill. Close behind came Southerners overrunning Captain Michael Wiedrich's Battery I, 1st New York Light Artillery. The gunners swung handspikes and fence rails in a hand-to-hand struggle for the cannon,

but the attackers' impetus carried them through Battery I and toward Battery F and G, 1st Pennsylvania Light Artillery, under Captain R. Bruce Ricketts. Again infantrymen battled gunners for possession of the prizes.

The swarm of graycoats held the crest and silenced two batteries, but Union officers had already reacted to the crisis. Two regiments from Colonel Wladimir Kryzanowski's brigade struck first, followed by Colonel Charles Coster's New Yorkers and Pennsylvanians. Hays' Louisiana "Tigers" and Avery's Carolinians repulsed the first two thrusts. It was a blind melee in the darkness; only the flash of rifles revealed the combatants' whereabouts. Colonel Samuel Carroll's brigade, sent by Hancock, finally hit the North Carolinians, driving them back. The Louisianans turned on Carroll, who changed the front of the 7th West Virginia and ordered a charge. This was more than the Confederates could stand, and on Hays' instructions they streamed down the hillside. Smoke and blackness shielded them and Hays reported, ". . . we thus escaped what in the full light of day could have been nothing else than horrible slaughter."

The Confederate lodgment on Cemetery Hill caused a temporary crisis, but lacked the strength for a decisive victory. The attackers expected support; that it did not arrive was another example of the flawed Confederate operations on July 2. Ewell, whose performance at Gettysburg was at best mediocre, had ordered Robert Rodes to coordinate his division's movements with Early's. But the corps commander did not personally oversee the execution of his instructions and Rodes, like he had on the 1st, gave another lackluster performance. During the afternoon, Rodes should have brought his large command forward to a position from which he could readily have assaulted Cemetery Hill. He did not. Ewell failed to prod him and when Early attacked, Rodes was just beginning the complicated maneuver through part of the town. By the time he was ready, Hays and Avery had been repulsed.

"The result of the day's operations," Lee stated in his report, "induced the belief that, with proper concert of attack," the Confederate army could achieve victory. Before he retired for the night Lee ordered a renewal of the offensive at daylight, with simultaneous strikes on both flanks of the Union line. He also directed Longstreet to bring up George Pickett's unused division and add it to his attack force. Lee, however, held no meeting with Longstreet or Ewell, missing a chance to clarify any misunderstandings.

Jeb Stuart had appeared at headquarters earlier on the 2d. When Lee saw his errant cavalryman, he said stoically, "Well, General Stuart, you are here at last." For Lee, the words represented a reprimand. The previous night Lee had told Major Harry Gilmore to select eight men to search for the missing cavalry brigades. These scouts carried sealed orders and rode on separate roads. James D. Watters found Stuart's troopers at Carlisle, resting after burning army barracks there.

Since their seizure of the wagon train at Rockville, Maryland, on June 28, the horsemen had been in the saddle almost constantly, covering miles and fighting Union cavalry. On June 30, Stuart's column crossed into Pennsylvania, colliding with Union Brigadier General Judson Kilpatrick's mounted division at Hanover. The Yankees drove the Confederates out of town. Stuart decided to save the wagons and detoured east through the town of Jefferson. But with Kilpatrick on his flank, Stuart waited until night before resuming his ride. His men rode all night, halting finally on July 1 in Carlisle, where Watters delivered Lee's orders.

Stuart's ride was "a useless, showy parade," claimed Lieutenant Colonel Gilbert Moxley Sorrel, Longstreet's chief of staff. Major Charles Marshall, Lee's military secretary, while drafting the campaign's report, urged a court-martial for Stuart. When Lee exorcised this recommendation, Marshall suggested Stuart be shot. The cavalry chief's vainglorious exploit was a leading factor in the Confederate army's failure on July 1 and 2, and unquestionably angered and disappointed Lee. The superior's remark, when they met, expressed this dissatisfaction. But Lee had use for Stuart on the 3d, so he ordered him to place four brigades beyond Ewell's left flank in a position from which he could assail the Union army's rear or its retreating columns if the Confederate infantry succeeded.

While Lee issued directives for July 3, Meade held a council of war at the Leister house. A dozen generals crowded into the room, which measured about 10 by 12 feet and was furnished with a bed, table, and one or two chairs. Chief of staff Daniel Butterfield, chief engineer Warren, all corps commanders—including Doubleday's replacement, John Newton, and Sickles' successor, David Birney—were present. Also invited were John Gibbon and Alpheus Williams, who had temporarily led the II and XII Corps, respectively, during the action.

The presence of Major General John Sedgwick meant the army's largest command, the VI Corps, had reached the field. Sedgwick's troops arrived about 5:00 P.M. after a harrowing thirty-four-mile forced march from Manchester, Maryland. Beginning

at 10:00 P.M. on the 1st, when orders arrived calling them to Gettysburg, the veterans trudged what seemed endless miles, hour after hour. It became a famous march, a feat the soldiers prided themselves on for many years. One of them, a Pennsylvanian, described it well while *en route*, telling comrades, "It's hell, boys, but if Lee's in Pennsylvania, I'd walk there on stumps." The march provided Meade with a vast reservoir of manpower for July 3.

The war council began about 9:00 and lasted nearly until midnight. Meade spoke infrequently and listened intently while officers discussed the army's condition and strength, merits and defects of the field position, and the number of rations for the troops. Some dozed occasionally; Warren slept through the meeting. Butterfield finally posed three questions: Should the army retreat or stay? Should it attack or remain on the defensive? How long should it wait for an enemy advance? All corps commanders voted to maintain their defensive positions, while a large majority agreed to remain at Gettysburg a day or two. With the voting concluded, Meade, according to Gibbon, said: "Such then is the decision." The generals returned to their posts for sleep.

One of those at the meeting, Alpheus Williams, got no rest that night. When he returned to the XII Corps position on and near Culp's Hill, he learned Confederates occupied trenches previously held by his division. Slocum and Meade gave him permission to attack. Williams planned carefully, for the Rebels lay behind log breastworks built by his men, and the swampy ground at the southeast foot of Culp's Hill at Spangler's Spring and Rock Creek protected the Southerners' left. The Federal timed his movement for 4:30 A.M.; ironically, that was the exact time Ewell set for a Confederate advance up Culp's Hill.

With a heavy bombardment, five Union batteries opened the third day's fighting on schedule. For fifteen minutes gunners lobbed shells into trees above the enemy lines low on Culp's Hill. When the cannonade subsided, and before the Federals moved, the Stonewall Brigade under Brigadier General James Walker went up the slope, initiating more than seven hours of infantry combat. The line of Brigadier General John Geary's division ran from the crest down the southern slope then curved west toward the Baltimore Pike. Geary's men met the Stonewall Brigade's attack and repulsed it. Johnson's four Confederate brigades, augmented by those of Junius Daniel and Edward O'Neal from Rodes' division and Brigadier General William Smith's brigade from Early's division, blistered the Federals with incessant fire.

A pattern of fighting soon developed: the Confederates attempted occasional thrusts, while the

Yankees shifted select regiments to dangerous spots to enfilade the enemy. At 8:00 O'Neal's Alabamans attacked, but were stopped and pinned down. An hour later Walker tried again with similar results. Finally, shortly after 10:00, Johnson ordered an assault by Steuart and Daniel. Both brigade commanders protested it would be suicidal but Johnson insisted and the troops were ordered to stand up. Steuart's men were cut to pieces before a wall of bullets and canister. Daniel fared better but made no breakthrough.

Williams, meanwhile, handled his Federals with skill. As Geary's troops tired he relieved them with regiments from other commands. Early in the fight, the 147th Pennsylvania, under Lieutenant Colonel Ario Pardee, Jr., charged across a field and seized a section of stone wall, from which the Keystone State volunteers slashed the Confederate left flank. The 20th Connecticut, assigned an exposed position, stood firm for hours. Rifles roared without abatement, without mercy, killing and maiming young men in a spot townspeople used for picnics. One dead Confederate was Wesley Culp, who as a teenager left Gettysburg for Virginia. He now came home, dying a few yards from his family's house.

Between 9:00 and 10:00, Slocum, believing the Confederates were retiring, ordered acting division commander Brigadier General Thomas Ruger to attack breastworks along the northern edge of the meadow around Spangler's Spring. Ruger wanted to test the position with skirmishers first but an aide garbled the verbal instructions while relaying them to Colonel Silas Colgrove, a brigade commander. Colgrove ordered the 2d Massachusetts and 27th Indiana to seize the works. Lieutenant Colonel Charles Mudge of the 2d heard the command with disbelief. "Well," he asserted, "It is murder, but its the order. Up men, over the works. Forward, double quick."

The Bay Staters and Hoosiers, 655 strong, swept across Spangler's Meadow. The enemy breastworks flamed in defiance, shredding the oncoming Union ranks. The Hoosiers on the right made it halfway before they gave up the hopeless mission. Mudge's veterans kept going in a remarkable show of bravery. They reached the entrenchments but four Confederate regiments raked them with gunfire. With Mudge killed and with more than half their comrades down, the Bay Staters retreated across the meadow. The next day, as 2d Massachusetts survivors filed past corps headquarters, Slocum and staff officers removed their hats in tribute.

Before noon the struggle for Culp's Hill ended. Williams retook his lost trenches and Johnson stopped his attacks. The fighting, some of the most brutal in the three-day clash, was only a prelude, a herald of the Battle of Gettysburg's bloody, dramatic climax.

Pickett's Charge and the Long Road Home

Robert E. Lee rose early on the 3d. Hearing the sound of Ewell's advance, he rode along Seminary Ridge, probably expecting to hear Longstreet's renewal of the offensive against Meade's left flank. But when Lee reached First Corps headquarters he found Longstreet ordering a flanking movement around Big Round Top. Longstreet had spent most of the night developing plans for a maneuver he strongly favored. Lee must have been startled by the general's alteration—without consultation—of the commanding general's definite orders for an attack. Longstreet had not even moved George Pickett's fresh division to the front as Lee instructed. Consequently, Lee scrapped his plans and began formulating a new offensive.

The Confederate commander took most of the morning to formulate a plan. From a point in front of Seminary Ridge, within Union artillery range, he, Longstreet, Hill, Heth, and staff officers scanned the Federal lines on Cemetery Ridge. They debated the best mode of attack and the composition of the force. Finally, Lee settled on a frontal assault directed toward a small clump of trees on the opposite ridge, in the very center of the Union front.

The Confederate attackers would have to cross nearly a mile of open fields into the muzzles of Northern cannon and rifles. The idea could chill the backbone of the bravest soldier, and the only plausible explanation for Lee's decision was overconfidence, borne from his belief that his army was invincible. As a prelude to the infantry assault, massed Confederate batteries would unleash a firestorm against the Union artillery on the ridge, with the intent of silencing the enemy cannon. When the infantry advanced, the Southern gunners would follow, giving support and protecting the flanks.

Longstreet, for one, could not believe his ears. As he later recounted, he told Lee: "General, I have been a soldier all my life. I have been with soldiers engaged in fights by couples, by squads, companies, regiments, divisions, and armies, and should know, as well as anyone, what soldiers can do. It is my opinion that no fifteen thousand men ever arranged for battle can take that position."

But Lee was not to be swayed. If his "incomparable infantry" succeeded, he might achieve the decisive victory he sought. What remained was the marshaling of an assault force.

Lee selected George Pickett's and Henry Heth's divisions, two of Dorsey Pender's four brigades, and Cadmus Wilcox' and David Lang's brigades from Richard Anderson's command. Except for Pickett, the other units had all been bloodied; Heth's four brigades had been critically weakened by the combat on the 1st and Heth was not in command. (Struck on the head by a bullet July 1, he was insensible for thirty hours. His life was spared because he had folded a newspaper into the new hat he wore, a hat that was too large for him.) Johnston Pettigrew, with no experience in commanding a division, now acted in Heth's stead. Hill or staff officers should have informed Lee of the battered condition of Heth's unit.

The select units formed on wooded Seminary Ridge and in a swale in front of the treeline, hidden from enemy view. The force, including Wilcox and Lang, numbered approximately 12,000, though figures conflict. Pettigrew filed his four brigades into place on the left. His left flank comprised the force's weakest command, John Brockenbrough's Virginians, and was unsupported. On Pettigrew's right, Pickett aligned his division in two lines. The brigades of Brigadier Generals Richard Garnett and James Kemper formed the front. Behind them, in close support, was Brigadier General Lewis Armistead's command. Pender's two brigades—those of Brigadier Generals James Lane and Alfred Scales (Scales' was under Colonel W. Lee J. Lowrance)—extended Armistead's left, supporting Pettigrew's right two brigades. Major General Isaac Trimble, a 61-year-old Marylander who joined the army during the campaign as a supernumerary, commanded these last two units. Wilcox's and Lang's troops lay in the fields south and east of Pickett, from where they could follow the main body to guard the right flank and rear. In all, there were fifty regiments from six Southern states assembled for the charge.

While the infantrymen settled in, awaiting the signal, artillery chiefs prepared their batteries for the cannonade. E. Porter Alexander posted seventy-five cannon of the First Corps along a 1300-yard front, in one continuous line from the Peach Orchard to the northeast corner of farmer H. Spangler's Woods. Sixty pieces of the Third Corps, under Major R.L. Walker, ringed Seminary Ridge south of the Hagerstown or Fairfield Road to a point near Spangler's Woods. Walker added two long-range Whitworth cannon on Oak Hill to his complement. Colonel J. Thompson Brown assigned forty-two guns to the operation, with thirty deployed on Oak and Seminary Ridges. At least 170, possibly 179 cannon were engaged during the bombardment.

Lee had given Longstreet overall responsibility for the assault and about 11:45 A.M. the lieutenant general sent Alexander the first of a series of notes exchanged between the two. In it Longstreet told the young artillerist that if the bombardment failed to "drive off the enemy or greatly demoralize him," Alexander should advise Pickett not to advance. The words stunned and upset the colonel, who asked the advice of Brigadier General Ambrose Wright, who stood nearby. The pair composed a reply, stressing that if Longstreet had an alternative to the cannonade and assault, he should consider it, for the long bombardment would drain the artillery chests. This response evidently snapped the corps commander back to the realization of his duties. He sent a second note about 12:15 P.M., vaguely directing Alexander to select the proper moment for the infantry to advance.

By now the fighting on Culp's Hill had ceased and the battlefield became relatively quiet. Soldiers on each side sweated in the midday heat, waiting for whatever was going to happen next—which, to most of them, was unknown. About 1:00 Longstreet sent a note to his chief of artillery, Colonel J.B. Walton, beginning: "Colonel: Let the batteries open." Minutes later two signal cannon from Captain M.B. Miller's 3d Company, Washington Artillery of New Orleans, fired. The line roared. More than 150 successive discharges fused into a thunderclap of war. Alexander said later it was precisely 1:00 P.M.; a Gettysburg resident timed it at 1:07.

The Southern cannoneers fired by salvos for deliberate precision, concentrating on the stretch of Cemetery Ridge marked by the copse of trees that Lee had chosen as the goal of his assault. To the Yankees lying on this parcel of Pennsylvania soil, it must have seemed as if the world were suddenly coming to an end. Howling shells exploded above them; solid shot caromed across the ground. One Federal described the metal storm as "the pelting of the pitiless gale." Another said, ". . . all we had to do was flatten out a little thinner, and our empty stomachs did not prevent this."

Union cannon—numbering about 118—responded quickly. The noise escalated; the din was unrelenting. "The atmosphere seemed to be as full of cannon balls, bomb shells, and flying missiles of death as a South Carolina millpond ever was of tadpoles," asserted a Rebel. "The whole country around seemed to be in a blaze of gunpowder." Most Southern gun crews overshot the target, their rounds engulfing the ridge's eastern slope instead. Meade's headquarters at the Leister house were subjected to severe fire. Sixteen horses were killed in the yard. Nevertheless, Meade stayed at the house until the cannonade was nearly over, and he returned shortly afterward.

George Pickett takes orders from James Longstreet to lead the charge across a mile of open, gently sloping farmland toward a clump of trees on Cemetery Ridge. (Library of Congress)

The firestorm lasted nearly two hours but for the Confederates it was more thunder than lightning. Their relatively inaccurate fire caused insignificant casualties and failed to demoralize the Union infantry on the ridge. The blue-clad gun crews suffered the worst, losing numerous caissons, limbers, and pieces disabled. But the firepower of most Federal batteries was not badly affected.

E. Porter Alexander, intently watching the bombardment, could not have known how little he had accomplished. Shortly before 3:00, when he saw some Union cannon retire, he scribbled a hurried note to Pickett: "For God's sake come quick. The 18 guns have gone. Come quick or my ammunition will not let me support you properly." Pickett, who was with Longstreet, read the note, handed it to Lee's "war horse," and asked, "General, shall I advance?" Longstreet bowed his head, then turned to mount his horse without a word. "I shall lead my division forward, sir," said Pickett.

George Pickett was a 38-eight-year-old Virginian whom history might have passed by had it not been for this day. He was friendly, a "good fellow," with no particular merit as a soldier. Once seen, however, he was unforgettable. A staff officer described him well: "The hair was extraordinary. Long ringlets flowed loosely over his shoulders, trimmed and highly perfumed." Longstreet* particularly liked Pickett and always "looked after" him. He was an unremarkable fighter but was a favorite destined for enduring fame only, perhaps, because he arrived last at Gettysburg.

When Pickett reached his division his men—Virginians all—stood, filed into their places in the ranks, and dressed the line. On their left, North Carolinians, fellow Virginians, Tennesseans, Alabamans, and Mississippians did likewise among the trees. Officers moved to their posts. The cannonade ended. A stillness seemingly deeper than the midday lull enveloped the field. It was a hot, humid Friday in July; the temperature was recorded in town at 87 degrees. The time was at or near 3:10 P.M. The order came: "Forward! Guide center! March!"

The Confederates stepped out, first the skirmishers, then the serried ranks. Pettigrew's line emerged from the woods. Pickett's rose out of the swale in front of the ridge. Across the fields a New Yorker shouted: "Thank God! There comes the infantry!" Even to less appreciative Yankees the sight must have been breathtaking. Before them, under a canopy of battle flags, looking like a mile-wide "glittering forest of bayonets," marched 10,500 members of the Army of Northern Virginia in lethal magnificence. In beautifully dressed lines, with parade ground precision, the Southerners advanced at route step—110 paces per minute.

Most Federals manning the portion of Cemetery Ridge toward which the Confederates were advancing belonged to Hancock's II Corps. Tough, experienced, they were members of John Gibbon's and Brigadier General Alexander Hays' divisions, and troops from two brigades of Abner Doubleday's I Corps division. They numbered about 5,750, hailing from ten Northern states. Five batteries from Hancock's artillery brigade and one from the III Corps stood among the waiting infantry. The foot soldiers huddled behind stone walls 2 to 3 feet high that were straddled by a rail fence that farmers had built to keep cows out of their fields. The wall began just south of the home of Abram Bryan and ran 1,000 feet south before turning west in a right angle. It then stretched roughly 250 feet down Cemetery Ridge before resuming its southward direction for another 800 feet. Gibbon's veterans held the section of the wall in front of the clump of trees, while Hays' soldiers—four deep along the wall—covered the right part of the line. Federal batteries on Cemetery Hill, the southern portion of Cemetery Ridge, and Little Round Top had a field of fire that allowed them to enfilade the enemy. This added significantly to the defenders' firepower.

Thirty-one cannon on Cemetery Hill greeted the Southerners at first, concentrating on Pettigrew's battle line soon after it emerged from the trees. The gunners hit the Confederates with every type of projectile they had. A Union gunnery officer reported, ". . . the havoc produced upon their ranks was truly surprising." Pickett's men were spared at first, as they beautifully executed an oblique left (a 45-degree turn) to adjust their attack path to Pettigrew's. Once they reached the Emmitsburg Road, however, cannon on the ridge and Little Round Top opened fire.

Pettigrew halted his line and dressed the ranks in the swale just past the W. Bliss barn, a building burned that morning by the 14th Connecticut. Many of Brockenbrough's Virginians, on the left, were already unsteadied by the artillery fire, and they remained in the protected ground when the battle line continued on. Union Lieutenant Colonel Franklin Sawyer, seeing the wavering brigade, launched an audacious charge with 160 members of his 8th Ohio, supported by seventy-five men from the 125th New

*James Longstreet's performance at Gettysburg has been the subject of much evaluation. To many fellow officers, he was one of the prime villains in the defeat. But much of this criticism resulted from his political apostasy after the war, when he joined the Republican Party. Lee, however, after Stonewall Jackson's death, regarded Longstreet as his most trusted, reliable subordinate, affectionately calling him "my old war horse." At Gettysburg, Longstreet thought Lee's tactics were poor. He argued against them vigorously and executed them grudgingly without his characteristic control and skill. Finally, he misused the latitude in Lee's commands by not implementing the commander's orders for July 3. But when Lee fashioned a new offensive that day, he left its execution to Longstreet, even though Old Peter again voiced opposition.

Above: Major General Winfield S. Hancock, commanding the II Corps, directs the defense of part of the Union line on the afternoon of July 3. One of many heroes to come out of this battle, Hancock ran for the U.S. Presidency in 1880. (CWTI Collection)

Below: Pickett's Charge—the climax of the Civil War. This painting by Philippoteaux is part of the Battle of Gettysburg Cyclorama located near the entrance of the National Cemetery.

York. The Federals ripped into the Virginians' flank, and Brockenbrough's command dissolved. Sawyer swung his men into line behind a fence, and they clawed at Davis' exposed flank.

Federal skirmishers lying in the grass stood, let go a round or two into the gray-clad ranks, and withdrew into the main line. Union artillerists rammed in charges, and the doors of hell flew open into the Confederates' faces. Batteries unleashed canister, cutting swaths in the Rebel line. The Southerners, said a Yankee, marched "in a half stoop" into the whirlwind of lead. Colonel Joseph Mayo, Jr., of the 3d Virginia said "everything was a wild kaleidoscopic whirl." Up the slope, behind the walls, Northerners yelled: "Come on, Johnny! Keep on coming." One Federal later admitted the Rebels were a "damned brave set of fellows."

When Archer's and Garnett's center brigades closed to within 250 yards, Gibbon's veterans stood on command and volleyed. The effect was fearful. Every member of the 1st Virginia's color-guard was shot; the flag of the 8th Virginia fell four times. Gibbon reported canister and musketry focused on the attackers' front line "melted it away, but still on they came from behind, pressing forward to the wall." Hays' men, 80 yards behind Gibbon's, held their fire until Davis' and Marshall's brigades began crawling over the high post-and-rail fences along the Emmitsburg Road. The slaughter matched what Gibbon had seen.

The Confederates, wrote one Southern officer, were a "mingled mass, from fifteen to thirty deep" on the slope. Kemper's brigade, hit front and flank, drifted into Garnett's ranks while Armistead's men pressed in on the rear. Kemper went down with a severe wound. But the graycoats finally started to shoot back. Suddenly, as if swept forward by a blast of wind, the "mingled mass" broke the deadlock and stormed toward a stretch of wall formed by the angle where the wall turned south—a spot known afterwards as the "Bloody Angle." Directly in their path was Alexander Webb's Philadelphia Brigade and two guns from Lieutenant Alonzo Cushing's Battery A, 4th U.S. Artillery.

With a yell, the Confederates rushed the wall. The 71st Pennsylvania broke under the onslaught. As a sergeant fired the last round of canister, Cushing, who was wounded in both thighs, took a Rebel bullet in the head and died instantly. Some Union gunners struck attackers "with hand-spikes and rocks and anything we could get our hands on." On their left, the 69th Pennsylvania fought desperately. "Everybody was loading and firing as fast as they could,"

one Keystone Stater remembered. "We thought we were all gone." But a volley from farther up the rise announced a shift in the balance of combat. The 72d and 106th Pennsylvania, which Webb had posted near the clump of trees, raked the gray swarm. Garnett died; Colonel John Magruder of the 57th Virginia was mortally wounded by two bullets, which crisscrossed in his chest as he stepped over a wall.

Confederate Brigadier General Lewis Armistead, with hat on sword, finally led a group of men toward the copse of trees and the two Pennsylvania regiments. The brigadier soon fell, fatally wounded by men serving under his former close friend, Winfield Hancock. Some of the Confederates following Armistead penetrated into the clump of trees but their stay was brief. Hancock and Gibbon were rushing reinforcements into the breach. The 19th Massachusetts and 42d New York swept through the trees, capturing or repulsing the Southerners. Then at ten paces the two Federal regiments exchanged staggering volleys with the approaching Confederates.

Just south of the clump another group of Rebels overwhelmed the 69th Pennsylvania—"We fell back, looking and praying for help," said one Federal. The Southerners drove toward Captain Andrew Cowan's 1st Battery, New York Light Artillery, yelling, "Take the guns! Take the guns!" Cowan's gunners loaded their last round of canister and yanked the lanyards on five pieces. Not one Confederate stood the blast.

Along Hays' front, the Southerners also charged in a mass across a field of clover. Union artillerymen and infantrymen unleashed hellfire. The 26th North Carolina surged to the forefront, as it had on July 1, toward Battery A, 1st Rhode Island Light Artillery. The gunners erased the Carolinians' line with their last round—a double load of canister. A sergeant and an enlisted man of the 26th reached the wall, where the Yankees ceased firing, reached over and said, "Come over on this side of the Lord." Hays swung some infantry and two cannon into the field, and they enfiladed the enemy's left flank. The North Carolinians and Mississippians broke and streamed back toward Seminary Ridge.

At the "Bloody Angle" and copse of trees, the agony was reaching a climax. Federals poured in. At places soldiers stood six deep, with the rear ranks hurling stones. "Men fire into each other's faces, not five feet apart," wrote an eyewitness. "There are ghastly heaps of dead men." Suddenly, near the clump of trees, the Yankees yelled and rushed the Virginians. More men fell in hand-to-hand combat; some even wrestled. But this final charge broke the impasse and Pickett's troops joined Pettigrew's in a flight to safety and sanity. Hundreds were taken prisoner.

The remaining units of the Southern assault force—the brigades of Wilcox and Lang—entered the action as the main attack was repulsed. They started late because of a mix-up in orders, then marched straight ahead instead of closing on Pickett's right. Union batteries shelled them from the beginning of their advance. Finally, with Pickett in retreat, regiments from Brigadier General George Stannard's Vermont brigade turned on Wilcox and Lang. The Vermont men had rendered valuable service by raking the Virginians' right flank at the stone wall. Now, the 14th and 16th Vermont charged Lang and Wilcox. The 2d Florida, on Lang's left, surrendered almost *en masse*. Wilcox, learning Pickett had failed, ordered a withdrawal. Along Cemetery Ridge the victors hurrahed in celebration.

In fields east of Seminary Ridge, Lee met the survivors. The commanding general was calm and patient, reassuring the beaten troops that all would be well. "All good men must rally," he said. "We want all good and true men just now." He spoke to James Kemper, who was being carried to the rear by some of his men. Cadmus Wilcox found Lee and reported on the condition of his brigade. "Never mind, General," Lee told him "*all this has been my fault*—it is I that have lost this fight, and you must help me out of it in the best way you can." Again and again Lee was heard repeating: "My fault! My fault!"

When Lee saw Pickett, he directed him to place his division behind the woods. Pickett, head bowed, replied, "General Lee, I have no division." Lee reassured him, taking the blame and adding, "The men and officers of your command have written the name of Virginia as high today as it has ever been written before."

Pickett's men achieved enduring glory but it was written in blood. Two of every five men in the command were casualties. Garnett was dead; Armistead mortally wounded; Kemper severely wounded. Scores of field officers fell and four regiments lost between 80 and 92 percent of their number. In Pettigrew's and Trimble's units losses were just as grievous. Pettigrew, wounded, counted approximately 60 percent of his men as casualties. Trimble, seriously wounded, lost slightly more than half his men. Altogether, of the 10,500 troops in the main assault force, about 54 percent, or 5,675, were either killed or wounded. A Virginian said it well: "We gained nothing but glory; and lost our bravest men."

Federal casualties amounted to approximately 1,500, or roughly 25 percent of those who met the attack. Hancock suffered a nasty wound in his abdomen from a deflected bullet and a piece of a ten-

penny nail. Gibbon fell with a bullet in his shoulder and several other valuable officers were dead or maimed.

Before seeking medical attention, Hancock sent Meade a message. "I have never seen a more formidable attack," he said, but he urged Meade to advance the V and VI Corps, predicting "the enemy will be destroyed." Lee expected such a counterattack but it never came. Critics, then and later, accused Meade of slowness or timidity. But, in fairness, the commander probably had only an hour to organize a force and determine where he should strike. Circumstances on the field—the disorganization and intermingling of Federal units, the loss of key officers, the fatigue of the men—made such an operation impossible in that time span. Meade ordered a reconnaissance-in-force with one brigade, supported by a second. These units crossed the Wheatfield, found the divisions of McLaws and Hood retiring to the western side of the Emmitsburg Road, then halted.

The day's final combat belonged to the cavalry. That morning, Jeb Stuart had posted four mounted brigades on Cress Ridge, about three miles east of Gettysburg. The wooded ridge commanded the cultivated fields between the Rummel and Lott farms, north of the Hanover Road. Union signalmen spotted Stuart's movement and alerted Brigadier General David Gregg, who located the Confederates after midday. The Union cavalry officer had his two brigades and George Custer's brigade from Judson Kilpatrick's division—4,500 troopers to face Stuart's nearly 5,000.

The engagement opened with an artillery duel between a Rebel battery of horse artillery and two Federal batteries. The Northerners, with better ammunition, had the best of it. About 3:00 P.M. Union Colonel John McIntosh saw Confederate horsemen forming, and charged with his brigade. The Southerners reacted, and the fighting swirled back and forth across the fields. Custer's Michigan brigade went in but crashed into another Confederate thrust. Repeatedly, attack was followed by counterattack, with neither side gaining an edge. Finally, Stuart's and Gregg's men withdrew to their original lines. Casualties were slight, though cavalry brigade Wade Hampton suffered a severe saber wound. Gregg's aggressiveness and his troopers' fighting spirit stopped Stuart, protecting the Union army's right flank and rear.

At the opposite end of the Federal position, in the area between Big Round Top and the Emmitsburg Road, Judson Kilpatrick's cavalrymen suffered a bloody repulse. On orders from Alfred Pleasonton, Kilpatrick advanced the brigades of Brigadier Generals Wesley Merritt and Elon Farnsworth against

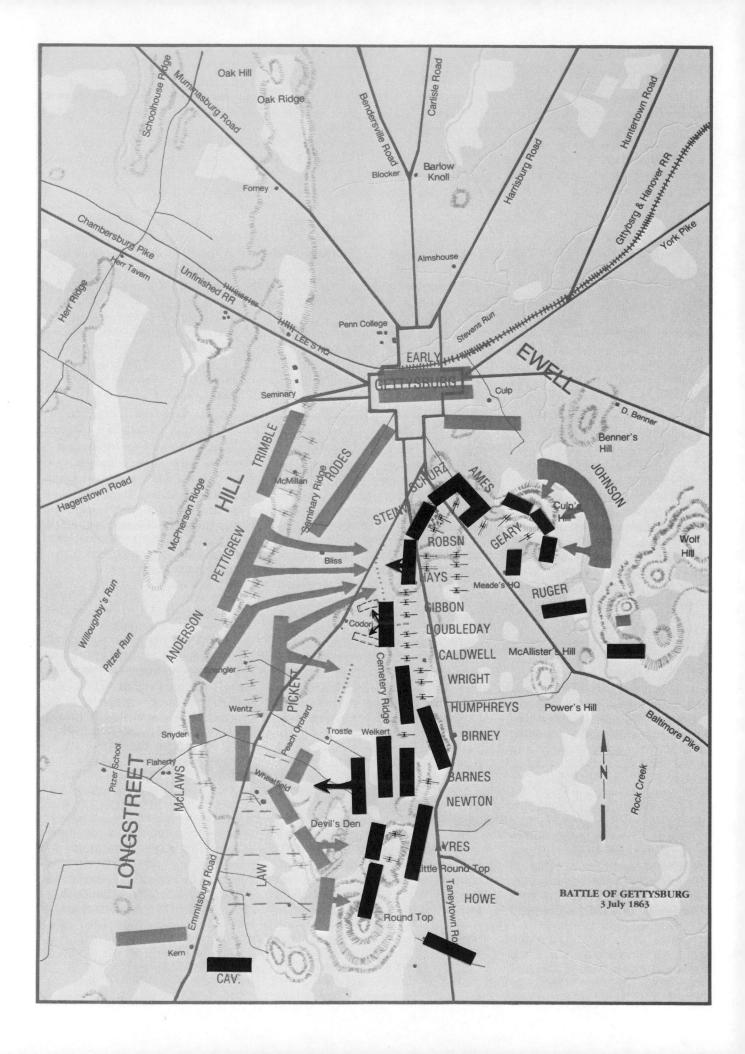

BATTLE OF GETTYSBURG
3 July 1863

Above: The cavalry fight on July 3 between Union troops commanded by David Gregg and Confederate soldiers led by Jeb Stuart. Neither side gained an edge. (CWTI Collection)

Below: Sergeant Edward S. Duffey and his gun crew firing what was, according to them, the last Confederate shot at Gettysburg. On the night of July 3, General Robert E. Lee praised the valor of his men, but said, "it has been a sad, sad day for us." The following day, he began the Confederate retreat southward. Sketch by Alfred Waud. (Library of Congress)

Union soldiers pursue Lee's retreating army through Maryland. (Library of Congress)

George Anderson's infantry brigade from John Hood's division, commanded by Evander Law. Merritt dismounted his men and pressed north up the road against Law's right flank, making little headway against those veterans. About 5:30 P.M. Kilpatrick ordered a combined attack by both brigades. But instead of sending Merritt's command in a mounted charge in the open fields, he told Farnsworth to attack on horseback across rugged terrain—a suicidal advance. The subordinate protested, but Kilpatrick insisted. Farnsworth led half his brigade toward the center of Law's line and into a hail of musketry. The young brigadier was killed and his men routed. Kilpatrick's blunder ended the fighting.

The Battle of Gettysburg, the greatest engagement ever fought in the United States had ended. Late that night Lee told a visitor to headquarters, ". . . it has been a sad, sad day for us." He praised the valor of his men but as he continued to speak his emotions swelled, and at the end he lamented, "Too bad. *Too bad.* O' Too bad!"

For the Army of Northern Virginia all that re-

mained was the journey homeward. Lee planned his retreat carefully on July 4, detailing departure times and order of march for each unit. During the day he proposed a prisoner exchange with Meade, who declined. About 1:00 P.M. a drenching rain swept in, stopped an hour later, then resumed in torrents at 9:00. The wagon train, seventeen miles long, started in the afternoon moving through Cashtown and Greenwood, escorted by Brigadier General John Imboden's cavalry brigade. The infantry marched after dark—Hill, then Longstreet, finally Ewell—on the Hagerstown-Fairfield Road. Stuart's other brigades rimmed the flanks and patrolled the rear.

Meade did not expect another attack from Lee, but he spent Saturday the 4th waiting and watching. He believed it imperative to rest his troops and have supplies and ammunition brought forward. At 4:15 P.M. he issued formal thanks to the army for "the privations and fatigue . . . and the heroic courage and gallantry it has displayed." He then reminded the troops that "our task is not yet accomplished," asking "for greater efforts to drive from our soil every vestige of the presence of the invader."

Late in the afternoon signal officers informed

Meade that indications pointed to a Confederate withdrawal. If he had wanted to disrupt Lee's movement, he should have moved forces that day to Fairfield, Pennsylvania, and into the South Mountain gaps beyond. But he missed this opportunity and the Southerners had a relatively unhampered route to Hagerstown, Maryland, and the Potomac River. Meade held another council of war with his corps commanders the night of July 4. Given the army's reduced strength and condition, a majority of the officers supported a pursuit by cavalry, with the infantry following on parallel roads. Before committing to such a major movement, though, Meade wanted clearer information on Lee's whereabouts, so he ordered a reconnaissance-in-force for the next day.

Early on July 5 Meade received confirmation of Lee's retreat, and a report from Judson Kilpatrick stating that George Custer's cavalrymen had struck Ewell's wagons near Fairfield after midnight. About midday John Sedgwick's VI Corps lumbered southwest toward Fairfield, where it encountered Ewell's rear guard. The rest of the Union army started toward Middletown, Maryland. On the 6th Sedgwick resumed his advance but Meade cancelled it and

directed the VI Corps to Emmitsburg. Meade kept a battery and a brigade each of infantry and cavalry on Lee's rear while most of the army marched toward Middletown.

Lee's army entered Hagerstown on July 7. The Federal pursuit quickened. Many of the infantry corps covered fifteen to twenty miles that day in a downpour. The same day, Meade learned of his promotion to brigadier general in the Regular Army and of Union Major General Ulysses S. Grant's capture of Vicksburg on July 4.

The Federals crossed South Mountain on the 8th, and late on the 9th were concentrated along a front running from Boonsborough to Rohrersville, Maryland. Additional Union forces, coming from the north and west, were *en route* but arrived too late to be of service.

The Yankees probed westward from their lines on July 10 and 11, sparking skirmishes. Meade's troops found the Southerners behind fieldworks that hourly grew more formidable. The rains that slowed the marches also swelled the Potomac, temporarily preventing a Confederate crossing. Forced to linger in Maryland Lee had selected a defensive position that covered the area of Williamsport and Falling Waters, Maryland. By the 11th engineers had laid plans, and the men began building earthworks with 6-foot-wide parapets. The line measured six to eight miles, its right anchored to the river at Downsville, and extending southwest of Hagerstown, covering the Williamsport road. The Conocoheague Creek protected the left flank. An inner line of works guarded the river crossing at Williamsport and Falling Waters.

Confronted with these works, bristling with muskets and cannon, Meade hesitated. He met with his ranking subordinates the night of July 12 and proposed a reconnaissance-in-force that could be expanded into an assault. Five of the seven corps commanders opposed the idea and Meade, still lacking confidence in his judgment as an army commander, acceded. He delayed the move for another day so he could personally examine Lee's position. He and Andrew Humphreys, now chief of staff, carefully studied the line on the 13th, and then Meade ordered a reconnaissance-in-force for the next day. But for the Union commander, time ran out. He should have attacked on the 13th.

Shielded by a pitch-dark night and heavy rain, the Confederate army re-entered Virginia July 13–14. Engineers had constructed a pontoon bridge and the river's waters had subsided. It was a masterful withdrawal and by 11:00 A.M. on July 14 all units had crossed except the divisions of William Pender (under James Lane) and Henry Heth. Before these last units could escape, however, the Yankees struck.

When Meade learned of the retreat, he ordered a general pursuit at 8:30 A.M. The cavalry divisions of John Buford and Judson Kilpatrick led the advance. Kilpatrick found Heth's troops at Falling Waters and charged with two squadrons before Buford arrived. The mounted Federals took the Rebels by surprise and a wild melee ensued. Southerners wielding rifles, fence rails, and axes unsaddled numbers of horsemen. Able brigade commander Johnston Pettigrew was fatally wounded. Kilpatrick sent in more units and Buford's troopers attacked Heth's right rear. Before the Confederates reached the opposite bank, 719 were captured.

With Lee's crossing of the Potomac, the Confederate campaign concluded. Exactly six weeks had passed since Lee's columns began their march north. This news soon reached Washington, D.C. At the White House, President Abraham Lincoln reacted to the report with anger and despair. Convinced Meade could have destroyed Lee's army, he told someone

that "we had them in our grasp. We had only to stretch forth our hands and they were ours. And nothing I could say or do could make the Army move." Secretary of the Navy Gideon Welles confided to his diary, "On only one or two occasions have I ever seen the President so troubled, so dejected and discouraged." When Meade learned of Lincoln's reaction, he tendered his resignation. It was refused, but the President never quite forgave the general for his cautious pursuit.

No criticism, however, could deny what George Meade accomplished. He won the decisive battle of the war in the East, a victory whose real meaning and significance people understood only with the passage of time. For three hot July days, Meade and the Army of the Potomac fought the Confederacy's best, the Army of Northern Virginia, and achieved a victory that may have saved the nation. At Gettysburg the Federals shattered the myth that Robert E. Lee and his legions were invincible. As one historian noted, the Confederates fought "the wrong kind of fight" at Gettysburg—taking the offensive against a superior and skillfully led foe that held a strong defensive position. Mistakes made on other fields proved fatal for Lee and his army those three days. His command system, which had functioned so brilliantly with Stonewall Jackson and James Longstreet, failed under the likes of A.P. Hill and Richard Ewell. In the end, Lee came close to victory only because of the men in the ranks. In his report, the general stated the truth: "More may have been required of them than they were able to perform."

A North Carolina soldier asserted "both sides got the worst of it at Gettysburg." In terms of carnage, the man was right. No other battle of the war exacted Gettysburg's price. Northern losses were 3,155 killed, 14,529 wounded, and 5,365 captured, for a total of 23,049. Lee officially listed his casualties at 2,592 killed, 12,709 wounded and 5,150 captured or missing, 20,451 in total. His actual losses probably exceeded 25,000, and one study places them at 28,063. Altogether, then, approximately 50,000 men were killed, maimed or taken prisoner at Gettysburg. Of every 1,000 Confederates, 301 were killed or wounded, and of every 1,000 Federals, 212 met a similar fate. Seventeen of the 52 Confederate generals who entered Pennsylvania, almost exactly one-third, fell in the battle. When the Confederates retreated, they left 6,082 wounded behind, including Brigadier Generals Isaac Trimble and James Kemper.

Not even the townsfolk of Gettysburg were spared. On July 3, 20-year-old Jennie Wade was baking bread in her sister's house on the Baltimore Pike when a

A dead sharpshooter in Devil's Den, at the foot of Little Round Top—one of some 50,000 men killed, maimed, or taken prisoner during the Battle of Gettysburg. (CWTI Collection)

stray Rebel bullet passed through two doors and struck her in the back. She died instantly. Unknown to her, her fiance had been killed in the fighting at Winchester, Virginia, three weeks earlier.

In the weeks after the battle Gettysburg's residents, led by attorney David Wills, confronted a question that followed every battle—what would be done with the dead? Southerners had been buried throughout the battle area. But locals wanted something more for the Federal dead. The group secured approval from the U.S. Government for a national cemetery. A State committee bought seventeen acres of land—five were added later—next to the Evergreen

96

Cemetery for $2,457.87. William Saunders, a landscape architect from Washington, D.C., was chosen as designer. He secured agreements from eighteen Northern states to fund the burials on a prorated basis and hired low bidder F.W. Biesecker to reinter the remains of Union soldiers at $1.59 per body. Black laborers performed the gruesome work, wrapping each corpse in an army blanket and laying the heads on wood shavings. Finally, Wills designated Thursday, November 19, as the day of dedication.

Governors, generals, congressmen, other government officials, dignitaries, and a crowd of 15,000 poured into Gettysburg on the appointed day. The ceremonies began at noon near the gravesites, with famed orator Edward Everett delivering the main address. When Everett finished his two-hour speech, President Lincoln stood, holding two sheets of paper. He had been asked to give "a few appropriate remarks."

Lincoln spoke only three minutes but his few choice words captured forever the meaning of Gettysburg and the war. He reminded his hearers they were engaged in a struggle, testing whether any nation "conceived in liberty and dedicated to the proposition that all men are created equal" could endure. "The brave men, living and dead," Lincoln continued, had already consecrated the ground at Gettysburg by their sacrifices. That November day of ceremony and remembrance, he said, should be a rededication to "the unfinished work," to "the great task remaining before us," resolving "that these dead shall not have died in vain; that the nation shall, under God, have a new birth of freedom, and that government of the people, by the people, for the people, shall not perish from the earth."

The President left the dais. The heroic drama of Gettysburg was now complete, though the war was far from ended. But the world, as Lincoln said, would "never forget what they did here."

"Our Other Late Successes"

In a letter of July 14 to General Meade that Lincoln composed but never sent, the president poured out his anguish at Meade's failure to attack Lee again on the north side of the Potomac. "My dear general," wrote Lincoln, "I do not believe you appreciate the magnitude of the misfortune involved in Lee's escape. He was within your easy grasp, and to have closed upon him would, in connection with our other late successes, have ended the war. As it is, the war will be prolonged indefinitely."

Among the "other late successes" mentioned by Lincoln, the principal one was the capture of Vicksburg. From then on, Lincoln would bear in mind the contrast between Grant's speed and boldness in that campaign and the caution and hesitancy of Meade after Gettysburg.

Sergeant Thomas Lawrence, Company F, 22d New York Infantry (left), and an assistant rest on boxes containing ammunition for the caliber .577 Enfield musket. (CWTI Collection)

"Looking for a Friend." On December 29, Sherman lost almost 1,800 men (to the Confederates' 200) in a bloody assault on Chickasaw Bluffs. (Battles and Leaders of the Civil War)

But Grant's reputation during the initial stages of the long struggle for Vicksburg almost sank into the mire of the Mississippi Valley swamps. A two-pronged thrust against the Confederate citadel in December 1862 had come to grief when Grant's force moving overland through Mississippi was compelled to retreat after cavalry raids destroyed supply bases in its rear while a riverborne force commanded by Sherman met a bloody repulse in an assault on Chickasaw Bluffs just north of Vicksburg.

These setbacks added to the gloom pervading the North in January 1863. And Grant did little to dispel this mood during the next three months, as he seemed to flounder around the Mississippi swamps making no headway while many of his men fell ill and died of disease. Criticism in the North rose to a crescendo. "Grant has no plans for taking Vicksburg," wrote an officer with important political connections. "He is frittering away time and strength to no purpose." Rumors began to circulate again that Grant was drinking. Pressure mounted on Lincoln to remove the general from command.

But Lincoln stood firm behind Grant. It was at this time that he supposedly told a delegation of congressmen who complained of Grant's alleged drinking that he would like to know Grant's brand of whiskey so he could send some to his other generals. Whatever the truth of this story, Lincoln did defend Grant against his critics. "I think Grant has hardly a friend left, except myself," said the president at this time. But "what I want . . . is generals who will fight battles and win victories. Grant has done this, and I propose to stand by him."

Lincoln's faith would soon be justified, in spectacular fashion.

—James M. McPherson

STRUGGLE
FOR VICKSBURG

Struggle for Vicksburg by Stephen E. Ambrose
Vicksburg: A Gallery of Rare Photographs
A Special Portfolio of Maps of the Vicksburg Campaign

AT A TIME when the Civil War went badly for the Union, President Abraham Lincoln looked at a map and commented to a visitor, "See what a lot of land these fellows hold, of which Vicksburg is the key . . . Let us get Vicksburg and all that country is ours. The war can never be brought to a close until that key is in our pocket."

By October 1862, the Federals had gained control of the Mississippi River from its mouth upstream to Port Hudson, in Louisiana, and from the river's sources down to Vicksburg, Mississippi. As long as the Confederates held the 130-mile stretch between those two towns, they could maintain communications with the western third of their nation and draw reinforcements and supplies. By denying the use of the great waterway to the Union, they prevented the reopening of normal traffic between the Northwest and New Orleans.

Lincoln was right. Vicksburg was the key and until that key was in the Federal pocket the war would continue. But wresting it from the Confederates seemed an impossibility.

WITH a population of nearly 5,000, the town stood on a 200-foot bluff on the eastern bank of the Mississippi, just downstream from where the river made a hairpin curve. Between there and Memphis the line of bluffs ran far inland, and the area adjacent to the river was low and swampy.

Across the river the ground was often inundated, and always nearly impassable for an army. From the north, the Yazoo River blocked the landward approach. To the east and south, staunchly Confederate Mississippians inhabited the countryside.

Soon after a Federal fleet seized New Orleans in April 1862, the Confederates began fortifying Vicksburg, first with batteries below the town to command the river approach from the south. Later, they mounted guns above the town and along the river, making Vicksburg impregnable to an attack from the water and creating a long gantlet past which boats found it dangerous to run. With good reason Vicksburg became known as the Gibraltar of America.

Long before Lincoln made his comment about Vicksburg, Ulysses S. Grant recognized its importance and began pondering how to secure this key that would both lock off the trans-Mississippi territory of the Confederacy and unlock the southern hold on the "Father of Waters."

NO ONE knows for sure just when Grant conceived his strategy for penetrating the heartland of the Confederacy by stabbing south along the great waterways leading into it. A visitor to the small Union headquarters at Ironton, Missouri in the summer of 1861 found the shabby, insignificant-looking new brigadier sitting under a tree in front of a cabin, drawing lines with a red pencil on a map. Grant explained that these were the invasion routes the high command should adopt and pointed out that one ran down the Mississippi past Vicksburg.

Two years were to elapse before Sam Grant was in a position to put his ideas into effect, but he never abandoned them.

The little spring beside which Grant dreamed his dreams now bubbles from a swale in the lawn of a Catholic school, and there is a simple shaft erected by his comrades of the 21st Illinois to mark the nearby site of his headquarters. But the greatest monument to this quiet little man is the fruition of

Vicksburg was vital to the South in the C

those early plans which he converted into one of the most decisive campaigns of all time.

IT IS a classic campaign, one that professional soldiers still study. With the single exception of air power, it contained the major elements of warfare later exemplified in World War II. There were mobile forces and even partisans striking far behind the lines of the main forces, and joint (Army-Navy) operations on a scale not seen again until the landings in North Africa in 1942. There were amphibious assaults, forced marches, pitched battles, field engineering of great resourcefulness, logistical triumphs, and intelligence and counterintelligence activity of a sophisticated nature. Finally, there was a siege in which courage and endurance were commonplace, and imaginative approaches to diverse problems were everyday occurrences.

STRATEGY OF THE CAMPAIGN

The scope of the campaign, the size and type of problems encountered and overcome, and its strategic importance are together enough to make it unique. But above all else, Vicksburg stands out because of the way in which one man dominated the entire campaign. Seldom in history has an individual so totally imposed his will upon his own forces,

ar. The Confederates defended it fiercely. (KA)

those of the enemy, and an operation. Ulysses S. Grant and Vicksburg are names that history will link together forever.

The campaign gave Grant an opportunity to show his skill in nearly every aspect of the soldier's trade. For each test he proved he was prepared and capable. His outstanding characteristic was flexibility of mind; he was always able to change his plans when confronted with a change in the situation. His relations with all but one of his chief subordinates were excellent. He was superb in handling troops. If throughout the long winter of 1862-63 he was not able to keep his superiors—a crabby General in Chief and an impatient President—completely satisfied, he

did convince them that a change in commanders would be a mistake. He solved a potentially explosive political problem with tact, delicacy, and understanding. He was keenly aware of the vital importance of logistics and saw to it that his men were never critically short of food or without ammunition. Though not an inspirational leader, he was ever steady and generated confidence and trust. In this campaign he managed his frontal assaults capably and broke them off before they became blood baths. His ability to maneuver large bodies of troops over great distances was truly outstanding.

FITTINGLY, Grant himself began the strategic campaign that culminated in the fall of Vicksburg when, in February of 1862, he captured Forts Henry and Donelson in northwestern Tennessee. Thus began the operations to open the Mississippi River, a task that would be the major objective of the Union forces in the West for the next year and a half.

Grant took command of the Department of the Tennessee on October 25, 1862. General in Chief Henry W. Halleck informed him that substantial reinforcements would soon come to the theater. It was characteristic of Grant that he started his campaign within a few days, and that he never turned back. His plans were flexible and he tried various routes of approach, but he kept his face ever toward his objective.

ON NOVEMBER 4 Grant started from Bolivar, in south-central Tennessee, with the idea of advancing along the axis of the Mississippi Central Railroad to Jackson, the capital of Mississippi. The Confederate forces facing him, commanded by Lieutenant General John C. Pemberton, fell back behind the Tallahatchie River. When this line, which Pemberton fortified, was outflanked by Federal cavalry and an infantry force from Arkansas that crossed the Mississippi at Helena, the Confederates retreated to Grenada and began digging in south of the Yalobusha River. Pemberton's retreat was almost a rout. Grant remarked after the war that had he known this he would not have been so meticulous in maintaining his supply lines and staying so close to the railroad, but would have moved right on to Jackson. But, being unaware of the enemy situation, Grant advanced cautiously, stopping to rebuild bridges, repair the railroad, and bring up supplies to advance depots. Although his cavalry made a dash into Holly Springs on November 13, his infantry did not arrive there until the 29th. By December 5 he still had not reached Grenada.

Perhaps Grant's reluctance to display the kind of boldness that had won him Forts Henry and Donelson was the result of a confused command system, one that made it difficult for him to advance

Ruined Depot of Shreveport and Texas Railroad.　　　　　Court-house.　　Washington Hotel.　　Uncle Sam House

with confidence. He was not sure at this time that he was being supported by the authorities in Washington. Essentially the high command there consisted of three men—President Lincoln, Secretary of War Edwin Stanton, and General in Chief Henry Halleck. Lincoln and Stanton were politicians who, with no prewar military experience, had handled well the administrative details of the largest war in which the United States had ever been engaged. Inevitably they were irritated when their generals were unable to use the large numbers of men they had raised and armed to conquer the South. Thus they were receptive when, in August 1862, John A. McClernand, an Illinois Democrat wearing a major general's uniform, had come to them, cursed the West Pointers for being too cautious, and said he could give them Vicksburg by Christmas. Lincoln and Stanton arranged for McClernand to raise a private "army" in the Northwest, with which he would launch an attack down the Mississippi River against Vicksburg. Even though he would be in Grant's theater, he would operate independently.

Evidently Lincoln and Stanton were embarrassed by what they had done, or else they feared the West Pointers would sabotage the operation, for they hesitated to tell Halleck about it and when they did they ordered him to keep it secret.

EVERYTHING was at cross-purposes. Halleck approved of neither the plan nor McClernand, whom he considered a pompous, foolish person and a poor general. Grant and his most esteemed subordinate, Major General William T. Sherman, distrusted McClernand as a soldier and disliked him as a man. McClernand in turn was outspoken in his contempt of all West Pointers.

Eventually Halleck spoiled McClernand's grandiose plans through a complex series of machinations that had a simple goal: to deprive McClernand of the force he was enlisting. As fast as McClernand raised troops in the Northwest, Halleck sent them to Memphis, where they were in Grant's Department and thus quite properly under the latter's control.

By early December Halleck had managed to tell Grant obliquely most of the "secret" (which had been discussed in the newspapers anyway), and Grant sent Sherman to Memphis to organize the new levies into units. The object was then to get them on their way to Vicksburg before McClernand became aware that he was being euchred. The latter, full of suspicion and indignation, finally hastened to Memphis, but he was too late.

INITIAL THRUSTS SOUTHWARD

Grant's plan had called for a single, overland thrust on Jackson and Vicksburg. He now changed it, possibly (at least in part) to thwart McClernand. The Union forces would make a two-pronged attack, one Grant's original overland drive and the other Sher-

— Church.   Prentiss House.   Battered Buildings.   Depot of Southern Mississippi Railro—

View of Vicksburg, Mississippi, from a drawing by F. B. Schell which first appeared in "Frank Leslie's Illustrated Newspaper."

man's amphibious effort down the river.

Three divisions of Sherman's force left Memphis on December 20, just a few days before McClernand arrived. All of Halleck's, Grant's, and Sherman's moves had been carried out more or less surreptitiously. For Grant this was risky; he did not yet have the press and public opinion solidly behind him, and the Government attitude was unknown. One aspect of the situation did give him reassurance: it had become obvious that Halleck was going to support him all the way. Halleck and Grant had had their differences early in the year, when Grant served under the other in the West, but now when it was a choice between McClernand and Grant, Halleck made his preference clear.

Grant might also have drawn comfort from the Confederate command structure had he known it. Pemberton, a native of Philadelphia and a graduate of West Point, had in mid-October assumed command of the Confederate forces in Mississippi and East Louisiana. A nervous man, Pemberton was unsure of himself and incapable of furnishing bold, aggressive leadership. When Grant started south Pemberton reported to Richmond that his situation was desperate. His statements caused such keen concern in the higher Southern echelons that President Jefferson Davis himself went west by rail to confer with Pemberton and inspect the defenses of Vicksburg. He was accompanied by General Joseph E. Johnston, whom Davis had appointed to command all forces between the Appalachians and the Mississippi. Considering the communications system available to Johnston, this was an impossibly large theater to control. An additional complication was that Johnston and Davis, both Military Academy graduates, hated each other.

Johnston vainly tried to avoid the assignment, protesting that no one could effectively control such a theater. He then asked Davis for more troops. Davis told him to transfer them from the other major army in his command, Braxton Bragg's, which was in Tennessee. Johnston argued that it would be easier and wiser to pull reinforcements from Arkansas, where Lieutenant General Theophilus T. Holmes had 20,000 men. Davis agreed; then to Johnston's disgust he wrote a friendly note to Holmes "suggesting" that he send some men. No troops came.

Before Davis returned to Richmond, Johnston had one more conversation with him. A pessimist by nature, Johnston must have sounded like a veritable Cassandra. He said the theater was too large, each of the two armies too small, and they were too far apart to support each other. All was lost. Davis told Johnston to do the best he could, and left.

Map 1. General area of operations during the Vicksburg Campaign. October 1862—July 1863.

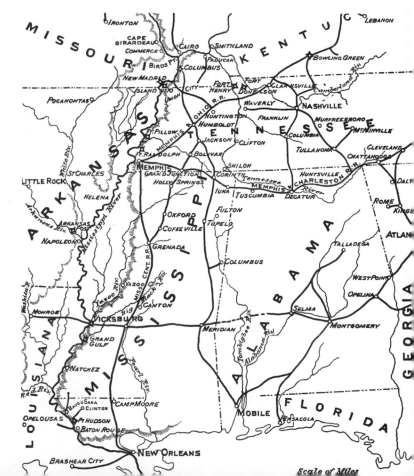

Scale of Miles

Major General Ulysses S. Grant, USA. (LC)

GRANT and Sherman, meanwhile, had paused to regroup. Major General Earl Van Dorn, commanding Pemberton's cavalry, and at the front facing Grant, decided to avoid a head-on collision. He slipped past Grant's left flank, got into his rear, and wrecked his supply base at Holly Springs. The Confederates destroyed or carried away a million dollars' worth of rations, forage, and ammunition.

Grant decided he had better pull back to Memphis and Grand Junction, where he could get fresh supplies by water from the big Union supply base at Columbus, Kentucky. Then he would rebuild the railroad from Memphis to Grand Junction which, because of its damaged condition, he had not used before, and repair any fresh damages caused by Van Dorn on the line. After a new supply reserve had been accumulated he would resume his overland advance. During the retrograde movement Grant restricted his men to short rations and sent out wagons fifteen miles on both sides of the road to scour the country for food and forage. To his amazement he found that even this narrow zone would support his force for two months.

Grant tried to inform Sherman of this withdrawal, but his wire communications to the rear had been torn down by Rebel raiders commanded by Brigadier General Nathan B. Forrest. Pemberton, unknown to

Sherman, reinforced the garrison at Vicksburg. Still, on December 21, Sherman learned that Van Dorn had captured Holly Springs. He might have guessed that this would cause Grant to turn back; but Sherman was determined to push on. He was so intent on reaching Vicksburg before McClernand that in his hurry to get away he had left behind part of a pontoon train. In the fighting that followed, this error of Sherman's cost the Union dearly.

SHERMAN arrived on the Yazoo eight miles north of Vicksburg on December 26. For three days he debarked his four divisions and worked them through the difficult swamps and bayous to a position from which he could assault across Chickasaw Bayou against the ridge just north of Vicksburg. He made this attack on the 29th. The Confederates, thanks to reinforcements which the suspension of Grant's overland drive had released, easily repulsed the Union troops with severe losses. Sherman fell back to Milliken's Bend.

There, on January 2, McClernand finally caught up with the expedition. In a towering rage he showed Sherman his orders from the President placing him in command. Sherman at once relinquished the command and, in his own words, "subsided into the more agreeable office of corps commander."

McClernand named his force "The Army of the Mississippi." He eagerly agreed to Sherman's suggestion that he move the army back up the Mississippi to the mouth of the Arkansas River, then steam up that stream to take the main Confederate position on it, the Post of Arkansas. McClernand had independently planned a similar campaign before he caught up with Sherman. Both generals felt this move necessary to relieve a growing threat to their right flank and rear, for the Confederates were preparing to descend the Arkansas with gunboats capable of raiding Union shipping. Indeed, one supply boat had already been captured.

McClernand got under way quickly, before Grant could interfere (Halleck had finally obtained from Lincoln orders that placed McClernand under Grant's general direction). On January 11 McClernand captured the Post of Arkansas. He then wrote Grant proposing that he penetrate deeper into Arkansas.

Grant was furious. He told McClernand to get back to the Mississippi immediately. He also wired Halleck that McClernand had gone off on a wild goose chase. Halleck telegraphed Grant: "You are hereby authorized to relieve General McClernand from command of the expedition against Vicksburg, giving it to the next in rank or taking it yourself." McClernand returned to Milliken's Bend. Grant arrived there on January 29. The next day he took personal command of all forces operating against Vicksburg.

WHEN Grant took command, McClernand protested bitterly. He had already told Lincoln, "I believe my success here [at the Post of Arkansas] is gall and wormwood to the clique of West Pointers who have been persecuting me for months. How can you expect success when men controlling the military destinies of the country are more chagrined at the success of your volunteer officers than the very enemy beaten by the latter in battle?" Lincoln, who was learning to rely more upon his professional advisers, especially Halleck, ignored the communication.

Grant's first act was to divide his forces into four army corps. He split McClernand's Army of the Mississippi into the XIII Corps under McClernand and the XV Corps under Sherman. His own forces were distributed into the XVI Corps (Hurlbut) and the XVII Corps (McPherson). Grant assigned to the XIII Corps the duty of garrisoning the Arkansas bank of the Mississippi. McClernand thought this was an attempt to relegate him to a subsidiary role in the campaign. He sent to Lincoln through Grant a formal complaint, citing Lincoln's original intention that he should command the expedition. Meanwhile in his personal contacts with Grant, McClernand was clearly insubordinate—and insufferable.

Grant wisely chose to ignore him and go on with his business, disregarding McClernand's insubordination. Grant realized that McClernand was an im-

Lieutenant General John C. Pemberton, CSA. (LC)

The head of the canal opposite Vicksburg cut by Grant's army. Although the project was a failure, the hard work toughened the Federals. (From a sketch by Henry Lovie in "Frank Leslie's.")

Principal Federals At Vicksburg

Maj. Gen. William T. Sherman

Rear Adm. David D. Porter

Brig. Gen. Eugene A. Carr

portant politician in Illinois, that Lincoln desperately needed the support of War Democrats, that McClernand was among the first members of Congress from the Democratic Party to pledge himself to a vigorous prosecution of the effort to save the Union, and that he had given up his seat in Congress to take the field. Such men are rare enough in any war, and Grant felt that he should make every effort to overlook McClernand's faults.

CAMPAIGN OF THE BAYOUS

By the time Grant assumed command winter rains had made the land around the river's banks impossible for any but the most limited operations. Still, Grant felt he could not stand idle for three months. Grant had good reasons for conducting a vigorous bayou campaign, although he was sure none of his efforts would be fruitful. The North had become discouraged. It was common talk, even among strong Union men, that the war would prove a failure. The elections of 1862 had gone against the Republicans. Voluntary enlistments had practically ceased. Had the North's second largest army stood idle over the winter or fallen back it would have fed the already rampant defeatism.

As Grant explained later, "It was my judgment at the time that to make a backward movement . . . would be interpreted by many of those yet full of hope . . . as a defeat, and that the draft would be resisted, desertions ensue, and the power to capture and punish deserters lost. There was nothing left to be done but to *go forward to a decisive victory.* This was in my mind from the moment I took command."

Through the winter Grant kept the troops busy, as he made four attempts to reach the high ground east and south of Vicksburg. The engineers tried to dig a canal that would divert the Mississippi and thus leave Vicksburg high and dry. The men labored for weeks in an effort to provide a water route from Lake Providence south to the Ouachita and then to Red River, which would allow the gunboats and transports to get below Vicksburg without having to run the Confederate batteries. Two attempts were also made to get into and along the Yazoo River above Vicksburg.

All these efforts involved an enormous amount of material and tremendous exertion by the troops. If they did no practical good in terms of the campaign itself, they nevertheless were of great benefit. The activity kept the generals from conspiring among themselves while the men, being constantly busy, had little time to grumble. The work gave newspaper reporters something to write about and stimulated the North's interest and morale. Perhaps most important, when spring came and Grant finally set

Maj. Gen. John A. Logan

Maj. Gen. John A. McClernand

Brig. Gen. Peter J. Osterhaus

Maj. Gen. James B. McPherson

Leading Confederate Officers

Maj. Gen. Carter L. Stevenson

Maj. Gen. Martin Luther Smith

Brig. Gen. John Gregg
Courtesy Ezra J. Warner

out, the troops he commanded were in good physical condition. Their muscles were hard, they were used to life in the field instead of the soft life of a permanent camp, and they had learned to get along on short rations.

GRANT BYPASSES VICKSBURG

At last, in late March, the river began to recede, the roads to dry out, and Grant concentrated his troops at Milliken's Bend, Young's Point, and Lake Providence "preparatory to a final move which was to crown the long, tedious, and discouraging labors" with success. By March 29 Grant had evolved his plan. He told Halleck he would move his army south of Vicksburg in barges and small steamers, through the series of bayous west of the Mississippi. Some overland marching would be necessary, but it should not be difficult in the drier weather. At the same time Rear Admiral David D. Porter's gunboats and large transports would run past the Vicksburg batteries. They would meet the troops south of Vicksburg and ferry them across the river. Grant had discussed the plan with Porter, who then approved it. This was fortunate for the army, since Porter's command was independent, and Grant could not give him orders. McClernand also agreed with the plan, but Sherman and McPherson strongly urged Grant to return to the overland approach east of the river.

Two months later, when Grant was besieging Vicksburg, he overheard Sherman telling the visiting governor of Illinois, "Grant is entitled to every bit of the credit for the campaign; I opposed it. I wrote him a letter about it." In his letter Sherman had said that by crossing the river south of Vicksburg, Grant would be putting himself voluntarily in a position that an enemy would be willing to maneuver for a year to get him into. Grant chose to regard the letter as unofficial and did not keep a copy. Years later Sherman himself gave a copy to Grant's biographer, General Adam Badeau, who printed it.

WHEN Halleck received Grant's plan he approved it, with the proviso that Grant should help Major General Nathaniel P. Banks before moving on Vicksburg. Banks, operating out of New Orleans, was attacking Port Hudson. Grant replied that once across the river he would send a corps to aid Banks, and Halleck was satisfied. As a diversion, Grant sent a small cavalry force, under Colonel Benjamin Grierson, on a raid through central Mississippi. Grierson's justly famous raid, which began on April 17 and ended on May 2, was a huge success. He broke railroad lines at a number of crucial places, frightened the citizenry, and caused Pemberton to send the Confederate cavalry and a division of infantry after

General Joseph E. Johnston

Maj. Gen. William W. Loring

Colonel Francis M. Cockrell

Maj. Gen. John S. Bowen

him in a hopeless chase.

Another, almost as important a diversion, was the dispatch, early in April, of Major General Frederick Steele's division to Greenville. Going ashore, the Federals drove inland to Deer Creek and then turned south, inflicting much damage in an area from which Pemberton's commissary drew much of its hogs and hominy. To counter this thrust, Pemberton's subordinate at Vicksburg, Major General Carter L. Stevenson, ordered out a strong column. Steele then retired and reported back to Grant at Milliken's Bend. Because of this expedition, Stevenson gave scant notice to intelligence reports telling of a Union advance southward from Milliken's Bend.

As a secondary diversion Grant left Sherman at Young's Point; late in April Sherman made a feint on the Yazoo that held some of Pemberton's force in place.

Throughout April, Grant's main force, led by McClernand's XIII Corps, worked its way down the west bank of the river. The area was flat bottom-land cut by numerous bayous. Road construction was a hard, muddy, disagreeable task that required much corduroying. The troops had to improvise a number of bridges, using whatever material was at hand and

Rear Admiral Porter's flotilla arriving below Vicksburg on the night of April 16, 1863. In the foreground General Sherman is going out in a yawl to visit the flagship "Benton." (BL)

their own ingenuity. By April 29 McClernand's and Major General James B. McPherson's corps had joined at Hard Times, where they met Porter's fleet, which in a spectacular movement had passed the batteries at Vicksburg.

Although the Federals had been moving south since the last day of March, Pemberton had done little to meet the threat. He did not even know about Grant's movements until April 17 and not until the 28th did he foresee a Union attack on Grand Gulf. Even then he sent the local commander, Brigadier General John S. Bowen, only some 5,000 reinforcements, raising Bowen's total force to 9,000—far inferior to Grant's more than 24,000 men. Pemberton had been begging Johnston for reinforcements, but disagreements at higher levels—Johnston wanted to take men from Arkansas, while Davis said he should make transfers from Bragg—prevented action.

Pemberton, however, could have done much more with what he had. But he was besieged with reports of the great damage being done by Grierson, had an exaggerated idea of Grierson's strength, and had consequently sent all his cavalry and thousands of infantry after the Yankee raider. He kept a large force north of Vicksburg to meet the threat Sherman posed, and hesitated to weaken the garrison at Port Hudson for fear Banks would pounce on the fort (this last was partly Davis' fault, as he had repeatedly stressed the importance of Port Hudson).

THE result of the poor intelligence work was that just when Pemberton should have been concentrating to meet and oppose Grant's crossing of the river, he had his force dispersed all over the state. Pemberton's subsequent discomfort was primarily due to his own indecision.

On April 29 Porter, at Grant's request, bombarded the Grand Gulf batteries. Grant hoped to cross his troops in the transports and assault craft, but the batteries proved too strong and, after consultation with Porter, Grant decided to land farther downriver. He planned to go to Rodney, but when a Negro informed him that a good solid road led inland from Bruinsburg he decided to cross there. On April 30 Grant got McClernand's corps and part of McPherson's corps across.

It would be impossible to improve on Grant's own description of his feelings at this point: "When this was effected I felt a degree of relief scarcely ever equalled since. Vicksburg was not yet taken, it is true, nor were its defenders demoralized by any of our previous moves. I was now in enemy territory, with a vast river and the stronghold of Vicksburg between me and my base of supplies. But I was on dry ground on the same side of the river with the enemy. All the campaigns, labors, hardships, and exposures from the month of December previous to this time that had been made and endured, were for the accomplishment of this one object."

GRANT MOVES TO ISOLATE VICKSBURG

From this point on, until the siege began, Grant moved with amazing speed. Brushing the Confederates aside with short, hard blows wherever he met them, he moved his force inland to Jackson, then westward to Vicksburg. He hardly ever took the obvious route, always left himself with alternatives, and kept Pemberton thoroughly confused. No other campaign of the Civil War, and few others in all military history, were so successful at such small cost. In view of this operation, it is difficult to explain the prevalence of the widely held view that Grant was slow and deliberate—a bludgeon general rather than the wielder of a rapier.

As soon as Grant was across the river he ordered Sherman to bring the bulk of his force south. Leaving Major General Frank Blair's division to guard his depots and supply line west of the river, Grant then set out inland with McClernand's corps and part of McPherson's.* The troops marched along the

---

*Grant's force numbered around 24,000 men; when Sherman joined him, on May 8, his strength was about 34,000. Pemberton had nearly 40,000 at all times; but while Grant was concentrated, Pemberton's force was badly scattered. Further, Pemberton received no substantial reinforcements, whereas by the end of the campaign Grant had over 75,000 officers and men.

LETTER FROM UNION SURGEON

The following letter was written by B. F. Stevenson, a surgeon with the 22d Kentucky, to his wife.

In hospital, in rear of Vicksburg, May 23, 1863.

Dear Wife, I have not, for more than two weeks, had an opportunity to write to you. New events have trod so rapidly on the heels of the old, that I have had no time for anything but my official duties.

Since my last we have passed through an exceedingly active period; on some part of our extended line a battle has been fought almost every day, and some days two or three. The conflict is determined and desperate, but I think we will ultimately win. We have been in our present position here four days, and the rattle of musketry and the roar of cannon have been unceasing during all that time. Our missiles occasionally go over the hills, on which the rebel works are erected, and into the city, on which the gun and mortar boats are pouring a ceaseless storm of shot and shell. I see no prospect of cessation short of exhaustion, as we have staked all on success.

The 22d has been engaged for three days, and suffered severely in wounded men yesterday. During the evening I amputated a leg for three of our boys above the knee and one below the knee, and four days before I did the same at Champion Hill for two of our men, and for one man of an Indiana regiment. In the same period I resected the upper third of the arm (humerus) for two 22d men, and for one of the 42d Ohio, and I have seen any amount of minor surgery. I am surfeited, sick, and tired of witnessing bloodshed, but nothing short of it would satisfy the insane men who would overthrow the government. I now think they have enough of it. In addition to our wounded of yesterday we had two men slain on the field.

Since reaching this side of the river, Grant's army has captured seventy-one cannon of all calibres, most of them brass field pieces. On the 17th twenty-two pieces were taken "at one fell swoop" at the crossing of Black River. In good time you will find in the papers full details of the operations of this army, so I will say nothing more than that on a field where there was anything like equal numbers we have whipped, and under like circumstances will continue to whip the rebels.

The defenses of the city are formidable and may require a regular siege, in which event we shall be here for some time to come. I fear you will charge me with thinking of nothing but sieges, and battles, and bloodshed, but surrounded as I am with such scenes, what else have I to think of? The weather here has been the most propitious for our operations possible. The wounded get on as finely as I have ever witnessed with wounded men anywhere. We have an occasional shower during the day which mitigates the heat, and the nights are cool enough.

I am worked up to my utmost capacity, but this you know I never object to. Love to all, with kisses to the children, and say that I soon hope to see them. Remember me kindly to enquiring friends.

Rodney road south of Bayou Pierre toward Port Gibson, a small village where there was a network of roads leading to Grand Gulf, Vicksburg, and Jackson. McClernand, in the lead, hoped to beat Bowen to the bridge over Bayou Pierre on the route that led to Grand Gulf, but he had wasted valuable time because of poor staff work. His men had not received their three days rations prior to crossing the river and he had to wait while they were issued. By the time he reached Thompson's plantation, five miles west of Port Gibson, it was after midnight.

In any case the Confederates were already there. Brigadier General Martin E. Green and an advanced detachment of Bowen's force had arrived late in the afternoon and taken up positions to contest the Yankee advance. Because the cavalry was off chasing Grierson, Bowen had no firm idea where the Federals were, but he guessed that they would try to cross the bayou and invest Grand Gulf. Therefore he sent one brigade to hold the bridge and cover Port Gibson, while he prepared to move with the other as necessary.

FOR General Green the night of April 30-May 1 passed slowly. All was silence about him. No scouts had reported in; he began to fear that Grant had taken a wholly unexpected route, or perhaps even reembarked his troops for another try at Grand Gulf. At 12:30 a.m. the tension became more than he could bear, and he rode forward to make sure that Lieutenant Tisdale and his outpost were alert.

Coming up to the Shaifer house he found a small area of chaos. Mrs. A. K. Shaifer and the other women of the house had panicked at the news the Yankees were coming. They were frantically trying to load their most valuable household effects into a wagon in which they proposed to flee to Port Gibson. The panic of the ladies allowed the overwrought Green to get control of himself. He calmly told them that the Yankees could not possibly arrive before daylight, and that they therefore had plenty of time to load their wagon.

He had hardly spoken the comforting words when a crash of musketry shattered the stillness. One ball smashed through the west wall of the house and several more buried themselves in the wagon-load of furniture. A brief horrified silence gave way to shrieks of dismay. Abandoning both household goods and dignity, the ladies scrambled into the wagon and whipped the team frantically toward Port Gibson and fancied safety. Green, both chagrined and amused, ordered Tisdale to contest the Yankee advance, then galloped back to make sure that the gunfire had alerted his command. The land campaign for Vicksburg was underway.

During the remainder of the night the troops exchanged sporadic fire with little result. The night was so dark and the country so broken that Brigadier General Eugene A. Carr, senior Union commander on the spot, decided to wait until dawn before deploying his division further.

BATTLE OF PORT GIBSON, MAY 1, 1863

Dawn revealed to General Carr a terrain of incredible complexity. It was an utter maze of ridges, each more or less flat-topped and of equal height, but running in all directions. Each ridge was separated from its neighbor by a steep-sided ravine filled with a jumble of trees, vines, and immense and almost impenetrable cane brakes. The ridge tops were chiefly cultivated fields except where there were groves of trees around plantation buildings. Visibility was excellent from the ridge-tops but the ravines were jungles that closed tightly about men moving through them, so that each man's world was a tiny green-walled room only a few yards across.

McClernand, nervous, eager, and excited, rode up at daybreak. He had just passed a fork in the road and had no idea which of the routes before him led to Port Gibson. The inevitable Negro "contraband" appeared to explain that both did, and that at no point did the two roads, which followed ridges, diverge more than a mile or two. They were separated, however, by a deep vine- and cane-choked ravine, so that one flank could not reinforce the other except by marching back to the junction of the roads. Bowen's men were in position on both roads, hoping to hold off McClernand until reinforcements under Major General William W. Loring could arrive from Big Black Bridge.

The old Mississippi River bed as it now appears from Fort Hill. The Water Battery lies in the center of the picture. (Courtesy Vicksburg National Military Park.)

Magnolia Church on the Port Gibson battlefield. (Margie Bearss collection.)

McClernand immediately decided to attack along both ridges and simply push the Confederates out of the way. He put the divisions of Hovey, Carr, and A. J. Smith on the right flank and that of Osterhaus on the left (Map 3). With an entire corps passing through one road junction there was not much room for maneuver, and it took a few hours to get everyone into position. Neither attack got off until after 8 a.m. By then Bowen himself had arrived. Instantly recognizing that he had the whole of Grant's army in front of him, he sent couriers to the rear to bring up all possible reinforcements.

IN RETROSPECT this was the critical moment of the Vicksburg campaign. Grant was still involved in an amphibious operation. His force was inevitably divided, with one of his three corps still on the west bank of the river and over half of another still engaged in disembarking and in unloading the transports. If Pemberton could have struck while Grant was thus off balance, with one foot in the water and the other on land, he certainly would have spoiled Grant's plans and he might have even destroyed his army.

But Pemberton utterly failed to take advantage of the opportunity. Because he had voluntarily given up his cavalry he was operating in the dark. Not until the battle had been joined did he learn that contact had been made. Then he sent elements of two divisions toward Port Gibson and telegraphed Johnston, demanding reinforcements. Johnston at once wired back: "If Grant's army lands on this side of the river, the safety of Mississippi depends on beating it. For that object you should unite your whole force."

As always, Johnston's strategic insight was impeccable. His advice, however, was worthless. Pemberton had five divisions scattered through the triangle formed by Port Gibson, Jackson, and Vicksburg. He had only one division and two brigades of another at the scene of the opening battle. He was simply in no position to prevent Grant from establishing himself on the east bank. Pemberton must have winced the next day when Johnston again wired him: "If Grant's army crosses, unite all your forces to beat it. Success will give you back what was abandoned to win it."

Johnston had been ill, and in any case never had his heart in the campaign. He approached it with the attitude that the result was a foregone conclusion, never showed any enthusiasm for his assignment, made no real effort to control or direct Pemberton, and was so weighted down with pessimism that he evidently felt that sending more troops to Pemberton was simply to waste them. There is no evidence that he ever made a determined attempt to get reinforcements to the hard-pressed Pemberton. In a typical "my hands are tied; there is nothing I can do" message to the Confederate War Department the day after the Battle of Port Gibson, he transmitted Pemberton's call for reinforcements and commented,

The Perkins house (now abandoned) still stands on the Port Gibson battlefield. It first served as Grant's headquarters and later was used as a hospital. (Photograph by Ken Parks.)

"They cannot be sent from here without giving up Tennessee."

THE upshot was that Bowen was left by his superiors to fight his battle alone. Grant, meanwhile, reached the field just as the battle was getting into full swing and inspected both flanks in person. McClernand's progress was slow but steady. He could not begin to deploy all his troops on one road, and in any case Confederate fire made a direct advance along the ridge unprofitable. He therefore sent men into the ravines on both sides to attempt to outflank Bowen. Once in the ravine, however, the smoke of battle, coupled with the vines and underbrush, made it virtually impossible to maintain any sense of direction, and regiments found themselves moving at odd angles to the direction their officers supposed. Great gaps opened at some points, while at others regiments jammed up. Still the weight of the advance was enough to force the enemy to give ground.

On the left Brigadier General Peter J. Osterhaus, a Prussian who was the most distinguished of the foreign-born generals who served the Union, was having great difficulty. At 8:15 he had tried to rush the Rebel position. He had gained about 400 yards, then had come to a sudden stop when he hit the main enemy lines. When he found time to check his position, Osterhaus discovered that his attack had carried his men into the middle of a concave system of ridges, and that the diverging movements caused by peculiar arrangement of the ravines had opened huge gaps in

Union troops marching toward the village of Port Gibson, where fighting would occur on May 1. (Harper's New Monthly Magazine)

his lines. The 42d Ohio faced the middle of the Rebel line with the 49th Indiana on an odd eccentric to the left. Between the Hoosiers and the 118th Illinois on their left there was a gap of more than 200 yards. A well-led Confederate counterattack might roll up his entire line. (Map 4)

But the Rebels had no fresh troops. Grant meanwhile, as soon as McClernand's men had passed the road junction, rushed elements of McPherson's corps forward. Throughout the day McClernand begged Grant for more men. Grant consistently insisted that McClernand, who had sent Brigadier General Alvin P. Hovey to help Carr, on the right, already had more men on his very limited front than he could use effectively. A brigade of Major General John A. Logan's division (which had crossed the river that morning) reached the Shaifer house about noon and Grant ordered it to support McClernand's right. Logan's next brigade to reach the field was sent to assist Osterhaus.

WHILE Union reinforcements reached the field in division strength, Bowen received his only reinforcements—about one and a half brigades coming up from Grand Gulf and Vicksburg. Osterhaus, with a superiority of over three to one, moved some troops into the ravine on his left, and sent a series of skirmish lines forward. There was a great deal of noise, tremendous confusion, and clouds of smoke before the Confederates fell back.

On the right McClernand, never a subtle general but a firm believer in applying the greatest strength

in the smallest space, prepared a direct frontal smash. He concentrated so many men on his narrow front that the regiments were stacked up two, three, and four deep. The two leading regiments got within eighty yards of the Confederate artillery before the men had to seek shelter. Two more regiments followed, the men shouting and forming a single irresistible mass. The Confederates had two batteries double-shotted with canister for a last telling volley, but before the gunners could fire their pieces the Yankees swept over them, capturing two guns of the Botetourt Virginia Artillery (Map 5). Gleefully the Union men manhandled these guns around and fired them at the backs of the fleeing Rebel troops.

McCLERNAND'S column moved forward along the Rodney road. About a mile beyond Magnolia Church the vanguard encountered a strong force of Confederates posted in a deep hollow. Here Bowen had deployed the brigade (William E. Baldwin's) that had just arrived from Vicksburg, after marching forty-four miles in twenty-seven hours. The half brigade (Francis M. Cockrell's) that had come from Grand Gulf that morning would constitute Bowen's reserve.

In this difficult country it took several hours for McClernand and his three division commanders to form their troops in line of battle. The Federals then advanced into the cane-choked hollow, but within minutes the enemy checked their forward progress. Bowen in the meantime had taken a desperate gamble. He sent Cockrell with his two regiments

far to the left. Taking advantage of the terrain, Cockrell was able to assail McClernand's right, which was not refused, and roll up one Union brigade. To counter this thrust McClernand was compelled to rush artillery and infantry to his right. Superior numbers soon told, and the Confederate success was nullified. But by this time dusk was at hand, and the day's fighting was over.

It had taken all day but the Confederate position was finally gone. Bowen had fought magnificently; no other Confederate leader would do as well in the campaign to follow. A West Point classmate of McPherson and the ablest general in Pemberton's army, Bowen was a severe disciplinarian. His jet black hair, bushy eyebrows, and luxuriant chin beard tended to draw attention away from his sleepy eyes and rather frail constitution. He was unable to withstand the rigors of the siege, contracted severe dysentery, and survived the campaign by only a few days. But he had made his contribution; it could have been decisive. For eighteen hours he had held up Grant's entire army, inflicting over 800 casualties. Had he received any help at all, Bowen might have driven Grant into the river. But Pemberton had let his best chance go by.

GRANT rode up to McClernand's headquarters just after the successful assault at Magnolia Church. Governor Richard Yates of Illinois was there; together the three men rode forward to inspect the captured position. The men cheered lustily as they passed along the line. Grant was impassive as always, but the cheers were heady to McClernand and Yates. The two politicians were so overwhelmed by the sight of all those voters that they simply had to stop and make brief congratulatory addresses to the troops. Yates said a few words, then McClernand shouldered him aside and exulted, "A great day for the Northwest!"

Grant watched quietly, then suggested that perhaps the advance should be resumed. McClernand, beaming, agreed, and got the pursuit started. Bowen had led part of his force over Bayou Pierre to cover Grand Gulf (which he evacuated the next night), while the remainder slipped northeastward over the Little Bayou Pierre, (South Fork of the Bayou Pierre) and then took a more northerly route toward Vicksburg, crossing Big Bayou Pierre (the Bayou's north fork) at Grindstone Ford. He fired the three bridges behind him. When darkness fell Grant let his weary men make camp.

The next morning Grant moved through Port Gibson to Little Bayou Pierre; he at once set his men to work bridge-building. Lieutenant Colonel James H. Wilson, two years out of West Point and soon to achieve fame as a cavalry leader, supervised

the construction. Using material obtained from wooden buildings, stables, fences, and the like, and going into the water himself to work as hard as the men, Wilson quickly had the bridge finished. Grant crossed, and by evening of that day (May 2) had reached Bayou Pierre.

A Bold Decision

Grant had planned to solidify his position around Grand Gulf and south of the Big Black, then send McClernand's corps to assist Banks at Port Hudson. Once that operation was completed, Grant would move north with his entire army reinforced by that of Banks. But on May 3 Grant learned that Banks was on a chase up Red River and would not be ready to invest Port Hudson for several weeks.

The news was extremely frightening. Grant had bet everything he had on this campaign only because he was convinced he could move faster than the Confederates. Outwardly taciturn, he was filled with an inner tension, a compulsion to get moving. The trouble was that he had no assured line of supplies. The road from Milliken's Bend down to Hard Times was so bad and so exposed to attack that Grant hesitated to supply his army that way. Material could not be brought up from New Orleans as long as the guns at Port Hudson were still firing. Transports and barges could run the batteries at Vicksburg, but only at what would be an increasing cost as the Confederate gunners improved with practice.

Grant made the boldest decision of the war. He declared that he would move inland without occupying the countryside. He would have the men carry enough hardtack, coffee, and salt to get by on, load his wagons to the bulging point with ammunition, and depend on the countryside for whatever else he needed. He did arrange to have heavily-guarded supply trains come out of Grand Gulf each day.

Grant's next problem was where to attack. McPherson, on May 5 had conducted a reconnaissance north of the Big Black River which revealed that Pemberton had finally concentrated his troops and was having them dig in to oppose an attack from the south. Grant may have known that Johnston was attempting to build up a force at Jackson, that President Davis had dispatched troops from the East, and that any reinforcements to Vicksburg had to come through Jack-

son. He therefore adopted a favorite Napoleonic maneuver and advanced so as to get between the two forces, hopefully to destroy the weaker one first, then turn on the stronger.

BY MAY 7 Grant had McClernand up to Big Sand Creek with McPherson at Rocky Springs. Sherman had reached Hard Times, crossed the river to occupy Grand Gulf, and caught up with the other two corps in a couple of days. On May 11 Grant pushed Sherman's corps out in front of McClernand's, which had halted near Cayuga, while McPherson prepared to advance on Raymond from Utica. Sherman and McClernand marched together to Auburn, where McClernand branched out almost straight north on the Telegraph Road toward Edwards' Station while Sherman moved on eastward to Dillon's plantation. If it proved necessary, Grant had lateral roads available so that any one corps could support another at any time. (Map 2)

Still, Grant was taking a risk. If Pemberton had organized the countryside so that spies and scouts could be reporting, or if he had retained his cavalry for reconnaissance, he might have descended quickly on the nearest Union corps and isolated and destroyed it. But he had neglected to make either of these elementary preparations and as a result was completely in the dark about Grant's movements. He was, in addition, under orders from Davis to hold Vicksburg and from Johnston to concentrate and attack Grant. Under the circumstances he decided to take an indecisive course, which suited his temperament in any case, collect his forces along the Big Black River, and await developments. He did send Bowen forward to occupy Edwards' Station and a brigade, Brigadier General John Gregg's, from Jackson to Raymond.

> One of the great myths of the Civil War is that Grant cut loose from his supply line when his army began its march inland from the Hankinson's Ferry-Willow Springs area. It was May 14 before the last train moved out of Grand Gulf. If Grant had been repulsed at Champion Hill, another train escorted by an infantry brigade would have been called up from Grand Gulf.—Edwin C. Bearss

BATTLE OF RAYMOND
(Maps 6 and 7)

When Gregg marched into Raymond on the afternoon of May 11 the populace hailed his men as saviors. The village seethed with rumors of the approach of a Yankee column from Utica. Gregg asked where he could find the headquarters of Colonel Wirt Adams, expecting to find the cavalry commander busy receiving reports on the enemy's movements. Gregg's request was met with blank stares—Adams had exactly five men in the village.

Adams' absence was due to a masterpiece of ambiguity by Pemberton. The latter, after ordering Gregg to Raymond, had sent a messenger to Adams: "General Gregg is ordered to Raymond. Direct your cavalry there to scout thoroughly, and keep him informed." What Pemberton meant was that Adams should take all his cavalry to Raymond and carry out this mission. Adams, however, read the message to say that the cavalry he already had in Raymond (five men) should scout thoroughly and keep Gregg informed. Adams therefore proceeded with his original plans and, while Gregg marched into Raymond, rode into Edwards' Station.

The result was that a Union corps was bearing down on an unsuspecting Rebel brigade, and again the Yankee forces, though outnumbered in the area, had overwhelming superiority at the point of contact. In the engagement that followed, the Southerners again showed that given equal numbers they were more than equal to their enemy. In part this was due to a misreading of the situation by McPherson, who overestimated his opponent's strength, a natural mistake—he just could not believe that a brigade would challenge a corps to pitched battle. He therefore advanced cautiously, enabling Gregg to engage the Union regiments piecemeal.

THE battle itself, on May 12, was even more confused than that at Port Gibson. The Confederates kept attacking, wildly hitting advancing Union regiments and forcing them to retreat. On two occasions John A. Logan personally rallied his men. Once the 20th Ohio, seeing a Texas regiment sweep down upon its flank, began to waver and prepared to run. Logan dashed up and with "the shriek of an eagle turned them back to their place." One Ohioan gave Logan his just due: "Had it not been for Logan's timely intervention, who was continually riding up and down the line, firing his men with his own enthusiasm, our lines would undoubtedly have been broken at some point."

The whole battlefield was a bowl of dust and smoke; no one could see what was really going on. The Confederates would probably not have fought had they known what they were up against. Considering some of the things they did, however, it is possible that a knowledge of the odds would have simply spurred them to greater efforts. For example, late in the day Colonel R. W. MacGavock found himself on a bare spur just as a pause occurred in the battle. As the smoke and dust lifted, he and his men were exposed to McPherson's entire corps artillery. Joyfully switching fire to the only visible target, the Union gunners began to rake MacGavock's ranks with shell fire. Meanwhile a blue line of infantry, sharpshooters thrown out in advance, began to come up the hill. MacGavock realized that if he fell back the entire Southern position would go with him. If he stayed, he would be cut to pieces by the Yankee artillery and the charging infantry.

Panoramic view of the battlefield of Raymond, situated about three miles southwest of Raymond along the Utica Road. The view is from the commanding ridge which was occupied by Federal forces during the battle. (Photo by Margie R. Bearss)

He could think of only one thing to do. A tall, commanding man who habitually wore a long gray cloak with a brilliant scarlet lining, MacGavock dramatically threw his cloak back. There he stood, a compelling crimson figure, at the head of his troops. Every eye on the battlefield turned toward him. He waved his arm forward and shouted for a charge. At that instant a Union sharpshooter cut him down, but his men rushed forward with irresistible force, screaming for vengeance. They broke the Yankee line and sent it running.

SOMEHOW this was not the way a battle between a brigade and a corps was supposed to go; in the end inevitably the weight of the Union attack made itself felt. The Confederates slowly fell back, even though Gregg continued to find the best defense was a good offense. Whenever a Yankee regiment appeared, the Rebels facing it would move forward threateningly, making as much noise as possible. Soon, however, the Confederates found themselves nearly surrounded, with the enemy well around both flanks. Gregg retired.

One Confederate brigade had held up a Union corps for half a day, at a cost of 515 casualties. McPherson suffered almost an equal loss in killed and wounded, but because his missing total was only 37 his casualty list ran to only 442.

The bone-weary, hot, dusty, thirsty 20th Ohio led the Union advance into Raymond. Coming into the shaded village from the brazen sun, they were astonished to find a tremendous picnic spread beneath the stately live oaks along the streets. The ladies of Raymond had prepared the feast for Gregg's soldiers, to be eaten upon their "return from victory." Gregg had moved through the village so fast, however, that the men had not touched the food. The boys from Ohio gratefully took their places and by the time the following regiment reached town the food was gone.

GRANT received McPherson's report of the battle while at Sherman's headquarters. He knew from his scouts that Pemberton was concentrating at Edwards' Station, partly to block the Federal movement to Vicksburg, partly to pose a threat to the Grand Gulf-Raymond road over which Grant was bringing up reinforcements and the heavily guarded trains. During the day, Sherman in the center and McClernand on the left had forced their way across Fourteen Mile Creek, as they turned their columns toward the Vicksburg-to-Jackson railroad. Grant also knew that a couple of Confederate regiments coming all the way from the eastern seaboard had reported to Gregg after he had retreated through Raymond. More would be coming and their route would be via Jackson. If Pemberton were finally going to

concentrate all his units, Grant wanted his pulled together too. He also wanted to cut Pemberton off from any possibility of receiving outside aid, and at the same time destroy the communications and manufacturing center of Mississippi, which was Jackson. Grant therefore "decided at once to turn the whole column toward Jackson and capture that place without delay."

Grant issued his orders on the night of May 12. He directed McPherson to Clinton, almost directly west of Jackson and astride the Vicksburg-to-Jackson railroad; once McPherson had occupied Clinton he would sever Pemberton's direct communications with Johnston, who was building up a force in the capital. Grant told Sherman to start at 4 a.m., marching through Raymond toward Jackson. McClernand would follow and occupy Raymond.

Grant was now deep in hostile territory, with large enemy forces on either side of him. The Union troops were in the position Sherman had said the enemy would be willing to maneuver for a year or more in order to get them into. Meanwhile General Banks, on Red River, was pleading for reinforcements.

GRANT had been in a similar position in February 1862, at Fort Donelson. Then as now he did not panic. (The modern slang expression is an excellent description of Grant in such a situation: "He kept his cool.") Neither did he take foolish chances. He kept his troops in supporting distance of each other, making constant reconnaissances to enable each corps to know at all times where the most practicable routes were in case it became necessary for them to concentrate. More important, he moved so rapidly, as well as audaciously, that he had the Confederates constantly and thoroughly confused.

Crocker's division at the Battle of Jackson on May 14, 1863. From a drawing by battlefield artist Theodore R. Davis. (HW)

McPherson reached Clinton early on May 13. The men immediately cut the telegraph line and began destroying the railroad. Sherman got into Raymond before the last of McPherson's command had left. McClernand had the most difficult mission; his spearhead, which had forced its way across Fourteen Mile Creek, was in contact with the formidable force Pemberton was concentrating at Edwards' Station. To keep the Confederates off balance while he broke contact, McClernand bluffed an attack, and the Confederates began digging in. McClernand, covered by this feint, sent three of his divisions eastward across Bakers Creek, and by the time Pemberton and his generals realized what had happened, McClernand's corps had stolen a day's march on them.

McClernand reached his encampment in good order. The next morning, May 14, McPherson marched at dawn for Jackson; so did Sherman. When the two corps reached the Confederate entrenchments around the city they would be about two miles apart. McClernand sent one division to Clinton, another behind Sherman, and a third to Raymond.

JOHNSTON GIVES UP JACKSON
(Map 8)

By the afternoon of the 13th Grant's position was as nearly perfect as the human mind and hard marching could make it. He had two corps threatening Jackson; a division, Hovey's, at Clinton that could either hold off Pemberton or reinforce McPherson; another division behind Sherman for support; a division at Raymond that could take either road and reinforce Hovey or Sherman; and two more divisions (one of which, Blair's, had recently crossed the river) farther back within one and one-half day's march of Jackson. These last divisions, under Mc-

Clernand's command, were threatening Pemberton and, if not needed at Jackson, were one day's march from there on their way to Vicksburg and on two different roads leading to that city.

The Confederate position, by contrast, approached the ludicrous. Johnston, who had arrived in Jackson on the evening of the 13th, had nothing like enough men to hold off two corps. Although the total Confederate strength in the whole area of operation was still greater than Grant's, the third battle of the campaign was about to be fought with the Union forces—who were invading and were in the heart of enemy territory—again in great superiority. Grant stood squarely between the two Rebel armies. Johnston ordered Pemberton to move on Clinton, where the two separated forces could unite. Pemberton, however, had other ideas. He was considering moving southeast to attack and destroy Grant's trains and the two divisions guarding them.

Within Jackson, Johnston had only some 6,000 men to defend the capital. "I am too late," he wired the Secretary of War. At 3 a.m. on May 14 he issued an evacuation order, even though he then was facing two corps, which had not yet begun their final advance on Jackson. In short, Johnston's pessimism was so great that he decided to retreat before any pressure was exerted and before he could possibly be certain that the Union concentration was aimed at Jackson.

AT 5 A.M. McPherson and Sherman started out for Jackson. It had rained most of the night; with daybreak the rain began to fall in torrents, turning the roads into sheets of mud. At places along Mc-Pherson's route the road was covered by a foot of water. The wheels of the ambulances, guns, and limbers quickly converted the road into a bottomless quagmire, through which the artillery horses strained in vain to pull the heavy caissons. The sodden infantrymen put their shoulders to the wheels. Curses quickly lost in the sound of falling water rang out whenever an officer or courier dashed past on his horse and splashed sheets of mud and water on the straining infantrymen.

Despite everything the men moved forward. By midmorning they had reached the outer Confederate lines. McPherson's leading division, Brigadier General Marcellus M. Crocker's, deployed. McPherson sent word back to the following division, Logan's, to hurry forward. Just then the rain abated slightly and McPherson organized an immediate assault. As he prepared to give the order to charge, another terrific downpour commenced, with the water coming down in buckets. McPherson, afraid to allow his men to open their cartridge boxes lest the water ruin the ammunition, called off the attack to wait for the rain to subside.

Sherman's vanguard, meanwhile, had worked its way forward and had reached Lynch Creek, which was nearly overflowing. A small Confederate force covered the bridge. As soon as he heard the enemy artillery contesting his advance Sherman rode forward, made a hasty reconnaissance, and ordered an immediate attack. Just then the rain ceased. It was 11 a.m. The men dashed forward, crossed the bridge, and drove the Rebels back. By early afternoon Sherman had forced the enemy into the main Jackson entrenchments (dug earlier by slave labor and citizen volunteers), where his assault came to a halt.

GRANT was with Sherman, and the two officers conferred on the next move. Sherman pointed out that the enemy trenches extended as far to his left as he could see. To the right his vision was obstructed, and he decided to send a scouting party to reconnoiter in that direction. Sherman, Grant, and some staff officers, standing in front of a cottage as they talked, presented an obvious target to the Rebels. Just as the scouting party rode away several shells whistled over the infantry line and exploded nearby. Neither Grant nor Sherman turned a hair.

The scouts, led by Sherman's chief engineer, Captain Julius Pitzman, found that the trenches to the right were unmanned. Pitzman returned to the main force and gathered up the 95th Ohio for a flanking operation. As the regiment was placing its flag as a symbol of victory on the earthworks, an old Negro ran up to the men waving his hat and yelling at the top of his voice, "I'se come to tell you-all that the

Rebels is left the city, clear done gone. You jes' go on and you will take the city."

With considerable difficulty the Ohio soldiers got the old man calmed down enough to ask him, "Why are the Rebs still firing their battery if they have left the place?"

"Ho!" he laughed, "there is only a few cannoneers there to work the guns to keep you back."

The Negro offered to guide them and the men agreed to follow. Sure enough, he led them right into the unsupported and unguarded rear of the Southern artillerymen. Shouting joyfully, the Yankees surged forward, through the backyards and over fences, pounced on the Confederates, and bagged themselves six guns and fifty-two prisoners. Sherman could now walk into Jackson.

THE northern jaw of the Union pincer was prepared to close. When the rains let up, Crocker decided not to waste time on such an inferior force, especially one that was challenging him two miles outside its earthworks. He sent his whole line charging forward on the double with banners unfurled, bayonets fixed, and the men cheering wildly.

The Rebels resisted for a few minutes, then retreated to their main trench system. Shortly after they arrived they pulled out of the city. Johnston had already left; Gregg was in command. Gregg, learning that Sherman had closed up against the Jackson fortifications, and of the repulse of the men facing McPherson, and receiving a message that the army's supply train had left Jackson en route to Canton, decided he had done enough. He ordered his remaining men, except for a number of artillerymen manning the guns, to retreat along the Canton road and protect the rear of the wagon train. It was these artillerymen whom Sherman's troops captured.

At 3 p.m. McPherson learned that the enemy had vanished from his front. He sent Crocker's division on into the city while directing a brigade of Logan's division to march cross-country and attempt to cut

Raising the Stars and Stripes over Jackson, Mississippi after Johnston's evacuation. Drawing by Theodore R. Davis. (HW)

off Gregg's retreat. Either the brigade did not march fast enough (the men had been marching or fighting in deep mud since 5 a.m.) or the order did not reach them soon enough. In any case Gregg escaped.

AT 4 P.M. Grant, McPherson, and Sherman met in the Bowman House to exchange congratulations, count the cost of victory, and plan new blows against the enemy. The Union forces had 299 casualties, the Rebels 845. In addition, the victors had captured seventeen cannon.

If Grant had been thinking of savoring his victory and letting his men rest for a day or two, McPherson gave him news that dispelled this notion. General Johnston had the previous day sent an order to Pemberton, dispatching it via three messengers. One of the couriers was widely known as a fire-eating Rebel civilian whom the Union authorities had expelled from Memphis some months earlier for making public statements threatening and disloyal to the Union. His expulsion and subsequent flight into Confederate-held territory had received considerable publicity. Actually the man was an undercover Federal agent, and the whole affair had been stage-managed. He became a trusted Confederate mes-

senger, and when Johnston sent him with orders to Pemberton, he took them first to McPherson. Thus the latter had the order before Pemberton, and showed it to Grant.

Grant eagerly grabbed the message. It directed Pemberton to proceed to Clinton and strike at Grant's rear. Johnston would try to unite with him there. Grant knew that Johnston's force was retreating to the northeast, but Pemberton did not. Presumably Pemberton would obey orders and should soon be setting out for Clinton.

Grant decided to concentrate at Bolton, the nearest point where Johnston could swing around and effect a junction with Pemberton. He told McPherson to march at earliest dawn and sent a courier to McClernand. After giving the tidings of the fall of Jackson, Grant ordered McClernand to "turn all your forces toward Bolton Station, and make all dispatch

Destruction of Confederate property in Jackson, one of the few towns in Mississippi. Drawing by Theodore R. Davis. (HW)

in getting there. Move troops by the most direct road from wherever they may be on receipt of this order."

One can only stand amazed at Grant's ability. The Confederates did not concentrate at Bolton or Clinton, which would have been their best move, so no battle was fought there. Had they done so, however, Grant would have fought them on at least equal terms—with his fresh troops in the forefront.

Grant told Sherman to occupy the rifle-pits around Jackson, and to destroy the railroad tracks in and about Jackson, and all the property belonging to the enemy. The conference then adjourned, and Grant retired for the night to sleep in the bed Johnston had occupied the night before.

BY 10 A.M. on May 15 all of McPherson's corps had gone and Sherman was ready to begin the destruction. The chief purpose was to eliminate Jackson as a communication center, since Grant did not have enough troops to leave an occupying force. Sherman therefore started with the railroads. He would line a regiment up in single file parallel to the tracks. At a given signal everybody would bend over, grab a tie, and heave, thus turning up on edge a section of track equal in length to the regiment. The men then piled up the ties, placed the rails on top of the pile, and started a fire. When the iron was cherry red in the middle, teams of brawny soldiers would grab the ends and twist the rails around a convenient tree. The results were called "Sherman's neckties."

Sherman burned all the factories in the town, many of the public buildings, and some private ones. His men found a supply of rum; the inevitable result was indiscriminate burning, against which Sherman protested bitterly.

During the morning Grant and Sherman visited a large textile factory. The plant manager and the employees, most of them women, simply ignored the presence of the two generals and went on working. The looms were producing tent cloth with C.S.A. woven into each bolt. Grant meditated on this industrious scene for a few minutes, then turned to Sherman and suggested that the girls had done work enough. Sherman told the girls they could leave, taking with them all the cloth they could carry. He then burned the factory.

BATTLE OF CHAMPION HILL
(Maps 9, 10, 11)

Sherman spent the night of May 15-16 in Jackson, marching for Bolton on the 16th. The Confederates re-occupied Jackson but the Union mission had been accomplished. Jackson was now worthless as a transportation center, her war industries were crushed, and the Confederate concentration that had

aimed at saving Fortress Vicksburg was scattered to the winds. And Grant, now well concentrated, was marching due west towards Vicksburg.

Pemberton, meanwhile, had finally started to move. He had so far committed the inexcusable blunder of doing nothing. When he received Johnston's order to strike Grant's rear at Clinton, Pemberton held a council of war. There, incredibly, he raised with his commanders the question, "Should we obey the theater commander's order?" A heated discussion followed. A majority voiced a desire to march to the southeast and destroy Grant's trains and the two divisions guarding them. Pemberton himself wished to hold the line of the Big Black, repulse the Federals, and then counterattack. Sensing the mood of his generals and soldiers, Pemberton announced he would ignore Johnston and strike out for Auburn and cut Grant's supply line.

The next morning, May 15, Pemberton set out. The rains, however, had swollen Bakers Creek, and

at the Raymond crossing the stream was unfordable. The Confederates spent most of the afternoon in waiting for the water to subside. Pemberton finally turned northeast and marched his troops into the main Vicksburg-Jackson road, where a bridge crossed the creek. They then marched eastward, turned into a plantation road, and after a seven-mile detour, the head of the column was back on the Raymond road. It was after midnight before the rear brigades had crossed Bakers Creek. When the army camped the troops lay down where they halted. Six miles separated the vanguard from the rear guard.

EARLY the next morning, May 16, Pemberton received a later order from Johnston, one written after the fall of Jackson. Again Johnston wished to attempt to unite the forces at Clinton. This time Pemberton decided he would do as ordered; he sent a message to that effect to Johnston.

Grant, meanwhile, had McPherson and McClern-

and converging on Champion Hill. The two contending armies were unaware on the night of May 15-16 that they were camped within four miles of each other. At 5 a.m. two railroaders reported to Grant that Pemberton was at Edwards' Station preparing to move east. His force was estimated at 25,000 men.

Grant's first thoughts were to get up reinforcements. He had planned to leave Sherman in Jackson for two days, in order to complete the destruction of the city. Now he sent orders to Sherman to move as soon as possible westward, and to put one division with an ammunition train on the road immediately. Sherman was to tell the division commander to march with all possible speed until he reached the rear of McPherson's corps.

The Battle of Champion Hill, the chief engagement in the Vicksburg Campaign. From a sketch drawn by a Union officer. (FL)

IN sharp contrast to the way in which orders were acted upon in the Confederate army, Sherman had a division on the road within an hour, and his other division was soon out of Jackson. A. J. Smith's and Blair's divisions on the 15th had marched from Auburn to Raymond. Passing out of Raymond, they had advanced a short distance up the Edwards road and had camped. Hovey's division of McPherson's corps had marched westward from Clinton. A clean-shaven politician from Indiana who had received a promotion for his good work at Shiloh, Hovey had spent the night at Bolton. McClernand sent Hovey forward, while Grant, who was preparing to ride forward from Clinton, sent a message to McPherson to clear his wagons from the road and follow Hovey as closely as possible. McClernand had two roads available for his four remaining divisions; Grant told him to move on the enemy by both, but cautiously and with skirmishers to the front to feel for the enemy.

A. J. Smith, leading McClernand's advance on the southernmost road, was the first to encounter the enemy's pickets. Shortly thereafter, Osterhaus, spear-heading McClernand's column on the middle road, and later yet, on the Vicksburg-Jackson road, bumped into the Rebels. McPherson, hearing the scattered fire, tried to hurry his men forward, but Hovey's wagons were occupying the road and delayed the advance. McPherson sent word back to Grant at Clinton, describing the situation. Grant immediately mounted his horse and rode forward. In a short time he had got the wagons off the road and cleared the way for McPherson. By then, too, Hovey's skirmishing had increased in intensity, and now amounted almost to a battle.

CHAMPION HILL,* Pemberton's accidental choice of a battlefield, was well suited to the defense. One of the highest points in the region, it commanded all the ground to the north and southwest. The position would be especially formidable against attack by columns advancing via the Raymond and Middle roads. As contact was made early with General McClernand's columns advancing via these roads, Pemberton concentrated his troops along the ridge extending to the southwest and commanding Jackson Creek. To reach the Confederates' main line of resistance, McClernand's troops would have to deploy and advance across fields commanded by Pemberton's artillery.

---

*The owners of the property prefer this usage to the usual form, Champion's Hill. Incidentally, if Pemberton had got across Bakers Creek farther south, he would not have disrupted Grant's movements but would have saved his army. Grant was moving straight west and was inclined to let Pemberton get away if he could capture Vicksburg cheaply.

The following quote is from "A Child at the Siege of Vicksburg," by William W. Lord, as it appeared in "Harper's Magazine," December 1908:

A bombshell burst in the very center of that pretty dining-room, blowing out the roof and one side, crushing the well-spread tea table like an eggshell, and making a great yawning hole in the floor, into which disappeared supper, china, furniture, and the safe containing our entire stock of butter and eggs.

It was not until midmorning that Pemberton and his generals learned of Hovey's approach. To meet this threat to their left, the Confederates rushed several brigades to hold the ridge extending northwestward from the crest of Champion Hill. Fronting this ridge were several ravines which ran north, then westerly, terminating at Bakers Creek. These ravines were overgrown with trees and underbrush. The weakness of this position was its length. So long as Pemberton was compelled by the presence of McClernand's troops on the Raymond and Middle roads to keep one half of his army posted on the ridges west of Jackson Creek, he would be unable to commit sufficient troops to hold the entire ridge overlooking Bakers Creek. Thus Pemberton's left flank rested in the air.

AS THE two armies confronted each other the stage was seemingly set for the climax of the campaign. After months (indeed, almost a year) of maneuvering in the west, the two major forces stood directly opposite each other. Pemberton had his troops on the field well in hand, but before the day was over he undoubtedly would wish that he had with him the two divisions he had left to hold the Vicksburg area, when he marched out to battle Grant. Pemberton's total strength on the field was about 23,000, opposed to Grant's 32,000.

To the winner of the battle that followed would go the final victory in the campaign for the Mississippi River. Champion Hill is thus, at first blush, one of the decisive battles of the Civil War.

Such a view of Champion Hill is superficial.

While Grant, through superior strategy and maneuvering ability, had gained a distinct advantage by splitting Pemberton and Johnston, all could be lost if he were defeated at Champion Hill. At this time Grant was deep in hostile country with a formidable force under Pemberton to his front and Johnston's rapidly growing army in his rear. By the 15th Johnston's scattered brigades outnumbered Sherman's two divisions at Jackson. In addition, there were two fresh Rebel divisions in Vicksburg, which on the morning of the 16th were as close to Champion Hill as Sherman. Grant, like Lee at Gettysburg, had to carry his ammunition with him. A two days' battle would have exhausted his supply of artillery ammunition.

If Grant were checked at Champion Hill, he would have to pause to regroup, and this would have allowed the Confederates to bring up fresh troops. The next battle would have found many of his batteries with nearly empty caissons. If Grant should decide to turn aside following a repulse at Champion Hill, he would either have to head for Grand Gulf or the Yazoo. Such a march would expose his flanks to Confederate attack.

As for the approach of Sherman's corps, it would have had little effect if Grant had been routed. Sherman's troops did not reach the Bolton area until long after dark on the 16th. The officers had pushed the men hard, and thousands had straggled. Some regiments in Tuttle's division melted to company strength. A thorough examination of diaries and journals offers convincing evidence that it would have been late on the 17th before Sherman's two divisions could have effectively interfered at Champion Hill.

WHEN the battle opened, Pemberton's men, who had been marching and constructing earthworks for the past two weeks, were tired but eager to come to grips with the Yankees. McPherson's, on the other hand, had been marching and fighting for more than eight straight days. McClernand's were not quite so hard pressed, but they too had done their share of tramping over the countryside. Sherman's, coming up in reserve, had done more marching than either of the others. In addition, the Union troops had been living on hardtack, fresh meat, and coffee for over a week. When the day ended, however, it was the Confederates who were exhausted, the Yankees who were ready for more. Grant's winter campaign to make the men work, in order to get into peak physical condition, had paid off.

As soon as Grant had cleared the road for McPherson he sent word to McClernand to push forward and attack. "These orders were repeated several times," Grant later recalled, "without apparently expediting McClernand's advance." The main weight of the battle therefore fell on Hovey and Logan.

Grant's criticism of McClernand may have been colored by personal feelings. It was about 2:30 before McClernand received the orders. He then issued instructions for his division commanders "to attack the enemy vigorously and press for victory." It was the division commanders who really failed to push the attack. Grant gives full credit to Hovey, whose division was, after all, a part of McClernand's corps. If McClernand is to be blamed for the failure of his

other division commanders, he should in all justice receive part of the praise heaped on Hovey.

By 10:30 Hovey's and Logan's divisions advanced to attack the Confederate left. Hovey on the left at 11:30 charged up out of a hollow and wrested from the Confederates a battery posted on the crest of the salient angle. (Brigadier General Alfred Cumming's Georgia brigade opposed Hovey's advance.) Pushing on, Hovey's men captured a second battery at the crossroads. Logan's division in the meantime was locked in a savage contest with S. D. Lee's Alabamians. On the extreme Union right, a brigade led by John Stevenson turned Pemberton's left, held by Seth Barton's Georgians, and captured two batteries. By 1:30 Pemberton's left had been mauled and hurled back almost a half mile with the loss of sixteen guns and several thousand prisoners.

THE Rebels of Bowen's division counterattacked with great dash and elan. Most of Pemberton's troops had stood helplessly by the past couple of weeks while Grant marched all through Mississippi, or so it seemed; now, unleashed, they fought as only men in a desperate situation can fight. At one point in the battle Colonel Francis Cockrell, commanding a Confederate brigade, led a charge holding his reins and a large magnolia flower in one hand while he brandished his sword with the other. The men followed, shouting gleefully.

The result of these attacks was to drive Hovey back, and he had to relinquish his captured guns. For the rest of the day the battle on Champion Hill raged, increasing in intensity. Hovey sent out innumerable pleas for reinforcements; he lost nearly one-third of his division. Hovey later called Champion Hill "a hill of death," and added that "I never saw fighting like this."

Grant did what he could to help. Crocker's division of McPherson's corps arrived just as it seemed that Bowen's Missourians and Arkansans would destroy Hovey's division and capture Grant's ordnance trains parked near the Champion house. Grant rushed one brigade into the breach torn in the Union line by the onrushing Rebels and bolstered Logan with a second. Hovey meanwhile got three batteries in action where they enfiladed Bowen's advancing lines.

THE advance by John Stevenson's brigade of Logan's division had carried it to a position from which, if he made a direct forward movement over open fields, he could get directly in Pemberton's rear and eliminate all possibility of escape. He did slide forward a little and got near the road leading down to Bakers Creek. Grant, who had been with Hovey, rode up, but neither he nor Logan realized the significance of Stevenson's position. Just at that

The Battle of Black River. Drawing by Theodore R. Davis. (HW)

moment a messenger arrived from Hovey with another plea for reinforcements—Pemberton had reinforced Carter Stevenson on Champion Hill after noting McClernand's disinclination to attack. Grant told Logan to rush John Stevenson to Hovey's aid, which uncovered Pemberton's line of retreat. Years later Grant admitted, "Had I known the ground as I did afterwards, I cannot see how Pemberton could have escaped with any organized force."

With Crocker moving into the breach the Confederate position on Champion Hill began to crumble. McClernand, meanwhile, had started to increase the pressure on the Confederate right. At the same time another brigade (Ransom's, of McPherson's corps), which had crossed the river at Grand Gulf a few days before, came up on the Rebel's right.

BY 4 P.M. Pemberton decided to withdraw. He had lost nearly 4,300 men, while inflicting on Grant losses of 2,400. As in all previous engagements the Confederate enlisted men had fought well, and the regimental and brigade commanders, along with one division commander, Bowen, had done good work. At the higher level dissension and incompetence had spoiled the effort. Early in the battle one division commander, Loring, said he would "be willing for Pemberton to lose a battle provided that he would be displaced," and Loring and other generals openly laughed at Pemberton's orders. Another Confederate officer said Pemberton was "to all appearances—so far as my judgment could determine—as helpless and undecided as a child."

Pemberton left Loring to cover the retreat. The withdrawal began smoothly enough, but soon took on the aspects of a rout. Organization was lost, men fled for Vicksburg's fortifications as individuals, officers galloped about frantically trying to find their units, while artillerists looked for their guns. One Confederate officer confessed that what he saw on Champion Hill "made it look like what I have read of Bull Run," and the dispirited soldiers chattered wildly that the Yankee-born Pemberton "has sold Vicksburg."

Carr drove across Bakers Creek, swung to the southwest, and was able to shell the Raymond road, along which Loring's division would have to pass if it were to rejoin Pemberton. Finding the Federals on his flank and rear, Loring drifted off to the southeast, made a forced march to Crystal Springs, during which his men abandoned their cannon and supply wagons, and finally moved north to join Johnston at Jackson.

ACTION AT BIG BLACK
(Map 12)

Pemberton rode through the already prepared breastworks guarding the Big Black and sent a fresh brigade in to man the works. He left instructions to move all the wagons to the left bank and to clear the roads for the passage of the defeated army. Then, thoroughly exhausted, he crossed the river with his staff, established his headquarters at Bovina, and settled down for a night's rest.

The men of Carter Stevenson's division were the first to reach the river; after their day with Hovey and Logan they were much too weary to do more fighting and they crossed the river. When they reached Bovina, Stevenson let the men flop down beside the road. They were instantly asleep.

Bowen's division came next. One of Pemberton's aides told him to defend the bridgehead until the whole force, including Loring's division (whose position was unknown to the Confederate main force) was across the river. Bowen's men, bone-tired and almost out of ammunition, were still—like their commander—of sound spirit. They filed into the trenches to extend the line.

AT THE same time, Sherman was on the road from Jackson to Bolton. He reached the Bolton area at 2 a.m. on the 17th; after four hours' rest he had the men on the road again, taking a route north of that followed by Grant's other two corps. Grant's idea was to send Sherman around to the left of the Confederate line, then have him swoop in behind Pemberton and keep him from getting back to Vicksburg. McPherson and McClernand would pursue the Confederates by the direct road to Vicksburg.

Grant's advance division, Eugene Carr's of Mc-Clernand's corps, began the pursuit at 3:30 a.m. (staff work in the Yankee divisions was outstanding, as was discipline; almost every day of the campaign the men were in full march when the sun rose). Shortly after daybreak they bumped into the main Confederate position. The east bank, where the Confederates were drawn up, was low bottom-land, with a bayou running irregularly across its front. The bayou was grown up with timber, which the Rebels had felled into the ditch, and there was a foot or two of water in it. The position was naturally strong; it had been strengthened by using cotton bales and throwing dirt over them to make breastworks. Carr came up almost on the exact center of Bowen's line; his left brigade (Benton's) anchored its left near the railroad, while his right brigade, under Michael Lawler, occupied the woods between Benton's right and the river, which at this point flows from east to west.

IF May 16 and Champion Hill belonged to Hovey and Logan, May 17 and the Battle of the Big Black was Lawler's. A mountainous man, weighing over 250 pounds, he fought in his shirt sleeves and sweated profusely. So huge was Lawler that he could not make a swordbelt go properly about his waist and wore his sword suspended by a strap from one shoulder. Grant once said of him, "When it comes to just plain hard fighting I would rather trust old Mike Lawler than any of them." A native of County Kildare, Ireland, Lawler was a veteran of Winfield Scott's advance from Vera Cruz to Mexico City. Lawler and his regiment had been mustered into service by U. S. Grant, then a captain serving on the

staff of the Adjutant General of Illinois. He enforced discipline in his young heroes by knocking down recalcitrants with his fists, feeding emetic to drunks in the guardhouse, and by threats of violence to officers and men alike.

This morning Lawler moved his brigade through the woods to within 400 yards of the enemy line. There, next to the river, was a meander scar, a scar deep enough to hide his brigade. From it he could launch a short, quick assault on the Confederate left center. To get to it, however, he would have to cross an open field exposed to fire from some detached rifle pits. Lawler did not hesitate. Leaving one regiment behind to protect his artillery, he dashed across at the head of the other three. Losing only two men, he was now safe and snug almost within a stone's throw of the Southern works. Lawler, after calling up the regiment left to protect the artillery, massed his four regiments in columns of battalions, with the brigades on a two-regiment front so that his attack would be a narrow battering ram rather than spread out in the usual manner. He told the men not to bother to fire, but to keep moving forward until they reached the enemy parapet. When his preparations were complete, he had the regimental commanders order "Fix bayonets." Pouring sweat, he heaved his great bulk up on his horse, jammed the animal in the flank with his heels, leaned forward to help his horse clear the scar, and bellowed "Forward!"

The regiments roared out of their shelter and ran toward the Confederate line. The dumbfounded Rebels barely had time to get off one volley before the assault column hit them. The charge was one of the shortest of the Civil War—it lasted just three minutes.

Completely outmanned, with bayonets and the stocks of muskets raining down on their heads, the Rebels fled. Lawler had broken the entire Confederate line south as far as the railroad. All along that line Rebels were scampering to the rear, desperate to get across the river before they were cut off.

The Indiana regiments and the Illinois units came over the barricade north of the railroad and captured a gun. Private James S. Adkins of the 33d Illinois, exhilarated by the bloodless victory, leaped astride the gun tube, waved his elbows up and down at his sides, and crowed like a rooster. Then, curious, he tugged at the lanyard. The gun went off, hurling a shell close over the heads of the units coming up in support, and bucking Adkins head over heels into the dirt. Miraculously, no one was hurt.

GRANT was near the middle of the Union line. Shortly before the charge began, a staff officer rode up and gave him a letter of May 11 from Halleck. In it the General in Chief ordered Grant to return to Grand Gulf and to co-operate from there with

Banks against Port Hudson, then return with the combined force to besiege Vicksburg. Grant quietly told the officer that the order came too late. Grant had served under Halleck before, and he realized that the General in Chief would not have given him the order if he had known Grant's position. The officer insisted that Grant had to obey, and was increasing the intensity of his argument when the sounds of an attack broke forth. Grant later described what happened: "Looking in that direction, I saw Lawler in his shirt sleeves leading a charge upon the enemy. I immediately mounted my horse and rode in the direction of the charge, and saw no more of the officer who had delivered the dispatch."

The Confederates on the west bank, before all the retreating men got across, fired the turpentine-soaked railroad bridge and the steamer *Dot*. Pemberton had ridden up from Bovina; he took one look and immediately decided against making a further stand along the Big Black. He just had too few men to prevent the Union troops from crossing. Sadly he ordered his division to withdraw the twelve miles to Vicksburg. Riding back to Bovina with a staff officer, he morosely muttered, "Just thirty years ago I began my cadetship at the U. S. Military Academy. Today, the same date, that career is ended in disaster and disgrace."

Grant's men spent the rest of the day (Lawler's charge ended at 11 a.m.) cleaning up the battlefield and building bridges over the Big Black. They had

★ ★ ★

Ruins of the Civil War railway bridge across the Big Black River under the present-day bridge. (Photo by Margie Bearss.)

captured 1,752 prisoners, 18 cannon, 1,421 stand of small arms, and 5 battle flags, at a cost of 39 killed and 237 wounded. The bridge building, as always in Grant's army, was superb. McPherson himself directed the construction of one of the four. He used bales of cotton to make a pontoon bridge. General Ransom supervised the building of another. He had trees felled on opposite banks of the river, dropped them into the water so that their tops interlaced. Taking lumber from nearby buildings, he then laid a roadway across the trees. Working through the night, the army had four serviceable bridges ready on the morning of May 18.

GRANT'S PINCERS CLOSE ON VICKSBURG

That morning Grant sent his three corps forward, McClernand's on the road paralleling the railroad, and McPherson's and Sherman's along the Bridgeport road. About three miles northeast of Vicksburg, Grant, who had pushed ahead, overtook Sherman's vanguard and turned it into the Graveyard road while a staff officer was left to point out the route McPherson was to take—the Jackson road. As the three corps approached the city, McClernand's would be on the left, McPherson's in the center, and Sherman's on the right.

By late afternoon on the 18th, Sherman's advance was in contact with Confederates posted on the ridge fronting Vicksburg defenses. Before darkness put a stop to the fighting, Sherman had discovered a road branching off from the Graveyard road and leading toward the Yazoo. Steele's division was turned into this road. Under the cover of darkness, Pemberton recalled the troops that had been contesting Sherman's approach, and they took position alongside their comrades on the earthworks extending from Fort Hill to Stockade Redan.

STEELE'S division early on May 19 resumed its advance. Grant and Sherman soon joined Steele. Grant was anxious to secure a base of supplies on the Yazoo above Vicksburg and Steele was headed straight toward Walnut Hills—the Confederate defensive position which Sherman had tried unsuccessfully to carry the previous December. So impatient were Grant and Sherman that they moved past the advance column and were riding well up with the advanced skirmishers. The enemy still occupied some detached works along the crest of the hill, although Pemberton had already decided to shorten his lines, and made no serious attempt to hold Walnut Hills. Shots rang out, and minie balls

A Federal's Recollection Of Vicksburg

Colonel Manning Force of the 20th Ohio Regiment, told of his experiences during the Vicksburg Campaign in an address in 1885 before the Ohio Commandery of the Loyal Legion. Following are excerpts from his address.

ON APRIL 25, Logan's division marched. The 20th Ohio had just drawn new clothing, but had to leave it behind. Stacking spades and picks in the swamp, the troops took their places in the column as it appeared, taking with them only the scanty supplies they had there. Six days of plodding brought them over nearly 70 miles to the shore of the river opposite Bruinsburg. I find in one of my letters: "We marched 6 miles one day, and those 6 miles, by evening, were strewn with wagon wrecks and their loads, and half-buried guns. At a halt of some hours, the men stood in deep mud, for want of any means of sitting. Yet when we halted at night, every man answered to his name and went laughing to bed on the sloppy ground."

Troops were ferried across the river to a narrow strip of bottom land which intervened between the river and the lofty-precipitous bluff. A roadway, walled in with high vertical banks, cut through the bluff, led from the river bottom up to the table land above. A small force could have held this pass against an army; but it was left unguarded, and the army marched up.

A Regiment in the Battle of Raymond
ON THE 12TH OF MAY, the 17th Corps marched on the road toward Raymond, Logan's division leading, Dennis' brigade in advance. The 30th Illinois was deployed with a skirmish line in front, on the left of the road, the 20th Ohio in like manner on the right. About noon we halted; the 20th Ohio in an open field, bounded by a fence to the front, beyond which was forest and rising ground. An unseen battery on some heights beyond the timber began shelling the woods. The 1st Brigade came up and formed on our right.

All at once the woods rang with the shrill Rebel yell and a deafening din of musketry. The 20th rushed forward to a creek and used the farther bank as a breastworks. The timber between the creek and the fence was free from undergrowth. The 20th Illinois, the regiment next in line to the 20th Ohio, knelt down in place and returned the fire. The enemy advanced into the creek in its front. I went to the lieutenant colonel, who was kneeling at the left flank, and asked him why he did not advance into the creek. He said, "We have no orders." In a few minutes the colonel of the regiment was killed. It was too late to advance, it was murder to remain; and the lieutenant colonel withdrew the regiment in order behind the fence. I cannot tell how long the battle lasted. I remember noticing the forest leaves, cut by falling rifle balls, in thick eddies, still as snowflakes. At one time the enemy in our front advanced to the border of the creek, and rifles of opposing lines crossed while firing. Men who were shot were burned by the powder of the rifles that sped the balls.

IN TIME the fire in front slackened. We ceased firing and advanced. The ground rose into a hill beyond the creek; dead and wounded were found there where they had fallen or crawled behind trees and logs. We emerged into open ground upon a hilltop, and were greeted by cheers of the brigade below at the crossing of the creek. The enemy was in retreat. A battery covering its retreat fired upon us. I made the men lie down behind a ridge, and the exploding shells sprinkled them with earth while the 1st sergeants were making out reports of casualties. Notwithstanding the admirable protection of the bank of the creek, 20 percent of the regiment were killed or wounded.

Soon the column advanced. We fell into place when it came up, and were halted on the hither side of Raymond. In a few minutes the earth was sparkling with fires, over which coffee was making in tin cups, and little chunks of salt pork were boiling. The sweet savor told that supper was nearly ready, when orders came to march through the town and go on picket on the farther side. Every man picked up his smoking cup, and the stick which bore his sizzling bit of salt pork, and we incensed the town with the savory odor as we marched through.

The 20th Ohio at Champion Hill
Champion Hill is a considerable eminence about a mile across from east to west. It is steep; its sides are roughened by knobs, gullied by ravines, and covered with forests. Low, flat land encircles the north and west faces. Hovey, following the road, attacked the northeast face; Logan's division, following, debouched upon the low land north of the hill. The 20th Ohio, being in advance, deployed, marched near to the base of the hill, and lay down to wait until successive regiments should arrive and form the line. A part of the enemy's forces, high upon the hill, kept up a dropping fire, and every few minutes a soldier would rise, bleeding, and be ordered back to the hospital to have his wounds dressed. There was in front of the line a very large and tall stump. The adjutant, Bryant Walker, and I, sending our horses away, stood behind this stump and observed that its shelter made a species of shadow of the fire. We found we could pace to and fro 50 yards, keeping in line with the stump; and while the rifle balls rattled against the stump and whistled through the air, we were shielded.

By the time the line was formed, a hostile line advanced from the timber at the base of the hill to confront us. We charged, pushed them into the timber and up the slope, and took position in a ravine parallel with a ravine in which the enemy had halted in our front. The firing was very heavy.

McPherson kept extending his line to his right, till Pemberton's line of retreat was endangered, and his army, abandoning the field, pushed in disorder for Vicksburg.

Rations Were Short
In 18 days Grant had marched 200 miles, won five battles, four of them in six days, inflicted a loss of 5,000 killed, wounded, and missing, captured 88 pieces of artillery, compelled the abandonment of all outworks, and cooped Pemberton's army within the lines of Vicksburg; while he had opened easy and safe communications with the North. During these 18 days the men had been without shelter, and had subsisted on 5 days' rations and scanty supplies picked along the way. The morning we crossed the Big Black I offered five dollars for a small piece of corn bread and could not get it. The soldier said the bread was worth more to him than money.

Life in the Trenches
On May 22 the 20th Ohio moved in support of the 1st Brigade of Logan's division. The brigade reached the base of an earthwork, too high and steep to be scaled, and could neither advance nor retreat. The 20th was placed in a road-cut which was enfiladed by one of the enemy's infantry intrenchments. But by sitting with our backs pressed against the side of the cut toward

Vicksburg, the balls whistled by just outside our knees. At sunset the company cooks came to us with hot coffee. They succeeded in running the gantlet, and the garrison could hear the jingling of tincups and shouts of laughter as the cramped men ate their supper.

After dark we were recalled and placed on the slope of a sharp ridge, with orders to remain in place, ready to move at any moment, and with strict injunction not to allow any man's head to appear above the ridge. There we lay two or three days in line. Coffee was brought to us at meal times. Not a man, those two or three days, left the line without special order. The first night Lieutenant Weatherby, commanding the right company, reported that the slope was so steep where he was that the men, as soon as they fell asleep, began to roll down hill. I had to give him leave to shift his position.

WHEN lying there, it sometimes occurred to me, what a transformation it was for these men, full of individuality and self-reliance, accustomed always to act upon their own will, to so completely subordinate their wills to the will of other men, many of them their neighbors and friends at home. But their practical sense told them that an army differs from a mob only in discipline, and discipline was necessary for their self-preservation. They had also perceived that military obedience is a duty enjoined by law, and in obeying orders, they were obeying the law.

One day when there was a general bombardment, I was told a soldier wished to see me. Under the canopy of exploding shell I found a youth lying on his back on the ground. He was pale and speechless—there was a crimson hole in his chest. As I knelt by his side, he looked wistfully at me. I said: "We must all die some time and the man who meets his death in the discharge of duty is happy." A smile flickered on his lips, and I was kneeling beside a corpse.

Fraternization

At night it was common practice for the pickets on both sides to advance unharmed, and sitting together on the ground between the lines pass the night in chat, banter, and high discussion. A watch was always left in the lines, and when an officer of either side came along on his tour, warning was given, the conference ceased, and the men on both sides slipped back to their places. When day came, work was resumed.

General Leggett was transferred to command the 1st Brigade, and I was assigned to his vacated place. The saps were made wide and deep enough for the passage of artillery, and batteries were constructed near the besieged works. General Ransom had a battery so close that the embrasures were kept covered by mantlets. A gun would be loaded and pointed, and then fired just as the mantlet was removed. The first time a gun was fired from it, a storm of rifle balls poured through the embrasure. A gunner jumped on the gun and shouted back, "Too late!"

When the working parties carried the saps to the base of the works, the besieged used to light the fuses of 6-pound shells, and toss them over the parapet. They would roll down among the working parties and explode, sometimes doing serious damage. A young soldier of Company C, 20th Ohio, named Friend, on detached service in the division pioneer corps, devised wooden mortars. A very small charge of powder in one of these would just lift a shell over the enemy's parapet and drop it within. After the surrender, there was much inquiry from the garrison how they were contrived.

whistled past the generals' ears. Ignoring them, Grant and Sherman rode to the crest of the ridge.

Sitting there on their horses, they took possession of the most important single piece of real estate in the Confederate States of America. As long as Pemberton held that chain of hills no Union force could approach Vicksburg from the upper Mississippi. For a year and a half the western armies of the United States had concentrated their effort on gaining control of these few square miles. As Sherman and Grant watched the men spread out over the heights, they felt the most intense satisfaction. Grant could now reopen his communications with the north, receive supplies and reinforcements, and conclude the campaign.

Sherman turned to Grant and said, quietly, that up to this moment he had felt no positive assurance of success. Now he realized that this was the end of one of the greatest campaigns in history. Vicksburg was not yet captured, and much might still happen, but whether captured or not, the campaign was a complete success.

Johnston agreed. He telegraphed Pemberton to cut his losses and get out. "If Haynes' Bluff be untenable Vicksburg is of no value and cannot be held," Johnston wrote. "If therefore you are invested in Vicksburg you must ultimately surrender. Under such circumstances, instead of losing both troops and place you must if possible save the troops. If it is not too late, evacuate Vicksburg and its dependencies and march to the northeast."

Pemberton held a council of war, which concluded that it was impossible to withdraw—a strange conclusion, considering that McClernand's force, on Grant's left, extended only a little south of the Southern Railroad of Mississippi. Pemberton decided to ignore not only Johnston's good advice but, once again, a positive order. When informed of Pemberton's decision, Johnston exhibited remarkable self-restraint—he advised Pemberton to hold out while he attempted to gather a relief force. His labors, however, were in vain.

BY June 4 Johnston had gathered a force of 31,000, and between them he and Pemberton outnumbered Grant. At this time he was notified by the authorities in Richmond that no more reinforcements could be diverted to Mississippi. Instead of boldly seizing the initiative, while the Confederates had numerical advantage, Johnston allowed one of his division commanders to go on leave. Not until June 22, when this officer returned from leave, did Johnston organize his army to take the offensive. At this time, thousands of reinforcements rushed from points as far away as Central Kentucky and Rolla, Missouri, had reported to Grant. The Federals now held a decisive

numerical advantage. As time for the Vicksburg defenders ran out, Johnston continued to drag his feet. It was July 1 before he put his troops in motion.

The threat of a move by Johnston against his rear forced Grant to keep forces on the Big Black guarding the crossing. On June 22 when reports, which were later proved untrue, reached Grant that Johnston had forced his way across the Big Black, he rushed additional troops eastward and placed Sherman in charge of a seven-division army. Sherman's task was to smash Johnston should he cross the Big Black.

ASSAULT OF MAY 19
(Map 13)

On the morning of May 19 Grant, figuring that the Confederates were so demoralized by the events of the past two weeks that they would crumble at the first sign of pressure, ordered a general assault. On the left and in the center the Union troops managed to gain some important positions for gun emplacements, but did not even come close to driving the Confederates out of their trenches. Obviously the Rebels could still fight. Sherman, on the right, learned this lesson best.

The key position in the enemy works opposite Sherman was the Stockade Redan complex. He gave Frank Blair's division the job of taking it. The ground in front of the redan was exceedingly rugged, consisting of a ravine covered with timber that Confederate working parties had cut six months earlier. Attempting to charge through this area, the men found it impossible to maintain a line of battle. As the Rebels poured small arms and artillery fire upon

A Union assault on defenses of Vicksburg on May 19, 1863. From a Prang chromolithograph by Swedish artist Thure Thulstrup.

them, they instinctively searched out a place of concealment and stopped there, pinned down.

On Blair's right the 1st Battalion, 13th U. S. Infantry, tried a charge. When the commander called out "Forward!" the Regulars sprang across the hill behind which they had formed. Charging on the double, they passed through a deadly beaten-zone that was being swept by canister and shell. Men began to fall, some killed instantly, others with an arm or leg torn off. Crossing the ravine, the Regulars were caught in a crossfire between the enemy in Stockade Redan and those in the 27th Louisiana Lunette on the left of the stockade.

Color Sergeant James E. Brown was shot through the head and killed. Another soldier instantly picked up the colors, and was immediately shot. In all, five different men were killed or wounded as they sought to carry the colors forward. The Regulars closed to within 25 yards of the Stockade Redan, began to falter, and finally scrambled back for cover behind fallen timber and stumps.

AFTER the battle a count revealed that the flag of the 13th U. S. Infantry had 55 bullet holes in it. The battalion had lost 43 percent of its personnel in the attack. Sherman called its performance "unequaled in the Army" and authorized the regiment to insert "First at Vicksburg" on its colors.

There were other acts of heroism that day. Sherman decided he could not withdraw his corps until it was dark; meanwhile the men fired by volley at any Confederate who stuck his head above the parapet. The Rebels replied by cutting short the fuses of their shells, then rolling them down the hill into the Yankee masses. Occasionally the Union men could catch the shell and throw it back; more often it ripped apart legs and arms.

Late in the afternoon the Yankees discovered they had almost exhausted their ammunition. Volunteers raced through the felled timber to fill boxes and hats with the cartridges rifled from dead and wounded men. Orion P. Howe, a 14-year-old musician in the 55th Illinois, volunteered to go to the rear and order up fresh supplies. While dashing through the timber he caught a minie ball in his leg. Undaunted, he staggered on. At the point of exhaustion he reached General Sherman himself and reported on the critical ammunition shortage. Sherman called for volunteers to lug the heavy boxes of cartridges forward, and every man of the nearby Company C, 12th Iowa, stepped forward. Musician Howe was subsequently awarded the Medal of Honor for his services on that bloody day.

At dark, the Union troops withdrew. Grant's attempt to storm his way into Vicksburg had failed. He had gained some advance artillery emplacements and some good staging areas for use in future attacks, but at a fearful price. He had lost 157 killed, 777 wounded, and 8 missing, as against a total Confederate loss of about 250.

GRANT TRIES AGAIN
(Map 14)

Following the failure on the 19th, Grant could either accept the situation and settle down for a siege operation or he could try another assault. He decided upon the latter course. Both he and his army were rather cocky at this point; five times they had met the Confederates in battle and routed them. The repulse of the 19th was an obvious fluke. The lesson of the campaign seemed to be that when Yankees attacked, Rebels ran. There were other more substantial reasons for another try. Johnston, in Grant's rear, was busily raising a relief force, and Grant wanted to destroy Pemberton's army before Johnston could come to his aid. If Grant could take Vicksburg immediately, he would not have to call upon Halleck for reinforcements and could, in fact, send men to the other theaters of war. Finally, in Grant's own words, "the first consideration of all was—the troops

believed they could carry the works in their front, and would not have worked so patiently in the trenches afterwards if they had not been allowed to try."

The attempt was to cost them dearly. Pemberton's men, given a decent chance, could fight as well as any men on earth. And, in their entrenchments, they were powerfully placed. One of McPherson's staff officers described the position: "A long line of high-rugged, irregular bluffs, clearly cut against the sky, crowned with cannon which peered ominously from embrasures to the right and left as far as the eye could see. Lines of heavy rifle-pits, surmounted with head logs, ran along the bluffs, connecting fort with fort, and filled with veteran infantry." On the slopes in front of the works were felled trees, with their tops interlaced, forming an almost impenetrable abatis. "The approaches to this position were frightful—enough to appall the stoutest heart."

Still Grant—and his men—wanted to try, and on the morning of May 22 they did. Grant had his corps

Inside the Federal lines at Vicksburg, May 22, 1863. From an on-the-scene sketch by battlefield artist F. B. Schell. (FL)

commanders set their watches by his, then called for a simultaneous assault at 10 a.m. The attack would be preceded by a heavy preliminary artillery bombardment. Sherman would aim at the Stockade Redan, McPherson at the stronghold on either side of the Jackson road, McClernand at the defenses flanking the railroad and Baldwin's Ferry road.

Sherman, who had failed in his direct attack across the ravine in front of Stockade Redan on May 19, decided to attack directly down the Graveyard road. He would spearhead his attack with a "forlorn hope," consisting of 150 volunteers. These men, carrying timbers in their hands, would move at the double down the road and fill in the ditch fronting the stockade.

THE attack moved off promptly at 10 a.m. The "forlorn hope" came through a curve in the road at full speed. The road at that point cut through a hill, then turned directly toward the redan. When the "forlorn hope" emerged from the extremely narrow cut they were 150 yards from the enemy and presented a perfect target. The Rebels cut loose, and most of the men were either killed or wounded. The remainder took cover in the ditch in front of the stockade. The 30th Ohio followed, to suffer the same fate. On their heels came the 37th Ohio. When that regiment started to emerge from the cut most of the men took one look and "bugged out," throwing themselves on the ground and refusing to advance farther. This choked the narrow cut, and Sherman's assault ground to an abrupt stop. Sherman made no further attacks that morning, even though only slightly more than 1,000 of his nearly 15,000 men had been engaged. After his experiences of the previous December and of May 19, he had had about enough of assaulting Fortress Vicksburg.

In the center McPherson never got any organized attack going. He put only 7 of his 30 regiments into action, and they all except those of John Stevenson's brigade stopped at the first sign of opposition.

Things went better on the left. McClernand sent

Landing supplies for Grant's army at Chickasaw Bayou on the Yazoo River, north of Vicksburg. Sketch by F. B. Schell. (FL)

Carr, who had the advantage of having Lawler's brigade in his division, storming the 2d Texas Lunette and the Railroad Redoubt. The 99th Illinois carried its flag across the Confederate works at a point 50 yards south of the lunette. Lawler, charging the Railroad Redoubt, drove the 30th Alabama out of its rifle pits and planted several Union colors there. Elsewhere McClernand's men pushed up to, although not through, the Rebel lines.

The enemy was soon able to contain the penetration McClernand's corps had achieved, and the Yankees were unable to do much about it. If Sherman and McPherson were guilty of not making strong enough commitments that morning, McClernand made the mistake of throwing everything he had into the first rush. With no strategic reserve he was unable to exploit his opportunities, and in fact could barely hold what he had gained.

WITH his entire corps engaged, McClernand appealed to Grant to have Sherman and McPherson resume the attack, arguing that he could achieve a breakthrough with more help. Grant thought McClernand was exaggerating his success (or so at least he claimed later), but felt he could not ignore the request and ordered Sherman and McPherson to renew their assaults as a diversion in favor of McClernand. At 3 p.m. Sherman sent Mower's brigade spearheaded by the 11th Missouri charging down the Graveyard road four abreast. As the regiment emerged from the fatal cut in the road it was riddled by Confederate fire. Those Missourians who were not killed dashed forward and took cover in the ditch alongside the survivors of the "forlorn hope" and the 30th Ohio. Sherman suspended the attack.

McPherson launched a half-hearted assault on the 3d Louisiana Redan, which got nowhere.

McClernand, meanwhile, was stuck. He could neither go forward nor disengage. At 5:30 counterattacking Confederates recovered the Railroad Redoubt.

Passing the Buck, *by Col. Manning Force*

ON MAY 3 our brigade found a road leading northeast toward Hankinson's Ferry. When we reached the road I was standing with Generals McPherson, Logan, and Dennis, the corps, division, and brigade commanders, respectively. McPherson said, "General Logan, you will direct General Dennis to send a regiment forward with skirmishers well advanced, rapidly toward the ferry."

General Logan said, "General Dennis, you will send a regiment forward, with skirmishers well advanced, toward the ferry."

General Dennis said, "Colonel Force, you will take your regiment forward with skirmishers well advanced, rapidly toward the ferry."

Finally, at nightfall, McClernand pulled his troops back. He was the only corps commander who really made an effort that day; if Sherman and McPherson had attacked with the same energy, the assault would probably have worked. But they did not, and later they—and Grant—were unduly skeptical about McClernand's penetration, which they claimed was a figment of his imagination. But in fact McClernand did get into the Rebel works and his report to Grant was accurate.

GRANT'S position in this affair is a strange one. If he really intended to try a full-scale assault, he should have been angry with Sherman and McPherson.

In any case Grant, in his report written on May 24, was quite unfair to McClernand. He showed a pettiness most uncharacteristic of the Commanding General. "General McClernand's dispatches misled me as to the real state of the facts," Grant said of the events of May 22, "and caused much of the loss. He is entirely unfit for the position of corps commander, both on the march and on the battlefield. Looking after his corps gives me more labor and infinitely more uneasiness than all the remainder of my department." Assuming that Grant really felt that strongly, that he did not immediately relieve McClernand can only be regarded as amazing. If McClernand was that bad, Grant was extremely derelict in his duty (not to mention his responsibilities to the troops in McClernand's corps) when he kept McClernand in command.

FALL OF McCLERNAND

McClernand smoldered. He was sure that if Mc-Pherson and Sherman—and of course Grant—had properly supported him his corps would be in Vicksburg. He was not, therefore, in a receptive mood when Colonel James Harrison Wilson visited him with an order from Grant directing him to send some troops to watch the crossings of the Big Black.

McClernand read the order, then snapped, "I'll be God-damned if I'll do it. I'm tired of being dictated to—I won't stand it any longer, and you can go back and tell General Grant." He added some more remarks of a similar character, then began to curse West Point generally. Wilson heatedly pointed out that McClernand was not only insulting the commanding general but Wilson himself, as Wilson was an Academy man, and offered to get off his horse and use his fists to get McClernand to apologize. The middle-aged general sized up the colonel in his mid-twenties and muttered, "I was simply expressing my intense vehemence on the subject matter, sir, and I beg your pardon."

Wilson, of course, reported the whole affair at Grant's headquarters, to everyone's great delight. Thereafter whenever anyone was heard using profanity—and it was a hard-cursing headquarters—Grant would laugh and explain, "He's not swearing—he's just expressing his intense vehemence on the subject matter."

McCLERNAND'S end came a couple of weeks later. He wrote an order of congratulations to the XIII Corps which, with some help from his headquarters, got into the papers. This violated a standing War Department regulation to submit such papers to army headquarters before publication; worse, Mc-Clernand had implied in the order that the XIII Corps alone had been responsible for the success of the campaign. Sherman bitterly remarked that the order was really addressed "to a constituency in Illinois," and McPherson said it was designed "to impress the public mind with the magnificent strategy, superior tactics, and brilliant deeds" of McClernand.

Grant asked McClernand if the order as published was genuine. McClernand said it was and he was prepared to stand by it. Grant finally decided to act and on June 18 relieved McClernand, putting E. O. C. Ord in his place.

Following the May 19 assault Grant held a conference with Porter and arranged for some good landing places along the Yazoo for transports and supply ships. He wired Halleck to say he was ready to receive reinforcements and supplies, which the General in Chief immediately began to send.

ONE afternoon a day or so later Grant took a ride along the rear of his fighting lines. Men began to glance at him as his horse moved slowly past. The soldiers generally did not love Ulysses Grant, nor were they awed by him—he was much too matter-of-fact a man to inspire such emotions. Besides, nothing about his personal appearance suggested greatness. The soldiers did respect him as a soldier, and as a man. He was the kind of person who invited honesty and was obviously approachable.

When Grant rode by a soldier who had looked up stared at his commanding general for a moment, then said in a conversational tone, "Hardtack." Other soldiers glanced at Grant and took up the call; soon everyone in the vicinity was yelling "Hardtack! Hardtack!" at the top of his lungs. They were not expressing a deep-rooted hatred of Grant, or anything like that, nor were they blaming him for the bland diet they had been on for the past month. They were saying that they were terribly proud of what they had done, especially considering the conditions under which they had marched and fought, but now the time had come to create a more regular existence. In short, it was time that Grant, who had done so well so far, get them something better to eat than a straight hardtack and meat diet.

Grant reined in and told the soldiers he had made all the arrangements and they would soon have fresh bread and coffee. The men laughed and cheered. The bond between Grant and the Army of the Tennessee had been strengthened.

Grant was very good at this sort of thing. Men in an Illinois regiment remembered that one evening Grant strolled out, sat down by their campfire, and "talked with the boys with less reserve than many a little puppy of a lieutenant." Grant assured the boys that he had everything under control, said that Pemberton was a "northern man who had got into bad company," and insisted that the Union position could be held even if Johnston raised 50,000 men.

THE SIEGE

The siege went forward. Grant's basic plan was to hold on until starvation forced Pemberton to surrender—the classic strategy of siege warfare—but he also wanted to end it as soon as possible, in order to release his troops for other theaters. In addition, the sooner Pemberton surrendered the sooner Grant could turn Sherman loose on Johnston, who had raised a relief expedition.

June, therefore, was an active month. Most of the work was designed to get the Union lines closer to those of the Confederates, so that the next time there was a general assault the troops would not have to cross a quarter-mile or so of rough terrain before reaching the enemy works. Grant had his engineers plan approach trenches and mines (which could be used to blow gaps in the Confederate position), which the men then dug. The whole thing anticipated the more sophisticated trench warfare of the Western Front in World War I.

The only trained engineers in the Army of the Tennessee were the West Point graduates, and most of them were high-ranking officers with other duties. The few full-time engineers discovered, however, that the Western soldiers were handy jacks-of-all-trades who could do almost any thing. One professional engineer declared that in the enormous task of constructing trenches, saps, batteries, and covered ways he could safely rely on the "native good sense and ingenuity" of the common soldier. "Whether a battery was to be constructed by men who had never built one before," he declared, "a saproller made by those who had never heard the name, or a ship's gun carriage to be built, it was done, and after a few trials well done . . . Officers and men had to learn to be engineers while the siege was going on."

AS SOON as Grant established his base on the Yazoo, the General in Chief began to feed him reinforcements. By June 18 Grant's army was up to 77,-000. Pemberton had no more than 30,000, all plagued by illness and malnutrition, and his supply of food and ammunition was strictly limited. Grant's lines ran from the Yazoo to the lowlands along the Mississippi above the city to the banks along the river to the south—twelve miles of camps, trenches, and gun emplacements on the hills and ridges. So tightly did Grant hold the ground that a Confederate defender wrote despairingly, "When the real investments began

a cat could not have crept out of Vicksburg without being discovered." Among other things, this meant nothing—especially no artillery ammunition—got in to Pemberton, so that on top of all their other difficulties his men were forced to endure the constant Yankee artillery bombardment without being allowed to reply in kind. They did, however, have a good supply of powder and minie balls. One Yankee wrote home to say that although the Rebels had not fired a cannon for seven days, at least fifty rifle bullets had whizzed over his head in the last ten minutes.

Taking pot shots at the Union lines was about all the Confederates could do. For the rest of their defense, according to one Yankee officer, was "far from being vigorous." The defenders seemed content to "wait for another assault, losing in the meantime as few men as possible."

THE waiting was hard, both because the Confederates were short of nearly everything and because of the Union bombardment. Food was so short that the citizens of Vicksburg and the soldiers defending it were soon reduced to eating mule meat and pea bread.* Medical supplies were almost non-existent. Water was so scarce that officers posted guards at wells

---

*In my eleven years at Vicksburg it was impossible to find a single primary document telling of eating rats, although statements to that effect appear in some histories. The origin of the rat story is with men of several Louisiana regiments who ate muskrats. Indeed, these men were eating muskrats before the investment.—Edwin C. Bearss

The Bombardment of Vicksburg

That night of the 13th we remained on the boat, which was anchored to trees on the shore. The boom, boom, of the mortar fleet every two minutes, the splash of the water against the sides of the boat, and the shrill saw-file notes of the myriads of insects on the shores kept one's eyes and ears open, so that sleep was almost impossible. The writer, with some others, sat on the bow of the boat till a late hour watching the shells as they fell into Vicksburg. We timed the shells as they left the mortars on their aerial flight, and found that it took about eighteen seconds for them to land in the city. Bombs do not pass so rapidly through the air as do shot or shell from cannon. The shell from the mortar passed at a considerable elevation—sometimes at an angle of forty-five degrees—making a curve like that of a rocket, and could be traced by the fire of the fuse till it exploded or dropped to the ground. When it did not explode in the air, it was easily dodged by an experienced veteran.

Most of the inhabitants of Vicksburg lived under ground during the siege, because the city was situated on bluffs of hard clay; and consequently comfortable rooms could be quite readily excavated. On a visit to the city after its surrender, the writer went into several of these subterranean rooms, and found them fitted up with the best furniture, removed from the houses, where nothing had been safe.

From "History of the Sixth New Hampshire Regiment in the War for the Union," Captain Lyman Jackman, historian, Amos Hadley, Ph.D., Editor. Concord, N. H. Republican Press Association, Railroad Square, 1891.

to make sure none was wasted "for purposes of cleanliness." On top of these privations, the citizens were forced to burrow underground or live in caves to avoid the well-nigh constant shell fire, which came both from Grant's artillery and Porter's fleet.

The ground was well suited to the building of caves, for it consisted of a deep yellow loess of great tenacity. Perpendicular banks cut through the ridges stood as well as if made of stone, and the citizens cut rooms for themselves in the embankments. In some cases two or more rooms were cut out, carpeted, and furnished with tables, chairs, and kitchen equipment.

IN TERMS of some of the sieges of the 20th century, most especially that of Leningrad, conditions inside Vicksburg were not so terrible. They were, however, bad enough—certainly the worst any large group of Americans have ever been asked to undergo. The citizens compiled a proud record. There was some complaining, but no pressure on Pemberton from the city to surrender and end the suffering. The people got by, as people under siege have done since war began, by joking about their condition. They even had a newspaper, which by the end was being printed on the blank side of wallpaper. The citizens of Vicksburg, in short, endured.

← *The Siege of Vicksburg, showing the struggle in the crater of the 3d Louisiana Redan after the explosion of the Federal mine on June 25. The Rebels held the line. By F. B. Schell. (FL)*

136

A July 4th to Remember

MEN in combat frequently are unable to assess the historical significance of the events of which they are a part. At Vicksburg, however, Grant's men knew they were engaged in a momentous undertaking. Because the siege lasted so long they received copies of Northern newspapers on a regular basis and thus knew that they were being talked about all over the world. Most of the men were from the Northwest, and the Mississippi River held a special fascination for them—they spoke and thought of it in almost mystical terms. The opportunity to participate in the campaign to open the Father of Waters was, they knew, a rare one, and few of them doubted that this was the most important thing they would ever do in their lives.

My great-great grandfather, Sergeant Pleasant W. Bishop of the 94th Illinois, expressed this feeling well. On July 4, 1863, early in the morning, he began a letter to his wife and children. "Since yesterday evening," he began, "there has been to some extent a cessation of hostilities between our forces & the rebels." He noted that the pickets had been "together all along the line *shaking hands*, trading pocket knives, exchanging papers, etc., etc." Rumors were flying, but Bishop found it difficult to evaluate them. He found it especially hard to believe that the Rebels were really existing on mule meat. Looking about him, Bishop reported that "the rebs have their white flags floating in many places," and a report had it that one was flying on the court house, "but I have lost all confidence in '*reports*.'"

AT THAT moment Bishop received orders to prepare to march. He broke off his letter, to resume it again on July 6. "Glorious news," he began. "I thank my God that I was permitted to *celebrate* the 4th of July by marching (at the head of Co. I) inside of the fortifications of Vicksburg." He examined the fortifications with a soldier's practiced eye and pronounced them formidable, reported that the mule meat stories were true, and thanked God for His blessings. "I would say that while I rejoice that Vicksburg is ours, it gives me no pleasure to see the destitution and the sufferings of fellow mortals in the rebble army, yet such must be their conditions unless they lay down their arms, and cease to fight against their God by fighting against their country. But I have been looking them over now for two days (feds and confeds being all mixed up together inside of the fortifications) and I find them to be just like people in other parts of the world, some of them are *men of sense* and some are not."

Bishop said the Yankees had been sharing their rations with the Rebels for the past two days, and were glad to do it. In a comment that speaks volumes for the efficiency of the Union high command, he added, "We have always had plenty to spare, for which I feel truly thankful."

THE possibility of an attack by Johnston must have been an active topic of conversation with the troops, for Bishop bragged that "our division inside these fortifications could whip all the Southern Confederacy . . . You can just tell our friends that the rebs' old Whistling Dick (a large gun they call by that name) is ours now, and I think he will whistle a tune they won't like to hear in taking the place."

No attack came, and the North held securely to the city and the river. For Pleasant Bishop, and for thousands like him, that hot afternoon was the greatest 4th of July they would ever celebrate, and the grandest in the nation's history.—Stephen E. Ambrose.

The troops on both sides did the same. On the picket line Johnny Reb and Billy Yank discussed politics, the siege, and philosophy, traded coffee and hardtack for tobacco, and got to know each other. Occasionally they sent personal messages back and forth. Each army contained regiments from Missouri; one day the picket at Stockade Redan agreed to informal short truces. This area, when soldiers in blue and in gray might visit briefly a relative or friend on the other side came to be called "Trysting place."

While the pickets got to know each other, under their very feet Grant's army dug tunnels. The Confederates counter-mined, but without success. Grant exploded the first mine, near the Jackson road, on June 25. The explosion of the mine was a signal for a heavy bombardment all along the line, accompanied by small arms fire. The mine blew off the top of a hill and created a crater into which an assaulting column charged, only to be checked by Confederates posted behind a parapet previously constructed to the rear of the work. A desperate battle ensued for possession of the crater. After twenty hours, Grant had McPherson recall his men, and another mine was commenced. On July 1 this mine was exploded. When this occurred, one of the Negroes who was counter-mining was thrown all the way into the Union lines. When asked how high he had gone, he replied, "Dunno, massa, but t'ink about t'ree miles." General Logan confiscated the Negro, who thereafter worked in his headquarters.

GRANT exploded another mine on July 1, again without significant results. His engineers, meanwhile, had pushed forward everywhere, so much so that at some points only ten yards separated the two forces. Within a week or so Grant would be able to simply overwhelm the defenders, sending his men over the top and into the Confederate lines so fast that the Rebels probably would not even get off a volley. Grant set July 6 as the date for the final rush.

Johnston had plans of his own. On July 1 he finally put his 32,000 men and 78 cannon in motion toward Big Black. He had no illusions about any great victories; he did hope to so distract the Army of the Tennessee that Pemberton could break out.

Pemberton circularized his generals to see if that was possible, asking specifically if their men could stand a battle and a long hard march. Most of the generals thought not. Their men could hold the lines a while longer, but a campaign in the field was impossible. Brigadier General Louis Hébert summed it all up: "Forty-eight days and nights passed in trenches, exposed to the burning sun during the day, the chilly air at night; subject to a murderous storm of balls, shells, and war missiles of all kinds; cramped

The arrival of General Grant at the Rock House just inside the Confederate line on July 4. Here he had a brief conversation with Pemberton, before riding on down the Jackson road to the Warren County Courthouse. The Rock House still stands. Sketch by Theodore R. Davis (BL). Note: Pemberton's headquarters were not at the Rock House, they were at the Willis-Cowan House. It also still stands.

up in pits and holes not large enough to allow them to extend their limbs; laboring day and night; fed on reduced rations of the poorest kinds of food, yet always cheerful . . ." All but one of Pemberton's generals told him it was time to surrender.

SURRENDER

At 10:30 a.m. on July 3, under a flag of truce, two horsemen approached the Union lines. One was a colonel on Pemberton's staff, the other General Bowen, who had fought so ably at Port Gibson and Champion Hill. Bowen was an old friend of Grant's, which may have influenced Pemberton's decision to send him on this mission. The Confederates carried a letter from Pemberton to Grant proposing an armistice and the appointment of commissioners to write a surrender formula. Pemberton knew that Grant wanted to get the whole business over in a hurry, and this knowledge gave him, he felt, bargaining power.

Bowen gave the note to A. J. Smith, who took it to Grant. The Union commander hoped to repeat his triumph at Fort Donelson and at the same time simplify matters, so his reply was short and to the point: "The useless effusion of blood you propose stopping . . . can be ended at any time you may choose, by the unconditional surrender of the city and garrison."

Bowen took the message to Pemberton at 3 p.m. Pemberton, Bowen, and a staff officer rode out. Grant, Ord, McPherson, Logan, and A. J. Smith, accompanied by several of Grant's staff, went forward to meet them. Grant and Pemberton walked away from the main group and had a conference near a stunted oak tree. Pemberton, excited and impatient, asked what terms Grant offered; Grant replied that he had said everything he had to say in his letter. Pemberton replied "rather snappishly" that in that case the conference might as well end immediately. Grant thought so too, and they walked back to mount up. Grant suggested that if he and Pemberton withdrew, per-

haps four of their subordinates (Bowen and Montgomery for the Confederates, McPherson and A. J. Smith for the Union) might be able to work out a satisfactory arrangement. Bowen patched things up, and before parting the two commanders agreed that at ten that night Grant would send another letter through the lines, one containing his final terms.

AT DUSK Grant called a meeting of all the corps and division commanders in the area—the nearest thing he ever had to a council of war. There was much to discuss. Vicksburg was unquestionably doomed—that was not at issue. The attack scheduled for July 6 would certainly be successful. But why pay the price? All Pemberton really wanted was to make sure his men were paroled instead of being sent north to a prison camp. Grant's officers urged him to make a deal, especially since shipping thirty thousand prisoners up the Mississippi would be an intolerable strain on Porter's fleet (something Pemberton already knew, as his intelligence service had intercepted and decoded messages wigwagged back and forth between Porter and Grant). Grant reluctantly agreed to abandon his unconditional surrender formula, and wrote to Pemberton proposing that the Southerners stack their weapons, give their paroles, and then go off to such camps for exchange prisoners as the Confederate authorities might suggest. Pemberton, who hoped that Grant would give generous terms in order to consummate the surrender on the nation's birthday, asked for some other minor concessions. Grant refused, and the deal was finally made.

Grant was later much criticized for allowing the Rebels to make their paroles. The critics contended that all, or most of Pemberton's 30,000 men would soon be fighting again. Grant's reply was that "I knew many of them were tired of war and would get

Interview between Grant and Pemberton to settle upon final terms for the surrender of Vicksburg and the Confederate garrison. (HW)

Entry of Grant's army into Vicksburg on July 4. The Warren County Courthouse is seen in the background. (FL)

Entry of Grant's army into Vicksburg on July 4. The Warren County Courthouse is seen in the background. (FL)

home just as soon as they could." Grant was mistaken, because many of the Confederates were back in ranks by November. A number of Carter L. Stevenson's soldiers were captured at Missionary Ridge, for instance.

ON THE morning of July 4 white flags began to flutter over the Confederate works. Logan's division and Sanborn's brigade were the first units to march into the city. Logan and Sanborn posted guards to keep unauthorized persons from entering or leaving and took charge of the captured people and property.

Sherman immediately moved his corps to the east in order to drive Johnston off. He took time to scribble a note to Grant before departing. "I can hardly contain myself," he exclaimed. "This is a day of Jubilee, a day of rejoicing to the faithful, and I would like to hear the shout of my old and patient troops." But duty called. "Already my orders are out to give one big huzza and sling the knapsack for new fields."

Grant, typically, was more subdued. Greatness can take many forms, assuming one shape with a Douglas MacArthur, another with an Andrew Jackson. It is most appealing, perhaps, when couched in directness and simplicity. At the conclusion of the most momentous and successful campaign on the North American continent, the architect of victory sent the following report to the War Department: "The enemy surrendered this morning. The only terms allowed is their parole as prisoners of war. This I regard as a great advantage to us at this moment. It saves, probably, several days in the capture, and leaves troops and transports ready for immediate service. Sherman, with a large force, moves immediately on Johnston, to drive him from the state."

IN HIS operations during May 1863, Grant used the classic ingredients of military success—surprise, speed, and power: *Surprise* of Pemberton, who could not believe that Grant would move independently of a protected supply line; dazzling *speed* in which his divisions marched upward of 200 miles in two weeks, fighting five battles; and the application of superior *power* at each successive, critical point. As historian Francis V. Greene wrote: "We must go back to the campaigns of Napoleon to find equally brilliant results accomplished in the same space of time with such small loss."

It is true that Pemberton was outclassed. Yet his soldiers, when given the benefit of good leaders such as Bowen and Gregg, fought with their customary skill and elan. As Grant said of them, when negoti-

ating surrender terms with Pemberton, "Men who have shown so much endurance and courage will always challenge the respect of an adversary." Again, he offered a line of thought that does not often occur to our people: Americans do not fight wars to make permanent enemies, but ever strive to convert their ex-foes into allies. Grant suggests this in his statement: "The men had behaved so well that I did not want to humiliate them. I believed that consideration for their feelings would make them less dangerous foes during the continuance of hostilities, and better citizens after the war was over . . . [Therefore]

when they passed out of their works they had so long and so gallantly defended, between the lines of their late antagonists, not a cheer went up, not a remark was made that would give pain."

INSTEAD, individual Yanks shared the food in their haversacks with Johnnies, and Grant ordered his commissary to issue ample rations to Pemberton's troops and to the citizens, both in the city and throughout the countryside recently passed over by the armies.

Tactically and strategically the results of the campaign were among the most decisive of the war. Abraham Lincoln, his cabinet, and the people in the North were enheartened after the previous long months of defeat and discouragement. The Confederacy, after Gettysburg and Vicksburg, never regained the military initiative. From hindsight, perhaps, the final outcome of the war was now inevitable. The commander at Port Hudson, on learning of the fall of Vicksburg, surrendered to General Banks. President Lincoln could now say, "The father of waters rolls unvexed to the sea."

Vicksburg: A Gallery Of Rare Photographs

Top, opposite page—A 7.44-inch Blakely rifle cast at the Low-Moor Iron Works in England and mounted with the Vicksburg River Defenses. In an engagement with the Union fleet on May 22 the Blakely burst and the muzzle was shortened. After the surrender of Vicksburg, the Blakely was turned over to the Federals and emplaced in the Castle Battery, where this photograph was taken. This gun was mistaken by the Federals for Whistling Dick, a rifled 18-pounder. (LC)

Below—Cave dugouts of Illinois troops during the siege of Vicksburg. The Shirley house, a landmark of the siege, is seen in the background. (Photograph from the J. Mack Moore collection, Old Court House Museum, Vicksburg, Mississippi.)

Above—The railroad depot for Vicksburg after the surrender of the town on July 4, 1863. (KA)

Below—The Market House in Vicksburg. The blurred figures seen along the street are Federal soldiers marching by. (LC)

Above—One of the Confederate batteries which defended Vicksburg. Ideally situated for the defense of the city and also virtually impregnable to direct assault, this battery was situated about 200 yards from the Mississippi. A Union encampment can be seen in the background of this photograph which was made soon after the surrender of Pemberton. (KA)

Federal transports along the levee at Vicksburg in February, 1864, seven months after the surrender of the city. (LC)

A Special Portfolio of Maps on the Vicksburg Campaign

The Maps

Except for the map on the next two pages the maps in this special portfolio are adaptations or simplifications by W. S. Nye of a very complete and detailed set prepared by the National Park Service, with troop positions by Edwin C. Bearss. Confederate units and routes are in black, Federals in brown. The small rectangles represent, in most cases, regiments; but except where otherwise labeled, units below brigade are not designated.

The Terrain

The Mississippi River, normally a half-mile wide, narrowed near Fort Hill and Grand Gulf to a quarter of a mile and at these points was 100 feet deep. As the levee system in 1862 was in its infancy, the mighty river frequently flooded the lowlands. The river near Vicksburg does not follow the same course today as it did a century ago, as may be seen by comparison with modern maps. Since the water level is now much lower, most of the tributaries then navigable are no longer so, and some, such as Deer Creek and Steele's Bayou, are now minor creeks. In 1862 Big Black and Bayou Pierre, both navigable, were formidable military obstacles.

The creeks east of the Mississippi were narrow, with steep banks and sandy bottoms and occasionally quicksand. Approaches to the creeks west of the river had to be corduroyed.

The Delta, the expanse bounded on the west by the Mississippi and on the east by the Yazoo and Tallahatchie, was an alluvial plain. The areas within the levees bounding the twisting waterways were the domain of the great planters, who during the Civil War grew more corn, hogs, and cattle than the money crop, cotton. Beyond these cultivated oases were great swamps in which grew cypresses, cottonwoods, Spanish moss, and all types of semi-tropical aquatic vegetation. All this and the numerous alligators greatly impressed the Northern soldiers, as did the mosquitoes and other insect pests.

The Vicksburg Bluffs were part of a limestone and sandstone escarpment that ran from Columbus, Kentucky to Baton Rouge. On this upthrust had been deposited windborne soil called loess, which near the river was 100 feet deep. The loess ridges near Vicksburg are hogbacks, but in most cases were not too steep to be cultivated near and on top. The ravines between were, however, cane brakes and jungles. East of Big Black the loess bluffs give way to a gently rolling tableland covered with a rich deposit of brown loam.

During the Civil War the bluffs and more level region between Big Black and Pearl River were much more heavily populated and cultivated than today, though the chief towns have grown. Vicksburg in 1860 had only 4,600 people, and Jackson 3,200. Both had some industry, including foundries for casting cannon and projectiles. Public buildings and some stores were of brick. The great plantation mansions were in the Southern tradition, while the homes of the poorer farmers were of the "dog-trot" type.

The few roads were all dirt, and after a rain were simply ribbons of mud. Since virtually no stone was to be found, roads and fields were lined with split-rail worm fences.

Snowfall was most infrequent in winter, but January through March was wet. Although the normal annual rainfall was fifty inches, Grant was lucky in having only two out of thirty-five significantly wet days, and this was a factor in the success of his campaign.

—Edwin C. Bearss

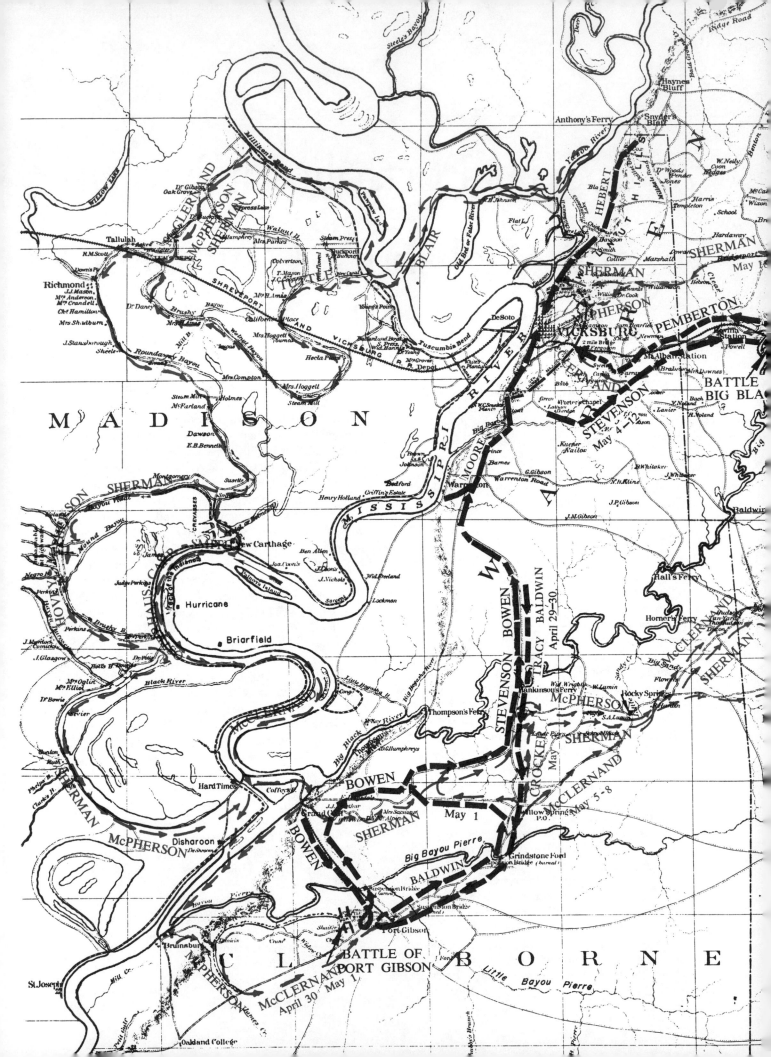

MAP
OF THE COUNTRY BETWEEN
MILLIKEN'S BEND, LA. AND JACKSON, MISS.

Map 2. The Vicksburg Campaign, showing the troop movements during April when the Federals were moving down the west bank of the Mississippi from Milliken's Bend to the crossing near Bruinsburg. Also shown are the routes of both armies from April 30, 1863 until Pemberton withdrew within the Vicksburg fortifications. The movements of major units only are plotted, the Confederates being shown in black and the Federals in brown. The basic map is from the Atlas to the Official Records, with a few corrections and additions furnished by Edwin C. Bearss. Mr. Bearss also supplied the routes and dates.

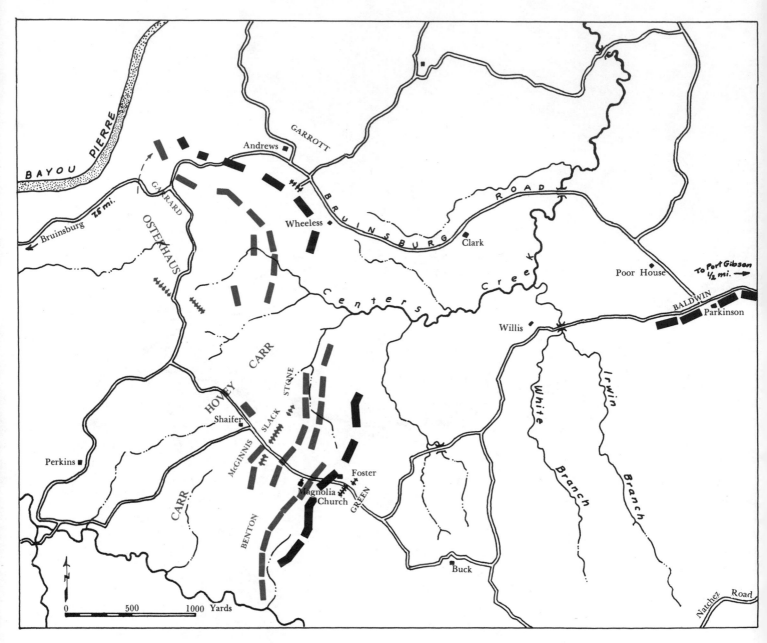

Map 3. Battle of Port Gibson, May 1, 1863—action from 8:15 a.m. to 10 a.m. This map portrays McClernand's initial assault on Bowen's Confederates deployed across two roads three miles west of Port Gibson.

On the plantation road Osterhaus' division gained 400 yards against Tracy's Confederate brigade (Tracy's command had made a 44-mile forced march from Vicksburg, during which a number of his men had straggled), then was stopped by heavy fire and made no additional advance until late in the afternoon.

Tracy was killed early in the engagement, and Col. Isham Garrott assumed command of the brigade.

On the southerly road Benton's and Stone's brigades of Carr's division diverged into the ravines while advancing to attack Green's brigade of Bowen's division, thus leaving a gap in the center of Carr's line. McClernand shoved Hovey's division into this space, and his men worked forward through the tangle of canebrake unitl 10 a.m., when they assaulted. After a desperate struggle, Green fell back across Centers Creek.

Map 4. Battle of Port Gibson; action from 11 a.m. to 4 p.m. Green's withdrawal was covered by Baldwin's brigade of M. L. Smith's division, which had just arrived from Vicksburg; and Baldwin took over the defense on this road while Green reorganized in rear. Bowen then sent Green to the north flank to assist Garrott.

Bowen's other brigade, Cockrell's, arrived about noon from Grand Gulf. Two of his regiments were sent to help Baldwin and one to reinforce Garrott. When, early in the afternoon,

Hovey's and Carr's troops came under fire of Baldwin's reinforced brigade, a severe fight ensued, which lasted an hour and a half. Bowen sent two of Cockrell's regiments to turn McClernand's right flank. Cockrell's Missourians mauled Slack's brigade, but they in turn were thwarted by Burbridge's brigade of A. J. Smith's division, which McClernand had fed into the line, and by enfilade fire from four of Hovey's batteries.

John D. Stevenson's brigade of Logan's division is reinforcing McClernand.

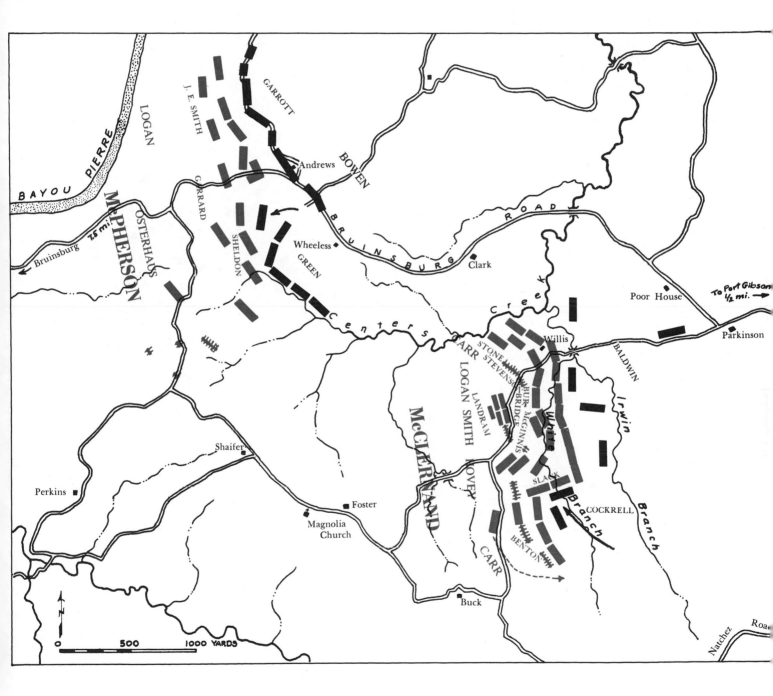

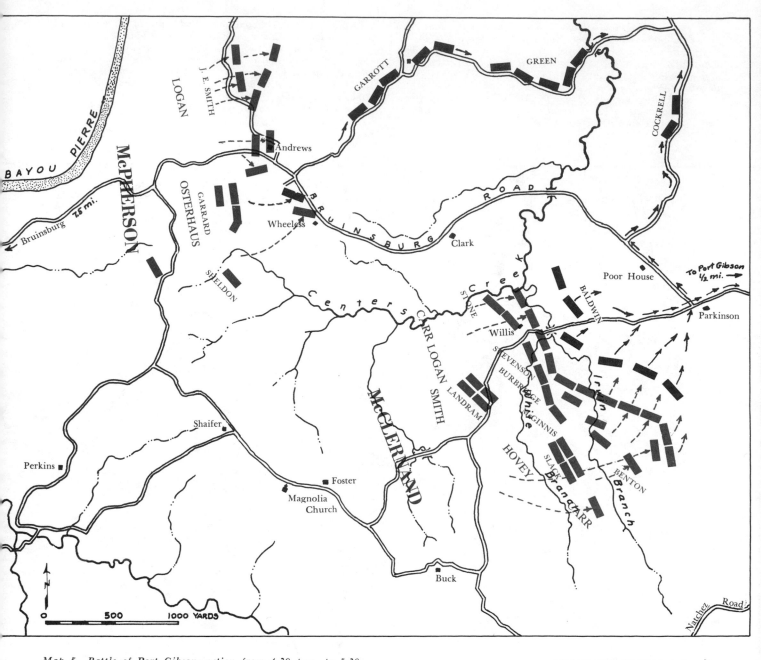

Map 5. Battle of Port Gibson; action from 4:30 p.m. to 5:30. Grant had sent in Logan's division of McPherson's corps to strengthen McClernand's drive. A general attack spearheaded by John E. Smith's brigade started at 5 p.m. and resulted in the defeat of the Confederate right flank followed by the collapse of the rest of the line. Bowen retreated in good order, resisting until dark, when pursuit ended. Accompanied by three brigades, Bowen crossed Bayou Pierre near the railroad bridge; Baldwin's brigade withdrew through Port Gibson and across the Little Bayou Pierre. The bridges were burned by the Confederate rearguard.

Map 6. Battle of Raymond, May 12, 1863. The situation from noon to 1:30 p.m., showing the Confederate attack. On May 11 Pemberton concluded that Grant was merely feinting toward Jackson and that his main force would head for Big Black Bridge, east of Vicksburg. He wired General John Gregg, at Raymond, to strike the Yankees in flank and rear as soon as they turned north. W. H. T. Walker was directed to move his brigade from Jackson to help Gregg.

Early on the 12th, Gregg's scouts notified him that a small enemy force was marching up the Utica road. Thinking that this was the "feint" mentioned by Pemberton, Gregg at once moved his 3,000 men to crush or capture the Yankees. The latter actually were the advance elements of McPherson's corps, 10,000 strong.

Gregg deployed a regiment each on the Gallatin and Utica roads, holding back a strong reserve. He emplaced Bledsoe's 3-gun battery to cover the bridge over Fourteen Mile Creek, which at 10 a.m. opened fire on the Union vanguard as it moved down the road toward the creek.

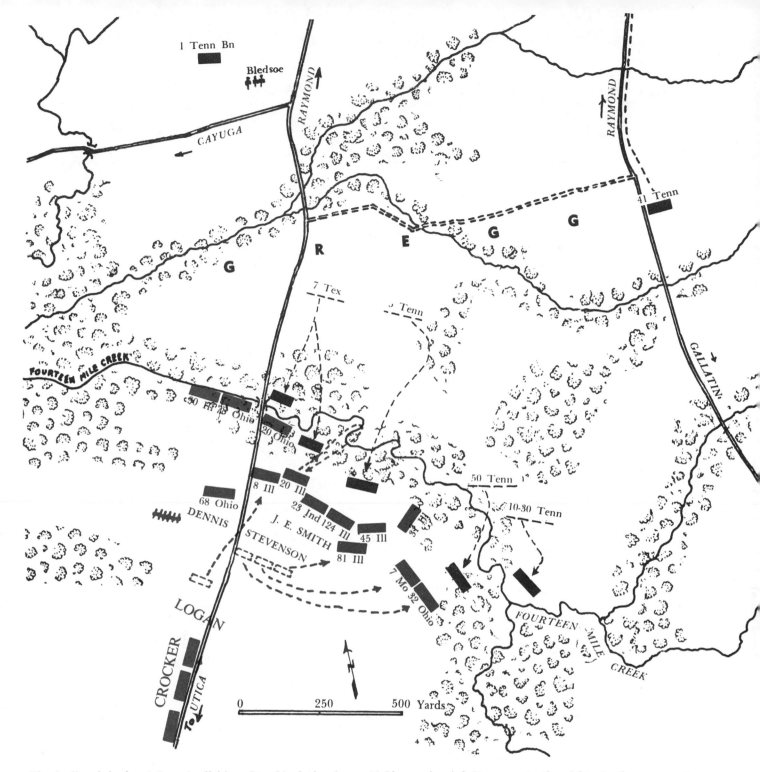

The leading brigade of Logan's division, Dennis', deployed astride the road and advanced, but the regiments were soon out of contact with each other and with the rear as they became entangled in the jungle bounding Fourteen Mile Creek. McPherson himself rode up and ordered two batteries into action. Smith's brigade was brought up on the right of Dennis'.

Gregg, still thinking he was facing a small force, decided to pin it in front with a secondary attack, and move a main force across the creek to the east and strike the enemy from flank and rear. He started the maneuver at noon, and his attack, as it developed, is shown on the map.

The Federals, still uncoordinated and confused by the dense woods and undergrowth, the dust and smoke, gave way in some instances, but Logan dashed up and "with the shriek of an eagle," as a participant described it, "turned them back to their place, which they regained and held." Stevenson, in reserve in the center, wanted to pitch in, but McPherson held his brigade back until the situation clarified. Then as the flank threat grew,

McPherson hurried Stevenson to the right. As the movement started, one regiment had to be diverted to shore up Smith's line in the center, and another to help Dennis on the left. Stevenson arrived with two regiments.

The smoke and dust still prevented Gregg from seeing the size of the enemy force, but as his attacking troops crossed the creek, Col. Beaumont of the 50th Tennessee, on the right, saw what appeared to be a division. He sent a staff officer posthaste to Gregg, who couldn't be found. The enveloping force advanced beyond the creek, to receive a shattering volley in the flank from Stevenson's regiments, which stopped the attack. About the same time Gregg, not hearing his units fire, realized that his attack was in trouble, as his troops on the west flank had been attacked savagely by the 20th Illinois. He ordered up the 41st Tennessee, but by the time they arrived the situation had changed drastically, and a general Federal counterattack was under way.

Map 7. Battle of Raymond. Union counterattack, 1:30 p.m. to 2:30 p.m. Smith's Union brigade launched a thrust at 1:30 p.m. that drove the 3d Tennessee back 500 yards, where it rallied in the ravine from which it had advanced at noon. At the same time, the three Federal regiments just to the right of the road assailed the 7th Texas, and in some of the bitterest fighting of the day forced it to retreat as shown. McPherson rushed Sanborn's brigade to assist Dennis, on the left, but two of the regiments not being needed there tried to help Smith and Stevenson. Their assistance again being declined, they drifted off to the southeast and pretended to be in reserve, but toward the end of the battle made an attack of their own volition.

The 50th Tennessee, on the extreme left, gave way and marched off up the Gallatin road. The 10th-30th Consolidated Tennessee under Col. McGavock, on being flanked out of position, marched northwest to a bare knoll where they came under artillery fire. The commander, instead of retreating, attacked. He was killed, and his troops were repulsed and withdrew up the Gallatin road.

The regiments on both sides were acting pretty much on their own, in a confused affair in which the dust and smoke prevented the senior commanders from knowing where their units were or what they were doing. After his right wing collapsed, Gregg ordered a general withdrawal, which was already in progress. The Confederates marched back through Raymond and bivouacked on the high ground beyond Snake Creek. They were reinforced during the night by Walker's brigade. The Federals stopped in Raymond.

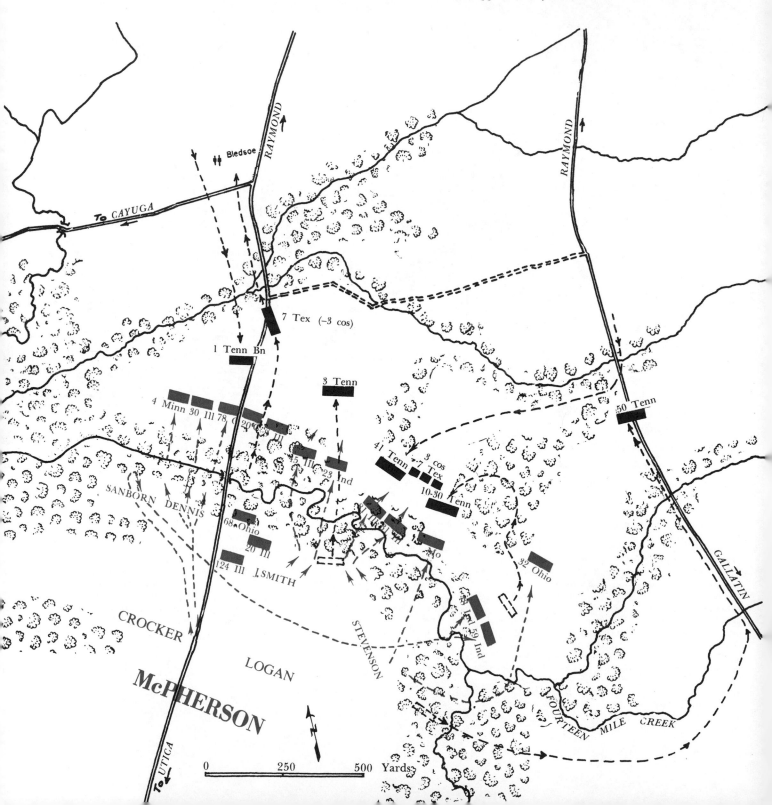

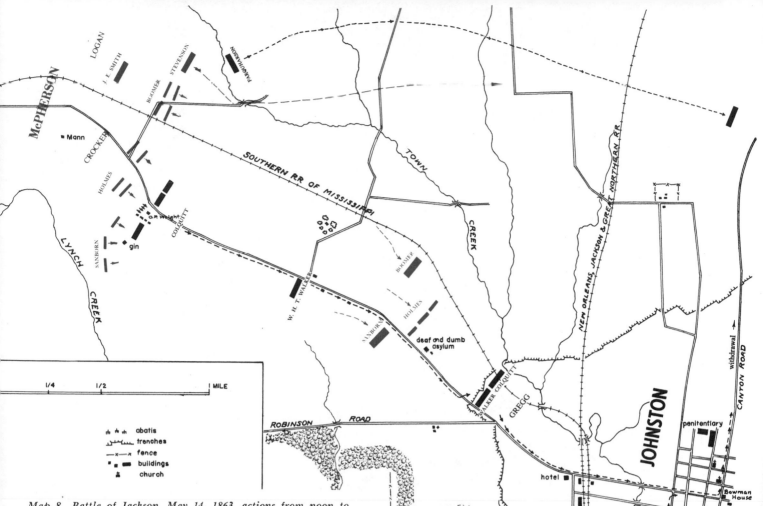

Map 8. Battle of Jackson, May 14, 1863, actions from noon to 3 p.m. When Gen. J. E. Johnston arrived at Jackson, he noted the size of the defending force, 6,000 men, and the imperfect intrenchments thrown up ten days earlier by slaves and citizen volunteers. At 3 a.m. on the 14th he decided to evacuate the city. He turned the command over to Gen. Gregg, whom he told to hold the town long enough to cover the withdrawal and the evacuation of stores.

At 3 a.m. Gregg led Colquitt's 900 men and a battery three miles out the Clinton road and deployed them on the high ground at the O. P. Wright farm. He placed Walker's brigade in support a mile to the rear; then when he learned that a Union column was advancing via the Raymond road, formed a task force of a reinforced regiment under Col. Thompson and sent it to guard the approach from the southwest. Thompson took a position behind a bridge over an unfordable creek. Finally, Gregg alerted his own brigade, under Col. Farquharson, to be ready to march from Jackson to any threatened point.

Starting at dawn in a heavy rainstorm, the Federal corps of McPherson and Sherman approached from Clinton and Raymond, respectively. Grant, well forward, rode with Sherman. The two columns kept in touch with each other so as to arrive near Jackson simultaneously.

Contact occurred on the Clinton road at 9 a.m. and the Federals came under artillery fire while deploying. During a short letup in the storm, McPherson organized an assault but had to postpone it because the rain started falling again and he was afraid that if the men opened their cartridge boxes their ammunition would become soaked. At 11 a.m. the rain ceased, whereupon Crocker attacked. Colquitt's men resisted strongly but were forced back, fighting bitterly. Gregg had Farquharson make a feint far out to the north flank, but this didn't deceive McPherson, who continued to push the attack. The withdrawal of Colquitt, and the sight of Stevenson's Federal brigade moving to get in his rear, caused Walker also to fall back within the fortifications. The Federals did not immediately pursue, but stopped to reorganize.

Meanwhile Sherman's column was held up by the bridge bottleneck and two Confederate batteries that were firing down the Raymond road. The Federals brought up twelve guns, which soon decided the contest, while the 95th Ohio, probing far around the left flank, passed through an unguarded section of the fortifications, and got in behind a row of Confederate guns inside the works.

At 2 p.m. Gregg was notified that the Confederate supply train had left en route to Canton. His mission accomplished, he ordered his troops to pull out to the north, screening the movement with cavalry and a few guns left behind the intrenchments.

The Federals presently found that the works were no longer manned, and they moved in. Grant and his victorious corps commanders had a celebration in the Bowman House at 4 p.m.

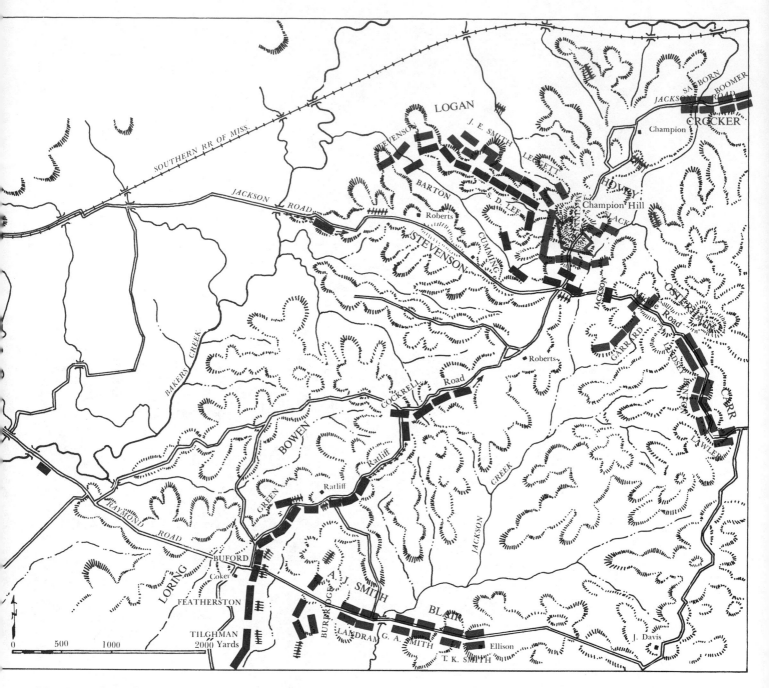

Map 9. *Battle of Champion Hill. Hovey's and Logan's advance, and the defeat of Barton's and Cumming's brigades, 10:30 a.m. to 1 p.m., May 16, 1863.* As soon as contact was established with the Union columns advancing via the Raymond and Middle roads, Gen. Pemberton posted his three divisions along the ridge commanding Jackson Creek. About 9 a.m. Pemberton learned from Gen. S. D. Lee (one of Stevenson's brigade commanders) that a strong Federal force was approaching along the Jackson road. To cope with this threat, Lee shifted his brigade to the left, moving to the crest of Champion Hill. Here he was reinforced by three of Cumming's regiments and parts of two batteries.

By 10:30 Gens. Hovey and Logan had deployed their divisions in the fields near the Champion house. Gen. McPherson gave the word and the two divisions advanced. Lee, seeing that Logan's right would outflank him, called for help. Barton's brigade was rushed cross-country from the Roberts house and formed on Lee's left.

A savage contest now ensued. Hovey's division, spearheaded by McGinnis' brigade, smashed Cumming's regiments at the salient angle, capturing four cannon. Stevenson's brigade of Logan's division routed Barton's brigade. With the brigades to their right and left in retreat, Lee's Alabamians retired to the Jackson road. Hovey's left brigade, Slack's, now drove ahead and at the crossroads scattered the 56th and the 57th Georgia and captured Waddell's battery. By 1 p.m. Pemberton's left had been mauled and hurled back; his army was threatened with destruction.

Map 10. Battle of Champion Hill. Bowen's counterattack, 1 to 3:15 p.m., May 16, 1863. Gen. Pemberton now realized that the four Union divisions feeling their way along the Raymond and Middle roads did not constitute as grave a threat to his army as Hovey's and Logan's bluecoats. Staff officers were sent by Pemberton to direct Generals Bowen and Loring to rush their divisions to the left to reinforce Stevenson's battered brigades. Bowen and Loring refused to go, pointing out that there were masses of Union troops to their front. When Pemberton repeated his order, Bowen at 1:30 put his division in motion for the crossroads.

As Bowen passed the Roberts house, he had Cockrell form his brigade to the left of the plantation (Ratliff) road; Green's brigade deployed on Cockrell's right. Storming forward, Bowen's troops overwhelmed Slack's brigade and recaptured Waddell's

battery. McGinnis' brigade of Hovey's division tried to check Bowen's onslaught, but was driven back in confusion. Bowen's troops swept on and reached the crest of Champion Hill, where they captured two guns of the 16th Ohio Battery. Lee's Alabamians now launched a savage counterattack on Logan's left. For a short time it looked as if the Confederates might rout Grant's right and capture the army's trains parked in the fields near the Champion house.

A fresh Union division, Crocker's, now reached the field. Sanborn's brigade was rushed to Logan's assistance, while Boomer's brigade plugged the gap ripped in the Union line by the retreat of Hovey's troops. Sixteen guns were massed by Hovey, so they could enfilade Bowen's line of advance. Once again, the tide of battle turned, and Bowen's troops were compelled to give ground.

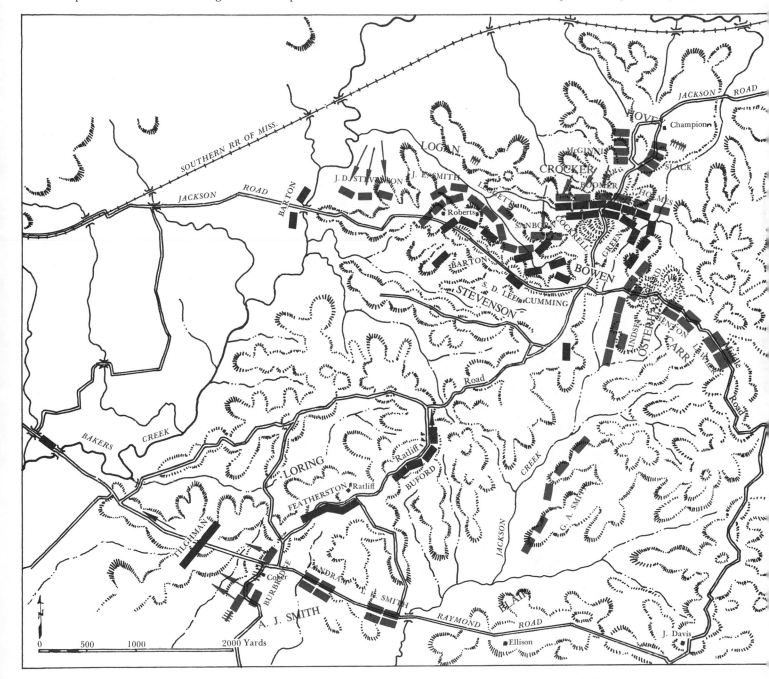

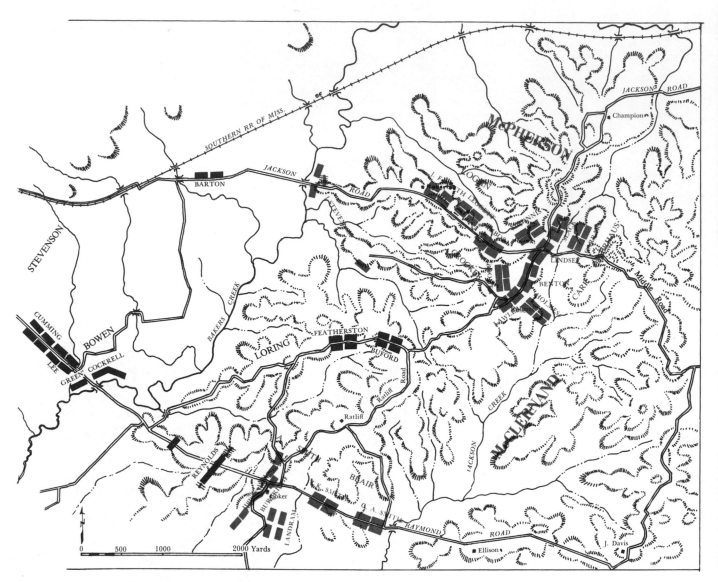

Map 11. Battle of Champion Hill. The Confederate retreat from Champion Hill, 4-5:30 p.m., May 16, 1863.

McClernand at 2:30, on receipt of Grant's order to press the foe, directed his columns on the Middle and Raymond roads to attack. Spearheaded by Osterhaus' division, the Middle road column overpowered Col. Jackson's roadblock. The advance of this force threatened to take in flank Bowen's division, which was struggling to hold onto Champion Hill.

By 4 p.m. Gen. Loring had finally decided to obey Pemberton's orders to march to the left. When he put his division into motion, Loring left Reynolds' (Tilghman's) brigade to hold the Raymond road. Loring reached the crossroads just as Osterhaus' vanguard came into sight on the Middle road. Buford's brigade was formed to oppose Osterhaus' march, while Featherston's brigade was posted to cover Bowen's withdrawal.

Pemberton at 5 p.m., seeing that the battle was lost, ordered his troops to retire from the field. Union troops of Stevenson's brigade having reached the Jackson road near Bakers Creek, Pemberton's troops retreated to the southwest via plantation roads.

If Pemberton's army was to escape across Bakers Creek, Tilghman's brigade, guarding the Raymond road, had to hold its ground. A. J. Smith, whose division had the lead, failed to attack with vigor as ordered by McClernand. Smith put two batteries into action, and they dueled with Tilghman's guns. Tilghman was killed, but his men held firm in the face of the bombardment, and Stevenson's and Bowen's divisions escaped

across Bakers Creek. By the time Loring was ready to follow, Carr's division had crossed Bakers Creek via the Jackson road bridge. When Carr's artillery shelled the Raymond road, Loring decided against crossing Bakers Creek at this point and marched his column down the left bank of the stream in search of another ford.

→

Map 12. Battle of Big Black, May 17, 1863. This shows the second phase of the action—the advance of the Federal units. Lawler's brigade earlier in the fight was in position with three regiments in the forward edge of the woods south of the position shown here for the brigade. Lawler's fourth regiment, the 22d Iowa, and the Battery A, 2d Illinois Artillery were east of the woods. From these positions, Lawler dashed forward to his final assembly area, as shown here.

The 56th Ohio at Vicksburg

The following are excerpts from the diary of Col. William H. Raynor, 56th Ohio.

June 12, Friday. Having received an order last night to take the regiment out to the rifle pits and relieve the 28th Iowa, I sent Co. D to the advanced post at three o'clock this morning, and after an early breakfast with the remaining companies, I went to our assigned position, posted the men in their proper positions, made all necessary arrangements for relieving them, and then I returned to camp.

Visited the pits occasionally through the day and in the evening I took out my blanket to remain all night in the ditches. After it became dark the firing ceased on both sides and then the men commenced talking with each other, the distance being only some 50 or 75 yards. The entertainment thus afforded was rich, many of the questions eliciting witty answers.

Gen. John A. Logan is very near one of their largest forts, and on our own line we are steadily advancing. Immediately to the left of our post the line of pits has been carried forward to within a very short distance of the rebel works.

June 24. In the evening I visited our advanced post and crept in the grass some distance outside. The enemy's picket came out just a few feet from me and were posted in line. I crept back a few steps and warned them not to come closer. The officer said they only wanted their own ground and did not intend to interfere with us as long as we remained outside their line; it made no difference how close we came. With that understanding, I posted our men a few feet only from them, and each stood watching the other till daylight. A Negro servant came to one of our posts. He belongs to an officer on Gen. Stephen D. Lee's staff.

June 25. In the evening I went to our advanced post and moved the pickets several yards nearer the enemy, and within a few feet of their line. The officer in command of the Rebel pickets advanced and conversed very sociably a few minutes and promised to bring me a Vicksburg paper tomorrow evening. The regiment immediately in our front is the 23d Alabama, the same regiment we charged and drove at Port Gibson; they were also opposed to us at Champion Hill. They manifest a great respect for the 56th Ohio, since they have had a taste of our fighting qualities.

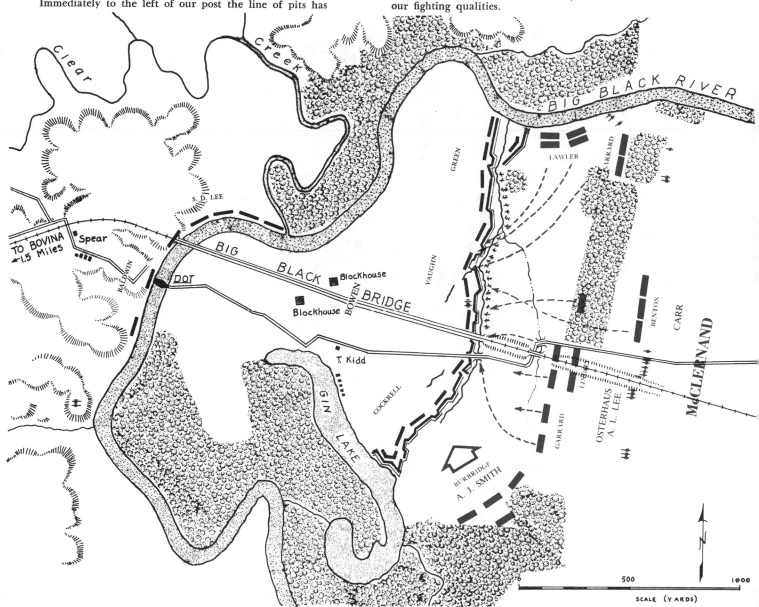

McPHERSON

QUINBY

LOGAN

LIGGETT

BOOMER

STEVENSON

J. E. SMITH

Shirley (White) House

3d La Redan

Great Redoubt

McCLERN

CARR

BENTON

A. J. SMITH

BURBRIDGE

LANDRAM

LIN

Two Mile Bridge

2d Texas Lunette

Railroad Redou

TUTTLE

MATHIES

RANSOM

HIGHLAND

Grant's Hq

BLAIR

K. SMITH

SHERMAN

G. A. SMITH

EWING

THAYER

Riddle house

Stockade Redan

SHOUP

COCKRELL

HEBERT

Rock House

MOORE

Confederate supply depots

FORNEY

BOWEN

S. D. LE

GREEN

BALDWIN'S FERRI

BALDWIN

M. L. SMITH

GRAVEYARD

City cemetery

JACKSON ROAD

STEELE

VAUGHN

GLASS ROAD

MANTER

MINT SPRING

FORT HILL

Yazoo City Road

BAYOU

VICKBURG

WOODS

BAYOU

Old Landing

MISSISSIPPI   RIVER

DE SOTO PENINSULA

SOUTHERN RR OF MISS.

0   1600   3200   4800 Feet

Map 13. May 19 Assault, 2 p.m. to dark.

By 2 p.m. one of Grant's corps, Sherman's, had occupied positions within easy striking distance of the Vicksburg earthworks manned by Gen. Pemberton's four divisions. Frank Blair's division, which was to spearhead the assault, had formed into battle lines on the ridges one-third of a mile east and north of the Stockade Redan Complex. When the brigade commanders passed the word, the troops advanced off the ridges into the abatis-choked ravines.

On the left, T. Kilby Smith's brigade was thrown into disorder as the soldiers worked their way through the felled timber. Several halts were called to enable the units to reform, before the brigade reached a ridge within 120 yards of the eastern face of Stockade Redan. Covered by the fire of the brigade, the 83d Indiana dashed to within a few yards of the

ditch fronting the Rebel works before being pinned down by the volleys of the 36th Mississippi.

Giles Smith's brigade advanced into the hollow north of Stockade Redan. Frightful losses were suffered by the troops as they scaled the steep slope toward their goal. A few men of the 13th U.S. Infantry reached Graveyard road, but they were unable to cross the ditch fronting the Confederate works.

Hugh Ewing's brigade, which had reported to Grant in March after service in the East, drove toward the 27th Louisiana Lunette. For a few moments, it looked as if the Easterners would succeed where Grant's veterans had failed. But like the brigades to its left, Ewing's was checked yards short of the Rebel works.

McPherson's and McClernand's corps, along with Steele's division of Sherman's corps, felt their way forward. At the beginning of the attack Albert Lee was wounded, and Keigwin took over his brigade. Rebel pickets were compelled to retire, and the Federals occupied ground within one-fourth mile of the Confederate fortifications.

As soon as it was dark, Blair's troops retired to the ridges on which they had formed for the attack.

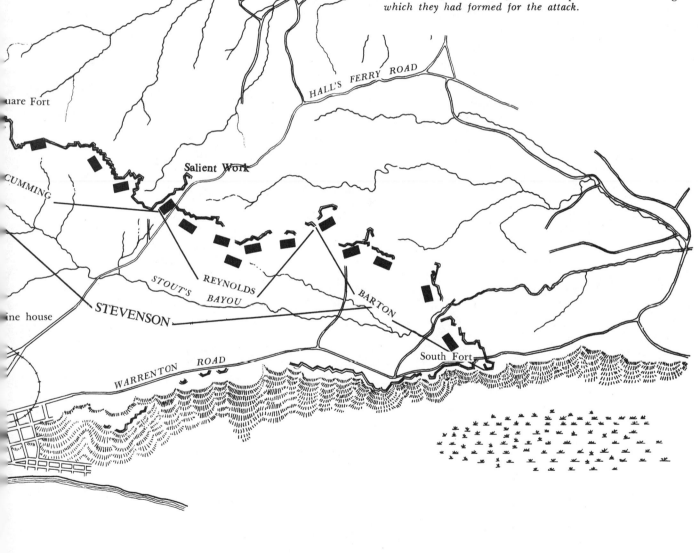

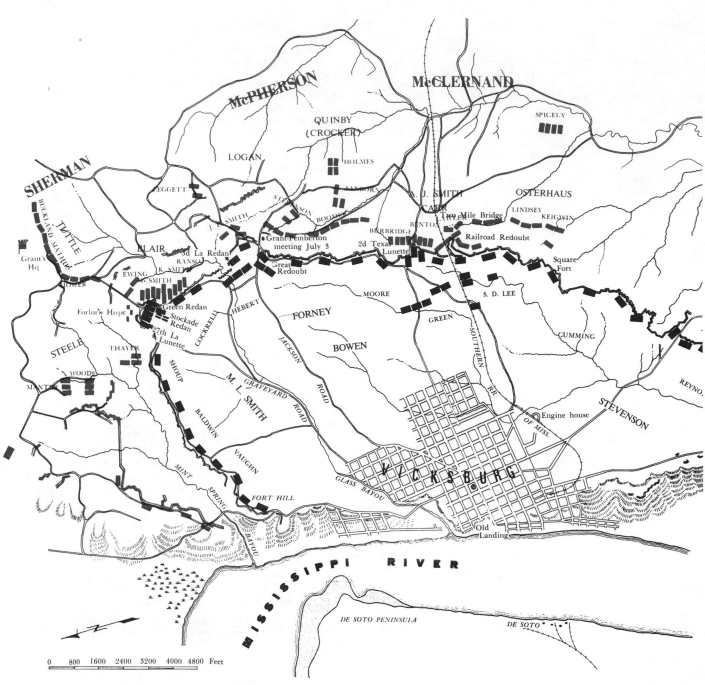

Map 14. May 22 Assault, 10 a.m. to 5:30 p.m.

After the Confederate fortifications had been hammered by a four-hour bombardment, Grant at 10 a.m. launched an all-out attack on the Vicksburg defenses. Preceded by 150 volunteers, Blair's and Tuttle's divisions of Sherman's corps advanced down Graveyard road, the soldiers four abreast. Confederates posted in Stockade Redan quickly blunted this thrust. McPherson sent a two-brigade column along Jackson road, but it was quickly checked by the fire of Rebels holding the 3d Louisiana Redan. Stevenson's brigade charged the Great Redoubt, only to be thrown back with heavy losses. Quinby's division halted after a feeble attempt to reach the Confederate rifle pits to its front.

McClernand was the only Union corps commander to fully commit his troops. Two brigades (Benton's and Burbridge's) rushed the 2d Texas Lunette and reached the ditch fronting the work before being checked. Lawler's and Landram's brigades advanced and compelled soldiers of the 30th Alabama to evacuate the Railroad Redoubt. Several Union colors were planted on this strong point. Osterhaus' division pushed to within 200 yards

of Square Fort. South of Vicksburg, McArthur, supported by the fire of Porter's ironclads, threatened South Fort.

If the Union army were to take advantage of the successes scored by McClernand's corps, Sherman and McPherson would either have to renew their attacks or divert troops to McClernand. It was midafternoon before Sherman launched the first of four poorly coordinated attacks on the Confederate works to his front. Ransom's brigade, Giles Smith's brigade, Mower's brigade, and Steele's division each in turn was repulsed in attacks delivered along a one-half mile front. McPherson's afternoon advance against the 3d Louisiana Redan was feebler than his morning's effort. Quinby was dispatched by McPherson to reinforce McClernand. By the time Quinby's troops were ready to go into action, the Confederates had counterattacked. At the Railroad Redoubt, men of Waul's Texas Legion recovered the work, capturing three stands of colors and many prisoners. A sortie led by M. E. Green rolled the Federals back from the 2d Texas Lunette. Grant's second assault on Vicksburg had failed.

The Summer of Southern Despair

Coupled with the Union victory at Gettysburg, the capture of Vicksburg and its 30,000 defenders formed a major turning point in the war. The fall of Vicksburg was followed a few days later by the surrender of the 7,000 Confederate defenders of Port Hudson. This opened the entire Mississippi to Union control and split the three westernmost states of the Confederacy from the remainder. The dual victories of Gettysburg and Vicksburg caused northern spirits to soar. "Copperheads are palsied and dumb for the moment at least," wrote a jubilant New York Republican. "Government is strengthened four-fold at home and abroad." From the American legation in London, Henry Adams wrote that "the disasters of the rebels are unredeemed by even any hope of success. It is now conceded that all hope of [European] intervention is at an end." By the end of July Lincoln had recovered from his disappointment with Meade's failure to follow up the Gettysburg triumph and attack Lee again before he could retreat to Virginia. "The Tycoon is in fine whack," wrote Lincoln's irreverent private secretary John Hay; "I have seldom seen him more serene."

As northern morale rose, southern spirits sank. "This is the darkest day of the war," wrote a Richmond diarist when he learned of the outcome at Gettysburg. Even the usually buoyant Josiah Gorgas, the brilliant chief of ordnance for the Confederate armies, wrote in his diary on July 28: "Events have succeeded one another with disastrous rapidity. One brief month ago we were apparently at the point of success. Lee was in Pennsylvania, threatening Harrisburg, and even Philadelphia. Vicksburg seemed to laugh all Grant's efforts to scorn. . . . Port Hudson had beaten off Banks'

A spirited attack by Harry Hays' Louisiana Tigers on a battery of the 11th Corps during the Battle of Gettysburg. Sketch by Alfred R. Waud. (Library of Congress)

Surrender of Port Hudson. Then, "the glorious old flag of the Union was unfolded to the breeze from one of the highest bluffs facing the river." (Harper's Weekly, August 8, 1863)

force. . . . Now the picture is just as sombre as it was bright then. . . . It seems incredible that human power could effect such a change in so brief a space. Yesterday we rode on the pinnacle of success—today absolute ruin seems to be our portion. The Confederacy totters to its destruction."

Southern woes in midsummer 1863 were compounded by the retreat of the Army of Tennessee from its namesake state. Simultaneous with the climax of events at Vicksburg and Gettysburg, Union General William S. Rosecrans finally got moving, after months of prodding by the War Department. Once started, Rosecrans moved quickly in a campaign of slash and maneuver that drove the Confederates into Georgia and captured the key rail center of Chattanooga. General Ambrose Burnside, transferred to Ohio after his defeat at Fredericksburg, recouped part of his reputation by advancing with a small army on Rosecrans' left and capturing Knoxville in September. All of Tennessee was now in Union hands. Suddenly, however, the Union juggernaut in this theater came to a violent halt at the battle of Chickamauga.

—James M. McPherson

THE BATTLE OF CHICKAMAUGA

by Glenn Tucker

IF, AFTER GETTYSBURG, the Southern Confederacy ever had a clear invitation to win the war and gain independence, it was lost, not in defeat, but spurned in an hour of glorious victory in the deep woods at Chickamauga.

There the rewards of two days of some of the most desperate fighting of American history were shamefully sacrificed by the hesitation of leadership. There a triumph so signal as to be almost unparalleled in this grim war between the two sections was cast aside not through any reluctance of the gray-clad soldiers to continue the fight and reap the full harvest of their success, but by the incapacity of the commanding

general of the Southern army, who was so out of touch with reality he was not even sure that a victory had been won!

Chickamauga, a word taken from the ancient Cherokee meaning "River of Death," is an appropriate name for this sanguinary, unplanned, almost uncontrolled clash of two great, groping armies, struggling with fervent zeal and ghastly sacrifice for the prize of Chattanooga, the rail center and heart city of the Middle South.

How desperately fought this battle truly was may be seen from the bare statistics. The combined casualties during the two days of fighting — on the 19th

and 20th of September, 1863 — were 37,129. They compare with total combined casualties of 23,582 at Sharpsburg (Antietam), known as the "bloodiest day of American history," where the fighting was confined largely to a single day. They compare with the reported casualties of 43,454 (perhaps more than 50,000) for the three days and the larger armies that fought at Gettysburg.

SOME HIGH POINTS

In truth, mere ground that few had ever heard of, much of it near worthless ground that lay uncultivated, vine-strewn, thicket-matted — stretches that had never known a saw nor heard the ring of the axe of man — was more recklessly fought for than almost any other of the world's acres. No ground was more coveted than those Georgian wastes, broken by a few cleared fields, running for five miles along the LaFayette Road between Lee and Gordon's Mill on the south and the McDonald house and Reed's Bridge road to the north.

It was a battle of peculiarly individualistic generals, Rosecrans and Bragg. Both are arresting studies in human behavior and the reactions of taut men under stress; neither is yet fully understood, despite the voluminous writing about them.

Major General William S. Rosecrans made a fatal mistake. (U.S. Signal Corps photo No. 111-B-3646 in the National Archives)

General Braxton Bragg could not believe that he had won. (KA)

Battle of rugged Pap Thomas, clinging doggedly to a convenient hill which ever after has been famous, named after the log cabin home of old man George Washington Snodgrass, near which Thomas slept with his portents and forebodings on the night of the 19th, using the knot of a tree root for a pillow, and where he held his line obstinately and heroically on the 20th until the grace of darkness relieved him of Longstreet's incessant hammering.

Battle of blunt and stormy Longstreet, newly arrived with five veteran brigades from the Army of Northern Virginia, who massed his attack and launched it in depth, and, like a tornado slashing a pathway in the woodlands, cut through the Federal right center, aided fortuitously by a momentary gap created by a misunderstanding and an ambiguous order. Longstreet broke Rosecrans' army into parts and drove substantially half of it — the better part of four divisions — with four division commanders, two corps commanders and the Union army commander himself from the field, back through McFarland's Gap into Rossville and the Chattanooga defenses.

Battle of Bushrod Johnson, the Ohioan in gray who pierced the Union center; of clear-visioned Nathan Bedford Forrest, whose pleas after the Confederate triumph that "every hour is worth ten thousand men," awakened in Bragg no quick response; of the gallant Cincinnati brigadier general and poet, William H. Lytle, whose lyric strains and battlefield fate were like those of Joyce Kilmer and Alan Seeger of a later war, who preferred to hold his brigade and die rather than follow his division commander Sheridan from the field.

Battle of the Hoosier ironmaster John T. Wilder, a sensational factor because his mounted infantrymen had armed themselves at their own expense with the new Spencer repeating rifles. Seemingly ubiquitous on the field was his efficient artilleryman, the young Greencastle and Lafayette, Indiana, druggist, Eli Lilly, whose triple charges of canister and grape caused Wilder to exclaim "it actually seemed a pity to kill men so."

Battle of the lovable, dashing Ben Helm, Lincoln's favorite brother-in-law, commander of the "Orphan Brigade," an intrepid Blue Grass aggregation also known as the "Blood of Boone," perhaps the most romantic unit of the Confederate Kentuckians. Helm fell from a Kentucky Unionist's bullet on the gory morning of the second day. His death, though he was an enemy of the Union, cast the Executive Mansion in Washington into the deepest gloom, and gave Lincoln probably as much anguish as any other event of the war.

THE PRESIDENT had offered Helm, who was a graduate of both West Point and the Harvard Law

Major General George H. Thomas, "Rock of Chickamauga." His stubborn stand saved the Union army from complete rout. (LC)

Lieutenant General James Longstreet. His men made the crucial ~breakthrough of the Union line. (Cook Coll., Valentine Museum)

School, and was a distinguished young representative of Blue Grass wealth and culture, son of a governor and descendant of earlier noted statesmen and famed pioneers, a Federal commission. But Helm had talked on that same day with reserved but inspiring Robert E. Lee, and had sided with the South.

"I feel like David of old when he was told of the death of Absalom," the grief-stricken Lincoln lamented to his caller and close friend, Judge David Davis, when he had word that Helm had died on this sanguinary field.

Battle of the "Bloody Pond," stained when the wounded soldiers crawled down and drank, and of driving thirst at night in the fields and dark woods where the masses of Unionists, cut off from Chickamauga Creek, were crowded into an area that had only a few weak wells and shallow springs, altogether inadequate for such numbers. "How we suffered that night no one knows," wrote a Federal officer. "Water could not be found. Few of us had blankets and the night was very cold." Some relief was provided by the 19th Mounted Indiana Infantry, which collected 1,000 canteens, filled them at Crawfish Springs three miles south, and brought them to sufferers at midnight.

"We had vermin in our clothing," wrote a soldier who lost his coat and went through the battle in his undershirt. "We did not take our socks off until they were rotten, and only removed our shoes once a week."

Battle that revealed the stanchness of the American character, where men of both sides submerged their individual identities and heedlessly threw their lives and fortunes into their causes, as a duty unsought, and often little understood, but nonetheless an overpowering duty. Battle of the vacant chair and the mother's anguish, about which nearly every Southern schoolboy once knew in the lines of the old song:

> One lies down at Appomattox
> Many miles away
> Another sleeps at Chickamauga
> And they both wore suits of gray. . . .

IN ONE respect Chickamauga was more similar to First Manassas than to any other battle. In no others were major Union armies put to such complete rout. Brice's Cross Roads was comparable but on a smaller scale.

Perhaps the two most obvious opportunities for the South to win a standoff war followed First Manassas, where the approaches to Washington were open and the city occupied by little more than a rabble; and Chickamauga, where able and aggressive Southern generalship might have taken the Army of Tennessee past Rosecrans, huddled in Chattanooga, and Burnside in Knoxville, and carried it to the Ohio, bringing the scattered Union forces behind it for the test in Kentucky of a second Perryville.

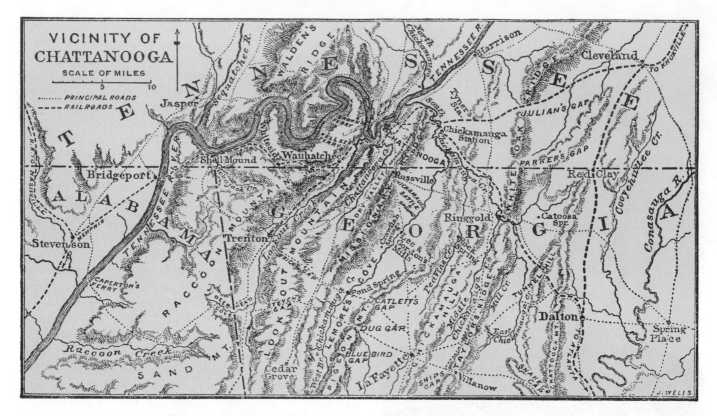

Map 1. Theater of operations during the Chickamauga Campaign. (From "Battles & Leaders, III, 640)

Chief of Staff Halleck kept the wires hot with messages urging more aggressive action and Rosecrans burned them as blisteringly with appeals and impertinences demanding the transportation facilities that would make feasible an advance into the heart of the Southland. Secretary of War Stanton heartily disliked Rosecrans and it is fair to say that this was a factor in the bad blood and low-key cooperation between the department and one of the largest Federal armies.

Rosecrans consulted with his officers. Thomas,

A panoramic view showing the Chattanooga region as it appears from Point Lookout, high point on Lookout Mountain. (B&L)

These things are clearer in aftersight, and it may be contended that the vast industrial and manpower superiority of the North made Southern independence impossible at this stage of the war; still, as is often demonstrated, bustling industries, teeming immigration, and monetary wealth are no substitutes for victory on the battlefield and a hot pursuit of the vanquished. Jackson, Forrest, Hancock, and others understood this well, and history abounds with examples of the triumph of weakness over strength. So it might have been after Chickamauga, this battle of the last opportunity, the last clear chance.

ROSECRANS' BLUNT DEMANDS

The campaign that culminated in the Battle of Chickamauga began at Tullahoma, Tennessee, into which Bragg had retired when Rosecrans advanced from Murfreesboro on June 23, 1863.

William Starke Rosecrans, commanding the Army of the Cumberland, had settled down in Murfreesboro on January 5, after the battle of Stone's River. At Murfreesboro he engaged in what was derisively termed "masterly inactivity." But the fault was more that of the War Department than the commanding general. He called loudly for the mules, horses, and equipment urgently needed for an advance, but the department was so indifferent that this became known as the "stepchild army."

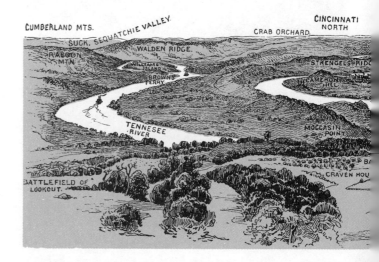

whose judgment few would question, agreed with the commanding general that the army could not move without adequate transportation. So did the other corps commanders. Only Chief of Staff James A. Garfield, who commanded no troops, voted for a prompt forward movement, about which Major General David S. Stanley, who had commanded the Union cavalry at Stone's River, said Garfield sought "cheap glory." Garfield wrote confidentially to his friend in Washington, Secretary Chase, about it, complaining of the delay, which was scarcely his role as chief of staff and the officer presumably closest to Rosecrans.

WHEN at length on June 23 Rosecrans felt ready, he conducted a series of brilliant strategical movements, perhaps unequalled and certainly unsurpassed for boldness and effectiveness in the Northern armies during the four years of war. By them he ousted Bragg from Tullahoma, and then from Chattanooga, a mountain-rimmed citadel with a wide river in its front, a stronghold which many regarded impregnable. He did this without losing a man in taking the town, and with the death of only six in the campaign, four of these by accident. The swift, sure procession of adroit flanking movements, which took the Army of the Cumberland over three mountain ranges in three weeks, startled the entire South, distressed Richmond, and caused rejoicings in the North like those that followed Gettysburg and Vicksburg.

BRAGG THOROUGHLY BAFFLED

Rosecrans' capture of Chattanooga on September 9, 1863, disclosed at its best his customarily dexterous handling of his army. Bragg was deprived of any reasonable opportunity to fight for the possession of the city, even had he been disposed to risk a battle or a siege.

He was simply outmaneuvered. Coming down through the Cumberland Mountains, the Union commander gave indication of a wide sweep to the left and a passage of the Tennessee River above Chattanooga. That would have appeared good judgment, for Major General Ambrose E. Burnside had arrived in East Tennessee with what was presumed to be a supporting army, and was on the left, where Rosecrans might be expected to make a juncture. Elements of Burnside's army captured Cumberland Gap and a neat bag of prisoners on September 9, 1863, and Burnside meantime had occupied Knoxville, 114 miles from Chattanooga, on September 6, three days before Rosecrans took Chattanooga.

Rosecrans' apparent swing to the left was merely a feint, well executed by elements of Crittenden's corps, aided by Colonel Robert H. G. Minty's cavalry brigade and the mounted infantry brigade of Colonel John T. Wilder of Thomas' corps. The Federals showed themselves frequently upstream, simulated the building of pontoons, pounded on empty barrels as though constructing boats, mounted batteries, shelled the city, and ingeniously baffled Bragg into maintaining a sharp watch and massing his troops upstream on his right, when all the while the menace was downstream on his left.

THERE, in late August and early September, Rosecrans' army crossed on pontoons, by pirogues, and at length by a hastily constructed trestle bridge. It passed over the river at or near Bridgeport and Shellmound, only twenty-five miles by air from Chattanooga, but hidden and remote either over the intervening mountains or by way of the winding river. For seven days the two great corps of Thomas and McCook, consist-

Col. Edward M. McCook commanded Union cavalry division. (LC)

But Bragg, though never popular, was not altogether stupid. When he saw he was flanked by the long swing of the Federal army to his left, and its crossing downstream and march into north Georgia, where it threatened his supply lines, he, too, resorted to stratagems. These were to emphasize to the now confident Rosecrans that the Confederates were in full and headlong retreat toward Rome and Atlanta. Bragg sent out scouts to be captured and give this false information. He imparted to country people and mountain dwellers the tale of woe that he was in full flight, and they in turn told Rosecrans. Rosecrans tended to believe the stories, and why not? Had not Chattanooga, the great prize sought in the campaign, fallen like a dead duck at an eager huntsman's feet? Were there not visible evidences that Bragg was baffled?

Success, so often dangerous to an impetuous, emotional man, now had its way with Rosecrans. If Chattanooga had tumbled to his ingenious flanking movements, Rome and Atlanta might be carried. When they were in his hands the communication lines of the South would be effectively severed. The Confederacy would be cut through the middle. A wave of optimism passed through the Federal army and sent its ripples into the Northern cities. "Old Rosey" might soon capture Atlanta. The war might be over by Christmas!

ALL of this went to make up one of the strangest dramas of the war, the covert reinforcement of Bragg to the utter surprise of Rosecrans. Bragg's retreat from Tullahoma deeply agitated President Davis and stirred repercussions through the Army of Northern Virginia, which was nursing its wounds and refitting behind the Rapidan after the tragedy of Gettysburg. Longstreet, prior to Gettysburg, had proposed to both Lee and the Richmond authorities that instead of heading north with Lee, his corps should be detached to reinforce Bragg, and that Joseph E. Johnston's Mississippi army be united with them. Combined, they would sweep Rosecrans aside, march to the Ohio River, and perhaps draw Grant back from Vicksburg to save Louisville and Cincinnati and prevent an invasion of Indiana and Ohio. Longstreet now felt that if Rosecrans overran Georgia the story of the Confederacy would end soon. He renewed his suggestion to Secretary of War Seddon that he go to Bragg. This time Lee and Davis assented. Both Longstreet and Davis preferred that Lee head the relief expedition in person but Lee declined, feeling that his more pressing duty was in Virginia.

ing of seven divisions, operating 300 miles from their "zone of the interior" base at Louisville (and 150 miles from Nashville, the main base in the theater of operations), but carrying with them rations for forty-five days and enough ammunition to fight two large battles, crossed the river behind the security of the Raccoon and Sand Mountain Range, and then Lookout Mountain, without Bragg being fully apprised of what was happening.

Friendly country folk who had watched from the ridges began to bring him more impressive reports than the earlier inklings he had been receiving by hearsay and rumor. He had thought the downstream movement the feint, the upstream the genuine danger, and in this was altogether mistaken. When he learned that Rosecrans was plunging south behind the cover of the Raccoon-Sand Mountain range, and might debouch at any moment in his rear and interpose the Federal army between his own and Atlanta, he had no course open but to retire.

The 92d Illinois mounted infantry of Wilder's brigade passed around the head of Lookout Mountain, following the curve of the river, on the early morning of September 9, 1863, and rode into Chattanooga without firing a shot. Dust clouds to the south showed Bragg's retreat route.

Had the Confederate War Department acted with alacrity, Longstreet might have arrived in time to save Chattanooga, for the direct railroad line ran through Bristol, Virginia, and Knoxville, to Chattanooga. Before the orders were issued and the rolling stock collected, Burnside had occupied Knoxville and cut the railroad. The transfer had to be made by a circuitous route mainly through Wilmington, North Carolina and Augusta and Atlanta, Georgia.

Longstreet's corps, heavy with Georgians, was elated. The men would get a chance to see their home state, possibly their home towns once more. Many did so on the transfer, even the celebrated and ancient Guards company from as far south as Columbus.

Lafayette McLaws wrote to his wife that the army had been "increasing daily in strength and efficiency" after the defeat at Gettysburg, and had regained its old self-confidence. The assumption was, as G. Moxley Sorrel explained, that when Longstreet left Virginia the Federal army would detach troops from Lee's front, but that Longstreet, having the short route, would arrive first. Meade was counted on to move cautiously and deplete his own army with great deliberation if he had to strengthen Rosecrans'. "His well known prudence and lack of imagination," wrote Sorrel, "might be trusted to keep him quiet during our great strategic coup."

AT FIRST it was judged Longstreet could reach Bragg with two divisions in two days. How inaccurate was this estimate! It depended on utilization of the railroad through Bristol and Knoxville. The more circuitous journey required upwards of ten days. Most of the rolling stock of the Southeastern states was pressed into service for this first transfer of a large army by railroad. (Joseph E. Johnston had transferred a much smaller force over a short distance in the First Manassas Campaign.) Longstreet's men, wrapped in carpets and blankets, filled passenger and freight cars and huddled together on the tops of flatcars and boxcars. They were fed bountifully by women who brought delicacies as they passed through the Carolinas and north Georgia.

The strangest aspect of this transfer was that Rosecrans, the man who would be the most concerned, was the last to hear of it. Richmond and Baltimore buzzed with gossip of an impending troop movement of major proportions, but the wires to Rosecrans were silent. Meade reported to the War Department the sudden disappearance of Longstreet's corps from his front. Stanton, Halleck, or some alert official in the department might have apprehended the danger to Rosecrans and told him about it, then sent him aid. But not until the last moment, when

it was too late, were orders issued to units scattered through the southwest to march to the support of Rosecrans.

Burnside in Knoxville turned in the opposite direction and reported to Washington that he was going to Jonesboro (in northeast Tennessee), which brought from Lincoln at the telegraph office the ejaculation, "Damn Jonesboro."

ROSECRANS himself did not accept at full value the report when he finally got it, that Longstreet was reinforcing Bragg. Not until he captured a captain of Robertson's brigade, Hood's division, on the battlefield was he willing to face actualities. Before that Colonel Atkins of the 92d Illinois had brought in a youth who had said he was from Longstreet's corps. Rosecrans "flew into a passion," Atkins said, "and upbraided the lad as a liar, frightening him into speechlessness."

Bragg was further strengthened by the return of elements that had been sent when Joseph E. Johnston's army was assembled at Jackson, Mississippi to succor Pemberton in Vicksburg. These included Breckinridge's veteran division of Hardee's corps; Bushrod Johnson's division, that would play a key role in the battle; and Walker's Reserve Corps which, with additions, aggregated two full divisions. Hardee, after the surrender of Vicksburg, had been sent to command in southern Alabama and the testy D. H. Hill, formerly of Lee's army, had been given a lieutenant general's rank and assigned to command Hardee's old corps, consisting of the divi-

Map 2. Rosecrans outflanked Bragg and maneuvered him out of Chattanooga. Minty and Wilder feinted near the city while the main Federal army crossed the Tennessee River downstream, then moved across three mountain ranges to bypass the city defenses. (From CHICKAMAUGA: BLOODY BATTLE IN THE WEST by Glenn Tucker, copyright © 1961 by the Bobbs-Merrill Co., Inc., used by permission of the publishers. Map by Dorothy Tucker.)

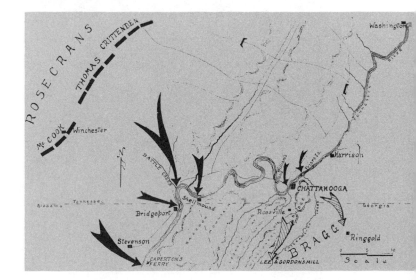

Gen. John B. Hood received crippling wound at Chickamauga. (LC)

Major General John C. Breckinridge led a veteran division in Bragg's army. (Cook Collection, Valentine Museum, Richmond)

sions of Breckinridge and Cleburne. Bragg, who had left Tullahoma with a force of about 35,000, now had a formidable army of 71,550 officers and men. Rosecrans was outnumbered, having a force of about 57,000.

Bragg might have waited for the arrival of Longstreet's full complement, but chose not to do so. Pickett's division had been left in Virginia, but Longstreet brought with him the divisions of Hood and McLaws, consisting of nine brigades. Only five arrived in time for the battle. The rest were scattered over north Georgia, making their way toward Bragg's army. McLaws was still in Atlanta forwarding his troops and did not reach the field until the day after the engagement ended; his division during the battle was commanded by E. M. Law. Some have thought that Bragg wanted to win a victory with his own army, now that the troops sent to Johnston had been returned, without having to share a triumph with Longstreet and his men. Bragg did try for an engagement two or three times prior to Longstreet's arrival, and began the main battle with Longstreet still absent. Another view is that Bragg went ahead without waiting for Longstreet because he hoped to catch and destroy Rosecrans' force while it was divided and in rough country.

NEAR TRAP IN McLEMORE'S COVE

His first effort was in McLemore's Cove. His opportunity there developed because Rosecrans in an impetuous movement farther south, such as had won him Chattanooga, caused his army to become gravely extended, whereas Bragg was concentrating in LaFayette, Georgia on Rosecrans' exposed flank. Rosecrans' army soon was strung out from Chattanooga to Alpine, Georgia, along a circuitous route and through mountain passes that left the wings three to four days' marches apart. Crittenden's corps occupied Chattanooga, with divisions thrown south toward Ringgold, and through Rossville toward LaFayette as far as Lee and Gordon's Mills.

Thomas' corps, in the center, crossed the Raccoon-Sand Mountain range and entered Lookout Valley; then the leading division trudged through Stevens' Gap into McLemore's Cove and began a movement toward LaFayette, not knowing of Bragg's concentration there. Crittenden was fifteen and more miles removed from him, out of prompt supporting distance.

Thomas had not wanted to proceed so hastily. He had recommended that the army occupy Chattanooga, refit itself, and consolidate its communications and defenses, then conduct a more orderly advance against Bragg in north Georgia. But Rosecrans, confident, overruled him and directed him into

McLemore's Cove, while McCook's corps was laboring far to the south through Winston Gap toward Alpine and Summerville, and Crittenden was extended south of Chattanooga. The army was about like the Army of Northern Virginia at the beginning of the Gettysburg Campaign, when Lincoln observed that Lee reached from the Rappahannock to beyond the Potomac, and commented that "the animal must be pretty slim somewhere in the middle."

BRAGG detected Rosecrans' thinness from his point of observation in LaFayette and determined to trap Thomas' advance units in the cove. Thomas' leading division, Negley's, passed through Stevens' Gap into the cove on September 9. McCook's corps was now forty-two miles to the south and Crittenden's fifteen miles and more to the northeast. When through the pass, Negley marched to Davis' Crossroads near the headwaters of Chickamauga Creek, moving without much caution, because he judged the cove, six to nine miles wide, unoccupied by hostile troops. Ahead of him was Dug Gap over Pigeon Mountain, through which he intended to march for the capture of LaFayette, believing that Bragg, shielded by the Pigeon range, was either unaware of his approach or was in flight.

But Bragg at that very moment was converging on Negley with vastly superior forces, consisting of Hindman's division to the north, supported by the balance of Buckner's corps, and D. H. Hill's corps in his front and to his right, with Cleburne's division in the lead. Bragg issued his attack orders and paced nervously along the crest of Pigeon Mountain awaiting the sound of his guns.

Two events happened that frustrated his carefully laid plans. First, Negley grew suspicious, having learned that Confederates were having lunch at a house a mile to the north. He withdrew to a wood, changed position to face north, and called on Thomas for reinforcements. Thomas, alert to the danger, sent Baird's division hastening over Lookout Mountain to Negley's aid.

THE other event was the reluctance or inability of Bragg's generals to obey his orders. Hill contended that Cleburne was ill, a matter which Cleburne himself did not seem to notice, and that Dug Gap was so barricaded that the obstructions could not be removed. Hindman claimed he was not supposed to attack until Hill had formed a juncture with him in the cove. For the better part of two days the opportunity to destroy Negley, and, in turn, Baird, continued to be neglected, however urgently Bragg called for action. Bragg later preferred charges against Hindman, but they were never pressed after

Hindman's brilliant performance at Chickamauga. Nor did Bragg have much to do with Hill thereafter, but placed him under the command of Polk and dealt with him mainly through that general.

Cleburne finally got into the cove, waded through Chickamauga Creek, and tried to cut off the retreat of the two Federal divisions, but reached the entrance to Stevens' Gap only to hear their artillery and wagons lumbering across the mountain. Thomas had extricated them instead of trying to support them. He understood Bragg's opportunity and was appalled by it. Negley's retirement was called "masterly," but Rosecrans seemed unperturbed that 10,000 of his men had been recklessly exposed to 30,000 of the enemy, and judged that Bragg was merely demonstrating to check the pursuit. His scouts still brought false reports that the Confed-

Map 3. Rosecrans plunged recklessly after Bragg on an extended front. Bragg, heavily reinforced, planned to trap and destroy the leading divisions of Thomas' columns in McLemore's Cove and of Crittenden's corps near Lee and Gordon's Mill, but was frustrated by the lethargy of Hill, Hindman, and Polk. Rosecrans, realizing on September 12, 1863, that Bragg had turned on him, began assembling his forces near Crawfish Springs and Lee and Gordon's Mill. (From CHICKAMAUGA: BLOODY BATTLE IN THE WEST by Glenn Tucker, copyright © 1961 by The Bobbs-Merrill Publishing Co., Inc., used by permission of the publishers. Map by Dorothy Tucker.)

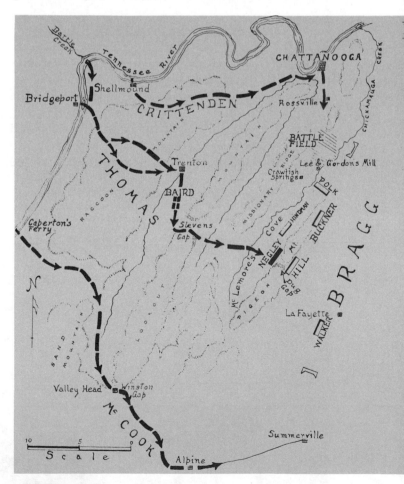

172

erate army was hastening from LaFayette en route to Rome.

Bragg was no more successful in operating against Crittenden's corps than he had been against Thomas. He issued and reiterated orders for Polk to attack Crittenden, who had now concentrated around Lee and Gordon's Mill, where he was isolated when Thomas retired from in front of Hindman and Hill. Polk merely requested more troops and the opportunity passed, and soon the great battle was impending.

These threats against his center and left caused Rosecrans to recognize reluctantly on the night of September 12 that Bragg was not in flight toward Rome and Atlanta, but was concentrated and distinctly menacing, while he, in turn, was dispersed and vulnerable anywhere along the line. His recourse was to effect the speediest concentration possible. For four days the Federal commander was bringing his scattered army together, while Bragg, baffled when his two fine chances were sacrificed by his unresponsive subordinates, stood by idly at LaFayette. Rosecrans brought McCook back by forced marches on Thomas, who issued again through Stevens' Gap into McLemore's Cove and moved down the cove and Chickamauga Creek to join with Crittenden at Crawfish Springs and Lee and Gordon's.

BRAGG'S BATTLE PLAN

Bragg, having given Rosecrans the grace of four days in which to concentrate, did not wait two or three more until he had all of Longstreet's two fine divisions in hand, and could assume an orderly offensive for the recapture of Chattanooga. He still hoped to catch Rosecrans in a disadvantageous position. But when Rosecrans was about concentrated around Lee

and Gordon's, Bragg determined to cut around his left, and, by moving up the right bank of Chickamauga Creek (which flows north) interpose between him and Chattanooga. If cut off from Chattanooga, Rosecrans would be deprived of any satisfactory line of communications with the North. To extricate himself he would have to go by the laborious routes through the mountain passes, by which two of his corps had come, and reach the Tennessee River at Bridgeport, being exposed to attack by Bragg and harassment by Forrest.

Bragg intended to deliver battle on September 18 but could not get his units into position in time. The delay allowed the advance units of Longstreet's command to reach him, and to fall in under Hood on his left. His plan was for Bushrod Johnson's division, accompanied by Forrest's cavalry and supported by Walker's corps, to move down the Chickamauga, cross at Reed's and Alexander's bridges, which were presumed to be beyond the Federal left flank, find and assail the flank, and roll Rosecrans' army back into McLemore's Cove. Meantime, as the battle advanced, Buckner's corps was to cross at Thedford's Ford, farther upstream, while Polk would cross and attack the Federals at Lee and Gordon's, and Hill's corps would serve as a support still farther upstream.

The plan appeared to be feasible. Bushrod Johnson and Forrest brushed aside Minty's cavalry on Rosecrans' left and took Reed's Bridge by an impetuous charge that prevented the Federals from destroying it. Johnson's division was on the west side of the creek at 4:30 p.m. September 18. Walker's corps was delayed at Alexander's Bridge by Wilder's mounted infantry with their repeating rifles and by Eli Lilly's battery, but Forrest was there and crossings were made above and below the bridge. Then at about the time Johnson was crossing downstream at Reed's Bridge, Forrest knocked the Federals off Alexander's Bridge.

First gun at Chickamauga, September 18, 1863. Confederates open fire upon Federal cavalry who have begun the destruction of Reed's Bridge. From original drawing by A. R. Waud. (LC)

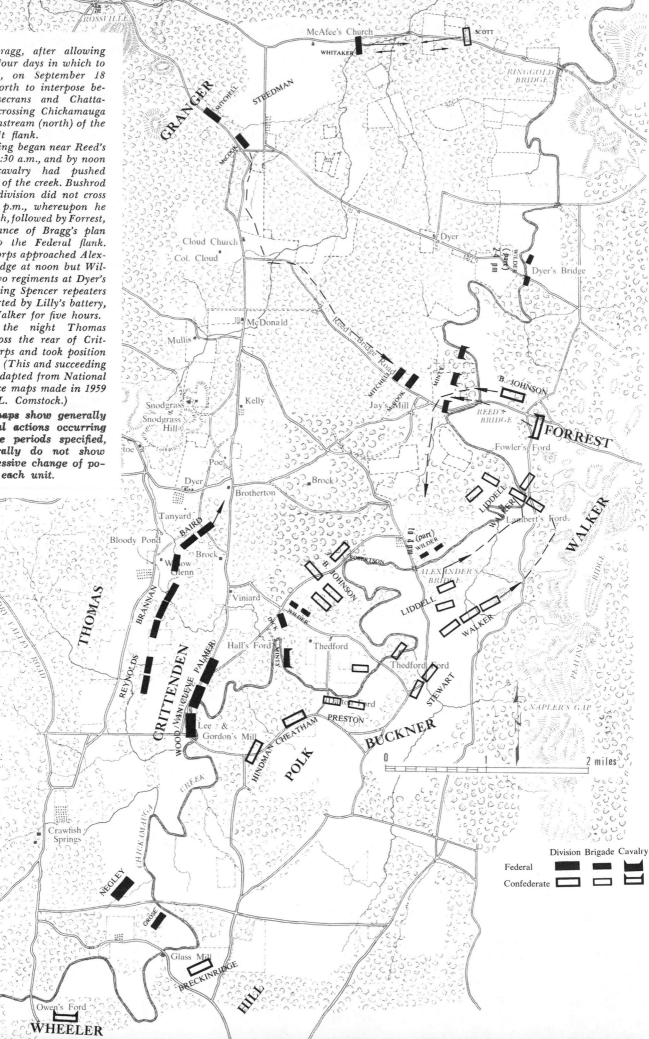

May 4. Bragg, after allowing Rosecrans four days in which to concentrate, on September 18 marched north to interpose between Rosecrans and Chattanooga by crossing Chickamauga Creek downstream (north) of the Federal left flank.

Skirmishing began near Reed's Bridge at 7:30 a.m., and by noon Forrest's cavalry had pushed Minty west of the creek. Bushrod Johnson's division did not cross until 4:30 p.m., whereupon he turned south, followed by Forrest, in furtherance of Bragg's plan to roll up the Federal flank. Walker's corps approached Alexander's Bridge at noon but Wilder (less two regiments at Dyer's Bridge), using Spencer repeaters and supported by Lilly's battery, held up Walker for five hours.

During the night Thomas passed across the rear of Crittenden's corps and took position on the left. (This and succeeding maps are adapted from National Park Service maps made in 1959 by Rock L. Comstock.)

These maps show generally the critical actions occurring during the periods specified, but naturally do not show each successive change of position for each unit.

	Division	Brigade	Cavalry
Federal			
Confederate			

Reed's Bridge (taken about 1890). It here retains its 1863 appearance. Reed's Bridge was a major creek crossing for the Confederates. Johnson's division crossed here after driving off Minty's cavalry.

FORREST, in the fight at Alexander's Bridge, was at his customary place in front of his men, where his beautiful steed was shot from under him — the mount that had been presented to him by the citizens of Rome, Georgia, after he had captured the Federal cavalryman and raider, Colonel Abel D. Streight.

Walker's corps consisted of the divisions of Brigadier Generals States Rights Gist and St. John R. Liddell, which, with Bushrod Johnson's division, gave Bragg three divisions on the west, or Federal side of Chickamauga Creek. Bragg all the while was pressing his army north in order to reach around the Federal flank, while Rosecrans, now understanding his adversary's intention, was moving his army north along the LaFayette-Chattanooga road, roughly parallel with Chickamauga Creek. Wilder, at Alexander's Bridge, finally finding his flanks were threatened by the Confederates who had forded the creek, retired beyond the LaFayette Road.

That night both armies prepared for the full-scale battle each saw was imminent. Rosecrans sent Thomas' corps to the left, to the region of the Kelly log cabin and a clearing called Kelly Field. Crittenden, whose rear Thomas had crossed in a hurried night march, was in the center and McCook's corps, as it arrived by forced marches, took position on the right. Be-

cause of the staggered arrival of the divisions marching from different positions to the concentration, the three Federal corps did not remain intact on the field. Reinforcements of divisions and brigades were continually sent to Thomas, who had the initial point of danger on the left, the flank Bragg was trying to turn.

Intelligence passed slowly in the wooded, thicket-grown area that chance was selecting for one of the most grueling battles of the war. As Thomas marched north to Kelly Field he learned from Wilder of the Confederate crossing at Reed's and Alexander's, but he later was informed by Colonel Dan McCook, who had been sent out from Gordon Granger's Reserve Corps at Rossville to help Minty, that a lone Confederate brigade was isolated west of the creek near Reed's Bridge. The brigade was McNair's, one of Bushrod Johnson's, which later would have a stellar role in the battle. It was not truly isolated, but was in the rear of Johnson's division, marching south.

Brannan Opens The Fray

Thomas, at 7:30 a.m. on the 19th, sent his left division, Brannan's, to pick up this stray brigade, and thereby opened the Battle of Chickamauga.

Brannan found that Bushrod Johnson had marched his entire division upstream. He encountered, not a stray brigade, but Forrest's cavalry and Gist's division of Walker's Corps, which now held Bragg's right flank. This first clash at Jay's Mill, at a road convergence upstream from Reed's Bridge, was of a nature that

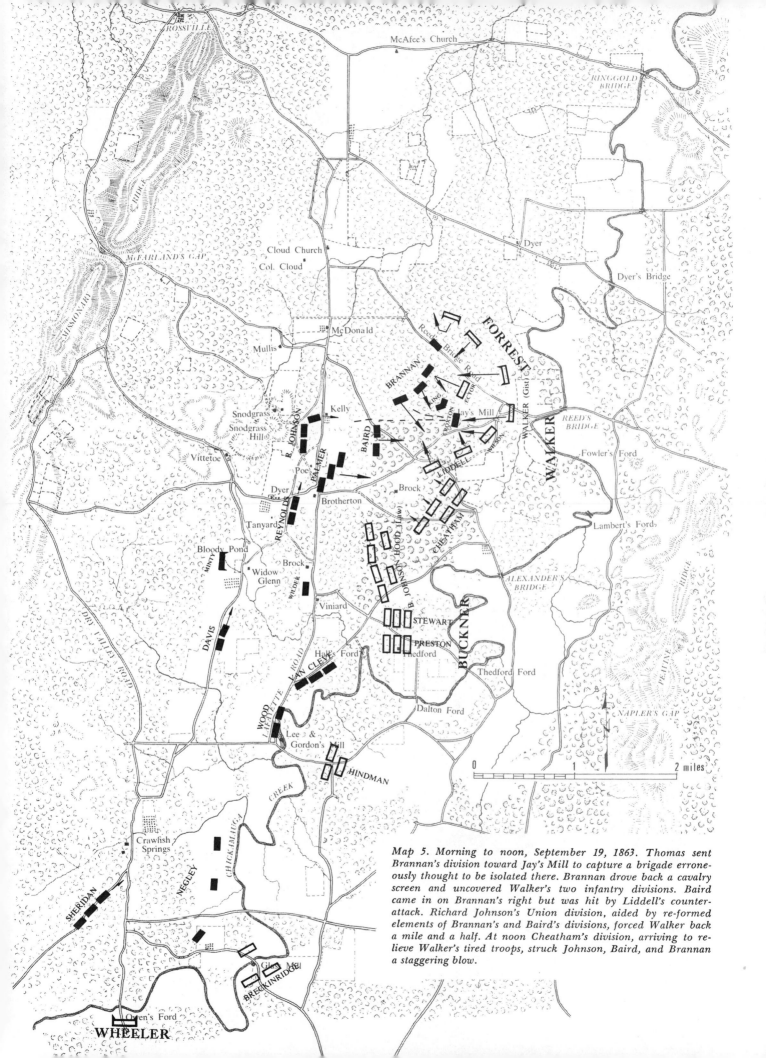

Map 5. Morning to noon, September 19, 1863. Thomas sent Brannan's division toward Jay's Mill to capture a brigade erroneously thought to be isolated there. Brannan drove back a cavalry screen and uncovered Walker's two infantry divisions. Baird came in on Brannan's right but was hit by Liddell's counterattack. Richard Johnson's Union division, aided by re-formed elements of Brannan's and Baird's divisions, forced Walker back a mile and a half. At noon Cheatham's division, arriving to relieve Walker's tired troops, struck Johnson, Baird, and Brannan a staggering blow.

presaged the desperate fighting of the next two days. Croxton's brigade of Brannan's division, which began the assault, sent back a facetious message asking which, of the many brigades in its front, was the one it was supposed to capture!

The battle of the first day was formless and inconclusive. Rosecrans established headquarters on his right, in the Glenn house, where he could dispatch into the action his divisions and brigades coming up on the roads from the south. He could have little influence over the battle there, though he tried to follow it by ear. The New York *Herald* correspondent, W. F. Shanks, poked fun at Rosecrans, who brought out some crude maps of the area and paced back and forth nervously, while his engineer officer tried to locate on the map with a compass the scene of the firing. "Never was anything more ridiculous," Shanks wrote. "When a gun sounded Rosecrans would ask the young widow, Eliza Glenn, where it was, and the country woman would say 'nigh out about Reed's Bridge somewhar,' or, 'about a mile fornenst John Kelly's house.'" (Fornenst was a good, colloquial word meaning beyond, but it seems to have no place in modern dictionaries.)

Divisions arrived on both sides throughout the day, marching north but going into action at the south end of each line. Thus the first day's battle was mainly a series of brigade clashes in the woods, and as the brigades became exhausted and the battle lulled toward the north, it was continued with renewed fury to the south. The armies were moving north but the battle was rolling south. During the afternoon Longstreet's first arrivals under Hood went into action.

The house of Mr. J. M. Lee, Crawfish Spring, Rosecrans' headquarters before the start of the battle and site of the field hospital for the right wing of the Federal army. (From B&L)

STEWART'S SPECTACULAR ADVANCE

Most promising for Bragg was the attack by the division of Major General Alexander P. Stewart, known as "Old Straight," more for his proficiency in mathematics than from his trim West Point bearing. Part of the time he had been Longstreet's roommate at the Academy, and after leaving the service he had been a fellow faculty member with Bushrod Johnson at Nashville University.

His excellent division of three well-led brigades, of Brigadier Generals William B. Bate, Henry D. Clay-

CONFEDERATE LINE OF BATTLE IN THE
CHICKAMAUGA WOODS.

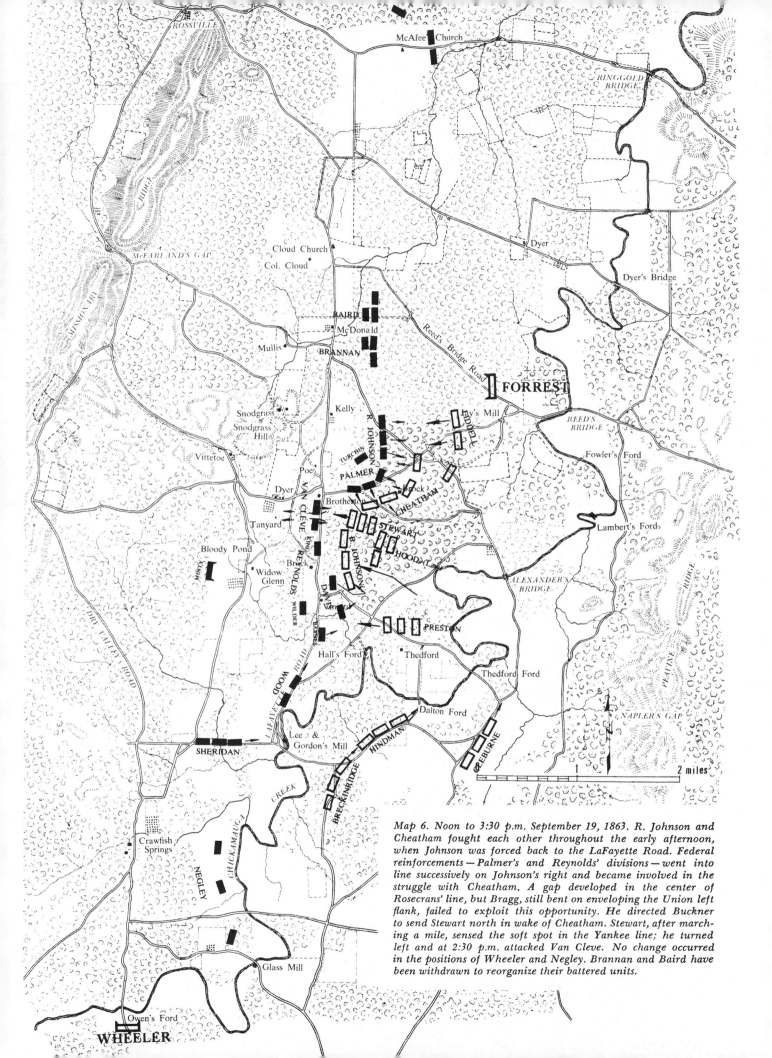

ROSSVILLE

McAfee Church

RINGGOLD BRIDGE

Cloud Church
Col. Cloud

Dyer

Dyer's Bridge

BAIRD
McDonald
Mullis
BRANNAN

Reed's Bridge Road

FORREST

REED'S BRIDGE

Fowler's Ford

Snodgrass
Snodgrass Hill

Vittetoe

Kelly

Ely's Mill

RIDDELL

R. JOHNSON
TURCHIN
Poe
PALMER

Dyer

Brock
Brotherton
CHEATHAM

VAN CLEVE
KING
REYNOLDS

STEWART

Lambert's Ford

Tanyard

Bloody Pond

Widow Glenn

Brock

B. JOHNSON

HOOD (Law)

ALEXANDER'S BRIDGE

MINTY

Brock
Van

WILDER

PESTON

PRESTON

Hall's Ford

Thedford

Thedford Ford

NAPIER'S GAP

Dalton Ford

WOOD

LEAVELL'S ROAD

SHERIDAN

Lee & Gordon's Mill

HINDMAN

BRECKINRIDGE

CLEBURNE

N

1   2 miles

Crawfish Springs

NEGLEY

CHICKAMAUGA CREEK

Map 6. Noon to 3:30 p.m. September 19, 1863. R. Johnson and Cheatham fought each other throughout the early afternoon, when Johnson was forced back to the LaFayette Road. Federal reinforcements — Palmer's and Reynolds' divisions — went into line successively on Johnson's right and became involved in the struggle with Cheatham. A gap developed in the center of Rosecrans' line, but Bragg, still bent on enveloping the Union left flank, failed to exploit this opportunity. He directed Buckner to send Stewart north in wake of Cheatham. Stewart, after marching a mile, sensed the soft spot in the Yankee line; he turned left and at 2:30 p.m. attacked Van Cleve. No change occurred in the positions of Wheeler and Negley. Brannan and Baird have been withdrawn to reorganize their battered units.

Glass Mill

Owen's Ford

WHEELER

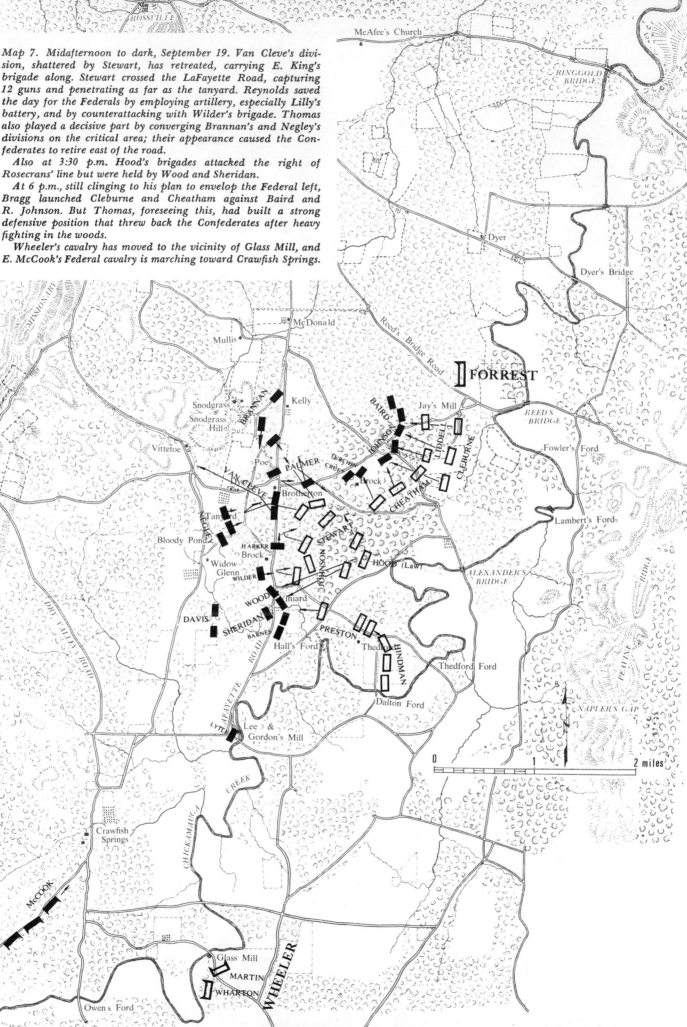

Map 7. Midafternoon to dark, September 19. Van Cleve's division, shattered by Stewart, has retreated, carrying E. King's brigade along. Stewart crossed the LaFayette Road, capturing 12 guns and penetrating as far as the tanyard. Reynolds saved the day for the Federals by employing artillery, especially Lilly's battery, and by counterattacking with Wilder's brigade. Thomas also played a decisive part by converging Brannan's and Negley's divisions on the critical area; their appearance caused the Confederates to retire east of the road.

Also at 3:30 p.m. Hood's brigades attacked the right of Rosecrans' line but were held by Wood and Sheridan.

At 6 p.m., still clinging to his plan to envelop the Federal left, Bragg launched Cleburne and Cheatham against Baird and R. Johnson. But Thomas, foreseeing this, had built a strong defensive position that threw back the Confederates after heavy fighting in the woods.

Wheeler's cavalry has moved to the vicinity of Glass Mill, and E. McCook's Federal cavalry is marching toward Crawfish Springs.

ton, and John C. Brown, was a veteran part of the
Army of Tennessee. It struck the Federal center at
3:15 p.m. in column of brigades. The assault caused
the recorder of the affair to question: "Did you ever
see the destruction of hail storms to a growing corn-
field? Did you ever witness driftwood in a squall?"
That was what Clayton's Alabama brigade looked
like as it closed with Van Cleve's Federal division,
with no breastworks for either and rifles being fired
almost muzzle to muzzle.

STEWART'S DIVISION was proudly termed the
"Little Giants" and here it proved itself worthy of
the name. The three brigades pressed back Van Cleve,
fought through the burning woods, crossed the La-
Fayette Road, and reached the tanyard of the Dyer
farm, in the heart of the Federal position. The situation was critical for Rosecrans because the LaFayette
Road was the link with Thomas battling under heavy
pressure with Walker, now aided by Cheatham on
the left. Stewart's division now held a segment of this
vital roadway. But the Federal center was saved by
the commander of one of Thomas' divisions, Major
General Joseph J. Reynolds, who had been Grant's
roommate at West Point, and was now one of Rosecrans' stanchest fighters. He posted his fourteen guns
to bear on Stewart's men and ordered every infantry
unit in the neighborhood to pour in their fire.

Wilder's mounted infantrymen again came to the
center of the fray and their repeaters compelled the
Confederates to give ground. Negley's division put in
its appearance. Before Negley could reach the fighting,
Stewart's intrepid division was pushed back to the
east side of the LaFayette Road. The jumbled Federal
center, now a confusion of units from all three of
Rosecrans' corps, was given time to reorganize.

CLEBURNE IS BEATEN BACK

The battle rolled farther south for desperate fighting at Viniard's farm, in front of Rosecrans' headquarters at the Widow Glenn's. Then it broke with
renewed vigor at the far opposite end of the line,
where Cleburne, who had been marching down Chickamauga Creek while the battle roared to his left and
had crossed at Thedford's Ford in the late afternoon,
made a desperate sunset attack on Thomas' strongly
held line.

Thomas had conferred with two of his left-wing
division commanders, Baird and Richard W. Johnson,
the latter detached from Crittenden's corps, and had
personally supervised the placing of the guns in
anticipation of a renewed assault. Apprehensive when
Stewart crossed the LaFayette Road and dented the
Federal center, he had detached Brannan's division
from the far left and sent it to the relief of Van Cleve.

There it remained, and came to have a distinct bearing on the fortunes of the second day.

Cleburne was at length repulsed. Darkness settled
early in the woods. Orders against campfires that
would reveal positions were enforced as rigidly as
possible. The moans of the wounded, who could be
given little relief, could be heard from the Reed's
Bridge Road to Viniard's farm. The weather was unusually cold for late September and both armies suffered from lack of fires and shortage of overcoats and
blankets. Perhaps on no other field of the war was
the suffering so acute as on the night of September 19.

THE ARMIES lay along roughly parallel lines, the
LaFayette Road dividing them except on the Federal
left, where Thomas crossed the road to the east and
defended a fortified position through the woods, which
he continued to strengthen by felling trees and hew-
ing abatis all night. The Federal divisions as aligned
roughly from left (north) to right were those of Baird,
Richard Johnson, Palmer, Reynolds, Brannan, (recently shifted from the far left), Wood, Van Cleve
(recessed), Negley (recessed), Davis, and Sheridan.
Facing them, the Confederate alignment from right
(north) to left was Forrest, Cleburne, Gist, Liddell,
Cheatham (recessed), Steward, Bushrod Johnson,
Hood, Hindman, and Preston.

Breckinridge's division, rated among the best, and
consisting of the brigades of Daniel W. Adams, Marcellus A. Stovall, and the "Orphan Brigade" under
Ben Helm, was reaching, with difficulty in the darkness, the position assigned to it on the far right, where
Bragg intended to renew his attack at dawn on the
20th, adamantly adhering to his plan to cut between
Rosecrans and Chattanooga and drive the Federals
back into McLemore's Cove.

Hood commanded a demi-corps, consisting of the
five brigades of the Army of Northern Virginia that
had arrived in time for a part in the battle. These
were two brigades of McLaws' division, those of Joseph
B. Kershaw, who assumed the division as well as
brigade command, and Benjamin C. Humphreys. The
latter had been Barksdale's, who had fallen at Gettysburg. The other division was commanded by E. McIver
Law and consisted of Law's old brigade commanded
by James L. Sheffield, Hood's old Texas brigade commanded by Jerome B. Robertson, and the brigade of
Henry L. Benning. Bushrod Johnson's division was
thrown into Hood's corps while the divisions of
Stewart, Preston, and Hindman were formed into
Buckner's corps. As it developed, the battle of the
second day was fought more by brigades and regiments
than by divisions and corps. A St. Louis newspaper-
man termed it a "soldiers' battle" and that term has
persisted because much of the time in the bush and
heavy timber the higher officers had little control.

"Old Pete" Reaches Battlefield

The most significant event of the night was the arrival of Longstreet. Bragg had made no arrangements to meet him when he reached the railhead at Catoosa Station, accompanied by his always reliable chief of staff, Colonel G. Moxley Sorrel, and his chief of ordnance, Colonel P. T. Manning. They waited for their horses that arrived on a second train, then made their way gropingly toward the sound of the firing, without a guide, and narrowly escaping capture by a Federal patrol that accosted them in the bright moonlight. Longstreet parleyed with the Federals, claiming to be a friend, rode quietly away, then with a dash avoided the delayed bullets.

Bragg was asleep in an ambulance but Longstreet aroused him and they talked for an hour. Longstreet, always combative and dominating, must have looked on Bragg with some contempt, though that did not become apparent until the next afternoon, when he had further opportunity to observe the army commander's generalship. Bragg's headquarters reflected a dismal air, which Hood had noticed when he arrived earlier. Longstreet's rank entitled him to high command on the field. Bragg consequently divided his army into wings, assigning Longstreet to command the left and Bishop Polk, also a lieutenant general, to command the right. It was noticeable that he did not divide the army into three elements and assign the remaining lieutenant general, D. H. Hill, to the center. Polk recommended that. Hill served under Polk and commanded a corps consisting of the divisions of Breckinridge and Cleburne. Bragg had not forgiven him for the failure to attack in McLemore's Cove.

THE DOWNGRADING of Hill unmistakably was an element in Bragg's ghastly failure to get the attack under way on time early on the 20th. His plan, as he outlined it to Longstreet, was for Polk to attack on the right at sunrise with Hill's two divisions. The battle would then move down the line through Cheatham's division and Walker's corps until it reached Longstreet, who would attack with Hood's and Buckner's corps in succession. Hood, who had participated with part of his command on the 19th, was elated over Longstreet's arrival. Longstreet was the first general he had met, he said, who was talking in terms of victory.

One detail Bragg had not attended to was to advise Hill that his corps had been placed under Polk. These two generals, Polk and Hill, had on the morning of the 20th one of the greatest opportunities of the war, and proceeded to bungle it. Polk had asked Hill to stop at his headquarters in an ambulance at Alexander's Bridge and had stationed sentries to keep

watch for him. Hill did not find Polk but two members of his staff did come and Polk entrusted the attack order to them. Hill had gone to Bragg's headquarters at the Thedford house after midnight but Bragg was not there, then had passed Alexander's Bridge, a mile away, at 3 a.m., but the sentries had been withdrawn at 2 a.m. He claimed he never saw the attack order until nineteen years after the battle. Perhaps the blame should fall equally on Hill and Polk; at any rate Bragg awoke early on the 20th, confident that the battle was about to begin, when all the while his orders were lost in the mechanics of transmission.

That night Rosecrans held a council of war, through which Thomas dozed. When his opinion was asked he would rouse himself and invariably deliver the same reply, "I would reinforce the left." He understood that Bragg would persist in his aim to get between Rosecrans and Chattanooga. The council settled little. When the business was completed, McCook entertained his fellow officers with a rendition of a mournful melody entitled "The Hebrew Maiden's Lament," a German song about a Jewish girl who sorrowfully rejected the suitor she loved to adhere to the faith of her fathers.

Bishop Polk Dallies

The critical moment of the battle of the second day came at 11 o'clock. Until then, the two armies

Longstreet's troops debarking from the trains below Ringgold, Georgia on September 18, 1863. They hastened from here into the Battle of Chickamauga which was already raging. (Reproduced from the booklet "Battlefields in Dixie Land" pub. 1928)

Thomas' bivouac after the first day's battle. The next was to be his great day. From a drawing by Gilbert Gaul in B&L.

were still fighting desperately and inconclusively in the deep woods. Bishop Polk failed to attack Thomas at dawn, as Bragg ordered. He got into action five hours late, at 10 o'clock, just as the church bells were ringing for morning services in Chattanooga ten miles away. Bragg said later that if his orders to Polk had been carried out, "our independence might have been gained."

When Bragg did not hear the guns on the right he sent messengers to Polk to learn the cause of the delay. One of them, Major Pollock B. Lee, told Bragg that he found Polk three miles behind his lines, about an hour after sunup, sitting on the porch of a farmhouse, reading a newspaper and waiting for his breakfast. When Major Lee told him that General Bragg was greatly disturbed, Polk was quoted as replying from his rocking chair. "Do tell General Bragg that my heart is overflowing with anxiety for the attack — overflowing with anxiety, sir."

Polk well before the war was one of the distinguished men of the country, Episcopal Bishop of the South, with his seat in New Orleans; handsome, with erect military carriage and large, intelligent face; close friend of the Confederate President, whom he had preceded by one class at West Point; a natural leader, inspiring by his presence as well as by his devoutness.

HE gave his life to the cause a little later near Kennesaw Mountain; but despite Polk's many high

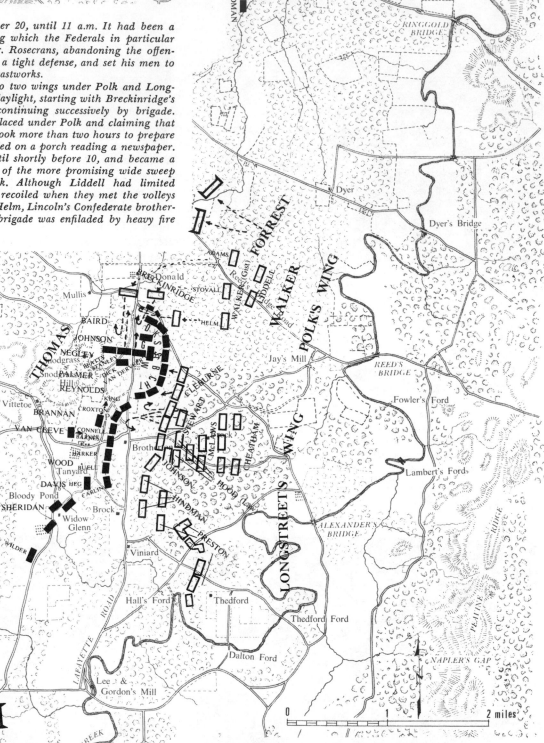

Map 8. Morning of September 20, until 11 a.m. It had been a miserable, frosty night during which the Federals in particular were able to find little water. Rosecrans, abandoning the offensive, contracted his lines into a tight defense, and set his men to work felling trees to build breastworks.

Bragg formed his army into two wings under Polk and Longstreet. Polk was to attack at daylight, starting with Breckinridge's division on the right and continuing successively by brigade. But Hill, irritated at being placed under Polk and claiming that the orders didn't reach him, took more than two hours to prepare for the attack, while Polk lolled on a porch reading a newspaper. The attack didn't get off until shortly before 10, and became a close-in envelopment instead of the more promising wide sweep around Rosecrans' left flank. Although Liddell had limited success, most of the brigades recoiled when they met the volleys at Thomas' log breastworks. Helm, Lincoln's Confederate brother-in-law, was killed when his brigade was enfiladed by heavy fire at close range.

Longstreet formed his wing for a concentrated blow at Rosecrans' center and was ready to jump off at 11 a.m.

Cheatham, Polk's reserve, on the 20th occupied the general position shown, but was not under Longstreet's command. This applies also to Map 9.

Steedman's reserve division covered the Union left at McAfee's Church, with Minty's cavalry brigade out in front. E. McCook's cavalry brigade guarded the Union right west of Lee and Gordon's Mill, while Long's cavalry brigade faced Wheeler at Glass Mill. Forrest's two divisions, covering the Confederate north flank, took no part in the action.

The Federal brigades in the tight center line, indicated by letters, are: D=Dodge; K=J. King; S=Scribner; St=Starkweather; B=Baldwin; C=Cruft; H=Hazen; T=Turchin; G=Grose; W= Willich; on Map 9, V=Van Der Veer.

qualities, President Davis' judgment is subject to question for entrusting him with a veteran corps and making him second in command of Bragg's army. One who had been at the top in authority, and the communicant with God for one of the leading faiths of the South, responded with lack of ardor to the severe and straightlaced soldier under whom he had been placed. He did not foment the cabal among the officers against Bragg in protest to that general's retreat after Stone's River, but he lent dignity and prestige to it by writing Davis personally over Bragg's head, a letter in which he told of the disquiet in the army and recommended that a new commander be appointed.

He had remained in the army only five months after graduating from the Military Academy, then turned to his religious studies and career. After thirty-four years as a churchman he was suddenly appointed a major general by his friend Davis. The Confederate cause never profited. He never fully cast aside the robe for the resplendent uniform he customarily wore.

Thomas repulsed the desperate but belated assault of Hill's corps, made by the splendid veteran divisions of Breckinridge and Cleburne, with Cheatham in support. Certainly no blame could attach to the division commanders. Thomas threw in a succession of brigades and called repeatedly on Rosecrans for reinforcements from the Federal right, which was then not engaged. Rosecrans said that to prevent Bragg from getting between him and Chattanooga he would reinforce Thomas with the entire army, if necessary.

Polk and Hill attacked by brigades in succession, and never with Polk's entire wing *en masse*. Instead of making a wider encirclement of Thomas' left, they wasted much power in costly assaults against Thomas' log breastworks.

ROSEY IS TOLD ABOUT A GAP

So it was around 11 a.m. Sometime between 10:30 and 11, probably near 11, Rosecrans had moved his headquarters, or at least some elements of it, to a ridge to the north that turned out to be in the path of Longstreet's breakthrough. Thus in modern military parlance the forward echelon of his headquarters was on this ridge while the rear echelon, consisting, perhaps, of his adjutant general and other staff members (and his "housekeeping arrangements") was still at Glenn's. But at 11 Rosecrans himself was on the ridge, following the battle mainly by ear. He had ridden along the lines in the early Sunday morning of the 20th. He was in many respects a magnetic personality, not unlike McClellan in his ability to inspire and win the affection of his troops. Most of them adored him, invariably cheered him.

"Old Rosey" — a handsome officer, neatly dressed, even nattily dressed, wore black breeches and a fresh blue coat, given a dash of elegance and swagger by his snow-white vest. His intelligent eyes, of dark blue, sparkled and danced with the excitement of battle. Well-read, a brilliant conversationalist, an inventor, an able engineer, he was in almost every respect up to that moment a successful general. He was regarded by his enemies as something of a genius, more to be feared than McClellan, Meade, Grant, or any other leader in the Northern armies. He had been triumphant in nearly all of his past engagements — in West Virginia, where the major credit had redounded to McClellan, at Iuka and at Stone's River, and in maneuvering Bragg out of Tennessee. His battles, unlike those of McClellan, Grant, Hooker, and some others, had been fought usually against superior or fairly equal numbers. Here at Chicka-

A SHELL AT HEADQUARTERS.

mauga he again faced a superior Confederate force.

At the Federal army headquarters (at Widow Glenn's), Chief of Staff James A. Garfield was marking the shifting positions of the Federal division on his improvised headquarters map. Even Garfield must have been confused, for no human being could possibly follow the devious course of the deadly brigade clashes occurring all along the line in the dense, vine-matted woods and jungle-like thickets.

SOMETIME around 10:30 o'clock one of Thomas' aides, Captain Sanford Cobb Kellogg, of Troy, New York, the young nephew of General Thomas' wife, arrived at Rosecrans' headquarters at the Widow Glenn's.

He was the thirteenth courier Thomas had sent that morning to report on conditions on the Federal left and to request more troops. Rosecrans all morning had been weakening his right and center to reinforce his left just as Meade had done on the second day at Gettysburg, and the center of the Federal army at Chickamauga was held by a line of divisions with no adequate reserve.

Captain Kellogg had ridden along the Glenn-Kelly road, then a woodland trail linking the Glenn farm with the Kelly farm. He did not see Brannan's division in line in the deep woods on his left as he passed. He reported to Rosecrans that there was a gap in the line between the divisions of Reynolds and Wood. This would mean that a dangerous hole existed in the center of the Federal army.

Although Kellogg is most frequently credited with it, there is no agreement on who first reported the existence of this supposed gap. Thomas' staff officer, Henry M. Cist, said the report of a gap came initially from Lieutenant Colonel Alexander Von Schraeder, an Ohioan on Thomas' staff, who reported to Thomas that there were no troops on the right of Reynolds, and that a long gap existed between Reynolds and Wood. Von Schraeder did not know that Brannan's division was in position there, slightly recessed from Reynold's front. According to Cist, Thomas at once sent this information to Rosecrans. Cist did not name the messenger but he obviously was Captain Kellogg.

VON SCHRAEDER, incidentally, was an interesting figure. He had eminent military connections. His father had been a lieutenant general in the Prussian army. The son, like many others who came to America in the late 1840's, had implicated himself in revolutionary activities of 1848, and when they collapsed was forced to flee. He reached Cincinnati, where he became a street car conductor. The war brought his military abilities into play and he became Thomas' assistant inspector general and eventually a brevet brigadier general.

Brig. Gen. James A. Garfield, Rosecrans' chief of staff. (LC)

Diorama in Chickamauga Battlefield Visitor Center showing action as Thomas held on Snodgrass Hill, September 20, 1863.

Whether the fault was initially that of the Troy, N.Y. volunteer, Kellogg, or the Ohio Lieutenant Colonel Von Schraeder, the message violently upset the Federal commander, Rosecrans.

One of Garfield's contemporaries and biographers, John Clark Ridpath, gives a picture of the conditions at Rosecrans' headquarters: "The information received at Widow Glenn's up to ten o'clock on the 20th showed that the troops, though wearied, were holding their own. Up to this time General Garfield, appreciating each emergency as it occurred, had directed every movement, and written every order during the battle. Not a blunder had occurred. His clear, unmistakable English had not a doubtful phrase or a misplaced comma. Every officer had understood and executed just what was expected of him. The fury of the storm had so far spent itself in vain."

Thus it was when the aide Kellogg galloped up and informed Rosecrans that there was a hole in his center.

ROSECRANS DICTATES CONFUSING ORDER

Here was the crisis of the battle. All of the resolute fighting being done on the left of the line by Thomas,

who was holding off the piecemeal attacks of Bishop Polk, was as nothing compared with the events of this fleeting instant inside the little log cabin where Rosecrans had paced nervously back and forth, issuing orders, trying to follow by ear the battle he could not see because of the forests. When he heard Kellogg's reports, Rosecrans turned to his staff. Garfield was not on hand at the moment. According to his admiring biographer, if Garfield had been there and if Rosecrans had spoken to him, the order which was about to be issued would never have been written down, because Garfield had been keeping a careful check on the location of each division, and he knew that Brannan was still between Reynolds and Wood, and that there was no gap in the line.

Brannan, it will be recalled, had been on the far left of the line when the battle opened. Later, after helping to repulse Stewart in the center, he had fitted his division into the heavy woods, along the line of a little trail called the Poe Road. At Rosecrans' council of war held on the night of the 19th, an agreement had been reached whereby Brannan would be returned to Thomas if required again on the left. This was the reason why Rosecrans was uncertain as to just where Brannan was at the moment.

Instead of dealing with Garfield, Rosecrans called to his aide, Major Frank S. Bond, and told him to write an order directing Wood to close the gap instantly by moving to the left. This apparently innocent, yet history-making dispatch, said: "Headquarters Department of Cumberland. September 20 — 10:45 a.m. Brigadier General Wood, Commanding Division: The general commanding directs you to close up on Reynolds as fast as possible, and support him. Respectfully, etc. Frank S. Bond, Major and Aide-de-camp."

That was all. But it was the determining factor in a great battle — one of the most desperately fought battles of American history.

AS this was the key situation in one of the most ghastly battles of the war, the order requires further examination. There is the customary difference in details, but there appears fairly general agreement that the order issued, as a result of the false intelligence brought by Captain Kellogg, was worded by Rosecrans himself and taken down by Major Bond as dictated. When he had the order in writing, Rosecrans rode to where Crittenden was mounted with his staff behind the army's right, and gave the order to Assistant Adjutant General Lyne Starling, chief of staff of Crittenden's XXI Army Corps. This account, which was testified to by Starling, partially absolves Rosecrans of the charge that he issued the order to General Wood directly, and not through corps channels, though Crittenden in person did not seem to know the details of it.

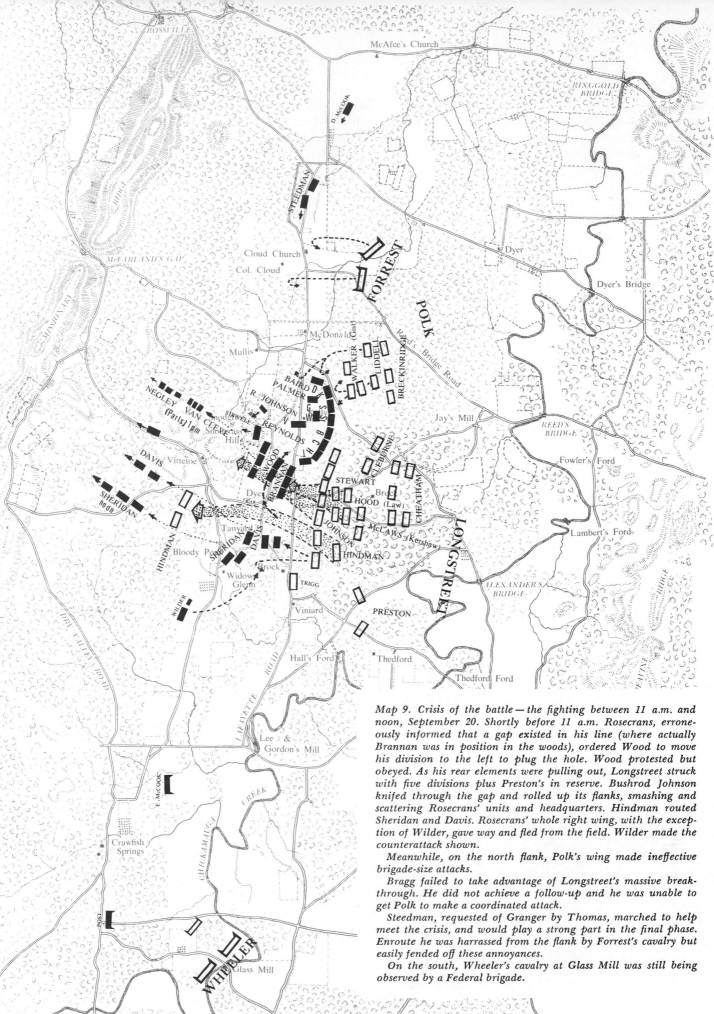

Map 9. Crisis of the battle — the fighting between 11 a.m. and noon, September 20. Shortly before 11 a.m. Rosecrans, erroneously informed that a gap existed in his line (where actually Brannan was in position in the woods), ordered Wood to move his division to the left to plug the hole. Wood protested but obeyed. As his rear elements were pulling out, Longstreet struck with five divisions plus Preston's in reserve. Bushrod Johnson knifed through the gap and rolled up its flanks, smashing and scattering Rosecrans' units and headquarters. Hindman routed Sheridan and Davis. Rosecrans' whole right wing, with the exception of Wilder, gave way and fled from the field. Wilder made the counterattack shown.

Meanwhile, on the north flank, Polk's wing made ineffective brigade-size attacks.

Bragg failed to take advantage of Longstreet's massive breakthrough. He did not achieve a follow-up and he was unable to get Polk to make a coordinated attack.

Steedman, requested of Granger by Thomas, marched to help meet the crisis, and would play a strong part in the final phase. Enroute he was harrassed from the flank by Forrest's cavalry but easily fended off these annoyances.

On the south, Wheeler's cavalry at Glass Mill was still being observed by a Federal brigade.

Starling said he hesitated when he had the order, not understanding the need for Wood to support Reynolds. There was no firing and the fighting had abated. But Garfield, who called out to him, according to his version, said the object was that Wood should occupy the vacancy made by the removal of Brannan's division, which had been ordered to the left of Thomas.

Starling rode to Wood, gave him the order, and told him the object of it. Wood stated at once that Brannan was in position and that there was no vacancy between him and Reynolds. Starling said he then told Wood "there was no order because there was no object for it." He turned, rode at once to Rosecrans, told the commanding general what Wood had said about there being no gap, and added the information that Wood "had a nice little breastwork in his front and ought not to be moved." He explained further to Rosecrans that the enemy was at the very moment in the act of attacking Wood's line and even while he was there, had driven in Wood's pickets.

IF the account of Starling is correct (it was given at the Crittenden court of inquiry and may have been unconsciously protective of his corps commander, Crittenden, though the chief of staff is not open to any charge of deliberate distortion), the responsibility and blame rests on the army commander Rosecrans. He neither countermanded the order nor rode to Wood's or Brannan's positions to ascertain personally the true conditions. The time was brief but he was only a few minutes away, probably not three minutes at a gallop. Still, Wood obeyed the order with alacrity, little knowing that his scrupulous execution of a written order would bring a storm of wrath down on his head.

Garfield's customary practice was to write an order as he thought it should be issued, then submit it to Rosecrans for approval or alteration. When, in this instance, Rosecrans took over the composition of the order himself, he left the wording vague. The meaning was subject to interpretation. But there was no escape clause, allowing the division commander to exercise his own judgment if circumstances differed. On the face of the order, the only course open to Wood was immediate compliance. That was emphatically the case in view of the fact that he had been severely, even rudely, censored, in the presence of his subordinates earlier in the morning, when Rosecrans felt he had not moved his division with wonted alacrity. Wood was supposed to replace Negley's division, which was to reinforce Thomas. When Negley was slow, Wood was also slow. Rosecrans placed the chief blame on Wood, denounced his "damnable negligence," loosened a torrent of ex-

pletives, as he could do so well when excited. Wood merely saluted and marched immediately. He could scarcely be expected to hesitate over execution of an order an hour or so later.

Particularly was that the case when the order carried the words, "as fast as possible."

WOOD'S SOLDIERLY OBEDIENCE

Wood's division consisted of but two brigades on the battlefield, both stanch and tested and commanded by officers of high merit. They were Colonel Charles G. Harker of the West Point class of 1858, who would be heard of later in the battle and would die in the attack on Kennesaw Mountain the next year; and Colonel George P. Buell, who would have later distinctions including a brevet for gallant service on Missionary Ridge. Wood's other brigade, that of Brigadier General George D. Wagner, had been left behind to garrison Chattanooga. This was one of the divisions which two months later would spearhead the attack and be one of the first, some say the first, to reach the summit of Missionary Ridge, and might therefore be accounted the division which more than any other, made Grant a lieutenant general and, in turn, President.

When Wood issued his orders he gained the customarily prompt response from his brigade commanders and in ten minutes after the departure of Starling the brigades were on the march to the left rear. Harker, who was on the left, moved first, instantly responsive, though, as he said, "we well knew the enemy was in our front ready to take advantage of any false step that we might make." He understood that McCook's corps, which was on Wood's immediate right, was ready to fill the gap caused by the departure of Wood. He marched to the left rear in search of Reynolds, but found Van Cleve's division gone and Brannan being broken, and looked about for the place where he could be of the greatest service. This was happily on what has since been known as "Harker's Hill," because of the notable use he made of it.

Buell followed Harker to the left and rear but was scarcely in motion — he had marched the distance of a brigade front — "when the shock came like an avalanche on my right flank." He was not allowed time to clear his brigade and keep pace with Harker. All about him was near chaos. As he watched, the entire right wing of the army and a part of the center gave way. "My own little brigade," he reported, "seemed as if it were swept from the field. The greater portion of my brigade was cut off from me and driven to the rear."

Down through the decades Wood had been condemned by one school and defended by another be-

Battle of Chickamauga. Repulse of Alexander P. Stewart's Confederate division at Crawfish Creek. Drawing by J. F. C. Hillen.

cause he obeyed the order. He has been accused of vindictiveness, a desire to avenge himself because of Rosecrans' censure of him earlier. He has been charged with stupidity, and with near criminality. But if there was an error, it was in the *order* and not in Wood's *response*. He did what any general ought to do on the battlefield. He obeyed.

Now, instead of the supposed gap reported by Captain Kellogg, an actual gap was created between the divisions of Brannan and Jefferson C. Davis. Wood's departure left a hole in the line a quarter of a mile wide.

LONGSTREET'S BREAKTHROUGH

Gaps have occurred in the lines on other battlefields and not been consequential, but in this instance there was a striking coincidence. At this very instant, at 11 a.m., Longstreet was beginning his massed attack against the Federal right center. Into the hole left by the departure of Wood he poured the divisions of Bushrod Johnson, Joseph B. Kershaw and McIver Law, supported on the right by Alexander P. Stewart and on the left by Thomas C. Hindman. As a general reserve he had the splendid division of William P. Preston, one of whose brigades was commanded by the brilliant young New Yorker, Archibald Gracie. Gracie, like Bushrod Johnson and a good many other officers of Northern birth, was fighting on the Southern side, as Thomas, the Virginian, was in major command of the Union fighting line.

Bushrod Johnson's attack was one of the most spectacular of the Civil War. He cut through Rosecrans' army with the ease of a razor severing a jugular vein. He cut off the Federal army commander from his main body north on the LaFayette Road. He advanced a mile through the center of the Federal position, scattering the fragments of Rosecrans' broken wing to the left and right. The divisions of Sheridan and Jefferson C. Davis collapsed and dashed headlong from the field. They were followed by the larger part of the divisions of Van Cleve and Negley. The right wing disintegrated and the efforts of officers to check the departure of the better part of four divisions was altogether futile. "We'll see you on the other side of the Ohio," some of the fleeing soldiers shouted.

D. H. Hill described the breakthrough and advance of Bushrod Johnson's three brigades: "On they rushed, shouting, yelling, running over batteries, capturing trains, taking prisoners, seizing the headquarters of the Federal commander, at the Widow Glenn's [this may have been the location of his staff; Rosecrans

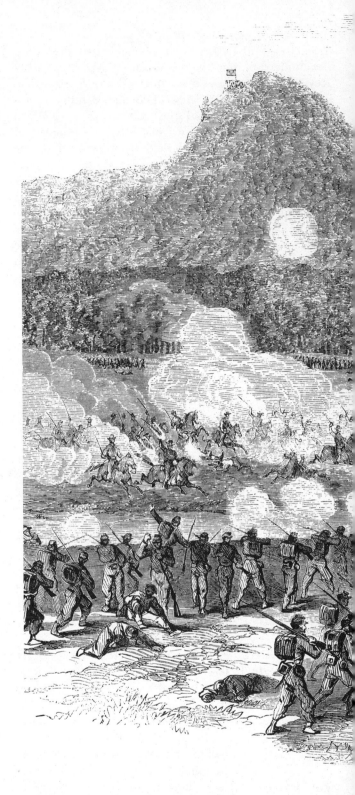

had left the Glenn house], until they found themselves facing the new Federal line on Snodgrass Hill."

WILLIAM M. OWEN of the Washington Artillery of New Orleans, who left such a splendid account of that extraordinary command's activities on many fields, and who was here attached to Preston's division, gave his version of the breakthrough: "Longstreet discovers, with his soldier's eye, a gap in their already confused lines and . . . short and bloody is

the work. We move steadily forward, no halting. The men rush over the hastily constructed breastworks of logs and rails of the foe, with the old-time familiar rebel yell, and, wheeling to the right, the column sweeps the enemy before it, and pushes along the Chattanooga road toward Missionary Ridge in pursuit. It is glorious!"

All the while Bragg did not seem to understand what was happening. Longstreet's attack in depth was a tactical masterpiece, comparable to Winfield

Scott Hancock's massed attack with the Federal II Corps at Spotsylvania. But Bragg made no effort to assist Longstreet by ordering a fresh attack with his right. At 2:45 Longstreet said, "They have fought their last man and *he* is running." That might seem to be the situation in his front, but Longstreet did not take into consideration the character of either Bragg or George H. Thomas.

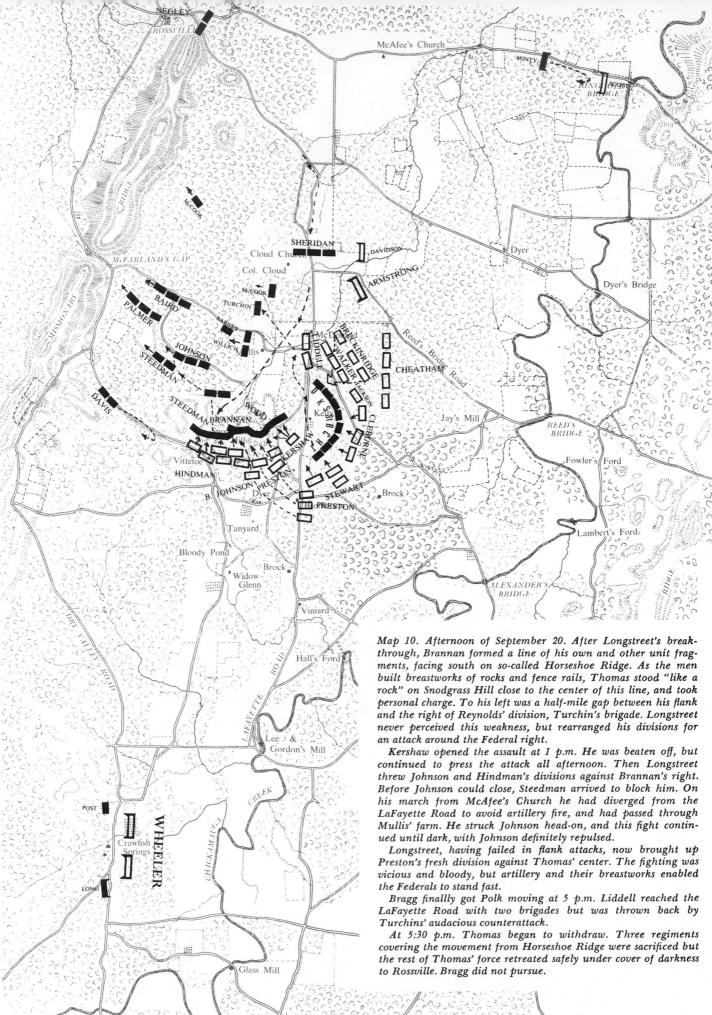

Map 10. Afternoon of September 20. After Longstreet's breakthrough, Brannan formed a line of his own and other unit fragments, facing south on so-called Horseshoe Ridge. As the men
built breastworks of rocks and fence rails, Thomas stood "like a
rock" on Snodgrass Hill close to the center of this line, and took
personal charge. To his left was a half-mile gap between his flank
and the right of Reynolds' division, Turchin's brigade. Longstreet
never perceived this weakness, but rearranged his divisions for
an attack around the Federal right.

   Kershaw opened the assault at 1 p.m. He was beaten off, but
continued to press the attack all afternoon. Then Longstreet
threw Johnson and Hindman's divisions against Brannan's right.
Before Johnson could close, Steedman arrived to block him. On
his march from McAfee's Church he had diverged from the
LaFayette Road to avoid artillery fire, and had passed through
Mullis' farm. He struck Johnson head-on, and this fight continued until dark, with Johnson definitely repulsed.

   Longstreet, having failed in flank attacks, now brought up
Preston's fresh division against Thomas' center. The fighting was
vicious and bloody, but artillery and their breastworks enabled
the Federals to stand fast.

   Bragg finallly got Polk moving at 5 p.m. Liddell reached the
LaFayette Road with two brigades but was thrown back by
Turchins' audacious counterattack.

   At 5:30 p.m. Thomas began to withdraw. Three regiments
covering the movement from Horseshoe Ridge were sacrificed but
the rest of Thomas' force retreated safely under cover of darkness
to Rossville. Bragg did not pursue.

Thomas Rallies The Fragments

The most stubborn phase of the battle was still to be fought. Thomas collected the remnants of the army's right wing on Snodgrass Hill where he was assisted by the timely arrival of Granger and Steedman with the Reserve Corps, small but resolute, and he held against the triumphant Confederates until he could withdraw under cover of darkness.

Longstreet hammered at Snodgrass Hill through the remainder of the afternoon. While he made occasional inroads to the crest, he was unable to break the stalwart defense, which earned for Thomas the title of the "Rock of Chickamauga." Buell's men, like Harker's, who composed Wood's division, were among the numerous heroic groups of the right wing who tarried to assist Thomas. Famous among the units of Wood's division was Colonel Emerson Opdycke's 125th Ohio, termed the "Tiger Regiment" after the fight on Snodgrass Hill. Opdycke gained later fame in larger commands fighting at Franklin and Nashville under Thomas, but is perhaps best remembered as the commander of "Opdycke's Tigers" at Chickamauga.

Rosecrans, Crittenden, McCook, and Garfield were swept from the field along with their retreating men, as were division commanders Sheridan, Jefferson C. Davis, Negley, and Van Cleve. Garfield returned later in the day with unnecessary orders for Thomas to hold and retire at nightfall. Thomas' retreat was hazardous, but the Confederate army was near exhaustion and he conducted it carefully. Polk's wing remained largely idle.

FOR the Confederates, a second crisis came after the battle had been won. The reluctant Bragg had found any number of reasons why he should not pursue Rosecrans, at a time when pursuit might have saved the Confederacy in the late afternoon of its power. Nearly everyone in the army except Bragg favored quick pursuit. Finally, by the next morning, Bragg also had been won to the obviously correct plan of crossing the Tennessee River above Chattanooga and interposing his triumphant army between Rosecrans in Chattanooga and Burnside in Knoxville. It is clear that both Rosecrans and Burnside would have been compelled to withdraw, unless Burnside, by chance, might have been captured.

Forrest, on Lookout Mountain where he had a good view of the Chattanooga area, pleaded with Bragg through Polk that "every hour is worth ten thousand men." But Bragg had been concerned over his appalling loss of horses in this in-the-woods fighting. From his vantage point Forrest wrote a message

General George Thomas at Chickamauga. Scene is set against a background of Tennessee hills, where battle smoke can be seen. General Gordon Granger, commanding a reserve corps of the Army of the Cumberland, occupied a position several miles from the battlefield awaiting orders. Finally, growing impatient, he said to a staff officer: "I am going to Thomas, orders or no orders," and advanced his troops toward the sound of firing. He is here pictured in the painting by Henry A. Ogden, at the moment of his arrival, shaking Thomas' hand.

to General Polk, saying the Federal trains were moving around the end of Lookout Mountain. Federal prisoners reported that two pontoons had been thrown across the river for the purpose of retreating.

This was the message which, in the opinion of Longstreet, sealed the fate of the Confederacy. Forrest cannot be blamed — he reported what he saw. But Bragg thought Chattanooga was being vacated. Instead of marching around the city, crossing upstream and threatening Rosecrans' communications and line of retreat, he advanced against Chattanooga, found Rosecrans entrenched, and began a protracted siege. The result was his ultimate defeat on Lookout Mountain and Missionary Ridge, by the host of Federal soldiers rushed against him from all directions. His delay gave the Federal armies time to concentrate and never again were they, as at Chickamauga, caught off guard.

CAUSES OF THE DEFEAT

Why did the North lose this battle, which may have prolonged the life of the Confederacy more than a year? The first blame must be lodged against Burnside, who failed to move down from Knoxville, as ordered, to join Rosecrans and shield his left flank, the flank Bragg was trying to turn to reach Chattanooga.

A second cause was the failure of the Federal War Department to send help from Grant's army, units of which were either idle at this period after the capture of Vicksburg, or were being dispersed. The surrender of Vicksburg released Joseph E. Johnston's army, which had been watching ineffectually at Jackson, Mississippi. Some of the best Confederate units in the West, including Breckinridge's division, were returned to Bragg, without Rosecrans receiving any compensating units from Grant. Sherman was idle with his corps in Mississippi and could well have been employed in Tennessee and North Georgia.

Burnside ranked Rosecrans. He has been excused on the ground that he did not want to join the Army of the Cumberland and supersede its commander. But Burnside could have waived the command, by direction of the War Department. A similar situation occurred when Meade sent Hancock to take command at Gettysburg after the death of Reynolds on the first day, though Howard ranked him. Meade issued orders which allowed Hancock the top command, and so the War Department might have done in this instance.

Thus, while Bragg was heavily reinforced, Rosecrans had to fight with substantially the same army he had commanded at Stone's River.

THE third major cause of the defeat was Rosecrans' poor tactical performance. This resulted in part because the battle was fought in the woods and, lacking communications, he lost control. His center and right were in a continual state of flux with units going to help Thomas. Against his weakened right center Longstreet massed his brigades for an attack in depth. Longstreet struck a weak spot and cut through the wide gap with ease, but had the gap not existed, is there not reason to believe that Longstreet could have overpowered McCook's weaker corps?

Rosecrans' failure resulted mainly from lack of an adequate reserve. Granger's corps, which finally gave Thomas some relief on Snodgrass Hill, was inadequate, and had another mission — guarding the Ross-

ville gap — besides that of acting as a maneuverable unit on the battlefield. Rosecrans showed capabilities, often brilliance, in his other battles. In the broader field of strategy he had few equals. His supreme error was in leaving the field while Thomas, with whom he could have gained contact and joined by a circuitous ride, remained. He can be termed "the general of the one mistake." But it was a mistake sufficient to allow his superiors, with whom one of his candid and fiery temperament had not been popular, to relegate him to a quiet sector.

THE BATTLE had a further bearing on the fate of the Confederacy because of the wounding of General Hood, whose leg was amputated on the night of the 20th by surgeons behind the lines. The stump was very short and the instance was one of the few in the war where a man lived with a lower member severed so near to the trunk.

Hood already had been grievously wounded at Gettysburg in an arm that was left near palsied and useless. Many wounded Civil War soldiers knew that when an arm or leg was amputated it continued to hurt. This writer has heard a veteran's account of an instance where a soldier insisted on having his leg dug up and packed with cotton between the toes before being reinterred. Some latter day doctors have

The wounding of General Hood at Chickamauga. From a sketch made by Frank Vizetelly for the "Illustrated London News."

Arrival of Union wounded from Chickamauga, September 23, at Stevenson, Alabama. From a sketch by J. F. C. Hillen. (FL)

diagnosed this pain as the result of fraying of the nerve ends, causing them to send false messages.

Hood suffered severe pain from his two wounds and for it, according to information that has been handed down, constantly took a laudanum derivative, believed by some who have studied his case to have been in sufficient quantity to establish a sort of euphoria, or unrealistic sense of well-being. That is a possible explanation for his belief that he could, in the closing stages of the war, take an army of 30,000 to 35,000 men, march with it to the Ohio, and draw Sherman back from Georgia. The shattering of his army by Thomas at Nashville was perhaps the supreme Confederate defeat of the war, and in different respects it was an outgrowth of Chickamauga.

Finally, in examining the causes of the Federal defeat, attention must be given to coincidence — the play of chance. Longstreet might have crushed Rosecrans' right wing in any event, but the realities are that he did it by taking advantage of the erroneous movement of Wood's division, a movement resulting from a messenger conveying misinformation to the commanding general, and that general's impulsive acceptance of it without making a personal reconnaissance, though he was close at hand.

Nor can any analysis neglect the over-all culpability of the Federal War Department for its failure to give Rosecrans a sufficient warning that Longstreet's corps was leaving Lee's army.

THE MEN STILL LOVED "OLD ROSEY"

Neither Thomas, nor Longstreet, nor Rosecrans, nor Bushrod Johnson have monuments on the battlefield. Perhaps Longstreet and Thomas do not need them, for anyone analyzing the battle will know of their achievements more readily from the written word than from stone. Bushrod Johnson rests in an obscure grave in a village cemetery in southern Illinois, where he went to do farming and grace an enemy countryside with his scholarship, mainly by giving lessons and lending books to farm lads he taught without pay. His is a delightful story that will some day be written more fully, for it has intrigued numerous Civil War buffs.

Rosecrans, the only commander of a major Federal army who has never been given a monument anywhere, lived in the hearts of his soldiers. He went to Congress from California, served as chairman of the House Military Affairs Committee, acquired wealth through his metallurgical enterprises, and had his moment of glory when he returned to the Chickamauga battlefield for the great reunion of blue and gray September 19 and 20, 1889. The barbecue feast was spread over ten acres, on thirty tables each 250 feet long, which on the two sides made 15,000 feet, close to three miles of seating room.

John B. Gordon, governor of Georgia, represented the veterans in gray. He and Rosecrans led the military procession, mounted on high-spirited steeds, with the 4th U.S. Infantry band playing "Dixie." Then they were lifted to a table top, where they spoke. Ten thousand men crowded around "Old Rosey" to take his hand. "Old veterans cried like infants," reported a scribe.

Then, at the final moment, the Rosecrans burial services in 1898, the most prominent personage on the stand was the broken old Georgian, Longstreet, shattered by his wound taken in The Wilderness and by the decades of abuse heaped on him by a coterie of enemies as the man who had lost the Battle of Gettysburg. More than any other, he was responsible for Rosecrans' defeat and relegation to military obscurity, yet was the chief mourner at the final parting.

AN UNRECOGNIZED JOAN

Nearly every war has its maid who longs to be a Joan of Arc. The Civil War's Joan died on the field of Chickamauga. She was a girl from Willoughby Street, in Brooklyn, who in early 1863, when Federal armies were meeting disaster and the Union appeared to many to be lost, believed she heard the call of Providence to save her country.

Her parents thought she was mentally unbalanced. They consulted their pastor and friends and decided to send her to visit an aunt in Ann Arbor, Michigan. There she was held a virtual prisoner. Escaping, but finding herself unable to reach Washington and tell President Lincoln of her mission, she concealed her sex, eluded detectives sent by her family to trail her, and enlisted as a drummer boy in a Detroit regiment.

Finding her way into Van Cleve's division, she sustained the rigors and rapid marching of the Tullahoma campaign. Her sex was not discovered until she was hit in the left side and fatally wounded by a minie ball on Sunday, September 20, at Chickamauga.

When the surgeons told her the wound was fatal, she dictated a letter to her father: "Forgive your dying daughter. I have but a few moments to live. My native soil drinks my blood. I expected to deliver my country, but the Fates would not have it so. I am content to die. Pray, pa, forgive me. Tell ma to kiss my daguerreotype. Emily."

"P.S. Give my old watch to little Eph."

She was buried on the field where she fell. Her story was contained in one of the unidentified clippings of anecdotes culled by Frank Moore in 1865 for his *Civil War in Song and Story*. Unhappily neither he nor the newspaper scribe left the maiden's name.

— G.T.

CURIOUS WOUNDS AT CHICKAMAUGA

An oddity of the battle was the wound of Private Edmund Brewer Tate, 15th Georgia, of Benning's brigade. He was one of eight brothers from Elberton, the marble town of east Georgia, who served in the Confederate army.

On the late afternoon of September 19 a minie ball hit him in the left breast. It went in at the nipple and ranged downward, then came out of his back left of the spinal column. The bullet made sixteen holes through the blanket that was rolled over his shoulder and chest, after the Confederate fashion. Those who saw him fall judged that the ball had passed directly through his heart.

That night his brothers looked for his body and discovered that he was still breathing. The army doctors found to their amazement that his heart was functioning normally, but on his right side, knocked there, they concluded, by the force of the minie ball. For the rest of his life he was known as "the man whose heart was knocked to the wrong side at Chickamauga."

His daughter, who confirmed the story for this writer, said the wound never curtailed his activities. He was a large, rugged man, lived into old age, even possessed the stamina to go into the ordeal of Georgia politics, and all the time his heart was on the wrong side. A biological authority, long a professor at a Southern university, explained for this writer that it was clearly, in his opinion, an instance of *situs reversis*, in which the heart and abdominal organs are transposed from birth, which happens, as he put it, "once in a blue moon."

An unusual coincidence befell Captain John N. Sloan, of Pontotoc, Mississippi, Hindman's division, who had some of his teeth and part of a jawbone ripped out by a bullet. Thirty-two years later at a reunion he and others of his company were going over the area where he had lain wounded. "Captain, here are your teeth," a companion called to him. Sure enough, there were three molars scratched from the dirt which he identified as his.

— G.T.

ABOVE: Bloody Pond, nameless cattle pond on a backwoods farm until the battle. ("Pennsylvania at Chickamauga and Chattanooga")

BELOW: The Snodgrass house (taken about 1890). This is how it looked in 1863 when Thomas made it famous with his stubborn defense.

ABOVE: Alexander's Bridge (taken about 1890). The bridge appears as it did during the battle. Alexander's Bridge was one of the two major Chickamauga Creek crossings used by Confederates moving onto the battlefield. Here Wilder's Mounted Infantry and Eli Lilly's artillery contested the crossing by Walker.

BELOW: The sloping ground of Kershaw's and Gracie's assault against Stanley's brigade at Snodgrass Hill, September 20, 1863. ("Pennsylvania at Chickamauga and Chattanooga")

THE
BATTLES FOR
CHATTANOOGA

by Glenn Tucker

Wellington said nothing is so melancholy as a battle won except a battle lost.

So it was after Chickamauga when the Confederate Army of Tennessee, triumphant and bloody, seethed with discord over the lethargy and ineptitude of General Braxton Bragg, its commander.

Gloom, fear, and near despair gripped its adversary, the Army of the Cumberland, as it retreated forlornly into Rossville and on through the mountain gap to Chattanooga, after the disorderly flight of one of its wings, along with its commanding general and two corps commanders, from a field long stubbornly contested, then lost in a twinkling by a chance mistake.

An army without food is better for a time than an army without heart, but Major General William Starke Rosecrans' beleaguered force of upwards of 40,000 exhausted survivors had neither. Morale was shattered; the supply lines were cut.

Only the tardiness of Bragg's pursuit spared the Union army. Spurred on by "Old War Horse" Longstreet, whose left wing had delivered the *coup de main* to the two Federal corps of Major Generals Alexander Mc-

Cook and Thomas L. Crittenden, and implored by the call of the discerning cavalryman, Nathan Bedford Forrest, that "every hour is worth ten thousand men," and importuned even by the Bishop-Lieutenant General Leonidas Polk, whose procrastination on the field had blunted Bragg's attack and possibly dulled his victory, the Confederate commander had buried his dead, counted his surviving artillery horses, taken counsel with his overabundant conservatism, weighed his restraints, and had finally drawn up in front of Chattanooga, having covered the twelve miles from the battlefield in what would have seemed an eon to Lee or Jackson—two and a half days!

On the day after the battle Major General George H. Thomas, who had saved the Federal army by his stubborn stand on Snodgrass Hill, laid out a fairly formidable defensive line across Rossville Gap and the Chattanooga Creek valley. Already the men were changing his nickname from the affectionate "Old Pap" to the more exalted "Old Hero."

Forrest and others believed Thomas' line could be broken or turned by the victory-stimulated Confederates,

but the test was not made. Rosecrans, instead of risking another battle on the outskirts, preferred to sustain a siege in the intrenched inner town. Though he toyed for a time with the notion of evacuating Chattanooga and retiring to Nashville (which might have involved another retreat through Kentucky and race for Louisville like Buell's the year before), he elected to hold fast and await succor. A retirement to Nashville or dash for Louisville would have left Major General Ambrose E. Burnside behind in Knoxville, ripened on the vine for Confederate plucking.

Last into Chattanooga was Cruft's brigade of Palmer's division, Thomas' corps, which during September 21, 1863, the day after the retreat from Chickamauga, had garrisoned the south end of Missionary Ridge. Its right rested on the road at Rossville and its left reached to the point part way up the ridge where Bragg later had his headquarters. When Bragg failed to pursue rapidly, most of the brigade was withdrawn into Chattanooga. Three companies of the 31st Indiana remained as rearguard. Finally only Company A was

left behind. The others, as they left in the darkness, shouted jocular requests to the Company A boys to "send home some souvenirs from [Belle Isle] and Libby Prisons." One sergeant said, as the tread of the last marching columns died away, "the loneliness seemed almost suffocating."

Polk's Confederates were at last coming up and all night the soft, drawling words sounded clearly from their bivouac at the foot of the ridge, while the Southern artillery rattled over the stones, and the heavy tramp of oncoming regiments could be heard from the roads leading from the battlefield. The dull gray of the new autumn day shone at length and with it came a courier with orders for the little company, the last fifty men of Rosecrans' battered army, to retire behind the Federal cavalry videttes three miles south of Chattanooga.

The company, after keeping guard all night, snatched an hour of sleep, then marched, and soon had rejoined thousands of bluecoats digging with spades a half circle of works reaching from the riverbank south to high ground north of the town.

Later that day (evening of September 23), a puff of smoke and a bursting shell gave notice that Polk's corps had reached the vacated crest of Missionary Ridge, while a similar announcement fell short from the top of Lookout Mountain. The siege of Chattanooga, the only investment suffered by a large Northern army during the war (Nashville a year later hardly rates as a siege), and in many respects one of the most peculiar affairs of American history, had begun.

Whether held by a Northern or Southern army, Chattanooga had been regarded as a citadel. It is a natural passageway between North and South. The Tennessee River flows down from Knoxville apparently intent on a course through Georgia, but the tossup of mountains around Chattanooga deflects it abruptly. Making almost an about-face—a sweep spectacular when seen from the peaks—it moves abreast its earlier channel, now churning and tossing northward.

Inside its graceful bend is a mile-wide projection, or virtual isthmus, called Moccasin Point. Here, where the river is so rudely deflected from the Georgia border, it manifests its discomfort by casting aside its former serene and placid surface and vexes itself with a series of what the pioneers called "boiling pots," or "sucks." They render navigation difficult until the mighty stream, comparable in beauty with the Hudson cleaving through the New York highlands, is well into Alabama, and until it is contemplating there the last long turn that directs it gently northwestward to the Ohio.

Chattanooga lay on the left or south bank, just above the coil of Moccasin Bend. The town was not an old

This wartime view of Chattanooga is from the Brady Collection in the National Archives. Lookout Mountain in the background.

The John Ross house, Rossville. Missionary Ridge on right. (NA)

Southern community like Nashville or Augusta, but had technically come into the possession of the United States only twenty-three years before the Civil War, after the ejection of the Cherokee Indians over the "Trail of Tears" in 1838.

Chattanooga is one of the Cherokee's half-anglicized words, derived from *chatta* (crow) and *nooga* (nest), but often given the loftier meaning of "eagle's" or "hawk's" nest. In days before the Revolutionary War, Spanish Roman Catholic priests from St. Augustine, Florida established a mission and school for Indians which long flourished on the ridge overlooking the "crow's nest." The religious outpost caused the height to be called Mission Ridge, later corrupted into Missionary Ridge.

The Indian towns along the nearby creeks were raided and burned by "Nolichucky Jack" Sevier, governor of the ephemeral state of Franklin, in 1793. Returning survivors of the devastation gradually assembled on the river and founded Chattanooga. John Ross, chief of the Cherokee, though only one-sixteenth Indian, built about 1800 a large log house, imposing by frontier standards, near the bold spring of clear mountain water in the pass between Lookout Mountain and the southern break of Missionary Ridge, five miles south of Chattanooga, and the second village of wigwams and huts that grew there took the name Rossville. Chattanooga, at first called Ross's Landing, had attained some importance as a trading post by 1830.

The Cherokee were removed after gold was discovered around Dahlonega, Georgia, and President Jackson had sided with the whites who had encroached on the tribe's southern Appalachian holdings. President Van Buren

sent General Winfield Scott and an army detachment to Missionary Ridge to transport the Cherokee (all except those who hid in the western North Carolina mountains) to reservations beyond the Mississippi. One of Scott's young subordinates who cast his eyes reflectively over the terrain and mused about the unsavory business at hand, who was already dedicating his career to the harassment of his superiors and to inflexible obedience to regulations down to the last punctuation mark, was a lieutenant from North Carolina fresh from the West Point class of 1837, Braxton Bragg.

By Civil War days Chattanooga had grown to be a town of 2,545 citizens with mixed sentiments about secession. The most important structure was the Crutchfield House, a rambling three-story hostelry at Ninth and Broad Streets run by Thomas and William Crutchfield, both strong Unionists. (William, during the war, served as a Union scout with an unofficial major's ranking and after the war was a Congressman from the district.) Possession of the Crutchfield House, the town's tallest building, signified possession of Chattanooga. The commanding general usually used the hotel as his headquarters, and the flag that flew above it would be seen from the surrounding heights.

When war came, the Stars and Bars floated atop Crutchfield's hotel, the town became a Confederate military depot, and the *Daily Rebel* told the news of Lee and Jackson in Virginia. At length, on September 9, 1863, Rosecrans arrived with his Federal army and his maneuvering skill that forced Bragg to evacuate the stronghold without a battle, until the bloody encounter occurred when the two armies stumbled into each other in the woods twelve miles south along Chickamauga Creek. Then the badly worsted Rosecrans came back to the town as a possible sanctuary.

One of the first acts of the beleaguered Union army was to tear down nearly all of the wooden houses. The town lay in valleys and on low hills, one being Cameron Hill, known also as Bell Mountain, in the western portion. There some large residences offered a degree of elegance. But lumber was scarce and the army engineers required it urgently for the bastions and lunettes being erected by Brigadier General St. Clair Morton, chief of engineers.

Within two weeks he had so mercilessly transformed a community of smiling homes and gardens into a forbidding gray fortress that another officer said of him: "If Morton needed earth for a fort, the fact that it was a gold mine would make no difference. He would only say, 'Gold dust will resist artillery—it will do.' " Homes were transformed into blockhouses. As one of the correspondents described it: "Black bastions sprung up in former vineyards; rifle pits were run through graveyards; and soon a long line of works stretched from the river above to the river below the city, bending crescentlike around it, as if it were a huge bow of iron, and rendering it impregnable. For a fortnight the whole army worked on the fortifications, and it became literally a walled city.''

Inside the citadel, the men tore down barns, sheds, and fences, along with the houses, and with the boards erected huts along orderly company streets. They used their shelter halves for roofs, which led to the observation that the town was not unlike the village of oldtime Indian days, the tented roofs being similar to wigwams. Day by day the ring of the ax rose to the Confederates on the nearby heights, as the Federal army cut, hewed, drove, and pounded, trying to make itself secure from the long-range enemy fire from Lookout Mountain and comfortable for the oncoming winter.

While he was entrenching in Chattanooga Rosecrans at the beginning made the inexcusable mistake of abandoning Lookout Mountain, which commanded the supply route from the river and railroad at Bridgeport and Stevenson to Chattanooga. As Bragg came up he seized eagerly the looming eminence, assigned Longstreet's corps to garrison it and guard Lookout Valley beyond it, and finally added the division of Major Gen-

"View of Chattanooga and Moccasin Point from the side of Lookout Mountain." This engraving from a photograph appears in B&L.

eral Carter L. Stevenson that had been part of Pemberton's army in Vicksburg, and two brigades of Cheatham's division. These last two brigades were the only ones left behind when the spirited fighting for the possession of Lookout developed.

The Confederate encirclement was not complete but was effective. The great Union army that a week earlier had threatened to take Atlanta and split the Deep South asunder, now needed food and the only means left open to supply it was by a wagon route to the north, over the worst of roads, across Walden's Ridge, a rugged spur of the Cumberland Mountains, thence via the Sequatchie Valley to the army base at Bridgeport and Stevenson, where the rails from Nashville met the river. By yielding Lookout Mountain Rosecrans had allowed Bragg to block the road and water route around Moccasin; all provisions had to be hauled over the miserable land route of sixty miles. The distance was such that the forage mules could haul only about what they required for strength to make the journey.

The army went immediately on short rations. Food conditions could not have been much worse, if as bad, at this stage of the war, in Florence, Salisbury, or Libby

Prisons. As the days passed, famine became a more pressing enemy than Bragg's army, and Bragg seemed content to employ it as his front line ally. The wagon trains lumbered heavily over the Cumberlands back and forth to Stevenson, along a road where the carcasses of dead mules gave grisly evidence that famine was surely winning. Groups of mules might be seen hovering about a small pond where, after drinking, they would die. Ten thousand horses and mules perished of starvation. The army was immobilized. Artillery horses, least needed, were fed less and died first. The batteries were sunk in the mud, stationary except for hauling by manpower.

Horses gnawed their hitching posts, their wagon spokes; some, the tails of other horses. A correspondent found that his mount's only feed was a pine board fence. Too exhausted to stray from it, though unhaltered, the animal finally stretched out and died. Guards had to be posted to keep the soldiers from stealing the thin fare rationed to the most urgently needed draft horses—those engaged in hauling food. The landscape, rolling and resplendent before the armies came, turned bleak and forbidding. Every shrub and blade of grass was devoured.

The men fared slightly better than the mules and horses. By the third week they were restricted to one-quarter rations. The only meat was bacon middling, with little or no lean, the size of three fingers. It was eaten with a four-inch square of hard bread called a "Lincoln Platform," and washed down with thin coffee. Wrote a correspondent: "I have often seen hundreds of soldiers following behind the wagon trains which had just arrived, picking out of the mud the crumbs of bread, coffee, rice, which were wasted from the boxes and sacks by the rattling of the wagons over the stones."

Citizens who remained in the town were even greater sufferers, huddled together in crowded huts under conditions described as worse than any tenement section of New York City. Finally the army fare was reduced to quarter rations for breakfast only. Roasted acorns became a delicacy. Men waited around the feed troughs to catch grains of corn that fell. Wood was scarce. The army shivered in the biting blasts of an early winter.

Bragg sent Wheeler with two cavalry divisions, Wharton's and Martin's, to break the sixty-mile "cracker-box line" by dashing up the Sequatchie Valley to a Federal depot at Anderson's Cross Roads. The raid at the outset was highly effective. He captured or killed horses and mules, destroyed 300 wagons, and burned a large quantity of supplies destined for the starving Federal garrison. Bragg really needed Forrest, who had a better touch in battle, but Forrest had sworn never to serve under Wheeler after they had lost heavily in a joint attack on Fort Henry, against which Forrest had advised; nor would he serve under Bragg either, after Chickamauga.

The Chattanooga Campaign. Dragging artillery over the mountains in mud and rain. ("Harper's Hist. of Great Rebellion")

After his initial success Wheeler sustained a series of sharp defeats by three Federal cavalry detachments under McCook, Mitchell, and Crook, and was fortunate to get back across the Tennessee River with a portion of his command, after he lost 800 mules he had captured. But his destruction of the wagons, followed by a season of heavy rains, was little short of a disaster to the Federal army.

Though famine was Bragg's strongest ally, time was his weakest; and time was running out. Events that were to control the destiny of the half-starved Federal army began to unfold back at the Soldiers' Home in Washington, when Secretary of War Stanton's messenger abruptly awakened President Lincoln with the disheartening news that Rosecrans, from whom so much was hoped, had been defeated and driven back into Chattanooga. Much as he had done when Stonewall Jackson was threatening in the Shenandoah Valley in the spring of 1862, Lincoln began personally the designation and dispatch of succoring forces that could most readily converge on the beleaguered town.

The first decision was to reinforce Rosecrans with two corps from the Army of the Potomac. Major Generals Oliver O. Howard's and Henry W. Slocum's, the XI and XII, were chosen and placed under the command

of Major General Joseph Hooker. Hooker's appointment to head the relief party caused immediate difficulty, because Slocum, one of the most effective of the Federal corps commanders, had been an outspoken critic of Hooker's conduct at Chancellorsville five months before. He promptly resigned, saying it would be "degrading in me to accept any position under him."

Lincoln, adept at adjusting personal relationships, declined to accept the resignation and arranged that Slocum with one division could hold the railroads open behind the lines and not act directly under Hooker's orders. Thus only one of Slocum's divisions participated in the Chattanooga fighting. Hooker's reinforcement, which reached Nashville in the remarkably short time of seven days, consisted of two of Howard's divisions under Adolph Steinwehr and Carl Schurz, and the single XII Corps division under John W. Geary, who had stubbornly defended Culp's Hill at Gettysburg.

As in the case of Jackson in the Shenandoah Valley, Lincoln wanted sufficient troops to counter the unexpectedly triumphant Bragg. He had Halleck telegraph to Grant to send all available troops to Memphis, thence east via the Memphis & Charleston Railroad to cooperate with Rosecrans. Grant, in turn, ordered Sherman in Mississippi to load the troops on transports—all except part of the XVII Corps under McPherson—and steam up the Mississippi River. Sherman, in fact, already was moving in response to an earlier call sent before the Battle of Chickamauga was fought. Grant then was ordered to meet "an officer of the War Department" in Louisville, but as his train was pulling out of the station at Indianapolis it was stopped by a messenger saying Secretary of War Stanton was at hand, and Grant tarried to meet him.

Stanton had a habit, amounting almost to a tic, of constantly wiping his eyeglasses with his handkerchief; but in the opinion of some of his subordinates, such as McClellan and Rosecrans, though he might clean his glasses he never could quite clear away the mist that obscured his thinking. Grant would find him easier to work with than did some of the others.

These transactions were requiring time while the Army of the Cumberland starved behind its trenches. Grant rode to Louisville with Stanton, heard a lengthy review of the military situation on all fronts, including the disappointments over some of the campaigns. Then Stanton divulged the results of the Cabinet meeting that had pondered the problem of extricating the Army of the Cumberland from impending disaster.

Left to right: Major General George H. Thomas (LC), Major General Oliver O. Howard (LC), Major General George Crook (LC), Major General Gordon Granger (LC)

Lincoln's decision, after the Cabinet members had talked, was to combine the three western armies of the Cumberland, the Tennessee, and the Ohio, under a single commander, Grant, still on crutches thanks to a fall from his horse.

The Cabinet thought that Rosecrans, brilliant but erratic, would have to go. Stanton detested him almost from the beginning, mainly because he treated the Secretary of War as an overly officious clerk, and a harassing one at that. The campaign that had been waged against Rosecrans by the highly articulate Assistant Secretary of War Charles A. Dana, who remained with the army and sent Stanton all the gossip, had been effective. Dana's reports were read aloud at the Cabinet meeting.

The soul of the Army of the Cumberland was in the ponderous form of the clear thinking and decisive but ordinarily self-effacing George H. Thomas. His men, whether he had led a division, a corps, or a separate army, had never yet acknowledged and never would know defeat. From Mill Springs at the beginning to Nashville at the end he was modest and triumphant. Now the "Old Hero," wearing about the only laurels that came to the high Union command from Chickamauga, was suddenly but inevitably and reluctantly about to be catapulted into the leadership of the military wreck that was once the glorious Army of the Cumberland.

Although the Cabinet favored the ouster of Rosecrans, Lincoln was reluctant to see him go. There were numerous

Left to Right: Brigadier General John W. Geary (LC), Major General William B. Hazen (NA), Brigadier General Montgomery C. Meigs (LC), Major General William F. ("Baldy") Smith (NA).

points in his favor that balanced off his ignominious departure from the field at Chickamauga. Finally Lincoln compromised. He left the decision to Grant. He had the War Department issue two orders, one relieving Rosecrans, the other continuing him in command, and gave Grant, the newly appointed commander of the Western armies, the privilege of tearing up one and issuing the other. Grant was not fond of either general but preferred Thomas. He tore up the Rosecrans order and on October 19 forwarded the other to Thomas. Rosecrans left Chattanooga quietly and becomingly, without giving notice to the men, most of whom idolized him even after he had lost at Chickamauga.

Grant upon assuming command received what he regarded as a suggestion from Dana that Rosecrans was considering evacuating Chattanooga. From Louisville he telegraphed Thomas to hold the town at all hazards. Thomas, who rarely made promises, gave assurance by ending his reply with the resolute words: "I will hold the town till we starve."

Back in Virginia General Lee was disproving the frequent expression of latter day recorders that he was concerned only with his own state and did not envision the war on a national scale. When informed of Bragg's triumph at Chickamauga he saw at once that time was of the essence. To Longstreet he dispatched his warmest compliments. To President Davis he expressed hope that the victory would be followed up; that Bragg would operate against the enemy's rear, push the advantage gained, open East Tennessee, and bring Major General Sam Jones, who commanded in southwest Virginia, into the Tennessee operations.

"No time ought now to be lost or wasted," Lee wrote. "Everything should be done that can be done at once." To Longstreet: "Finish the work before you, my dear general, and return to me. I want you badly and you cannot get back too soon."

Meade had heard in early September of Longstreet's departure from Virginia to reinforce Bragg in north Georgia. Sensing an opportunity, he began to menace Lee's left. The VI Corps troops who had been sent to quell the New York draft rioters were returning to the Army of the Potomac. Lee heard trainload after trainload of these regiments arriving to strengthen Meade, then learned after Chickamauga that Meade had detached the bulk of two veteran corps, the XI and XII, to hasten as succor to the penned-up Union army in Chattanooga.

Lee issued orders to Jones to occupy Knoxville, which Burnside had vacated after Chickamauga in order to move belatedly toward Rosecrans and give him some relief. Jones marched but did not reach Knoxville in time. Then Lee struck out on an offensive that took him past Bristoe Station and on to the old lines at Centreville. This was mainly a demonstration in favor of Bragg. His aggressive movement, the first since his return from

General Ulysses S. Grant led the besieged Union forces to victory at Chattanooga. ("Photographic History of the Civil War")

Then-Major General William Tecumseh Sherman was stopped at Tunnel Hill by the stout defense of Cleburne's men. (From LC)

"Longstreet reporting at Bragg's headquarters," by A. R. Waud.

Gettysburg, was designed to block any further reinforcements for Rosecrans and Burnside, and to develop any weaknesses resulting from Meade's dispatch of the two corps. One of these, Slocum's XII, had a splendid record in the Union army, culminating in its resolute defense of Culp's Hill at Gettysburg, which was as responsible as any other factor for Meade's repulse of the Southern invasion.

In front of Chattanooga, the Army of Tennessee still muttered rebelliously against Bragg, even more flagrantly than it had when that commander failed to press his prospects after the drawn battle of Stone's River.

While several generals criticised Bragg and signed a petition to have him replaced, the exasperating friction remaining after his removal of Polk was between the commanding general and Lee's "Old War Horse." Reports of their controversy spread through the ranks. It was evident to all from the incident described by one of the officers present at the first stormy session after Chickamauga. One of his men called him over to within hearing range. A group of high generals was assembled, among whom were Longstreet and Major General John C. Breckinridge towering on their mounts above the others. Bragg was afoot. Longstreet and Bragg were talking spiritedly and Longstreet's words were clearly audible.

Bragg held his poise, spoke slowly, in low tones, though Longstreet assailed him angrily. "General," said Longstreet, "the army should have been in motion at dawn today." Bragg's reply was muffled and Longstreet continued: "Yes, sir, but all great captains follow up a victory." The conversation apparently grew more heated for Longstreet concluded: "Yes, sir, you rank me, but you cannot cashier me."

Longstreet worked off his anger in a letter to Secretary of War Seddon, saying Bragg had done only one thing right—ordering the attack on September 20—but everything else had been wrong. "I am convinced," he wrote, "that nothing but the hand of God can save us . . . as long as we have our present commander." Then he put his finger on the crux of the whole situation: "Can't you send us General Lee? The Army in Virginia can operate defensively, while our operations here should be offensive—until we recover Tennessee at all events. We need some great mind as General Lee's (nothing more) to accomplish this."

Little consideration was given to Longstreet's suggestion—a reiteration of one he had made when he left Virginia—to transfer General Lee temporarily to Tennessee as the person who could now best gather the fruits of the Chickamauga victory. Lee rejected the proposal but his letter to Longstreet on October 26, answering three letters from Longstreet, saying that President Davis, now being on the ground, could take a broad view of the whole situation, did carry the sentence: "I will cheerfully do all in my power." Possibly Lee was not importuned strongly enough to take him, in a desperate hour, to Chattanooga and to the employment of the Army of Tennessee in an aggressive campaign of motion, instead of a siege doomed to failure if protracted.

Apart from their mutual distrust, Bragg and Longstreet were in sharp disagreement over methods. Bragg favored the investment, which he felt might lead to the capture of the entire enemy army; Longstreet still urged by-passing the Federals, operating against their rear, throwing them into retreat, then capturing or dispersing Burnside's army in Knoxville. In the discussion that nearly wrecked the army, Longstreet had the support of virtually all of Bragg's subordinate officers, as well as those from his own corps from the Army of Northern Virginia.

The balance of Longstreet's corps that had been unable to reach Chickamauga in time for the battle arrived immediately thereafter: Lafayette McLaws with the brigades of Brigadier Generals W. T. Wofford and Goode Bryan, and the two missing brigades of Hood's old division, those of G. T. Anderson and Micah Jenkins. When the army began its advance, two days after the battle, Bragg was thinking more of marching triumphantly through Chattanooga with banners aflutter than of heading again toward Kentucky and pulling the invaders after him. As the unsympathetic Longstreet stated it: "The praise of the inhabitants of a city so recently abandoned to the enemy, and a parade through its streets with bands of music and flaunting banners, were more alluring to a spirit eager for applause than was the tedious march for fruition of our heavy labors."

While Longstreet did not foment the discord that was at the boiling point in Bragg's own Army of Tennessee, a recurrence of the near-mutiny that had agitated the

Left to Right: Lieutenant General Leonidas Polk (NA), Lieutenant General Daniel H. Hill (B&L), Major General Benjamin F. Cheatham. (LC).

officers after the criticised retreat from Stone's River, his concurrence in it and his standing in the Confederacy, gave it such elevation that Bragg was almost a pariah among his own subordinates. Meantime, Bragg's principal quarrel in the Army of Tennessee had been with his second in command, Lieutenant General Leonidas Polk, to whom he wrote two days after the battle, demanding an explanation of why he had failed to attack the Union left, as ordered, at dawn on September 20.

Polk, engaged in troop movements, failed to answer. Bragg gave him three days, prodded him, and this time got a reply he characterized as altogether unsatisfactory. Thereupon he removed Polk from his command and

sent him back to Atlanta. Similarly, he suspended Major General Thomas C. Hindman, who had contributed measurably to the triumph at Chickamauga, and sent him back to Atlanta, giving his division to the capable Brigadier General Patton Anderson.

D. H. Hill, stormy and combative, who nearly always saw the merits of his own way instead of his commander's, was relieved from corps command, replaced by Breckinridge, and the lieutenant general's commission Davis had granted him before Chickamauga was not even sent to the Senate for confirmation. Though one of the South's toughest fighters, he passed from an active combat role. William Bate of Tennessee, who won plaudits at

Left to Right: Lieutenant General James Longstreet (LC), General Braxton Bragg (LC), Lieutenant General William J. Hardee (LC).

Chickamauga, strengthened the army by taking command of a division. Forrest's abuse of Bragg to his face was in language which for intemperance probably was never duplicated by a subordinate to a chief. He impulsively walked out to independent command and later triumphs.

Discord was sapping Bragg's effectiveness but not his self-respect or self-confidence. His had been a lifetime of quarreling. He still enjoyed the President's support and shook off his detractors. In the case of Polk, he was undertaking to disgrace the President's old favorite of Military Academy years. The treatment of Polk, the President said, was no less than a "public calamity." He held that Bragg might arrest Polk and prefer charges but did not have the authority to proceed further and pack him off to Atlanta without a trial. Then he gave Bragg, who shared his close friendship from Buena Vista days, much gratuitous advice about his conduct. Bragg, in turn, protested that Polk's disobedience had been flagrant. "I suffer self-reproach from not having acted earlier," he told Davis, but the President pigeonholed the charges.

The army was cast into greater turmoil and shrouded in deeper gloom at this stage when the rumor went around that Polk was to be replaced by John C. Pemberton, a Pennsylvanian in Southern gray, who appeared at Chattanooga. Pemberton's recent surrender of Vicksburg had made him, whether or not justifiably, the most disliked and discredited military figure in the South. Such an appointment would have been a clear provocation for mutiny in an army already rebellious in everything except an overt act. In the end, Lieutenant General ("Old Reliable") William J. Hardee, Davis' West Point classmate, and probably with Stonewall Jackson and Longstreet a part of the triumvirate of the best corps commanders in the Confederacy's experiment in arms, was a compromise who suited everyone. He returned from his independent command in Mississippi to the army that had long known him favorably, to take command of Bragg's largest corps which was strung out for five miles along Missionary Ridge.

Colonel James Chesnut, the President's military secretary, did not overestimate the crisis in command when he telegraphed to President Davis on October 5 that his presence with the army was urgently demanded. Never had a large element of an American army mutinied since the revolt of the Pennsylvania Line under St. Clair's command in the Revolutionary War, but the closest approach undoubtedly was with the victors of sanguinary Chickamauga only two weeks after the enemy had been driven from the field. The clash of personalities sometimes resounds above the din of arms, and campaigns are lost as often by discord as by defeat.

Lookout Mountain, seen from the Federal works on Chattanooga Creek, commanded the supply route from the river and railroad at Bridgeport and Stevenson to Chattanooga. (CWTI Collection)

President Davis was at Bragg's headquarters by October 9, a rapid railroad journey by the circuitous route imposed by the loss of Knoxville. He had been in Chattanooga before, once to advocate secession to the Tennesseans, and it proved a day of notoriety for innkeeper William Crutchfield. After Davis spoke, Crutchfield the Unionist disputed his words and heckled him with vigor. Pistols were drawn all around and a shootout was threatened. It could have cost the South its emergent political leader had not Tom Crutchfield hurried his brother away and silenced him.

This time Davis quickly entered into one of the most peculiar councils of war ever conducted, in which he gathered the top officers of the Army of Tennessee, together with Longstreet, who stood next to Bragg in seniority, and with Bragg seated before them, demanded that they voice their opinions about their commander's generalship and qualifications to lead a great army. Longstreet was nonplussed, since as senior he would have to speak first, but he was never a man, even with General Lee, to be anything but blunt.

If Davis had a faint notion that he could still any covert denunciation of Bragg by bringing it into the open, he should not have begun with Longstreet, who, though he knew that what he said would alienate him thereafter from the Confederate President, did not hesitate when pressed. He later indicated he regarded the whole procedure improper and gave therefore at first an evasive answer, but when Davis was dissatisfied, he stated that Bragg could be of greater service elsewhere than as commander of the Army of Tennessee. Buckner, Cheatham, Cleburne, and D. H. Hill, who had not yet been dismissed, expressed the same conclusion, Hill speaking "with emphasis." One of his testy temperament would not pass over such a likely opportunity for complaint. Many thought that he had authored the round-robin letter to Davis requesting Bragg's dismissal.

Davis was not appeased. Clearly he had wanted an expression of confidence in Bragg such as he had obtained from Joseph E. Johnston after the Stone's River haggling. He had not expected the unanimous condemnation of one of his choice army commanders. On the next morning he took Longstreet for a walk, and according to Longstreet's version (the only one extant), the Old War Horse offered his resignation for the sake of harmony. Of course, it was declined. Longstreet then must have thrown cold water into the President's face by suggesting that Joseph E. Johnston, the ranking general in the West, be substituted for the nauseous Bragg. Longstreet said the thought increased the President's displeasure. The conference accomplished little more than to confirm some intra-corps transactions, the most important of which was to give Micah Jenkins command of the wounded Hood's division. When they parted Longstreet thought he detected behind the President's gracious smile, "a bitter look lurking about its margin," and felt that clouds were gathering over the headquarters of the First Corps.

Still ruffled, Davis called a second conference at Bragg's headquarters but this time talked more about operations. He asked for ideas. Some good plans were presented as substitutes for a prolonged siege. Already it was known that Grant's troops were being hastened across Mississippi and Tennessee and others were near at hand from the Army of the Potomac, all for the relief

of beleaguered Chattanooga. There was no future in delay. Longstreet favored changing the army's base to Rome, Georgia, marching out to capture Bridgeport, where the Union supply route would be cut, then crossing the Tennessee River and forcing the Union army into either a battle or full retreat. Even Bragg talked some of crossing the river and gaining the enemy's rear. Maps were laid out and scrutinized. But nothing eventuated and, according to Longstreet, Davis left the army more despondent than he found it. He took Pemberton back with him and Hardee arrived to supplant Cheatham, who had held temporary command of Polk's old corps.

Davis' visit, in truth, accomplished nothing. He supported Bragg on all counts and confirmed him in command of the army, which was probably the worst possible course. The only lasting effect of the President's visit probably came from the address he made to a part of the army on Lookout Mountain shortly before his departure. An unusual formation of one of the outcroppings ideally suited for a rostrum had long borne the name of "Pulpit Rock." This the President ascended and with his customarily happy phrases inspired the soldiers. After the Federals captured Lookout and learned of the incident, they changed the designation of "Pulpit Rock" to "Devil's Pulpit," a name that has been more enduring.

Jefferson Davis addressed Stevenson's division from Pulpit Rock on Lookout Mountain. Tripod signal in this 1864 photo erected by officers of U.S. Coast Survey. (Brady Coll., LC)

Davis spoke, apparently on the advice of some of the officers, to quiet the apprehension being felt in Stevenson's division, which had surrendered to Grant as a part of Pemberton's army, at Vicksburg on July 4. The division was now back in active service, irregularly, the Federals maintained, because the men had not been exchanged. Davis thought otherwise. If they had not been properly exchanged and were captured with guns in their hands, they were, under the rules of war, liable to the death penalty. What he said was described by a Northern scribe as "a flight of fancy as to what Bragg was going to do, when the proper time arrived, in the way of scattering the vile invaders who ravaged the beautiful valley below." Later developments showed that some trepidation remained with the men of Stevenson's division even after the President's reassurances.

What a strange walk Davis' undoubtedly was with Longstreet. Here was the scholarly President, gifted in the law, gifted in administration, gifted in legislative affairs, gifted presumably in military leadership, who could examine the delicate tendrils of a legal point down almost to abstraction and, given sustained life, prolong an argument into infinity, walking along the mountain ridge with tough, dominating Longstreet, who usually cut through the outer skin and muscle of a problem to see the naked heart, then became impatient of those who sought further assurance by feeling the pulse, lifting the eyelids, and examining the color of the tongue. Personalities could not have offered stronger contrast: the debater and the doer, the pedant who claimed alliance with reason alongside the unflinching disciple of force.

ABOVE: "Sutlers' Row" in Chattanooga, probably 1864. (LC)

———————————

BELOW: Thomas' headquarters at Chattanooga. (NA)

As might be expected, there was no meeting ground. The walk helped seal the fate of the Confederacy. On it Davis came to recognize that Bragg and Longstreet could never work under the same yoke. Here, largely to rid Bragg of Longstreet, he committed the major error of the Chattanooga Campaign, determining that they should be parted. Bragg then, with his consent, committed a trifle later that cardinal blunder of dividing his army in the face of a vigilant and increasing foe. He sent Longstreet to Knoxville to capture an enemy force of comparable size, Burnside's Army of the Ohio, while he, Bragg, pursued the investment with little more than the bloody remnants of the army that had fought so desperately at Chickamauga. Longstreet said he acceded to the plan reluctantly, though it freed him from Bragg's irksome presence. He did not know at the time that the author of it was President Davis.

For the moment, however, Longstreet was on hand and to him went the first combat assignment at Chattanooga. He commanded Bragg's left, as Hardee did the right, and Breckinridge, who had borne the heavy load of much of the Chickamauga fighting, the center.

G rant reached Chattanooga on October 23 and at once put into effect the plan that had been developed by Rosecrans and his chief of engineers, Major General William F. ("Baldy") Smith. Much has been made over the authorship of this plan but as one looks at the map, it becomes so simple an expedient that any private in the ranks might well have devised it;

Rapids on the Tennessee River. Steamboat "Chattanooga" being warped up the "suck" at head of rapids. (Brady photo from NA)

it cut off the great Moccasin Point loop of the Tennessee River so as to utilize only the portion of the river not commanded by Confederate guns. The cutoff here was from Brown's Ferry, thence by wagon road to the pontoon crossing at Chattanooga. This meant free passage from the town to the bank well below the area within range of the Southern battery atop Lookout Mountain.

The plan, as carried out, was for two brigades, Hazen's and Turchin's, plus three batteries under Major John Mendenhall, to move on Brown's Ferry, Hazen by boat and Turchin by marching across Moccasin Point. The ferry was just below one of the "sucks," where the

The move that opened the Chattanooga supply lines. Hazen's men landing from pontoon-boats at Brown's Ferry. (From a wartime sketch by T. R. Davis in "Battles & Leaders of the Civil War")

river rushed between gorges and the current at high water was so swift that the sidewheeler river boats of the day could not make headway against it. They had to be warped upstream. More frequently their cargo was unloaded at Brown's Ferry and transported by wagon road across the neck of Moccasin Point, then into the town.

Grant's operation was designed to capture and employ this oldtime high-water route across the neck. It would have to be done by surprise or else Longstreet, who held Bragg's left across Lookout Mountain and into Lookout Valley, between Lookout and Raccoon Mountain, could readily concentrate sufficient men to hold the left bank of the river all the way to the spurs of Raccoon Mountain and the road over it. Secrecy was imperative and was emphasized in the orders. Fairly close timing was required, because the plan called for cooperation between Hooker coming across Raccoon Mountain from Bridgeport, and the two of Thomas' brigades coming separately down from Chattanooga, the one by boat and the other marching across the neck of land.

Hooker, under orders from Thomas, concentrated at Bridgeport and marched into Lookout Valley. Though Corps Commander Palmer accompanied Turchin's brigade, the operation was put under the direction of the chief engineer officer, "Baldy" Smith. He selected fifty details from Hazen's brigade, each being a boatload of twenty-four men—the boats were pontoons—and with Colonel Timothy R. Stanley of the 18th Ohio in charge and Captain Perrin V. Fox, commanding a detachment of the 1st Michigan Engineers, supervising, they pushed off at 3 a.m. and floated silently down the river, hugging the tree-fringed right bank opposite the enemy.

Turchin, marching on the hidden road across the neck, was at the river at Brown's Ferry ahead of them. The little flotilla was observed by Confederate pickets at the ferry, but the troops landed at 5 a.m. in good order, scattered or captured the enemy pickets, en-

Major General Hooker and staff—Lookout Valley, winter 1863-64. (1) Capt. Hall, (2) Gen. Geary, (3) Gen. Butterfield, (4) Gen. Hooker, (5) Gen. LeDuc, (6) Capt. Kibler. (Photo courtesy of Chickamauga-Chattanooga National Military Park)

trenched on a knoll, and immediately, as they labored, resisted a spirited attack by 1,000 of the enemy with three pieces of artillery, before they had established a secure bridgehead on the Confederate side. Turchin crossed by 10 a.m. and the pontoons were laid under Confederate artillery fire. On the next day, October 28, Hooker arrived by the road through Raccoon Mountain and the Union army held the Tennessee River crossing in force.

By capturing Brown's Ferry and commanding the lower Lookout Valley, Grant's army effectively broke the siege, as far as victuals were concerned, though the haul and transfer were still more difficult than any army enjoys. But the "cracker line" was shortened to where it would carry much more than "Lincoln Platforms," and Sherman was coming on. That assurance, plus an abundance of better food, and the appearance of draft animals that began to come down from Nashville following Hooker, lifted the morale of the Federals and eased the restiveness of Lincoln and Stanton in Washington.

Steamers soon began bringing a good supply of vegetables, which the army craved, and other provisions, clothing, and forage for the animals. Hooker now had on hand the complete requirements of an army for land transportation, nor had his teams been starved or overworked. Grant pointed out—it must have been with high satisfaction—that within five days after his arrival in Chattanooga the way to Bridgeport was open, and that within a week the men were receiving full rations. Whatever else might be said about Grant, he was a general of restless action. He saw how the troops were lifted: ". . . an abundance of ammunition was brought up, and a cheerfulness prevailed not before enjoyed in many weeks. Neither officers nor men looked upon themselves any longer as doomed. The weak and languid appearance of the troops, so visible before, disappeared at once."

When Hooker entered Lookout Valley he moved by the railroad station at Wauhatchie, where he left Geary's XII Corps division as a rearguard, then marched down the valley three miles with the XI Corps under Howard to cooperate with Palmer's brigades at Brown's Ferry.

Bragg had discredited reconnaissance reports that numerous Federals (Hooker's two corps) had arrived at Bridgeport, close at hand. Bragg was a chronic doubter. Only when Longstreet led him to the vantage point of Signal Rock, whence he could survey the western country

MAP # 1   *The opposing armies at Chattanooga as they appeared on the morning of September 24, as the siege began. Rosecrans has withdrawn his army into the city—the concentration of the units permits showing only the placement of the several corps on this map—and Bragg has invested him, lining his corps up from the northern point of Missionary Ridge, south along the ridge, across Chattanooga Valley, and almost to the slopes of Lookout Mountain. It should be noted that Hood's division is now commanded by Jenkins, while Longstreet's part of the line includes the two divisions of Preston and Stewart, actually still part of a small corps commanded by Buckner. Meanwhile, Rosecrans has a single brigade near the Craven House which had tried to keep Wheeler from taking Lookout, and another two brigades guarding his tenuous escape and supply route along Moccasin Point and through Brown's Ferry. This and the following maps were specially prepared by historian William C. Davis, and are based on maps in the archives of the Chickamauga-Chattanooga National Military Park, reports in the "Official Records," and the "Atlas" in the "Official Records."*

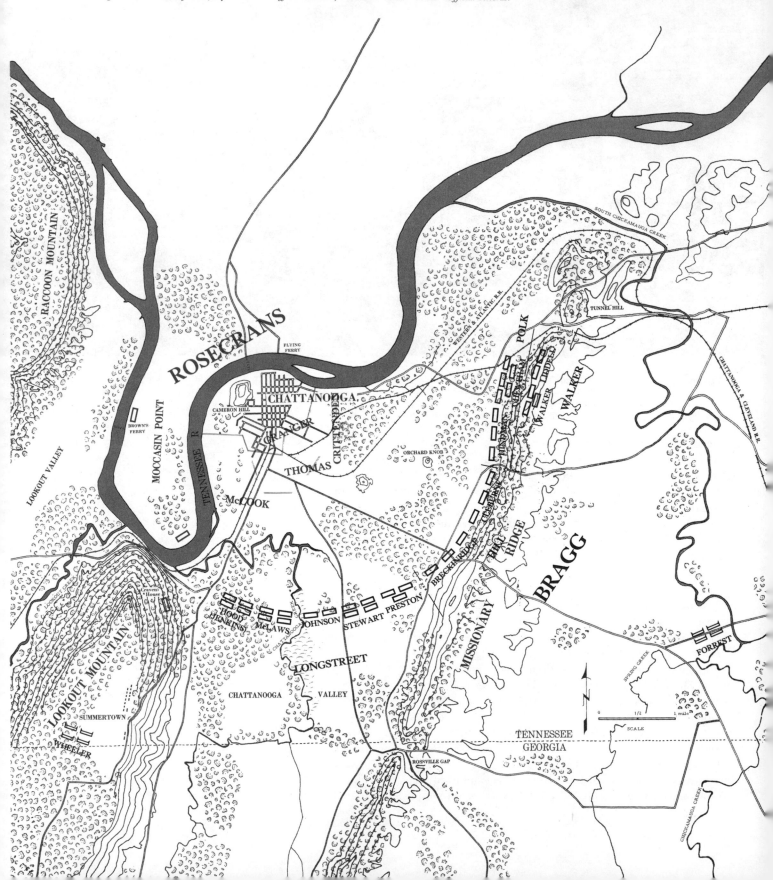

and see the long blue column marching into Lookout Valley below him, did he concede that his own signal corps gleanings had been more accurate than what he had termed them, "sensational."

As darkness came on that night, the Confederate officers could look down on Hooker's campfires disclosing exactly how the Federals had divided their forces between the river and the railroad depot at Wauhatchie three miles up the valley. About 1,500 Federals remained at Wauhatchie while Hooker and Howard went on with 5,000.

Bragg ordered an attack on the weaker party at Wauhatchie. He left the details to Longstreet but took charge of giving orders to the two divisions that were to participate—those of Jenkins and McLaws. According to Longstreet, he changed his mind about sending McLaws but did not inform Longstreet about it.

Jenkins formed his division and designated Law's brigade to hold Howard's main body at the Lookout Creek crossings to keep it from assisting Geary at Wauhatchie. So necessary was this that Longstreet intended that McLaws should reinforce Law with his entire division. As Longstreet described his actions, he waited at the mountain observation point until midnight, then rode to the stepoff point of the attack, and learned there that McLaws had not even been ordered by Bragg to participate. Thus virtually half of the force that was to bag Geary had not been ordered up by Bragg at all.

Longstreet here made the improper assumption, as he acknowledged later, that because McLaws would not appear, Jenkins would not attack. Instead, as he put it, "the gallant Jenkins decided that the plan should not be abandoned." He determined to carry it out with his single division. As this was his only chance to command in a battle in his short and brilliant life he deserves attention.

Micah Jenkins was one of the several young Southerners in Longstreet's corps—Evander Law, Joseph B. Kershaw, Moxley Sorrell, William C. Oates, and others among them—who showed an aptitude for command. He was from Edisto Island off the South Carolina coast—a lad who stood first in his class of 1854 at South Carolina Military Academy, now The Citadel. Then with a classmate, Asbury Coward, he founded and conducted the King's Mountain Military School at Yorkville, South Carolina. He rose in the Southern army from colonel of the 5th South Carolina at First Manassas to command one of Lee's stellar brigades and, by the time of Chattanooga, to lead Hood's division after Hood had his leg shot off at Chickamauga. (Jenkins was killed in the later fighting in the Virginia Wilderness by the unhappy Confederate blast that also grievously wounded Longstreet.)

At this juncture, when Bragg had neglected or refrained from ordering up the reinforcements and Longstreet had departed without countermanding the original attack plan, but when nobody else seemed to believe the attack would be launched at such a late hour, Jenkins decided to charge Geary with his single division. The battle that ensued was bitterly fought and brutal, and lasted until the streaks of dawn lighted the east, with Jenkins the decided loser. As he wrote about it the next day, he called the odds against him immense and the fight "terrible." That was true of the broad action, but not of his initial encounter, for at first he appeared successful.

Geary was surprised both by the suddenness and the vigor of Jenkins' attack. His three New York regiments, the 78th, 137th, and 149th, and two Pennsylvania, the 27th and 111th, served him well, stood firmly, and finally rolled the Confederates back. Thirty men from the 27th Pennsylvania rushed to Knap's Federal battery when all the horses had been killed or disabled, and dragged a gun to a point where it could arrest Jenkins' flanking column. All officers of the battery were either killed or wounded. The Confederates charged repeatedly for an hour and a half.

In his letter to his wife next day Jenkins told that the creek he had to cross (Lookout) had two bridges, both of which had had their planks removed. The men crossed on the stringers to get between Howard's main body (of 12,000, as he numbered it) and Geary's. Jenkins' entire command numbered about 4,000. His old brigade, all South Carolinians, was under its senior colonel, John Bratton. Jenkins contended that instead of encountering 1,000 Federals as expected, he ran into the XII Corps

Brigadier General Micah Jenkins. (Coll. of Library of Congress)

216

numbering about 5,000, which had come up in the night prior to the attack.

Nevertheless, Bratton's men stormed in splendidly, captured wagons, trains, and the enemy camp "and in a few minutes would have had the whole Yankee force routed and their guns captured." But the Federals in reserve under Hooker, numbering by Jenkins' count 12,000, moved to the rescue, pressed against the holding brigade of General Law, encircled his flank, and so threatened him that he had to pull back.

There were points of disagreement about Wauhatchie. Grant wrote that "the night was so dark that the men could not distinguish one another except by the light of the flashes of their muskets." In the palpable blackness Hooker's teamsters became frightened, abandoned their teams, and allowed the animals to break loose. The mules, according to Grant, dashed directly toward the enemy and stampeded them. The incident gave occasion for the oft-repeated famous "Charge of the Mule Brigade," a parody on Tennyson's more distinguished account of the British horse at Balaclava. It must have related to Benning's brigade, the only Georgians present. Major J. L. Coker, assistant adjutant general of Bratton's brigade, denied the mule-charge story and said the brigade retired in good order.

The character of the simple burlesque may be seen from the opening stanza:

> Half a mile, half a mile,
> Half a mile onward,
> Right through the Georgia troops,
> Broke the two hundred.
> "Forward the Mule brigade.
> Charge for the Rebs!" they neighed;
> Straight for the Georgia troops
> Broke the two hundred.

Jenkins reinforced Law with Robertson's Texas and Arkansas brigade and Benning's Georgia brigade.

ABOVE: View of Chattanooga from north bank of the Tennessee River. (From "Harper's History of the Great Rebellion")

BELOW: Knap's Pennsylvania battery suffered heavy casualties in what Geary called "Wauhatchie's bloody glen," where his son Edward, an officer in the battery, was killed. (Photo from NA)

When Howard marched to Geary's relief with his main body, Law was brushed aside. With the help of Benning, Jenkins skillfully extricated Bratton and the famed battle of Wauhatchie, a bit overrated because it was the first of the Chattanooga engagements and because of the literature about the charge of the mule brigade, ended. Said Longstreet of the withdrawal: "The conduct of Bratton's forces was one of the cleverest pieces of work of the war. . . ." Jenkins said he had to recall his men "in the midst of success."

Major Coker of Bratton's staff, who disputed the story of the mule brigade charge, as did others, accounted the battle of Wauhatchie of minor importance, as lasting an hour and a half and being a single brigade action, with none but Bratton's men firing a shot, but it did confirm possession of Lookout Valley for Hooker's Eastern army and brought him up facing Lookout Mountain, one of the two keys, the other being Missionary ridge, if Bragg was to keep the Federal army under siege. The Federal loss in killed and wounded was 416. Bratton's brigade loss was 351; the Confederate total, 408. The battle secured the supply line via Brown's Ferry.

For Geary, later governor of Pennsylvania, it was a signal triumph in which he could not have taken much personal satisfaction. His son, a lieutenant in Knap's Pennsylvania battery, was shot through the brain while aiming a piece after most of the other officers and gunners had fallen in their exposed position during the initial Confederate attack.

A striking discrepancy occurs in the accounts with respect to the nature of the night. By one well-established story, Longstreet could be seen clearly atop Lookout Mountain directing the attack. This is of some interest because the Union cryptographers had broken the Confederate signal code and were able to decypher every one of Longstreet's messages.

The circumstance was given high significance to the outcome of the battle and campaign by one of the correspondents present because, as he related it, Geary was heavily outnumbered and would have been driven had he not been able to anticipate each Confederate move.

The promontory on which Longstreet stood, looking westward from Lookout Mountain, was known thereafter as "Signal Rock." Alongside himself Longstreet stationed his signal corps men with their flares, and with them repeatedly signaled down to Jenkins. No doubt it was true that his large form could be seen in front of the

MAP #2 Chattanooga after two months of siege. Thomas now commands the Army of the Cumberland, Hooker has arrived, and Sherman is approaching. This map shows positions as of the evening of November 23, and a number of changes have taken place. Longstreet and Buckner are gone. Hardee has come, and now commands one corps, and Breckinridge the other. Cleburne, detached from Breckinridge to go north to protect Bragg's right, has been ordered back, and is approaching the ridge, while Hindman's division, under Patton Anderson, is transferred to Breckinridge. Over on the left, Stevenson and Cheatham face Hooker at Lookout. Hooker's command has been augmented by Cruft's division from Granger's corps, and will soon be joined by Osterhaus, who has accidentally been cut off from Sherman. Meanwhile, Sherman, with Davis' division of Palmer's corps, is making a pontoon crossing of the Tennessee on Bragg's right, while Howard's corps moves to communicate with him. In the center, Wood has advanced and taken Orchard Knob, setting the stage for the next two days' battles. Palmer has succeeded to command of Thomas' corps, while McCook's and Crittenden's have been combined under Granger. Howard's corps, which came west with Hooker, is now part of the Army of the Cumberland.

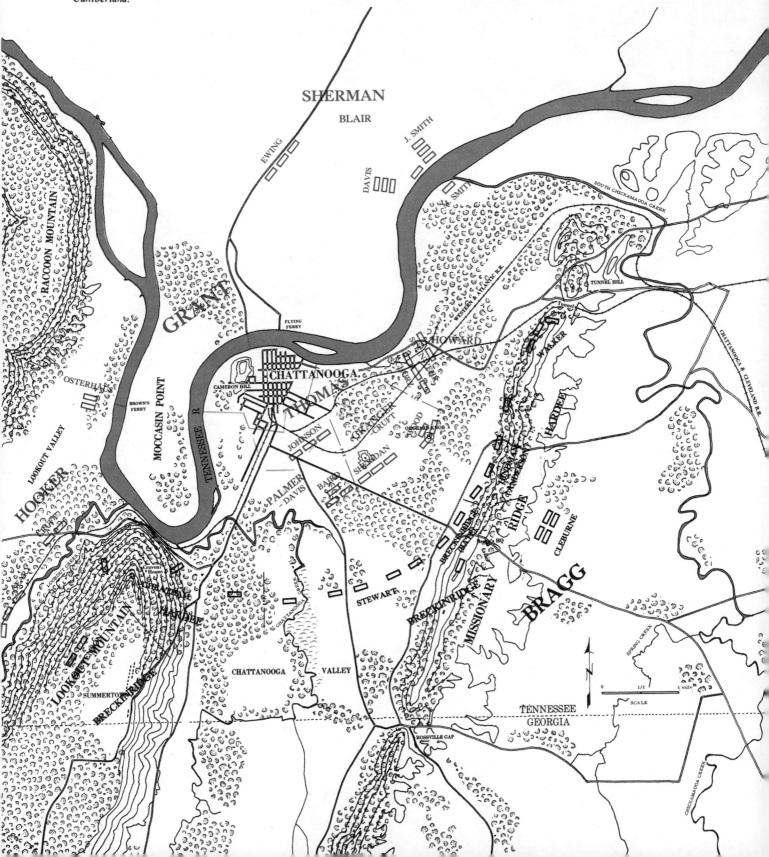

flares. "During the whole battle," ran the correspondent's account, "the flaming torch of Longstreet flashed orders that showed his increased desperation, and finally, much to Geary's gratification, he saw it signal the recall. All the while the figure of Longstreet on 'Signal Rock' standing out boldly against the dark back-ground, was plainly visible in the glare of the signal torches to the combatants below."

John S. C. Abbott, who wrote as the war progressed and published his two-volume history in 1866, made a point that "the night, illuminated by nearly a full moon, was almost as bright as day. . . ." It seems more credible that Longstreet at such a distance could be seen by moonlight instead of by the beams of his signal torches. Records of the U.S. Naval Observatory show that on the night of October 28, 1863, the night on which Wauhatchie was fought, the moon had receded only two days from full, having been at full October 26. Thus the John S. C. Abbott account appears more accurate in this respect than Grant's.

Longstreet left Chattanooga on November 5 to force Burnside back into Knoxville, then to besiege him there. He took the divisions of McLaws and Jenkins and was joined later by that of Bushrod Johnson, the division that had been the entering wedge that split Rosecran's army at Chickamauga. Longstreet confronted Burnside with fairly equal numbers at the beginning but as he built his force with the acquisition of Johnson, Jones from western Virginia, and others, Bragg was deprived of 20,000 good soldiers at the very time Grant was strengthening step by step and making formidable the Federal army in the valley below him.

The Confederate commander had no such preponderance of numbers as to warrant his detachment of Longstreet however cordially President Davis may have assented to it. Bragg appears at this point in the campaign to have been naively sanguine. At the time he was losing Longstreet he was losing also his strongest ally, famine, yet he did not undertake to invest Chattanooga by regular approaches, by storming, or by any measure whatever that might lure the Northerners from their position so that he might meet them again in open battle. He merely waited, as he had done at Murfreesboro, then at Tullahoma, for the capricious element of time to assert itself in his favor.

Longstreet, when he heard the rumor that he was to be sent toward Knoxville, could not give it credence. "At the moment," he wrote, "it seemed impossible that our commander, after rejecting a proposition for a similar move made just after the battle, when flushed with victory and the enemy discomfited, could now think of sending an important detachment so far, when he knew that, in addition to the reinforcements that had joined the Union army, another strong column was marching from Memphis under General Sherman, and must reach Chattanooga in fifteen or twenty days." Longstreet's

second thought was that Bragg's move "might, after all, be in keeping with his peculiarities," and took up the plan with the belief he might be given a strong enough force to crush Burnside and be back in front of Chattanooga before Sherman's arrival. But he did tell Bragg the detachment of his force would indeed be hazardous.

Longstreet took the trains to Sweetwater, Tennessee, en route to Knoxville. As soon as Grant learned that he had left Bragg's lines, the Federal commander was eager for action, even though Sherman's corps was as yet at some distance.

Two days after Longstreet left, Grant completed a reconnaissance and was satisfied that he could dislodge Bragg from Missionary Ridge by attacking his right flank, then moving south down the crest of the ridge. Success might bring Longstreet back, since he had not yet reached Knoxville nor gained contact with Burnside en route. Longstreet's departure exercised Washington and Grant was being urged to protect Burnside, who had become almost a liability to the Union side.

Grant ordered Thomas to make the attack on Bragg's right with the Army of the Cumberland. The operation Grant contemplated was precisely the same that Sherman with his fresh army and much other help was to fail in signally later in the month. Thomas, with his 40,000, knew his force was insufficient to hold the Chattanooga lines at the time he was hurling a heavy bolt against Bragg's entrenched lines facing the Union left on Missionary Ridge. Grant on the other hand, thought it possible even to cut Bragg's communications between Dalton, Georgia, and Cleveland, Tennessee, which would sever Bragg from Longstreet. But he was dealing in Thomas with a methodical general who never took the long chance.

Thomas told Grant frankly that the attack would invite disaster. In this opinion he had the support of his chief engineer officer, "Baldy" Smith. Grant yielded, but the incident did not impress him with Thomas' zeal or flexibility. The weight of opinion, however, has remained with Thomas. Colonel Fred Knefler of Beatty's brigade, Wood's division, commented, like others: "There is no doubt if General Thomas had undertaken to execute that order, and at the same time attempted to hold Chattanooga with the limited numbers at his command, he would have disastrously failed."

Grant's disappointment was evident when on November 14 Sherman finally arrived. Grant told his leading lieutenant, as Sherman later stated it, that the defeat at Chickamauga had left the Army of the Cumberland so demoralized "he feared they could not get out of their trenches to assume the offensive." He thought they would

fight well after the Vicksburg men supplied the initial impetus.

They remained, as they had been termed for a year, the "stepchild army."

Sherman, leaving Memphis on October 11, moved his corps partly afoot and partly by railroad to Corinth, Mississippi, his progress impeded by Confederate cavalry. A more aggravating cause for his slowness was an order from Halleck to repair the railroad as he went. As he moved from Memphis, he had visions of cutting a swath across north Alabama and southwestern Tennessee that would be a sort of barren bastion protecting Kentucky and the North. The call for haste saved the countryside.

Grant had grown anxious well before Longstreet pulled away from Chattanooga. He wanted Sherman and he wanted him at once. Impatient of the railroad mending, he ordered Sherman on October 27 to stop it, drop everything else and hasten to Stevenson. Sherman had been slowed also by a superabundance of wagons, his belief at the outset being that he would have to haul provisions to the starving army in Chattanooga. Each division marched with its train immediately behind it, which slowed the whole.

Stevenson, Alabama, early Union supply base in the Chattanooga Campaign. ("Harper's History of the Great Rebellion")

The army struggled through rain and mud. Finally the infantry was free of its impedimenta, leaving the wagons to follow. At Eastport, where the Memphis & Charleston Railroad reached the Tennessee River, he obtained abundant supplies which Grant had caused to be collected at St. Louis and sent by boat up the Tennessee. So anxious had Grant become that he sent the orders for Sherman to hasten by a messenger who paddled his craft down the Tennessee past the "sucks" and "boiling pots," over Muscle Shoals, and on to Iuka, Mississippi, where they were handed to Sherman on October 27.

Grant feared the Confederates might be intending to march on Nashville, as Longstreet had suggested, and Sherman's was the only force near enough to be interposed. All was haste now with Sherman. On November 1 he was in Florence, Alabama; on the 14th he rode into Chattanooga ahead of his troops.

Grant, concerned that the single-track railroad from Nashville would be inadequate to supply the several Federal armies that were converging on Chattanooga, plus Burnside's force in Knoxville, ordered Sherman to detach a division led by G.M. Dodge an old-time railroad constructor. He was to rebuild the railroad linking Decatur, Alabama, with Nashville, so that everything would not depend on a single track between Nashville and Stevenson. That deprived Sherman of a division, but it was an assurance the army would not starve.

MAP #3   The Battle of Lookout Mountain, November 24, 1863. The three divisions under Hooker have attacked Stevenson and Cheatham and driven them from all but the eastern slopes by evening. They will be withdrawn after midnight. Meanwhile, Sherman has crossed the Tennessee on the right with some resistance from one of Cheatham's brigades, while Cleburne has been moved to meet him.

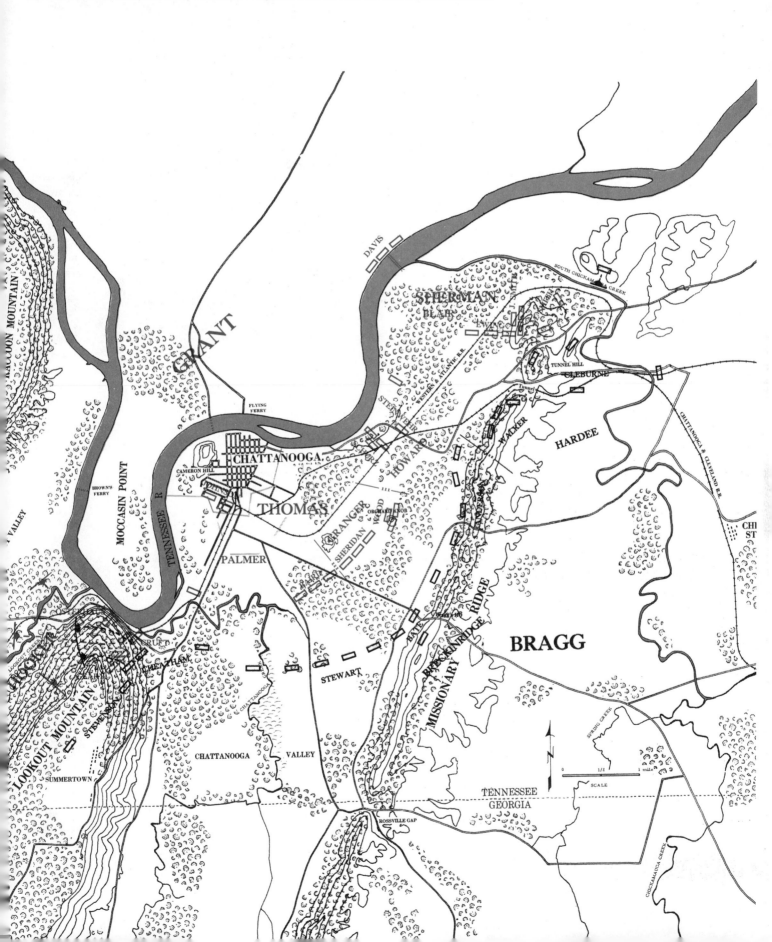

Union Army transports on the Tennessee River below Chattanooga. (From the Collections of the Library of Congress)

On the Union side, the main role in the great drama that was now unfolding was to be played by the "Old Hero's" cast-aside Army of the Cumberland, stripped down to four divisions after Jefferson C. Davis' had been sent to help Sherman, and much of Palmer's XIV Corps, Thomas' old command, had gone to co-operate with Hooker after he had parted with Howard, who came into Chattanooga. To use the theatrical phrase, Thomas, the bit-part player, was about to emerge the star.

First came Orchard Knob, Monday, November 23. The corps of Major Generals Crittenden and McCook that had been worsted and driven from the field at Chickamauga had been consolidated into the IV Corps under Major General Gordon Granger, who had marched to the relief of Thomas on Snodgrass Hill. Two divisions of this corps, Thomas J. Wood's and Philip H. Sheridan's, were paraded in the early morning much as though for a grand review, and such the Confederate onlookers from Missionary Ridge believed to be in progress.

Bragg's forward elements reached to rising ground about a mile in advance of the Federal Chattanooga defenses. They held Orchard Knob, a foothill, that looked out toward Missionary Ridge and was almost a nettle beneath the Union army's underwear, an irritant that would have to be removed before Grant or Thomas could exercise themselves freely and come to grips with Bragg's center.

The demonstration of the two divisions was begun as a reconnaissance in force. It was exploratory, to see how strongly Orchard Knob was held. The divisions left their artillery behind. Absalom Baird's division was stationed *en echelon* in support of Sheridan and Richard W. Johnson's division of the XIV Corps in support of Wood.

Quickly Bragg's spectators were disillusioned of the idea that they were watching a mere pageant, or witnessing a Union chest thumping, or display of power, now that Sherman's reinforcements were at hand. A cannon signaled from Fort Wood and, while most of two great armies observed, the divisions of Wood and Sheridan, with Willich's brigade of Wood's division in advance, rushed the Confederate lines on Orchard Knob. Almost before anyone was aware of what was happening, they overran and captured this strong point of Bragg's front line. Grant was at Fort Wood, with Thomas and others, and could not repress his admiration of the maneuver, or of the élan of the two Cumberland divisions. Thereafter the commanding general had no misgivings about the stanch fighting qualities of Thomas' men.

"Old Hero" Thomas was elated. When he saw the battle standards of Wood's division atop the Confederate ramparts he signaled Wood to hold fast. Though this was merely a feeling movement, the advantage could not be relinquished. His signal corps flag wavers spelled out the words: "You have gained too much to withdraw. Hold your position and I will support you."

The support he sent consisted of Blair's division on the right of Sheridan, who had moved through timber and had not kept abreast Wood, and Howard's corps on Wood's left. The story was told that the unemotional Thomas, when he saw some of his men falling on Orchard Knob, surveyed the terrain through his glasses and remarked with some feeling, "What a beautiful place for a cemetery." He kept it in mind and later caused to be established the one the visitor may see there today.

With Orchard Knob in Grant's possession, the entire army moved forward and intrenched along a new line, which caused rejoicing for several causes. One was that the new works enclosed a much larger area, parts of it heavily wooded. No longer was there crowding. The famine of firewood was ended and loggers at once began felling trees. That very night Orchard Knob sent up red flames from the great fires around which men and officers clustered, warming muscles and sending heat to bones that had been chilled for two months.

Before morning Bridge's Sixth Illinois Battery of Wood's division rolled up behind the infantry. Under cover of darkness, lunettes were added to the field works. The men bivouacked beneath open skies, without shelter, but the fires were a welcome exchange for the dingy, crowded huts and dugouts in the town. By this time the town, according to one description, was a "completely gutted, useless wreck." From Missionary Ridge the Con-

federates tossed shells onto Orchard Knob but the fire was ineffectual and sporadic.

There, along the Orchard Knob line, the Army of the Cumberland, possessing a higher status but still the cast-offs alongside Sherman's men from Vicksburg, passed in idleness the stirring day of November 24, 1863, while Grant was getting his forces into final position for the attack he would launch on the morrow. The plan was simple, with Sherman holding the lead. Bragg's army would be assailed on both flanks. Sherman would attack the Confederate right at the north end of Missionary Ridge. Hooker, who on the 24th was fighting for Lookout Mountain, would cross Chattanooga Creek and valley, take Rossville, and strike Bragg's left at the south end of the Ridge.

Thomas, with the Army of the Cumberland, who was already in position, would be the reserve, would threaten Bragg's center, and assist either Sherman or Hooker. Thomas was not to participate in the initial attack. Grant himself made it clear that "Thomas was not to move until Hooker had reached Missionary Ridge." Grant took his position with Thomas on Orchard Knob and gave orders to him directly. When Sherman became impatient a bit later that Thomas did not coordinate his movements with those of the Army of the Tennessee, he was exhibiting a lack of understanding of Thomas' role in the battle.

Although the Army of the Cumberland had an excellent view of Lookout Mountain and Missionary Ridge, neither end of the ridge was visible from its position in the center. The men could follow the action only by ear except where it might reach a momentarily clear summit. On the 24th the rain fell, sharply at times, but mostly in intermittent drizzles, and Lookout Mountain was obscured by the mist. The wind blew down in gusts from the north, bitter and searching, chilling especially Thomas' men, who had no huts, no shelter halves, no blazing fires in the heavy wind and rain, and no assigned activity to exercise them and cause them to forget the cold.

All day the heavy mist hung over the peak of Lookout and during most of the day Missionary Ridge was blotted out by the fog. Down where Sherman was getting into position there were bursts of firing and toward Lookout, in Thomas' right rear, the rattle of Hooker's musketry could be heard, rising to a crescendo in the afternoon.

Most eyes were turned in that direction. Sometimes when there were breaks in the mists along the mountain sides, or when the fog lifted sufficiently from the shelvings, they could see blue-clad soldiers working their way up the mountain. The Cumberlanders thought they could distinguish some of their own men, members of Brigadier General Charles Cruft's First Division of Granger's IV Corps, who had been detached to help Hooker. The Federal batteries on Moccasin Point joined in the cannonade of Lookout. Using some of Sherman's horses—the Army of the Cumberland no longer had any—Brigadier General John M. Brannan, commander of the Cumberland army's artillery, hauled forty pieces down to the Point to give Hooker artillery coverage as he stormed up the Lookout slopes. Through the day the cannon roared with their deep voices, but little more destructively than the Confederates' fire through the fog from the mountain shelves and summit.

The "grapevine telegraph," the 1863 name for "scuttlebutt" or "latrine rumor," carried wild stories of victory and defeat along the lines. Finally the dank November day grew duller and darkness came down from the surrounding heights, without anyone being sure of what had happened on Lookout. But the Cumberlanders did get one cheering bit of intelligence: that Sherman had crossed the Tennessee and was in position to launch his assault, which was to be the *coup de grace* of the battle, at daybreak. Grant was so pleased with this development that he sent a telegram to Washington saying the fight had progressed favorably, that Sherman had taken the end of Missionary Ridge, and that Hooker was high up the eastern slope of Lookout. Still, the men knew little, Grant was unduly optimistic about Sherman, and the earnest fighting had not yet begun on Missionary Ridge.

In contrast with the 24th, November 25 dawned bright in the valleys, though a light fog still hung on the summits. The mist was soon burned away. Nearly every eye of the Cumberland Army was turned intently toward the craggy top of Lookout Mountain. The sun's rays appeared suddenly to dissipate the fogginess. Then, simultaneously

Hooker's men bridging Lookout Creek. It was here that Hooker's attack bogged down. From a wartime sketch by H. E. Brown. (B&L)

from the entire army, rose a mighty shout. As a Federal colonel described it: "At the point from which rebel batteries had thundered upon Chattanooga for weeks, the Stars and Stripes, gloriously radiant in their gorgeous beauty, were proudly floating in the morning breeze."

The flag was the battle standard of the 8th Kentucky Volunteers, Colonel Sidney M. Barnes commanding, of Whitaker's brigade, Cruft's division, Granger's corps of the the Army of the Cumberland. The division of the castoffs that had been lent to Hooker were the first to reach the mountain top. Cheers rolled back and forth along the lines, especially among the Cumberlanders. Lookout Mountain, believed by Bragg and many others to be impregnable, had been won.

What had happened on Lookout? The Confederates had strengthened their defenses both before and after the departure of Longstreet. Brigadier General John K. Jackson took command on November 14 and drew a formidable line around the Craven house situated on a shoulder of Lookout. Jackson had 1,489 of Edward C. Walthall's brigade and 1,205 of John C. Moore's, both of Cheatham's division. Walthall was above on the shelf and Moore, whose men were poorly armed, was below on Walthall's right.

At foggy daybreak on November 24 Geary, still at Wauhatchie, received Hooker's order to cross Lookout Creek and assail the enemy on the mountain. Geary had three brigades, recently experienced in fighting over rough terrain on Culp's Hill at Gettysburg. They were the brigades of Colonels Charles Candy, George A. Cobham, Jr., and David Ireland. As they stepped off they were reinforced by Brigadier General Walter C. Whitaker's brigade of Cruft's division, Granger's corps, and later by the balance of Cruft's division. Then, still later in the day, came Peter J. Osterhaus' division of Sherman's Army of the Tennessee.

The units are of interest because they represented the three army groups that had been hastily assembled to avert a Union disaster in Chattanooga—portions of the Army of the Potomac, of the Army of the Tennessee, and substantially all of the Army of the Cumberland. Upon

Hooker's advance, Geary held the right, Cruft the center, and Osterhaus the left. Howard's corps had been moved from Lookout Valley to cooperate with Thomas and Sherman.

Hooker's battle for Lookout was effective but not spectacular. Due to the weather it was not as thrilling as Thomas' capture of Orchard Knob. Brigadier General Montgomery C. Meigs, the efficient Georgia-born Quartermaster General of the Union army, who observed such of the fighting as was visible while he was in Grant's party on Orchard Knob, called it the "Battle Above the Clouds," a name that appealed so much to the soldiers and press that it became a fixture, but usually it is awarded no more historical accuracy than the Barbara Fritchie legend or the negotiations under a "famous apple tree" at Appomattox. Still, since a fog is merely a low-lying cloud, and since the fog shrouded the mountainside, the title, one of the most renowned of the war, was not altogether a fantasy of the down-to-earth engineer, Meigs, noted for his practicality.

A coincidental phase of the fighting was that as the battle developed, Grant sent Brigadier General William P. Carlin's brigade of Richard W. Johnson's division, Palmer's corps, to further reinforce Hooker. Carlin's main function was to carry extra ammunition to replenish Hooker's dwindling supplies. Carlin, as night was falling, captured the most readily seen house on the mountain side.

The man who lived here was a well-known ironmaster of that locality, Robert Cravens, and he had painted his house white and it is referred to in the accounts as "the white house." Carlin's capture of it signaled Federal triumph. That night the Confederates withdrew to Missionary Ridge.

The significance of the capture of Lookout Mountain was that it gave Grant a straight line of battle with Lookout on the right, extending to the outer works at Chattanooga, through Orchard Knob, and on to where Sherman had come into position facing the north end of Missionary Ridge.

Grant's plan gave preference to Sherman. Quite naturally he turned to a corps and a general whose methods and responses were familiar to him all the way from Shiloh through Vicksburg. Naturally, as well, he wanted the major glory to go to his own men. He woefully misjudged Thomas, but that was not to become evident until the battle was joined and nearly over. As will be recalled, Sherman was to attack on the northern end of Missionary Ridge and sweep down the crest. Hooker would carry Chattanooga Valley, cross Chattanooga Creek, take Rossville, and sweep up Missionary Ridge from the South. Thomas with four divisions of the Army of the Cumberland would hold the center in front of Orchard Knob and create any necessary diversion required to accelerate the advances of Sherman and Hooker, and assist either. His was to be the more passive role.

MAP #4 *The Battle of Missionary Ridge, November 25, 1863. Breckinridge has pulled back his line to the ridge, while Stevenson and Cheatham have gone to the right to join Hardee. There Sherman, reinforced by Howard, strikes, meeting stiff resistance at Tunnel Hill from Cleburne and Stevenson. Meanwhile, Hooker has moved forward from Lookout to assail Rossville. By mid-afternoon he has driven Breckinridge's left up the ridge some distance, just as Thomas' attack on the center unfolds. Most accounts indicate that the first break in the main line came at Deas' brigade of Hindman's division, though other points gave way almost simultaneously. By late afternoon, unable to hold the position, Bragg's army retreats behind spirited rearguard actions by Cleburne and portions of Breckinridge's command.*

The dramatic storming of Missionary Ridge without orders by Thomas' "stepchild" Army of the Cumberland. Confederates a bit late withdrawing guns. ("Harper's Hist. of Great Rebellion")

The plan had some defects, the first being lack of proper reconnaissance. Missionary Ridge at the northern end was presumed to be a continuous range when in truth it was broken into smaller hills with one highly difficult valley before the ascent to the main ridge. An important eminence was Tunnel Hill where the Western & Atlantic Railroad that connected with Knoxville and, when unobstructed, with Richmond, Virginia, passed through the Missionary Mountain range. To the south the ridge was continuous all the way to Rossville Pass.

Another development of the plan, which proved its greatest obstacle, was that just before Sherman assailed the northern extremity, Bragg garrisoned it with Cleburne's division, which became his army's right division under Hardee's right wing command. What ensued here gave warrant to Hardee's later statement: "When Cleburne's division defended, no odds broke its lines; where it attacked, no numbers resisted its onslaught, save only

once, and there is the grave of Cleburne."

Cleburne reached north Missionary Ridge under fortuitous circumstances, with a thin margin of time. When Longstreet moved on Knoxville with 12,000 infantry and a few horses and found that he was supposed to be besieging an army of superior numbers, under Burnside, of 12,000 infantry and 8,000 horses (or so he thought), he called on Bragg for reinforcements. That general, compounding an original error, sent him Buckner with Bushrod Johnson's division, then ordered the division of the Irish-born Arkansan, Pat Cleburne, which was without peer in the Western armies, to go. What Bragg truly had in mind in so wantonly weakening his army at a time when Grant was drastically strengthening his, is anybody's guess, but the distrustful Longstreet gained the impression that the commanding general was out to destroy him when the truth was Bragg was destroying himself. The generals became at heart almost as much at war with each other as with the diligent and gathering foe. One by one Bragg had stripped his own command of nearly every top-ranking general who had recommended his dismissal to President Davis: Longstreet, Polk, Hill, Buckner, and now Cleburne. Bragg paid no attention to

anything that Longstreet recommended, though he was indebted to Old Pete for a glorious victory and might have wanted to share with him counsels about the succeeding steps.

No moment could have been less appropriate for Cleburne to depart from Bragg to join Longstreet. He boarded the cars on November 23, the day Grant was preparing the last details for the grand assault he proposed to begin on November 24. When Bragg saw the Federals in motion and realized his mistake, he telegraphed Cleburne in frenzied haste, caught him at Chickamauga Station, halted him, then ordered him to move in desperate speed to the army's headquarters. By that time the preliminaries of a large-scale battle were already in progress.

Bragg had been proceeding on the theory that because of the formidable nature of Missionary Ridge a weak line could hold it. In even greater indifference, he had weakened his defenses on the right despite evidences of Sherman's concentration there, until the ridge was all but stripped at the north end, and now that was about to become the main object of the enemy offensive.

Cleburne on the morning of November 24, a great day of Chattanooga, was rushed hurriedly to the right. He stationed Lucius E. Polk's Tennessee and Arkansas brigade to hold the Chickamauga Creek crossing just below the confluence of the creek with the Tennessee River, and to the east side of Missionary Ridge. With his other three brigades, those of Lowry, Liddell, and the Texans first under James A. Smith, who was wounded, then under Colonel (later General) Hiram B. Granbury, he fortified himself on a strong line on the ridge. (Granbury and Cleburne were to die within a few paces of each other next year at the Battle of Franklin.) This brigade had been under Brigadier General James Deshler, who fell with 418 of his men killed or wounded at Chickamauga. When General Lee, who had commanded Deshler in western Virginia early in the war, learned he had been killed, he wrote "There was no braver soldier in the Confederacy than Deshler." Now his old brigade, one of Bragg's best, was due for another blood bath.

Cleburne, with a good eye for terrain, had his brigades in strong position after preliminary skirmishing on the night of November 24. He was far up the ridge to the north and had no understanding of Bragg's intentions until he had sent his aide, Captain Irving A. Buck, several miles south to Bragg's headquarters. There Hardee, who was just leaving the council, gave notice: "Tell Cleburne we are to fight; that his division will undoubtedly be heavily attacked, and they must do their very best." Buck reassured Hardee that the division had never yet failed and would not do so on the morrow. The words of both general and captain were prophetic.

That night the moon was in eclipse, a not infrequent attendant of battles. When sufficient light was restored, Cleburne further strengthened his lines. Hardee arrived between 2 and 3 a.m., solicitous about the flank, which all believed Grant would try to turn in the morning. They rode the lines, directed Lucius Polk to occupy an additional hillock, then Cleburne himself determined to cover another spur of Missionary Ridge rising above Chickamauga Creek. The dispositions were important to his defense, which was one of the spectacular features of the oncoming battle.

Smith's and Granbury's brigade of Texans, working busily to complete some new trenches, met the first fire of Sherman's batteries which, with much preliminary skirmishing, told that an attack of major proportions was at hand. At 11 a.m. Sherman assailed Cleburne's lines with his customary impetuousness. He carried the assault forward to within a few yards—fifty paces at best —of Swett's battery that guarded Tunnel Hill. Sherman sent Hugh Ewing's division in first but that was not enough.

Sherman here proved what many Civil War students including his most noted biographer, Lloyd Lewis, have discerned, that he was not a great battle leader. Having at his disposal two corps of the Army of

230

the Tennessee, plus Howard's corps of the Army of the Potomac, and the two divisions of Jefferson C. Davis and Absalom Baird of the Army of the Cumberland, he still could not drive Cleburne who, according to his assistant adjutant, Captain Irving A. Buck, "seemed omnipresent, watching and guarding every point, and providing for any contingencies." All morning Sherman sent in his ample divisions that were, as Buck stated it, repulsed at all points. Grant thought that Bragg was shifting heavy reinforcements to his right, a deduction also of many others, but the fact is that Cleburne fought with no more than his own division, under the general supervision of the right wing commander, "Old Reliable" Lieutenant General Hardee.

Satisfied that the Confederate right was secure, Hardee moved off to the left, to where he quickly summoned Cleburne and Brigadier General States Rights Gist, commanding Walker's old division. An appalling situation had developed in the army's left center.

The roar of battle sounded over the rolling hills of the little town and reverberated from the circle of mountains. In the center there was no assurance that Sherman was doing well on the Union left. Sherman was reported to be holding his own—only that. The rattle of his musketry died down; even the field artillery fire (most of the army's guns were concentrated there) was sporadic and gave the impression the attacks were localized and piecemeal and not one overpowering assault down the crest of the ridge.

There was likewise cause for concern from the army's right under Hooker. He had swept around the foot and

forward down the mountain summit majestically, but had come up against the simple little matter of crossing Chattanooga Creek, where Cheatham's men had destroyed the bridge after retiring from Lookout, and there was no earthly manner for an army to cross until Hooker could build pontoons. That was a process of hours.

To those in the center, the outlook seemed dismal. The center was being stripped continually of supports. Howard's corps marched from Wood's left to help Sherman; then Baird followed. He had to pass from Sheridan's right and move across the rear of two Cumberland divisions. Grant was determined to crush Bragg's right around Tunnel Hill and was employing the better part of his infantry and artillery in the effort. A man not easily rebuffed, he intended no half measures.

Sherman called repeatedly for Thomas to take up the assault. Grant, nearby, had not yet given the signal. Thomas had three divisions left, Wood and Sheridan from left to right, Johnson in support *en echelon* behind Sheridan. When Howard moved off to Sherman, Wood's left was up in the air, but none worried as they watched the grand spectacle of the large bodies of troops—Howard's corps and Baird's division—marching north with banners waving. Still, there were no cries of victory, no huzzahs along the lines, only depressing uncertainty, perhaps another defeat. The shadows of the late November day lengthened. The sun hung perilously close to the summits of the western ridges.

It was 3 p.m. Two other generals, along with Thomas, were about to take the battle of Missionary Ridge into their hands. They deserve a brief introduction. Philip H. Sheridan's role in the war to this time had been passably good, not distinguished. He weighed 115 pounds, stood 5' 5" and was known in the army as "Little Phil." Bow-legged, by nature a thorough cavalryman, though he now commanded an infantry division, he was devoted to horses. When he was dying on Rhode Island Avenue in Washington and could look out on Scott Circle, he expressed an ardent wish that if he were ever monumented (as other generals were being honored at that time) the sculptor would give him a better horse than Scott's docile animal. He can rest unvexed; the spirited mount he sits astride on Sheridan Circle, supposed to depict him at the moment he reached Cedar Creek from Winchester (the theme of Thomas Buchanan Read's famous "Sheridan Twenty Miles Away") to turn the tide of fleeing Federals and defeat Jubal Early (which many regarded no great task), is often rated the most handsome mount in the capital city.

Sheridan was self-confident to the point of being pertly conceited, though he had been, like the Confederate Lieutenant General A. P. Hill, a five-year man at West Point. Health was something of a factor in both cases. At this stage of the war the quality of his generalship was in as much question as was in later years his birthplace. President Rutherford B. Hayes claimed him for Perry County,

Major General Patrick R. Cleburne (LC)

Ground of Cleburne's defense at Tunnel Hill, north end of Missionary Ridge. ("Pennsylvania at Chickamauga and Chattanooga")

Ohio. General Charles Devans, Jr., who delivered his eulogy before the Loyal Legion, said he was born in Somerset, Ohio, where he did spend his youth, and is now handsomely monumented. Some obituaries say he was born in Ireland, as was his father. He wrote in his memoirs that he was born in Albany, New York, the year after his parents reached the United States. The standard biographies accept this, though a man is not always the best authority on his birthplace. New Jersey is given at times.

He was tough and worked his way up through adversities, mainly, perhaps, because of his self-confidence, his willingness to take responsibilities, an understanding that war is a brutal trade. He was roughly handled at Stone's River, and driven from the field at Chickamauga. He saved his reputation partly by turning at Rossville and starting back toward the field, but the battle ended before he got there.

The past was now of little moment, because he was having, like Hooker, a fresh opportunity, and this time under the eyes of the man of destiny, Grant, who could not have been enamored with him yet, because he had preferred at Corinth to leave that uncertain general, then apparently shelved, and join Buell's army in the pursuit of Bragg into Kentucky and the Battle of Perryville. The future appeared more promising with Buell. Thus, he worked into division command under Rosecrans, Buell's successor, when he might have been with Grant at Vicksburg.

At 3 p.m. November 25, he had his division in sharp alignment to the right of Wood's, whose reputation likewise was shaky. Wood had appeared (and would do so

later) in some of the stirring situations of the war, yet he never seemed to gain the lasting attention to his performance that went to some of the others. Now, at the age of 40, there was a spot on his record, transparent when examined closely, because he obeyed Rosecrans' order, pulled his division out of line at Chickamauga, and opened the gap through which Longstreet drove his massed attack, to scatter the Union right wing and send it helter-skelter back into Rossville and Chattanooga.

Wood had a reputation for extreme diligence. He hastened from West Point, ignoring his leave, to get to General Zachary Taylor and haul up the guns at Palo Alto, then conducted an enterprising reconnaissance and won distinction at Buena Vista. As lieutenant colonel of dragoons he went with Albert Sidney Johnston on the Utah campaign. He was on leave in Egypt and rushed home by the first boat when the Civil War erupted. He held the center and held it firmly in the fast moving battle of Stone's River.

Thomas had confidence in him and that was about as good a recommendation as one could have in this war. He responded to it the next year at Nashville, commanding Thomas' largest corps and the center of the Union army in what not a few have accounted the most complete Union battle victory in the conflict. He was a Kentuckian from Munfordville. Now his division, disciplined and given restored confidence by two months of drill under three highly capable, battle-tested brigade commanders —Willich, Hazen, and Samuel Beatty—stood at attention and dressed with that of Sheridan, each division having a front of two brigades and each brigade a front of two regiments, except Willich's, with a four-regiment front. From the base of Orchard Knob, they looked up the 600 feet to the crest of Missionary Ridge.

A cloud of skirmishers was out in front and each division had one brigade in reserve, the same formation

Major General Philip H. Sheridan (KA)

George Pickett had employed in his assault four and a half months before on Cemetery Ridge at Gettysburg. One of the participating colonels confirmed that as the divisions aligned themselves no one seemed to have the impression that they were to storm the forbidding ridge. This was to be only a demonstration in force "to relieve the pressure against Sherman" when the truth was that Sherman was not under pressure, but was himself applying the pressure against Cleburne—unsuccessfully.

All morning and through the early afternoon Grant had been waiting and listening, inwardly disappointed, no doubt, but outwardly composed and mostly silent. When he did turn to Thomas, he disclosed no concern, merely said calmly, "Don't you think it is about time to advance against the rifle pits?" It was half a question, half an order. Thomas took it as an order and as such issued it to the corps commander, Granger, who worded it clearly, so that when it got to Wood verbally it was: "You and Sheridan are to advance your divisions, carry the intrenchments at the base of the Ridge, if you can, and if you succeed, to halt there." Thus Wood wrote it from memory later. Then Granger continued: "The movement is to be made at once, so give your orders to your brigade commanders immediately, and the signal to advance will be the rapid, successive discharge of the six guns of this battery." (Bridges' six 10-pounder Parrott rifle guns.)

Sheridan in turn got the same order. The men had long been waiting for it and they responded with alacrity.

What a transformation! Arms that had been stacked all day were seized; groups that had been idly watching fell into line; and as far to the right and left as the eye could reach, the Army of the Cumberland, or three splendid divisions of it, was beautifully aligned for the massed infantry assault, one of the old-time masterpieces of warfare, (but dying surely with the coming of improved artillery and the repeating rifle). Theirs was the tactic of Lee at Malvern Hill, of Pickett at Gettysburg. Now it was to be employed by Thomas at Missionary Ridge.

Again, let one of the colonels describe it: "There was no trepidation in the ranks of these formidable soldiers as the lines dressed up, as if preparing for a . . . ceremony. There was oppressive silence in the ranks, impatiently intent upon the signal for the advance."

Just then, almost at the moment of the stepoff, Baird's division came up, returning from Sherman. It fell in on Wood's left but was not fully in position when the six signal guns spoke, the sounds everyone had been awaiting. Then the four divisions of the Army of the Cumberland, Wood and Sheridan in front in the center, Richard Johnson and Baird *en echelon* on the right and left, respectively, stepped off. The late afternoon sun glistened off burnished bayonets; muskets were at the carry on right shoulders, the men in solid formation, shoulder to shoulder. All about them the battle had nearly ceased. Hooker was making his bridge across the Chattanooga Creek and was no longer engaged; Sherman was licking his wounds off to the north, biding his time for a fresh assault. Now in the center of the great stage of battle, the scene changed as the fresh cast entered: Thomas, Wood, and Sheridan, in major roles, and in the lesser, Baird and Richard Johnson.

Bragg's army had three defensive positions on Missionary. The first was at the base, consisting of a strong line of rifle pits; another was halfway up, much weaker than the first and intended to give security to those who might be forced from the base. The third was at the physical summit, where in most places the ridge is razorback thin, which meant that the Confederate army had to hold steady or run down the reverse slope, there being no other place to go, no plateau on which to form again and hold. The position was one of the strongest, in that it could be reached only by an arduous climb, yet one of the weakest, in that there were no adequate positions on the crest of the ridge to afford a satisfactory field of fire commanding the western approaches.

Orchard Knob was a salient close to Bragg's pits at the bottom of the mountain. As the two Federal divisions marched, the Confederates in the rifle pits at once opened fire. Behind, Federal guns roared from Orchard Knob at targets on the summit, where groups of Confederates were observed viewing the spectacle through their glasses. The slanting sunrays struck the forbidding cannon which the gray artillerymen were now beginning to serve; lines of Confederate infantry could be observed forming for

"Cleburne's repulse of Sherman at Missionary Ridge, Nov. 25, 1863." Alfred R. Waud drawing. ("Battlefields in Dixie Land")

battle along the thin crest. The incredible feature of it all was that an extraordinary attack was beginning without anyone, from Grant down to the lowest private, knowing just where it was going. Said one of Beatty's colonels: "There was not the slightest intimation of an intention that the ridge was to be attacked and taken by storm. . . . nothing of the kind was in contemplation." Such was clear from Granger's orders. Such was clear from almost every participant's account noted.

Nearing the rifle pits, the Federal lines halted and fired a volley that thundered along Missionary Ridge and echoed from more distant Lookout. Then the two divisions charged together, keeping their lines fairly well dressed, but rushing impetuously, "like a raging torrent," someone said, "shouting eagerly, boisterously." Some called out, "Remember Chickamauga! Remember Chickamauga!" The great mass of men captured the pits and inundated Bragg's forward position.

The line of Confederates, too thin to withstand such an attack in depth, fell back, those who could, and began laboring up the mountain. Many were captured. Although, as it developed, Bragg's lines were not well engineered, his artillery had not been idle during their two months on Missionary Ridge and had the ranges accurately calculated and tested. Even as the gray-coated infantry struggled upward, the well-served artillery blazed from the ridge, pounding the rifle pits with "frightful precision." The pits gave protection from the front, none from the rear.

It is often true that a battle is won or lost in a twinkling. Here was the crisis of Chattanooga. Here, in fact, was the crisis in the career of Ulysses S. Grant, of George H. Thomas, Braxton Bragg, and other high

officers of both armies. And not one of them had the slightest influence in shaping the ensuing course of events. Chance? Coincidence? Providence? Here, many have contended, was the hour of destiny for the American Republic.

The fate of two nations, the old Union and the new Confederacy, was suddenly taken from the grasp of the generals and thrust into the hearts and hands of the farm boys and office clerks, the college students and blacksmiths, the youthful lawyers and factory hands of Ohio, Indiana, Illinois, and a number of other states, who stood during a few fleeting seconds in the Confederate trenches in the midst of the hail of canister and shells sweeping down on them. Nobody had been able to reconnoiter the Confederate trenches. Nor did they calculate how grievously the captors of them would be exposed if this "demonstration" in Sherman's favor, this feeling-out of Bragg's center, ended at the bottom of the ridge.

No army could remain there, Alexander's, Caesar's, Napoleon's—nor that of Thomas. Thus exposed, any army would wither and rapidly disappear. The men had three choices: they could stand and be slaughtered, they could retire, which was foreign to their nature and would bring taunts of the Eastern and Vicksburg soldiers, or they could follow the retreating Confederates up the mountain.

As if by one impulse the entire line swept up the steep slope after the retreating enemy.

Nobody issued an order. None was needed. As Colonel Knefler, commanding the 79th Indiana, Beatty's brigade, Wood's division, explained: " . . . nothing could live in or about the captured line of field works; a few minutes of such terrific, telling fire would quickly convert them into untenable hideous slaughter pens. . . . There was no time or opportunity for deliberation. . . . Something must be done, and it must be done quickly."

The common soldier did what Bragg after Chickamauga failed to do. He followed the retreating enemy. Sheridan took out his silver whiskey flask, waved it at the Confederate gunners, shouted pleasantly, "Here's to you," and took a swig, only to be acknowledged by a close shell that scattered the dirt over his uniform. "That's damned ungenerous," he again shouted, and added that he would retaliate by capturing those guns. They were christened after the wives of Confederate generals—Lady Breckinridge, Lady Buckner, and the like. His men, like Wood's, plunged forward instinctively.

The mountain side became half gray with the uniforms of the retreaters, then half blue with the pursuers. Now and then the Confederates halted and turned to loose a blast of musketry. Necessarily the artillery fire from the summit subsided when friend became intermingled with foe. The slope is steep; it has every appearance of being impregnable, but just as the Confederates had pulled themselves up the almost sheer side of Round Top and the formidable incline of Little Round Top at Gettysburg, here the two armies struggled upward, now climbing, now battling with clubbed muskets and rocks, now halting and sending volleys into each other. No exaggeration could be involved in the statement that this mountain combat was as difficult as any fought during the war, perhaps more difficult than Malvern Hill in Virginia, Culp's Hill, Little Round Top, or Cemetery Ridge at Gettysburg, or along the Bloody Lane at Antietam, or Snodgrass Hill at Chickamauga, or anything except possibly the ghastly slaughter in front of Lee's trenches at Cold Harbor during the bloody affair where roughly ten thousand men fell in ten minutes.

One officer could be followed easily by friend and foe because he wore a bright red sash, a beautiful target for a sharpshooter, and waved his glittering sword, giving notice to the world that he commanded. The Confederates quickly got the message and a marksman's bullet crashed into his middle.

Perhaps the improbability of it all was what helped to panic the Confederate division on the summit, which looked down half helpless on the tide of friend and foe that struggled and panted step by step, and bush by bush, toward the crest. The crude and unfinished second line of rifle pits halfway up the steep slope was of little worth. It was overrun after a brief defense. By this time the smoke, the infantry soldier's godsend before the era of smokeless powder, was beneficently wrapping the mountain side. Even through the smoke, there was not much doubt at the top of the ridge, though considerably more back on Orchard Knob, where the high Union command tried to follow every detail, of how the fray was going.

Grant, standing with Rawlins and others, was close to Thomas, who had ordered the Army of the Cumberland forward to the bottom pits, and Granger, the corps commander who executed the movement. All were appalled. Then Grant was highly angered. Visions of Chickasaw Bluff must have passed through his mind. Troops could not storm so forbidding a mountain held by a formidable and up to this time victorious enemy army, well officered, well disciplined, battling to repel an invader from their homeland. Turning to Thomas, Grant inquired sharply, menacingly:

"Thomas, who ordered those men up that ridge?"

The "Old Hero" answered slowly, without excitement, "I don't know, I did not." Granger likewise disavowed it. Thomas, seeing Grant's displeasure, sent his Chief of Staff Joseph S. Fullerton to Wood and another staff officer to Sheridan to learn if they had ordered the men up the ridge. But Thomas told them—and here Thomas'

capacity for command disclosed itself—"if they can take it, push ahead!"

As Grant turned from Thomas, he muttered, as several heard him, that if the assault failed, someone would pay dearly for it!

The exchange brings to mind the declaration of General Douglas MacArthur after a later war that "there is no substitute for victory." Grant's statement showed there would be an accounting for violation of orders, or for exceeding orders, only in case of failure. The test was success. One may have heard the old story of the baseball rookie, who in the last of the ninth, with the score tied, none out, and a man on first, was told by the manager to bunt. Instead, he lashed out a long double and won the game. Returning to the bench to get the manager's warm applause, he received instead a blow on the chin, and a remark, "When I say bunt, I mean bunt."

Not so in warfare. Victory excuses anything—every-thing. When one is ordered to take a trench and wins a battle, all is usually forgiven and a new star appears on the culprit's shoulder. Had he not seen at the front, an opportunity the commander in the rear could not apprehend? In this instance, about 18,000 stars would be merited. Not only Grant, but "Old Hero" Thomas, plus Meigs, Dana, and others, all doubters, but all thrilled with the magnificent sight of the blue coats scaling the heights, were frightened that the effort was too audacious. All seemed convinced the men would be hurled back at the crest. Only Granger, who, like Thomas, disavowed giving the order, appeared sanguine. "When these men get going," he told Grant, "All hell can't stop them!"

Still, Grant reflected doubt. Because of his attitude, a wave of staff officers dashed forward from Orchard Knob to check the advance of the reckless men. But the hail of bullets was too steady for their mounts to penetrate it.

Most of them fell or, battle trained as they were, rebelled when the incline became sharp. How fortunate this was for the cause, some of the attackers recalled later. But the order did reach Sheridan's command, caused a trifling delay like a sand hill built by children in front of an advancing wave, and then the blue tide swept past the cautioning aides. No countermanding order reached Wood's division.

For the attackers, the going was a trifle easier as they neared the crest. Occasionally there were areas of dead space not commanded from the summit. Bragg, though he had had plenty of time, had not engineered his main defensive line to the best advantage. The works were generally on the thin topographical crest, and not on the military crest, usually some distance below, free from any shoulders or rises protecting the oncomers. That and the heavy smoke, the wave of retreating Confederates immediately in their front, and the inability of the gunners to depress the artillery—most of which eventualities the Federal high command could have anticipated—were the principal factors that made the assault feasible.

Working toward the summit, color bearers falling right and left, bending forward like men walking into a fierce rainstorm, sinking momentarily into pits and depressions, the "foxholes" of later wars, the stormers at length found themselves immediately in front of the Confederate works, where most of them dropped for a moment, exhausted, protected by the blessings that the artillery could not reach them and that the enemy's infantry fire was abating. Soon they were puzzled by the stillness in the Confederate trenches.

By this time, seeing his men so close to the top, Thomas had confirmed their audacity and ordered the entire line forward, which sent the divisions of Baird and Richard Johnson laboring on the flanks of Wood and Sheridan, giving protection from any enemy movements against the advancing and exposed flanks, such as were disastrous to Pickett when his flanks were enfiladed at Gettysburg.

There was fighting at the summit, to be sure, but it quickly became isolated and sporadic. The advance from the rifle pits at the base to the trenches at the summit was indeed an accomplishment with few parallels. As a participant described it, "Never in the history of our country, in battles on sea or land, was the American flag greeted by such a furious tempest of fire."

But why the sudden calm? Why no counterattack? Why no effort at a flanking movement? The Confederate division on the line where the Federal assault had its full impact suddenly left its works and rushed down the reverse slope of the mountain. Just then a heavy explosion sounded in the Confederate rear. It seemed to shake the mountain like an earthquake. The concussion beat heavily on the eardrums of the blue and gray soldiers. Two ammunition chests of the Washington Artillery of New Orleans had exploded. It seemed to serve as a signal for the half-rested Federal brigades. They rose and dashed with bayonets and clubbed muskets into the Confederate trenches, capturing guns, shouting in exultation, turning the cannon about to fire at the fleeing enemy. The summit in the center of Bragg's army was won.

Colonel Fred Knefler, of the 79th Indiana, mentioned before in this account, was born in Hungary in 1834. He went to military school there, and as a youth carried a musket in Kossuth's army for the liberation of the Magyars from the Hapsburgs. He learned drill, discipline, and the duties of a soldier. When Kossuth's cause failed he came to America, reached Indianapolis, worked as a carpenter, learned to speak beautiful English without the help of a teacher, studied Shakespeare, and eventually won the friendship of General Lew Wallace, later the author of *Ben Hur*, who at the outbreak of war made him his adjutant general. Later Colonel Knefler fought at Chickamauga; later he marched with Sherman to the sea. Now, in Beatty's brigade, Wood's division, as the attack moved against the ridge, he commanded two regiments, the 86th Indiana and his own. At their head, he stormed over the parapet and was credited with leading the first Federal units into the Confederate works.

There was no race track camera nor yet a finish-line tape on the crest of Missionary Ridge that evening and the claimants for first into the works were numerous. Henry M. Cist, the careful chronicler of the Army of the Cumberland, awarded first place to Sheridan's division, but conceded that "almost simultaneously" the crest was won in six places. Sheridan did have favorable ground toward the finish but was slowed a bit by the unhappy injunction brought by the aide to obey orders. Wood in elation when his men were at the top, declared feelingly: "Soldiers, you ought to be court-martialed, every man of you. I ordered you to take the rifle pits and you scaled the mountain!"

In later years when the question was raised of who first entered the main Confederate line, Wood assembled such a impressive sheaf of eye-witness testimony, some from other than his own command, that it has been difficult to assign the credit elsewhere, despite Cist's view and despite the fact that for this performance Grant came to dote on Sheridan instead of his old-time West Point roommate, Wood. Still, what seemed to impress Grant mainly was Sheridan's quick pursuit of the worsted and retreating enemy. Little Phil awaited no orders, as Ewell and Jubal Early did while the precious minutes sped by when they looked up at Culp's Hill and East Cemetery Ridge on July 1 at Gettysburg.

Colonel John A. Martin of the 8th Kansas, Willich's brigade, Wood's division, claimed the honors for his regiment as first to break the Confederate line, as did some of the Ohio men for their units, indicating that there was indeed what was later known as a photo-finish. The fact was that the Confederate line was soft at the point of impact, due in a measure to Bragg's faulty distribution of his troops.

One of Sheridan's conspicuous youths was first lieutenant and adjutant of the 24th Wisconsin, a Milwaukee regiment of Colonel Francis T. Sherman's brigade. Eighteen years old, he won a forecast in the regimental report that he would have "an honorable career." That, he surely did.

He was laboring up the mountain at the head of his regiment when the color bearer fell. Grasping the flag-staff as the line wavered, he rushed forward with great courage and planted the regimental standard on the Confederate works, an act of such signal heroism that he was one of the seven Union soldiers in this battle awarded the Congressional Medal of Honor.

He became a lieutenant colonel at 19 and fulfilled his commander's forecast by rising to be a lieutenant general in the American Army, and its commander in the Philippines. His name was Arthur MacArthur, Jr. His son, likewise a wearer of the Congressional Medal of Honor won in World War I, was General of the Armies Douglas MacArthur, destined to one of the distinguished careers of American military history.

Grant said the Confederate army was thrown into such disorder that the officers lost all control. That clearly was the case except for Cleburne's, Bate's, Gist's, and Stewart's divisions, or with other units that maintained their formation and made a passably orderly withdrawal. Still, Bragg had little to say in praise of his men.

He and Hardee made gallant efforts to rescue his army from disintegration. They tried to form a new line of Gist's, Bate's, and Cleburne's divisions and hold on the right, but the wound in the left center was irremediable. Someone recorded an adjutant's remark at the time of the Federal breakthrough: "I shall never forget the look of anguish on General Hardee's face."

View of Lookout Mountain from the hill to the north. Military road winding over north slope of Lookout was built after Hooker captured the mountain. From a wartime photograph. (B&L)

Hardee, the wing commander, assigned to Cleburne the task of safeguarding the army's retreat across Chickamauga Creek and through Ringgold Gap. No officer could have more ably conducted a rearguard that had to keep its formation and battle frequently and sometimes win, to save a confused, fleeing host.

Cleburne sent off his artillery across Chickamauga Creek. Colonel Hiram A. Granbury, commanding Cleburne's Texas Brigade, was the last to leave the ridge. Night had fallen but by 9 p.m. the last of the division was over the creek save for the pickets, who then crossed without the loss of a man.

The late November night turned bitter cold. Cleburne's heroic division of scarcely more than 4,000 waded Chickamauga Creek through water waist deep and in the early morning of November 26 spread across Ringgold Gap. Here the Chattanooga Campaign ended. Sheridan had followed to the Chickamauga Creek crossing but was halted by darkness, though he captured prisoners, small arms, and artillery and won Grant's hearty commendation. Hooker finally forded Chickamauga Creek without his artillery, captured Rossville, and took some prisoners, but the Confederates retreated before he got into the main action.

Bragg, writing his report a few days later, said: "A panic which I had never before witnessed seemed to have seized upon officers and men, and each seemed to be struggling for his personal safety, regardless of his duty or his character. . . . No satisfactory excuse can possibly be given for the shameful conduct of our troops on the left in allowing their line to be penetrated. The position was one which ought to have been held by a line of skirmishers against any assaulting column. . . ."

More vivid still is the account of Captain Buck:

"The scene of disorder at Chickamauga Station beggars description; it can only be appreciated by one who has seen a freshly beaten army. Regiments were separated from the brigades, the latter from divisions, and com-

Confederate prisoners at Chattanooga (LC)

manders from commands, and in great part army organization seemed lost. . . . It is difficult for those acquainted with the unflinching bravery of these same soldiers—tried and never found irresponsive to the call of duty upon every field of battle from Shiloh to Chickamauga—to realize, much less to understand, the unaccountable, shameful panic which seized them, and for which no apology can be found."

Unstinted was the praise of Cleburne. Bragg: " . . . Cleburne, whose command defeated the enemy in every assault . . . and who eventually charged and defeated him . . . who afterwards brought up our rear with great success, again charging and routing the pursuing column at Ringgold . . . is commended to the special notice of the Government."

And Hardee: "In the gloom of nightfall Cleburne's division, the last to retire, sadly withdrew from the ground it had held so gallantly. . . ."

Bragg in a letter to President Davis conceding his "shameful discomfiture" claimed the fault was not entirely his, charged that Breckinridge was drunk and "totally unfit for duty" for five days during the crisis of the battle, said it was a repetition of his conduct at Murfreesboro, and implied that Cheatham "is equally dangerous." But he feared "we both erred in the conclusion for me to retain command here after the clamor raised against me." That last, at least, was true.

T he Battle of Chattanooga had momentous results. It confirmed indisputable possession by the Federal army of Chattanooga, the rail center and heart city of the South, a community which more than any other tied the sprawling Confederacy into a nation of accessible parts. It led to the promotion of Grant to lieutenant general and commander in chief of the United States armies. It revealed

Battle of Ringgold, Ga., Nov. 27, 1863. Cleburne stationed his troops on the ridge; their fire was destructive; huge rocks were rolled down the mountain slope; confusion and heavy losses were inflicted on the attacking Federals who withdrew to await reenforcements. Cleburne's command retired unmolested.

again the sterling qualities and tactical abilities of Thomas. It launched Sheridan on the notable role he would play in the later stages of the struggle in Virginia. More indirectly, it led to the promotion of Sherman as the over-all commander of the Western Federal armies.

For the South it was a shattering blow from which the Army of Tennessee never fully recovered. If it did open any beam of sunshine through the clouds looming over the cause of Southern independence, it was in ending Braxton Bragg as an army commander and sending him off to Richmond to become the personal military advisor of his friend, the President. The command passed in a few weeks through Hardee and Polk to the strategically able General Joseph E. Johnston, who succeeded in delaying the collapse of the Confederacy in the West by another year.

Grant in his later writings thought he moulded the battle a little more decisively than was actually the case, and became persuaded in his recollections that he had ordered the movement he so roundly condemned when it was being executed. But it was more a soldier's than a general's victory. Or did it, like so many battles, turn on the whims of the Goddess of Chance? Still, Grant with his simple directness, never made matters more difficult than they were, and did his part with a determined, unruffled calmness, an attitude that was a reassurance to those about him and, in turn, to the army.

Bragg, on the other hand, ratified again Longstreet's comment made after Chickamauga, that almost everything he did was wrong—that almost everywhere he should have done exactly the opposite. Bragg, the subordinate who had come out of the Mexican War with the highest reputation, ended his Civil War career as an army commander with the lowest. A man of such high principles and unfailing integrity deserves pity, more than the violent upbraiding history has accorded him. Few made more enemies needlessly, none struggled more tirelessly than he did to succeed.

Grant regarded his victory as well-nigh epochal: "If the same license had been allowed the people and the press in the South that had been allowed in the North, Chattanooga would probably have been the last battle fought for the preservation of the Union."

NUMBERS AND LOSSES

The loss in neither army in the Chattanooga battles was as severe as at Chickamauga two months earlier. Grant gave the size of his Chattanooga army as 60,000, his losses as 752 killed, 4,713 wounded, and 350 captured or missing. He probably underestimated his army's size, because the Army of the Cumberland alone numbered about 40,000, to which should be added Sherman's two corps of the Army of the Tennessee and the XI Corps and one division of the XII Corps of the Army of the Potomac serving under Hooker. A more realistic figure would appear to be in the neighborhood of 70,000.

Bragg suffered fewer killed, being on the defensive, but many more captured. His army numbered about 65,000 over-all, but lost 12,000 when he and President Davis sent Longstreet to Knoxville. Other reinforcements were sent to Longstreet, leaving Bragg about 50,000 for the final battles. His over-all loss was 361 killed and 2,160 wounded.

His loss in prisoners and missing is less certain. Grant reported that he sent north 6,100 prisoners and that many others must have deserted due to Bragg's unpopularity. The Confederates reported 4,146 missing. Using the latter figure, the over-all loss in the Chattanooga battles was Federal, 5,815; Confederate, 6,667. The total of 12,482 casualties compares with the over-all loss of both armies of 37,129 at Chickamauga, 23,582 at Sharpsburg, and 43,454 at Gettysburg.   —G.T.

Artillery captured by Army of the Cumberland at Chattanooga.